HEALTH CARE RISK MANAGEMENT

HEALTH CARE RISK MANAGEMENT

ORGANIZATION AND CLAIMS ADMINISTRATION

GARY P. KRAUS, M.B.A., J.D.

PROFESSOR, PROGRAM IN HEALTH SERVICES
MANAGEMENT
DIRECTOR, PROFESSIONAL LIABILITY AND RISK
MANAGEMENT
UNIVERSITY OF MISSOURI-COLUMBIA HOSPITAL AND
CLINICS
COLUMBIA, MISSOURI

FOREWORD BY KURT DARR, J.D., SC.D., FACHA

NHP NATIONAL HEALTH PUBLISHING

A Division of RYND COMMUNICATIONS

Printed in the United States of America
First Printing
ISBN: 0-932500-43-9
LC: 86-61053

To
Meredith,
Kyle, and Colin

CONTENTS

Chapter 1   Introduction to Risk Management *1*

Gary P. Kraus

Definition and Purpose *1*   The Risk Management Process *3*   Summary *16*
Chapter Exercise *16* Questions *18* References *19*

Chapter 2   Risk Management Program Design *21*

Thomas S. Gaudiosi, Gary P. Kraus, and Joan T. Rines

Organizational Models *22* Interinstitutional Relationships *31* Risk Management
and Quality Assurance *35* The Role of the Medical Record Department in Quality
Assurance *40* Internal Office Organization *47* The Risk Management
Committee *50* Summary *54* Chapter Exercise *55* Questions *55* References *56*

Chapter 3   The Risk Manager *57*

Gary P. Kraus

Role of the Risk Manager *57* Educational and Experience Prerequisites *63* Job
Descriptions and Compensation *68* Professional Societies and Credentialing *71*
Summary *75* Chapter Exercises *75* References *75*

Chapter 4   The Risk Management Information System *77*

Gary P. Kraus

Risk Management Communications *77* Incident Screening *86* Computerized
Filing and Report Systems *89* Summary *95* Chapter Exercises *95* References *96*

Chapter 9 The Medical Record and Risk Management *227*

Joan T. Rines

Chapter 10 Risk Management in the Future *259*

CONTRIBUTORS

Thomas S. Gaudiosi, M.A.

Mr. Gaudiosi is Senior Vice-President of the Milway Corporation, consultants in risk management, Radnor, Pennsylvania.

Jacquelyn L. Goldberg, J.D.

Ms. Goldberg is a risk management consultant for Multi-Risk Management, Inc., Chicago, Illinois. She was formerly a risk management specialist with the Chicago Hospital Risk Pooling Program.

Gary P. Kraus, M.B.A., J.D.

Mr. Kraus is Professor, Program in Health Services Management and Director, Professional Liability and Risk Management, University of Missouri--Columbia Hospital and Clinics, Columbia, Missouri. He is also past President of the Missouri Association of Hospital Risk Managers.

Joan T. Rines, M.S.(R.), R.R.A.

Ms. Rines is Director of the Health Information Management Program, Stephens College, Columbia, Missouri.

Phyllis S. Solomon, B.J.

Ms. Solomon is a second year law student at the University of Missouri School of Law and served as Mr. Kraus's legal research assistant.

Herbert Squire

Herbert Squire is Director of Risk Management and Quality Assurance, St. Joseph's Hospital, Kansas City, Missouri, and is past President of the Missouri Association of Hospital Risk Managers.

Nancy J. Sublette, R.N.

Ms. Sublette is Director of Patient Relations, University of Missouri—Columbia Hospital and Clinics, Columbia, Missouri.

David Tapp, M.Ed., A.R.M.

Mr. Tapp is Director of Risk Management, Cox Medical Center, Springfield, Missouri, and is past President of the Missouri Association of Hospital Risk Managers.

FOREWORD

As diagnosis related groups and other prospective payment mechanisms and an increasingly competitive environment put more pressure on health services organizations to be efficient, managing risk of all kinds through prevention or minimization will be critical. The author of this book has thus chosen a timely and important topic. Managers who learn these lessons early will be among the successful. Those who do not may find themselves otherwise employed.

In the mid-1960s, the concept of risk management did not exist. Hospitals and other health institutions followed the industrial model and typically included a safety officer on their staffs. Larger organizations sometimes employed someone in this capacity full time. More likely than not this individual was also director of engineering and the physical plant. The safety officer's role was almost exclusively one of preventing accidents to employees, and to a lesser extent to patients and visitors. By contemporary measures, this was a narrow view of the potential for risk to which the organization was exposed. For better or for worse, this has all changed—with much of the credit, or blame, attributable to the dramatic changes in medical malpractice during the past 20 years.

All the elements were present in health services organizations of that era, especially hospitals: insurance, safety, prevention, medical audit, workers' compensation, and management responsibilities and accountabilities. Lacking was the common thread to tie the disparate elements into a total concept. For the health services field that thread is now known as risk management, and this book makes major progress in drawing the elements together and making them usable for the health services manager.

The book is exceptionally well balanced because it combines the theory of risk management with its implementation, and the law of risk management with practical implications for managers. It is an appropriate book for the didactic setting for many of the same reasons it is useful in operations, and it is suitable for a specialized course on risk management or in conjunction with a general management text. The net effect is to provide managers and students alike with a useful tool. For both, the exercises at the ends of chapters and the extensive use of references will be of significant benefit.

Chapters especially worthy of note are those on risk management information systems, particularly the use of computerized filing and reporting systems; the investigation of potentially compensable events; and settlement strategy and litigation defense. The sections on education for risk management, medical staff members as joint defendants, high risk areas, and no-fault liability are required reading for everyone who is or wishes to become a risk manager.

I am particularly pleased that the author addresses the various ethical considerations raised by any risk management program. Although the subtleties of ethics often escape the manager, it is imperative to be informed and thus better able to avoid these difficult questions or to minimize their negative consequences. Since early settlement is an imperative of risk management, this approach may run counter to what is reasonably seen as the manager's duty to respect the patient and his or her rights. A balance here is crucial.

Kurt Darr, J.D., Sc.D., FACHA
The George Washington University
Washington D.C., September 1985

PREFACE

The purpose of this text is to provide students of health administration, management, and other health professions with a book that summarizes the broad and divergent areas that collectively are called risk management. A secondary purpose is to offer the health provider a handbook that can be used for applied risk management.

The reader should understand that risk management is management, and therefore the traditional management elements of planning, organizing, directing, staffing, and controlling are all incorporated, albeit under different titles. It would take several volumes to deal effectively with every process of health care risk management; however, this text was designed to provide balance and to expose the reader to an organized overview of the subject.

For practitioners of risk management or those anticipating careers in the field, the text offers didactic material necessary for an understanding of the subject. Although the text touches upon most areas of risk management, emphasis is given to those processes collectively known as risk prevention, since it is here that practitioners currently focus most of their attention. To understand the driving force that motivates risk managers, some knowledge of law is necessary, and therefore a summary of relevant legal principles is included, so that the reader will be familiar with the legal parameters within which risk managers operate.

Instructors in health law, quality assurance, and risk management as well as related disciplines may find the text of value for its pedagogical content and exercises. Coupled with the companion instructor's manual, the text provides the necessary tools for instruction in the subject.

Last, the text offers an alternative to the traditional advocacy form of dispute resolution by suggesting other ways of handling such conflicts.

Gary P. Kraus, M.B.A., J.D.
Columbia, Missouri
January 1986

ACKNOWLEDGMENTS

The author wishes to acknowledge those who have contributed chapters or sections to this text.

Ms. Joan T. Rines, M.S., R.R.A., the Director of the Health Information Management Program of Stephens College, Columbia, Missouri, was most generous of her time in contributing part of Chapter 2 and most of Chapter 9 on medical records. One cannot overemphasize the importance of medical records in risk management.

I wish to thank Mr. Thomas S. Gaudiosi, M.A., Senior Vice-President of the Milway Corporation, consultants in risk management, for his contribution of the section in Chapter 2 on "The Risk Management Committee," and part of the section in Chapter 3 on "Professional Societies and Credentialing."

I wish to thank Ms. Phyllis S. Solomon, B.J., my legal research assistant, for her work in researching and writing much of Chapter 5.

Mr. David Tapp, Director of Risk Management, Cox Medical Center, Springfield, Missouri, and past President of the Missouri Association of Hospital Risk Managers, was of particular value for committing his considerable practical experience to paper in Chapter 6 and much of Chapter 7.

Ms. Jacquelyn Goldberg, Risk Management Consultant for Multi-Risk Management, Inc. in Chicago was very generous in contributing Chapter 8 and the section in Chapter 7 on ethical issues.

I would also like to acknowledge the assistance and cooperation of Mr. Herb Squire, Risk Manager of St. Joseph's Hospital, Kansas City, Missouri, and Ms. Donna Mouse, Risk Manager of Research Medical Center, Kansas City, Missouri, both of whom are past Presidents of the Missouri Association of Hospital Risk Managers.

I wish to thank Ms. Nancy Sublette, R.N., Director of Patient Relations, for her assistance with the sections on "The Potential Compensable Event" and "P.C.Es and Occurrence Screening" in Chapter 6.

I would like to thank Mr. David Meyers, the Director of the American Society for Hospital Risk Management, for his encouragement and for letting us use material from the Society.

Last, I wish to thank my secretary Mrs. Caroline Major for taking the time and effort to type and organize the manuscript.

Gary P. Kraus, M.B.A., J.D.
Columbia, Missouri
January 1986

CHAPTER ONE

INTRODUCTION TO RISK MANAGEMENT

Definition and Purpose

Risk management is a series of tasks and functions the purpose of which is to reduce unplanned or unexpected financial loss to an organization. Although various authors define risk management differently, most usually agree on the combined tasks, functions, and processes that collectively make up risk management. Williams et al., in their book *Principles of Risk Management and Insurance,* refer to the risk management process as loss exposure handling.[1] Other authors suggest that risk management in a health care environment should be directed primarily toward improving patient care and secondarily toward financial considerations.[2] Although this altruistic position is admirable, it is inconsistent with the purpose of risk management and represents a frequent misunderstanding of the total risk management process. The improvement of patient care is the objective of quality assurance, which is a subpart of the risk management process of risk prevention, to be addressed later in this chapter.

By unplanned or unexpected loss we mean those incidents that we know occur, but are not predictable in terms of time and scope. Predictable losses associated with routine business practices, such as the failure to meet financial expectations due to circumstances within the industry, are not within the purview of the risk manager. For example, if a restaurant incurs financial loss and subsequent insolvency because it could not serve sufficient customers as a result of poor management, location, competition, or other factors the resulting loss is not theoretically unplanned or unexpected, since it is predictable by financial and other standards. However, if the same institution experiences a shutdown because the kitchen was closed as a result of a grease fire, then the event is unplanned and unexpected and thus falls within the purview of risk management.

The tasks and functions carried out by risk managers are frequently very broad in scope and often appear unrelated. However, close analysis of the functions of risk management shows that they fit together like the fibers of a cloth, which viewed in total presents an artistic pattern. The label of risk manager as it is applied in hospitals and other health care facilities appears to be a misnomer, since the tasks and functions as well as the expectations, mission, or goal of the office

1

would seem to call for a more descriptive title. For example, the label of loss control or quality assurance coordinator is more descriptive of the actual function of many hospital risk managers, as in essence they attempt to control (i.e., reduce and prevent) losses by coordinating the efforts of others within the organization rather than by carrying out the task themselves.

Risk management is a logical process, and the steps designed to achieve its objective are aligned in a series of functions that is equally logical and predictable. From the historical perspective, the development of the risk management process and the migration of risk management from blue-collar industries to health care is also both rational and logical.

Although risk management is rather new to health care, it has been in place in various blue-collar industries since early in this century. As the law of workers' compensation and product and general liability developed and expanded, industries began to experience losses beyond the traditional casualty claims associated with weather, fire, and other events. The insurance industry naturally expanded into these markets and, to reduce losses, attempted to influence management by offering such activities as safety programs designed to prevent accidents. These and other functions evolved into the processes that, incorporated together, we call risk management. As time passed, insurance companies offered incentive programs for their customers in an attempt to have them carry out some risk management processes from within the organization rather than from outside. An example of such an incentive is reduced premiums to organizations that establish internal risk control programs.

Before 1965, losses to the hospitals from casualty, workers' compensation, and professional liability were generally low, resulting in manageable premium levels. However, with the development of a line of law cases beginning with *Darling v. Charleston Community Memorial Hospital*,[3] hospitals found themselves experiencing increased claims resulting from the negligent acts of their medical and nursing staffs. Parallel with this development, many states began liberalizing their workers' compensation laws, making this exposure area a virtual no-fault program. In the late 1960s and early 1970s, health care providers began experiencing what has now been called the first medical malpractice crisis. The principal effect of the crisis was dramatic. There were large increases in insurance premiums, and many carriers withdrew from the medical malpractice insurance market.[4] Many hospitals then found that their insurance costs were substantially increased or that they were unable to purchase insurance altogether.

A natural result of the crisis was an attempt by many states to lessen its impact by passing statutes aimed at reducing the number of frivolous claims. Several states passed laws requiring a claimant to present his or her case before a screening committee or panel of judges, attorneys, and health care providers, before filing a claim in court. As a result, there appeared to be a leveling off in the number and severity of claims against health care providers. In the late 1970s, however, many of these statutes were declared unconstitutional, and the courts were again available to aggrieved parties. Simultaneous with the overruling of many of these statutes was the education of the plaintiff's bar and the infusion of large numbers of attorneys into the liability market. Consequently, some observers have labeled the situation in the 1980s as the second malpractice crisis. It appears from recent statistics that the primary effect of the new crisis is not a withdrawal of insurance companies from the market, but steady increases in premiums. Another effect of the crisis is an increase in the number and the size of losses, particularly in a few specialities of medicine such as obstetrics and gynecology. Although insurance is available, the cost is extreme. Another and perhaps more insidious result is the abandonment by many doctors of all or a part of their practice, particularly in the area of obstetrics. In Florida and California, it appears that as many as 15 percent of obstetricians now refuse to deliver babies.[5]

The first medical malpractice crisis stimulated the development of risk management programs in American health care facilities. Program designs were taken directly from other industries, although different nuances and professional standards required different approaches to the same mission and goal, which is the prevention of financial loss. Many within the health care industry misunderstand the purpose of risk management. This is perhaps because the goal to reduce financial loss sounds selfish and has a negative connotation in a traditionally non-profit industry dedicated to relieving the suffering and pain of patients.

The Risk Management Process

Identification of Exposure Areas and Risks

The first step in the risk management process is to identify exposure areas and the risks within each area. Risk or exposure identification is an ongoing process, which requires continual monitoring, since the health care industry is in a constant state of change. As changes occur within the system, risks that heretofore did not exist can develop and must be identified, measured, and dealt with. For example, as health care facilities develop multi-institutional plans and strategies, they also expose themselves to risks associated with antitrust law. In the past, when statutory exemptions were available, exposure to antitrust liability was almost unknown; however, in recent years it has become one of the more serious and prevalent forms of liability exposure.

The exposure to new risks within health facilities occurs as a result of developing technology, according to Ben Reagan. "Risk managers should take the lead in ensuring that their hospital's technology—lasers, magnetic resonance imaging devices, and ultrasound, for example—doesn't outstrip the staff's abilities and that risk doesn't overwhelm protection."[6]

There are many areas of risk exposure within a health care facility. Many of these require substantial technical expertise to identify and analyze risks. The average risk manager cannot possess the degree of experience needed to identify and analyze all the risks associated with every area, simply because risk managers lack knowledge of all professional and technical departments and functions. Therefore, it may be necessary for outside experts to analyze a particular exposure area in order to accurately identify the risks therein. The following list contains some common exposure areas found in health care facilities.

1. Liability associated with medical, nursing, or other forms of professional malpractice, including corporate liability for acts of the staff and employees

2. General liability exposure for injuries to patients, guests, visitors, and others

3. Workers' compensation exposure for employee injuries and occupational diseases

4. Property and casualty exposure associated with the physical plant and equipment

5. Exposure associated with chemical and nuclear wastes and other environmental hazards

6. Exposure associated with vehicular transportation such as company automobiles, trucks, ambulances, and aircraft

7. Exposure to defamation actions among medical staff, administration, and other personnel

8. Exposure to financial losses in the business office through embezzlement and thefts

9. Exposure to antitrust actions against the corporation and individuals by medical staff, applicants for staff membership, and competing organizations

10. Exposure to contract, warranty, and similar actions associated with the purchase and use of goods and services

11. Exposure of the trustees or directors to actions by individuals or groups with divergent political or community interests, including actions by stockholders over fiduciary issues

12. Fraud and abuse exposure associated with federal and state third-party reimbursement programs

13. Exposure to federal and state securities violations associated with capital funding programs

14. Exposure to losses associated with employee and staff hiring, promotion, and termination practices

15. Exposure to losses of intellectual property such as copyrights, patents, and trade secrets

16. Exposure associated with the loss of a key employee by death or disability.

An in-depth analysis of each of these exposure areas is necessary in order to identify all the possible risks within each. For example, a close analysis of the transportation exposure area might reveal the primary risk to be collision with another vehicle or with a pedestrian. The risks within this exposure area are somewhat simple to identify and usually do not require outside assistance, since the risks are known to most individuals. On the other hand, an analysis of the risks associated with exposure to professional liability requires substantial expertise and knowledge of the health care delivery system and of nursing and medical procedures. To accurately identify the risks in this exposure area, the hospital risk manager must have knowledge of hospital practice. Frequently the use of outside consultants is necessary.

There are many techniques offered by authors in the area of risk management to identify risks in the various exposure areas. A common technique is the flow chart method. In their text, *Handbook of Risk Management,*[7] Carter and Doherty recommend the use of production flowcharts to identify subtle hazards in manufacturing and production activities. This technique requires the diagramming of every activity within a process so that a close analysis of each can be done. An example of a flowchart of a hospital process for a reporting system for patient care equipment failure is shown in Figure 1-1. Flowcharting is a common technique used in many activities such as computer programming, and its use has developed into a fine art. Flowcharting should be used by risk managers to identify potential risks in an exposure area or to analyze an area once incidents have occurred in order to identify weaknesses within a system.

Another common technique to identify potential loss areas is the questionnaire. This technique, described by Pfaffle and Nicosia in their text *Risk Analysis: A Guide to Insurance and Employee Benefits,*[8] is used for risk analysis in business activities. The method attempts to create a dependable list of significant exposures by answering two questions: first, What does the business stand to lose? and second, What exposures are significant in the business? The first question relates to the assets of the company—physical, financial, or human—that could be damaged or lost by any act, direct or indirect, including litigation. The second question seeks to recognize significant exposures by comparing the firm's assets against existing perils and weighing each existing peril against all assets. From the answers to these questions, a comprehensive picture of the operation of the business will be drawn. Several major sources may be used to obtain information, including but not limited to operating statements such as sales reports, income statements, labor reports, and risk policies and procedures. Also included are balance sheets, annual reports, flowcharts, contracts and other forms of agreements, major contracts for services, computer analysis of operations, and risk surveys, including analysis reports similar to the flowcharts described above. Once the data have been collected, the risk manager can put together a questionnaire listing the

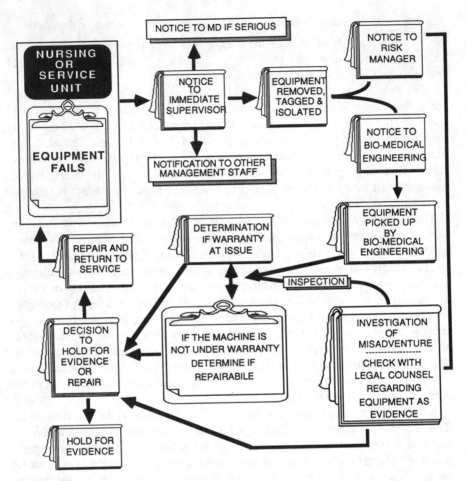

Figure 1-1 Flowchart of a common hospital process.

institution's assets along common lines such as physical assets, financial assets, and human assets. As the reader can imagine, this process involves a lot of data— just the list of equipment in a health facility can be a very lengthy document. The physical assets, such as cash on hand, accounts receivable, notes, profit and loss statements, and securities are somewhat easy to identify, as are key personnel, including research staff, administrative staff, and medical staff.

After reviewing the tangible and intangible risks associated with this information, the risk manager can assign a probability of loss to each. A simple way of doing this is to assign probabilities according to categories of definite, moderate, slight, and no risk. Once these probabilities have been assigned, the risk manager will be in a position to answer some questions, such as: What are the annual expected losses? What is the maximum probable loss during specific time periods from all exposures? What is the maximum possible loss from all exposures?

Inspection is another risk identification technique common to many businesses. It involves a detailed inspection of the firm's premises, of each process, and of the goods and services produced. It also includes the analysis of operations carried out away from the facility, such as home health care programs, convenience clinics, and other services controlled by the primary organization. The inspection process should also include analysis of transportation systems, security services, research endeavors, and other activities, and should identify key employees whose loss could disrupt the organization. Last, the inspection process includes an analysis of the loss prevention program itself, which is an ongoing function.

Risk Measurement

Once the risk identification process has been completed, the risk manager can move on to an accurate measurement of the potential losses that the organization could incur. The probability data supplied through the risk identification technique of using questionnaires is particularly valuable in this process. Some theorists, including Williams et al.,[9] suggest that the probability assignments mentioned in the risk identification questionnaire are actually part of the risk measurement process. We, however, prefer to place probability in the category of risk identification, since measurement entails the application of a parameter, which in risk management is measured in dollars, whereas probability simply states the likelihood of an event occurring.

The risk measurement process requires the risk manager to measure, analyze, and evaluate data in order to make an intelligent and appropriate decision regarding how to deal with the risks and the potential financial losses to which the organization is exposed.

Risk measurement consists of a series of activities that involve highly technical and analytical tasks. Williams, et al. suggest that four concepts must be understood and considered in order to carry out the risk measurement process. First is the risk identification process, which we have discussed above. Second is the likelihood of a loss occurring. The third concept deals with the variation in potential losses. This relates to the range of possible outcomes and the degree of severity that can be attached to each. The last concept deals with the uncertainty concerning a loss or simply the inability to predict the future.[10]

Other theorists have offered different approaches to the risk measurement process. Richard Prouty has published an approach that includes three basic steps.[11] The first step is the assessment of the likelihood of a loss. This is essentially a probability analysis. The second step is the estimation of the severity of a loss. The third step is factoring in the dollar loss. Prouty uses four degrees of likelihood to define the probability of an event occurring: almost nil, slight, moderate, and definite. Almost nil means that the exposure cannot be avoided, but the chances of the event occurring are more theoretical than realistic. Events with a slight likelihood are those that could occur but have not done so in the past. Events with a moderate degree of likelihood are those that occur once in a while, and definite events are those that occur regularly.

Once the likelihood of one of the above loss-cause combinations is attached to the exposure area and the risks within it, Prouty suggests that it is then necessary to factor the measurement of severity into the equation, such as the *maximum possible loss* and the *maximum probable loss*. By the maximum possible loss he means the worst dollar loss possible for the lifetime of the activity. By the maximum probable loss he means the worst dollar loss that is *likely* to occur. Prouty also suggests a third measurement of loss severity, called the *annual expected dollar loss indicator.* This measurement has a time factor as a parameter, as suggested by its title, and is based on historical data of the organization and the industry. It is generally the average amount of loss that can be expected.

The risk measurement process requires the application of the fundamentals of probability analysis, according to George L. Head. He suggests that a risk management specialist can select proper risk management techniques only on the basis of reliable predictions of (1) future losses, and (2) the effectiveness of alternative risk management techniques in safeguarding against the effects of these losses.[12] The fundamentals of the laws of probability are beyond the scope of this text, and readers are referred to the literature of the insurance industry and actuarial science for details of their application in risk measurement for health care facilities.

This discussion of the risk measurement process is an oversimplification of a highly complex task. Many hospital risk managers may find that they lack the necessary skills or expertise to carry out this activity completely. For example, to measure the potential loss of the physical plant one would have to have knowledge of architectural, engineering, and construction costs associated with the hospital building industry. These data are relatively easy to obtain through individuals and organizations within the relevant professions and industries. Real estate appraisers routinely supply information regarding the value of a structure. However, risk measurement of more nebulous exposure areas, such as professional liability for malpractice, is frequently nothing more than educated guesswork. It is almost impossible to predict with any degree of accuracy what a jury might award an individual who sues over an incident of medical malpractice. Data are available from closed claims studies produced by insurance companies and organizations such as the National Association of Insurance Commissioners[13]. Often, however, these data are outdated by the time they are published. Data published by other sources on economic factors such as inflation should be considered, so that a reasonable ballpark figure can be established for the purpose of estimating potential loss more accurately. Still, with all the data and experience available, it is difficult to place realistic parameters on the risks to which an organization is exposed. For example, in the short period of two years (1984-1985), jury verdicts in Kansas City increased astronomically. Recently a jury returned a $10 million verdict in the wrongful-death case of a 91-year-old woman who died from a drug overdose in a Kansas City hospital.[14] The size of the judgment was so large and out of proportion that the loss transcends the most speculative maximum dollar loss that a risk manager would have applied for that particular risk. That case and several other large awards have resulted in Kansas City being referred to by the insurance industry as having ,"the Hyatt Regency syndrome," referring to the famous skywalk collapse, which resulted in a battery of suits and claims, most of which were settled for amounts that, many critics claim, were too large in relation to the damages many claimants sustained. More seriously, however, these awards have driven excess insurers out of the market, and many hospitals have found that secondary umbrella coverage is not available.

Risk Handling

Once the probability, severity, and expected dollar losses have been projected, the risk manager is ready to pursue the next process of risk management, which is essentially deciding what to do about risks that have been identified and measured. This process is called risk handling or risk treatment.

Risk handling or risk treatment generally includes a battery of tasks and functions that can be placed under the broad categories of risk financing and risk control. The difference between risk financing and risk control relates to the objectives of the techniques used in each. The objectives of risk financing pertain to the funding of real or potential losses, whereas risk control objectives pertain to controlling the events that give rise to the real or potential loss. Although most of the tasks and activities included in risk financing and risk control are separate and distinct, some activities are common to both. For example, the use of contract clauses designed to shift the liability for a loss from one party to another can be characterized as both a risk financing and a risk control technique, as will be explained later.

Risk financing is further divided into three subcategories: risk retention, risk transfer, and risk self-financing. Head defines risk retention as those methods of financing an organization's losses that use funds which originate within the organization. He defines risk transfer as methods of financing the organization's losses with funds from outside the enterprise. Most experts do not place self-financing in a separate category but include it with risk retention, except in cases where the firm loses control and management over the fund, in which case it is placed in the risk transfer category. We prefer to consider risk self-financing as a separate, third category, because the title highlights the distinctive features among the three categories.

A common element shared by all three subcategories of risk retention, transfer, and self-financing is that they represent conscious decisions by the risk manager or the administration to finance those risks to which the organization is exposed. For example, risk retention represents a decision to retain the risk of a potential loss and, if the loss occurs, to fund it by one of several techniques using resources within the organization. One such technique is to pay losses as a current expense out of operating income.

A second technique is the use of a deductible, which represents that part of a loss not covered by insurance or some other funding program. Most automobile insurance policies have a deductible, usually in the range of $50 to $500, which does not cover part of a claim. A third technique is to pay off losses through the establishment of a funded reserve account. A fourth method is borrowing to pay losses when incurred.

The most common risk transfer technique is to purchase insurance from an unaffiliated insurer. A second technique is to enter into contracts with a noninsurer third party, who agrees to pay for losses that otherwise would be paid by the transferring organization. An example of this technique is an indemnity agreement supported either with or without bonds.

Risk self-financing techniques involve the purchase of insurance from an affiliated insurer, such as a captive company. A second method is to establish a trust fund designated to pay for losses in certain exposure areas. A third technique of self-financing is participation in insurance cooperative groups.

The primary difference between risk transfer and risk self-financing is in the method of financing; in self-financing, managerial control and ownership of the funds are retained. For example, when an organization purchases insurance on the open market, the premium is paid and the risk is transferred to the insurer. The premium for the coverage is spent and for all practical purposes represents a business expense to the organization. However, if the premium is paid to a captive insurer, the funds are used to cover the exposure area, and if not used, remain for future periods until either paid out in claims or returned as dividends.

For a thorough understanding of all forms of risk financing, the student should consult texts on insurance. However, it is appropriate to mention a few concerns regarding various risk financing systems that are important for risk managers.

The size of the deductible that an organization elects to retain is an important decision, which must be made after thorough analysis of the financial position of the firm balanced against the potential loss. In some exposure areas, such as medical and hospital professional liability, the size of the deductible can be formidable. This is particularly true when purchasing secondary or umbrella insurance. Because of the large number of recent multi-million-dollar judgments, organizations that are self-insured for primary coverage have found that secondary insurers are only writing policies with large amounts of self-retention, often in amounts of $1 million and $2 million. Organizations that experience the necessity of retaining large deductibles should have sufficient coverage or cash reserves in their primary plan to finance any large loss or should have a source of ready credit.

Cash funding techniques should be used only for exposure areas where small losses are probable, either individually or in total at the end of the funding period. For example, cash funding is frequently the mechanism used to reimburse patients for lost personal items in hospitals and other facilities. Considering the cost of processing claims and the value of the items for which reimbursement is demanded, it is usually more economical and represents an important goodwill gesture to reimburse patients for these losses through a funded line item account or from a funded reserve account.

Borrowing to cover losses is not recommended as a technique of risk retention unless no viable alternative exists. When one considers the fees for loan processing, interest, and the repayment of the principal, borrowing can be an expensive form of risk financing to be used when no alternative exists or the likelihood of a loss is extremely remote.

The concept of insurance is familiar to most students; less well known, however, is the difference between *occurrence-type* and *claims-made-type* insurance policies, particularly in relation to professional liability. An occurrence-type policy provides coverage for misadventures as long as the event occurred when the policy was in force. A claims-made-type policy provides coverage for misadventures as long as they are reported during the time of the policy period. When one considers such exposure areas as professional, general, or product liability, where the statutes of limitations are very long and claims can be brought against the organization years or decades after the time the event or misadventure actually occurred, the distinction and the advantages and disadvantages to both the insurer and the insured become self-evident.

Hospitals and other providers prefer occurrence-type policies because they then feel secure for the policy period against all events and misadventures that may arise, even if they are not filed until years later. Administrators and risk managers can plan effectively for a given time period, knowing that coverage is in force and that changes in the economy, the law, and the social environment will not impact on them. Insurance companies, however, feel less secure with occurrence-type policies because planning for them becomes difficult, if not impossible. Rates set now must be adequate to cover losses incurred in the distant future within the exposure area. A brief look at the rapid changes in medical malpractice in the last two decades provides an example of the difficulty of accurate insurance planning. Low rates set in the late 1970s and early 1980s for occurrences arising out of those years but only now being awarded have proven to be inadequate to cover claims. This in part has contributed to the high cost and unavailability of liability insurance for some health care facilities.

Insurers naturally feel more secure selling claims-made-type coverage for many of the same reasons that the insured like occurrence-type policies. Insurers can establish rates on a period-to-period basis knowing that, once the time period has lapsed, they know what claims have been filed. They can then adjust rates for subsequent periods with a fair degree of accuracy, knowing that their "tail" is not extended for a prolonged period of time. For insured organizations, the problems are somewhat the reciprocal of those of the insurer under occurrence-type policies. They must make sure that the long "tail" is properly covered by either locking themselves into another claims-made-type policy or buying retroactive tail coverage. Rates can be high and coverage may not be available in some high-risk exposure areas.

Regardless of the type of insurance purchased, the risk manager must have a clear understanding of the details of the contract. Particular attention must be paid to definitions in the language. This is critical as it pertains to reporting language in claims-made-type policies. One must know without debate what must be reported so that the event will be covered by the contract. For example, some contracts define a "claim" as a happening or event characterized by the misadventure coupled with the actual making of a demand by way of litigation or other formal process. Other contracts may define a claim as being made when the provider notifies the insurer of the happening or misadventure, even if the injured or aggrieved party has not made any overt demand and may never do so. In this situation, the importance of an early incident detection and reporting system within the institution is self-evident. Chapter 4 which deals with risk management information systems, discusses incident reporting.

The use of contracts as a method of risk transfer must be seriously considered before being implemented as a viable technique. Agreements with third-party organizations or individuals to indemnify one for a loss that may accrue and be paid by the organization, with the understanding that the third party will reimburse the organization for its loss, are risky from the outset. If the third party should refuse to honor the agreement to indemnify the primary party, the latter may have to resort to costly litigation to enforce the contract. The contract could contain technical flaws that render it useless, and then the organization would incur an uninsured loss. Also, the third party may not have the resources to support the agreement and could resort to bankruptcy or other forms of relief to stave off insolvency. Consequently, any contract of indemnification should be supported by a requirement that it be enforced by insurance or a performance bond.

Risk self-financing techniques have become very popular among health care providers in the last decade. This resort to self-financing is primarily a result of the high insurance premiums experienced by hospitals and physicians. Many institutions felt that the rates being charged were far greater than the risks they desired to transfer to commercial insurance firms and that some better mechanism of risk financing could be created. Many institutions resorted to establishing their own insurance companies, called captives. These affiliated-owned companies are usually located in jurisdictions with no taxes and few, if any, insurance regulations.

Many of these jurisdictions are independent sovereign island nations or colonies located off the United States coast, such as Bermuda, the Bahamas, or certain of the Caribbean islands; thus they are frequently referred to as "offshore corporations." Captive companies are corporations in which the insured hospital or provider organization is the sole shareholder. Since the captive company issues only one contract or a small number of contracts of insurance to its affiliated owner, there is little or no risk spreading, and therefore the premiums must be large enough to cover all potential losses.

Another common source of self-financing, particularly for nonprofit organizations, is the use of trust funds. A trust fund has three entities: a maker, a trustee, and a beneficiary. In trust funds used for self-funding, the maker is usually the hospital, or in multi-institutional organizations, the parent firm, which places the money into the fund. The maker essentially makes the contribution to the fund on the recommendations of insurance consultants and actuaries. The money is placed in an account under the control of a trustee, usually a bank, which is the legal owner of the fund but manages it according to the trust document. The beneficiary of the trust fund is the covered person or organization, which may also be the maker. Institutions that desire to establish trust funds for risk self-financing purposes must meet legal, tax, and other reimbursement laws and regulations. The trust document serves as the authority and contract for operation of the self-financing program and therefore must be specific regarding all aspects of the plan.

Regardless of whether the risk is transferred through commercial insurance, an indemnity contract, or self-financing through an affiliated-owned captive or trust fund mechanism, the use of an umbrella insurance program to ensure the viability of the primary coverage is highly recommended. In recent years, however, excess or umbrella insurance has become very expensive, and in some areas, it is unavailable, or if available, not in the amounts desired. Also, retention levels are frequently high, placing stress on the primary coverage.

The unavailability and high cost of excess insurance may be the primary characteristics of the current medical malpractice crisis, whereas unavailability and high cost of primary coverage were the features of the first medical malpractice crisis of the mid-1970s.

Risk Control

The majority of tasks and activities that the average hospital risk manager performs fall within the area of risk control. One can argue that quality assurance is simply the implementation of risk control techniques, primarily in the area of risk prevention. The relationship between quality assurance and risk management will be explored in Chapter 2. Risk control incorporates three major categories: risk avoidance, risk shifting or reciprocation, and risk prevention. The objective of risk control techniques, as suggested by the names of the three categories, is to avert losses by fostering policies, decisions, and actions designed to achieve the desired result. Risk control techniques must be implemented in order to reduce losses from unplanned events, notwithstanding the fact that they have been anticipated and funded by the risk measurement and risk handling programs described above.

Risk avoidance is a policy and decision process that, when successful, achieves the result of averting losses by avoiding the risk or exposure area altogether. For example, if a hospital wishes to avert catastrophic losses from malpractice suits brought on behalf of children who sustain brain damage at birth, the hospital administration may decide to forego obstetrics services. Risk avoidance may be particularly easy to implement if the risk to be avoided is associated with services that are financially marginal or traditional loss centers. Risk avoidance is not usually feasible when the exposure or risk area is a good profit center for the organization. Head states that risk avoidance is a very complete risk management technique, because if a risk can be completely avoided, the organization can be absolutely certain that it is safe from that specific loss area.[15] Also, it stands to reason that if risk avoidance is successfully implemented, no other form of risk control or risk financing is necessary because the organization has avoided the risk.

Risk shifting or reciprocation involves techniques of moving an organization's risks by shifting or reciprocating the responsibility for them to other persons or organizations by contract. Some authors refer to risk shifting or risk reciprocation as another form of risk transfer. Risk transfer, however, as it is found in risk financing, does not transfer the risk itself but only the financial burden associated with it. We feel that risk shifting or reciprocation is a more accurate descriptor, since both the risk and the associated financial responsibility are moved from one party or organization to another.

An example of a risk shifting or reciprocation technique is the use of a contract clause whereby a subcontractor accepts the risk of liability for misadventures associated with the subcontracted activity. If a hospital desires to contract with a physician group to operate the emergency department, the parties might include an agreement whereby the doctors would assume all liability. The contract should be supported by an indemnity clause and evidence of insurance containing an endorsement for the hospital.

Risk shifting or reciprocation agreements should be arrived at through arm's-length negotiations. However, some risk managers frequently incorporate "hold-harmless" agreements into various documents they prepare. Hold-harmless agreements can be legally problematic if they are not reasonable or do not meet the requirements of contract law. The risk manager should consult legal counsel before incorporating hold-harmless agreements into documents. However, if used properly, such agreements can be an effective risk shifting tool in the risk manager's arsenal.

Risk prevention consists of a battery of techniques, activities, and programs primarily designed to prevent the adverse event that would result in a claim or lawsuit and subsequent financial loss. Although a large part of this text deals with risk prevention, it is important to review all the different categories and activities at this time and understand their place in the overall risk management process.

Risk prevention can be subdivided into two major parts: preoccurrence activities and postoccurrence activities. Preoccurrence activities include all tasks and functions associated with preventing incidents that might give rise to losses. Postoccurrence activities are those tasks and functions that can be carried out after the incident to help mitigate the potential or real loss.

Preoccurrence activities can be further subdivided into education programs, process and methods analyses, and policy and procedures design. The various educational programs implemented by risk managers are planned specifically to make others in the institution aware of and sensitive to preventing adverse events from occurring. Process and methods analysis studies and analyzes the way tasks are accomplished throughout the organization. The objective of this analysis is the critical evaluation of methods so that flaws in the system that might give rise to adverse occurrences can be discovered and corrected. Many of the techniques used and the data generated in the risk identification process can and should be used in risk prevention. This category incorporates many of the techniques used by industrial psychologists and time and motion experts. One can argue that an industrial psychologist whose mission is to increase job satisfaction is also carrying out a risk prevention program, because if the psychologist should find and correct a potential for job-related injuries, this will prevent financial loss as well as improve employee morale.

Policy and procedures design consists of the planning techniques used to design ways of carrying out tasks within the organization to prevent adverse events from occurring. The differences between policy and procedures design and process and methods analysis is more a matter of semantics than of substance. The former deals with establishing rules of behavior, and the latter deals primarily with analytical skills of performance. Establishing a hospital policy requiring nurses to check intravenous solutions every hour throughout the night would be classified as a risk prevention technique within the framework of policy and procedures design. Using the services of a fire safety specialist to identify and correct hazards is an example of a process and methods analysis function. In terms of general management theory, one can label policy and procedures design as a planning function, whereas process and methods analysis can be seen as a control function.

Postoccurrence activities can be subdivided into pre- and postlitigation techniques, tasks, and strategies. Prelitigation activities are those carried out immediately upon learning of an incident and are designed to head off potential or real claims or lawsuits by the use of one of several mitigation techniques. Many of the tasks used in this category are strategic in nature, and the success of the technique may never be quantifiable. For example, the waiver of a hospital bill of a patient who was critical of the care rendered is a common prelitigation technique. If the waiver is granted without the patient's signing a release from liability, and litigation never results, then one might assume that the strategy was successful. However, one can never really be sure, since the patient might not have filed a claim even if the risk manager had refused to waive the charges.

Many of the prelitigation techniques discussed in later chapters are controversial. However, given the source of the criticism, one must consider whether admitting human error and offering to mitigate the damages without the involvement of a paid third-party advocate is legitimate or just sour grapes.

Postlitigation techniques are those that a risk manager can carry out after the adverse event has occurred and the individual who sustained the injury or his or her representative has filed a claim or lawsuit. By and large, these tasks involve settlement techniques and attempts to reduce the potential loss through various strategies designed to lessen the financial, emotional, political, and public relations impact. Later in this text, various aspects of postlitigation risk prevention will be discussed in detail.

Summary

The risk management process is a complex set of tasks, functions, and decisions carried out with the objective of reducing unexpected financial loss to the organization. The process involves three major areas: exposure or risk identification, risk measurement or evaluation, and risk handling or treatment. Exposure or risk identification is simply the analysis of an exposure area of an organization so that risks contained within it can be identified. Risk measurement or evaluation is the process of applying analytical skills and decision-making techniques to the risk or exposure areas, to ascertain their potential for happening and the financial impact, should they happen.

Risk handling or treatment deals with how the risks that have been identified and measured are dealt with by the organization. There are two major categories: risk financing and risk control. Methods of risk financing include retention, transfer, and self-financing of risks and exposure areas. Risk control includes the avoidance, shifting, and prevention of risks to eliminate or reduce the financial impact of an occurrence to the organization. Figure 1-2 illustrates the risk management process and elucidates the various divisions and their relationship to each other.

Chapter Exercise

Community Hospital is a not-for-profit, 500-bed general hospital located in a typical American city of one-half million people. There are 15 members on the

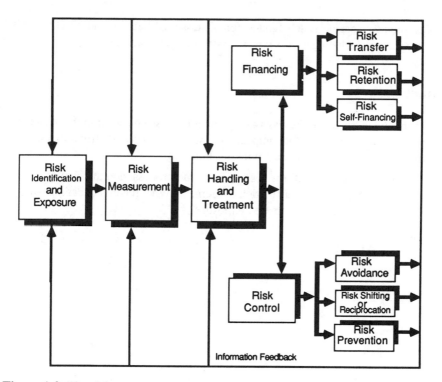

Figure 1-2 The risk management process.

board of trustees of the hospital, who represent a cross-section of all professions, and most of whom are prominent members of the community. Three members of the hospital board also sit on the board of trustees of a local college.

The risk manager is called into the office of the hospital administrator and told that, at the recent board meeting, the possibility of developing an affiliation with the local college was discussed. From unofficial sources the administrator has learned that the college needs more clinical teaching sites to expand the size and scope of its health programs. The college is particularly interested in Community Hospital because of its size and location, the quality of its medical staff, and its reputation for excellence. The hospital administrator has learned from the board that if approval is forthcoming, the college would like to send 25 students from the B.S. nursing program each academic semester, and about 10 students from each of the college's allied health programs which include respiratory therapy, medical technology, physical therapy, and dietetics. The risk manager is asked to prepare an assessment of the impact of such an affiliation on all aspects of the risk and loss control programs of the hospital.

Community Hospital is self-funded for professional liability and purchases all other insurance including excess coverage on the open market.

Questions

1. Using the overview of the risk management process presented in this chapter, prepare an assessment of the impact, if any, of the proposed affiliation on the exposure areas and risks to Community Hospital.

2. Assume that the board of trustees approves the proposal and that you are asked to help prepare the affiliation agreement. What recommendations will you make regarding the increased exposure?

References

1. C. Arthur Williams, Jr., George L. Head, Ronald C. Horn, and G. William Glendenning, *Principles of Risk Management and Insurance,* vol. I (Malvern, PA: American Institute for Property and Liability Underwriters, 1981), 4.

2. Bernard L. Brown, Jr., *Risk Management for Hospitals: A Practical Approach,* (Germantown, MD: Aspen Systems Corporation, 1979), 2.

3. *Darling v. Charleston Community Memorial Hospital,* 33 Ill. 2d 326, 211 N.E. 2d 253 (1965).

4. U.S. Department of Health, Education and Welfare, *Report of the Secretary's Commission on Medical Malpractice.* (Washington, DC: Government Printing Office, No. (05) 73-88, January 16, 1973), 39.

5. Barry M. Manuel "A Surgeon's Perspective on Professional Liability," *Bulletin of the American College of Surgeons,* vol. 70, no. 3 (March 1985): 6.

6. Ben Reagan, "Technology Creates New Areas of Hospital Liability Exposure," *Hospital Risk Management,* vol 7, no. 2 (February 1985): 1.

7. Robert L. Carter and Neil A. Doherty, *Handbook of Risk Management* (Middlesex, England: Kluwer-Harrap Handbooks, 1974), 4.3-01-4.3.05.

8. A.E. Pfaffle and Sal Nicosia, *Risk Analysis Guide to Insurance and Employee Benefits* (New York: AMACOM, 1977), 6-9.

9. Williams et al., 155.

10. Williams et al., 156.

11. Williams et al., 157.

12. George L. Head, "Fundamentals of Probability Analysis," in *Readings in Risk Management* (Malvern, PA: Insurance Institute of America, 1980), 116.

13. M. Sowka, (ed.), *N.A.I.C. Malpractice Claims: Medical Malpractice Closed Claims 1975-1978* (Brookfield, WI: National Association of Insurance Commissioners, vol. 2, no. 2, September 1980).

14. *Claude Woods v. North Kansas City Hospital et al.,* Clay County Circuit Court, unpublished case, 1985.

15. George L. Head, "Using Risk Avoidance," in *Readings in Risk Management* (Malvern, PA: Insurance Institute of America, 1980), 177.

CHAPTER TWO

RISK MANAGEMENT PROGRAM DESIGN

Thomas S. Gaudiosi, Gary P. Kraus, and Joan T. Rines

This chapter discusses how risk management programs are organized and designed in various health care facilities. Various organizational models found in hospitals and multi-institutional systems are described, and recommended models are provided based on the location, role, and function risk management plays within the organization.

We have seen in Chapter 1 the breadth and detail that the risk management process encompasses. It is obvious that the sheer complexity of the risk management process will preclude any one individual from carrying out the total program. However, it is the responsibility of the institution's board of trustees to see that the chief executive officer (CEO) implements a sound risk management program. It is not unusual for the CEO, members of the medical staff, and the board members to become actively engaged in parts of the process, which we shall explore later in this and other chapters.

We shall see in the section on "Interinstitutional Relationships" the necessity for establishing relationships between the risk management office and other departments within the organization. A sound risk management program depends on a positive and supportive attitude throughout the organization, with special emphasis given to risk management by those at the top of the organizational structure.

Much has been said and written about risk management and quality assurance. Unfortunately, confusion and disagreement exist over the role and purpose of the two and their relationship with one another. The section on "Risk Management and Quality Assurance" will explore the evolution and objectives of the two and the and relationships between them, offer models for strengthing the relationships, and provide suggestions for their integration when that is desired.

The functional and physical organization of the office of risk management must be well designed to achieve optimum efficiency. The section on "Internal Office Organization" will provide models with recommendations for organizing a risk management office.

A final section will explore the need, rationale, and function of the risk management committee. An explanation of how such committees function in health care facilities will be presented, and recommendations for a model committee will be provided.

Organizational Models

There is a truism in business that states that the higher an individual or office is on the organization's chain of command, the more influence and power that individual or office will be able to wield throughout the enterprise. One has only to look at the White House staff to realize that the incumbents are able to wield substantial power over various government agencies, even though they may have no legal authority over them, simply because they have access to the President. This same truism applies to risk management. If an office of risk management is located high within the organization's structure—for example, reporting to the board of trustees—then it will be in a better position to influence the behavior of those within the organization than if it were located at a lower point in the hierarchy.

The American Society for Hospital Risk Management (ASHRM), through a survey conducted among their members in 1983, has identified the ranks within the organizational hierarchy that many risk managers occupy.[1] Table 2-1 illustrates the hierarchical rank of reporting organizations. The professional positions to which the individual with responsibility for risk management reports were also assessed by the ASHRM, which found that the chief executive officer/vice-president is the most frequently identified office, with 44.4 percent of responses (Table 2-2). The organizational setting in which most risk managers have responsibility is the parent company or institution. Over 80 percent of respondents in the ASHRM survey identified the parent organization as their place of responsibility (Table 2-3). Regardless of the organization model used or the office to which the risk manager reports, strong interinstitutional relationships are necessary, since the risk

Table 2-1 Administrative Reporting Level Occupied by Individual with Responsibility for Risk Management

Administrative Level	No. of Respondents	Percentage
Highest	309	10.2
Second	1295	42.6
Third	854	28.1
Fourth	366	12.2
Fifth	109	3.6
Sixth	34	1.1
Seventh	16	0.5
Missing responses	54	1.8
Total	3037	100.0

Source: ASHRM-SRS, p. 6. Percentages do not sum to 100 because of rounding.

Table 2-2 Titles of Risk Management Professionals' Supervisors

Supervisor Title	Number	Percentage
Chief Executive Officer/Vice-President	1347	44.4
Senior Officer/Vice-President	917	30.2
Board of Trustees Member/President	140	4.6
Financial Officer	93	3.1
Chief Medical Officer	63	2.1
Nursing Administrator/Director	63	2.1
Personnel Officer	35	1.2
Chief of Engineering or Safety/Security	31	1.0
Quality Assurance Coordinator/Director	31	1.0
Operations Officer	22	0.7
Administrative Assistant to CEO/Senior Officer	20	0.7
Legal Services Officer	15	0.5
Director of Risk Management and Quality Assurance	9	0.3
Risk Management Coordinator/Director	7	0.2
Medical Records Manager/Director	5	0.2
Marketing/Public Relations Officer	1	0.0
Other	18	0.5
Missing responses	220	7.2
Total	3037	100.0

Source: ASHRM-SRS, p. 7.

Table 2-3 Organizational Setting in Which Individuals Have Responsibility for Risk Management

Organizational Setting	Number of Individuals	Percentage
Parent Organization/Institution	2436	80.2
Satellite Facility or Division	468	15.4
Other	64	2.1
Missing responses	69	2.3
Total	3037	100.0

Source: ASHRM-SRS, p. 14.

manager is primarily a coordinator of others. A risk management policy must be drafted by the organization, and the CEO must support it. Each department must know its role in the risk management process through the published risk management plan.

One can generally ascertain the importance and therefore the effectiveness of a hospital risk management program by its location on the organizational chart. If one categorizes programs by location, most hospital risk management programs fall within one of the models illustrated in Figures 2-1 through 2-7.

The board model shown in Figure 2-1 is one in which the risk management

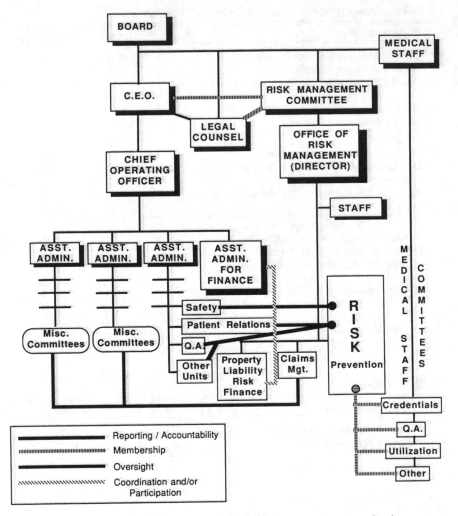

Figure 2-1 The board of directors model of risk management organization.

program comes under the direct control and authority of the board of directors of the organization. The legal structure of the institution may refer to the board members as trustees, directors, curators, or some similar term, but whatever the names used, we are referring to the legal body entrusted with the overall direction of the enterprise. Note that the line of authority leads directly to the risk management committee and that the risk manager reports to it. The CEO is a member of the risk management committee, as are the legal counsel and members of the executive committee of the medical staff.

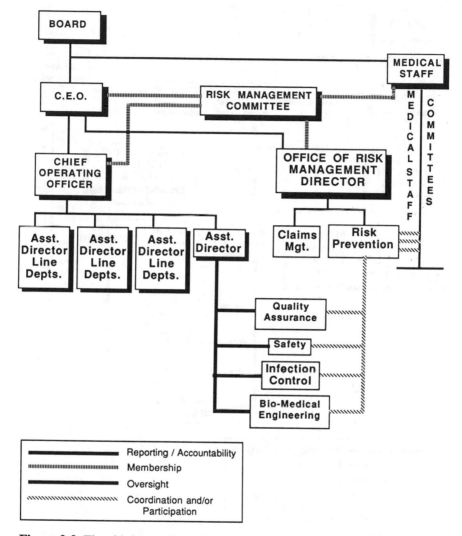

Figure 2-2 The chief executive officer model.

In this illustration, the risk management office maintains oversight responsibility for several functions including quality assurance, safety, and patient relations. The office also coordinates and/or participates in several committees and activities throughout the institution and its medical staff.

In Figure 2-2 we see a common example of a risk management program organization, the CEO model. Note that the risk manager serves as a staff person to the facility's CEO and has no line authority over any department. In this model the

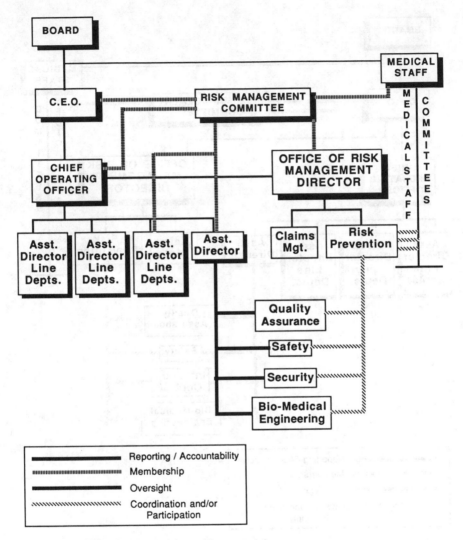

Figure 2-3 The chief operating officer model.

risk manager's role is one of coordination of activities and oversight. Any authority to carry out specific tasks will be identified by policy and procedures. The risk management committee is strictly an advisory body, and its membership includes individuals from the medical staff and hospital administration. The effectiveness of the CEO model will depend to a great extent on the importance the institution's chief executive places on risk management.

Figure 2-3 illustrates another common form of risk management organization,

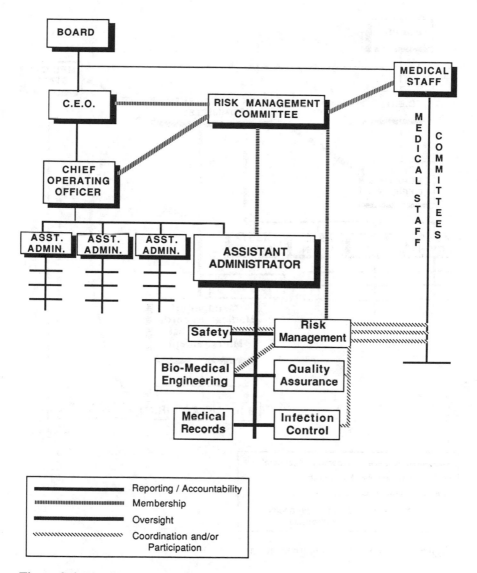

Figure 2-4 The department model.

wherein the office reports to the chief operating officer of the facility. In essence, the office functions in a fashion similar to that of the CEO model. The placing of the risk management office under the chief operating officer rather than the CEO is usually a matter of functional convenience.

Figure 2-4 illustrates another common example of risk management organiza-

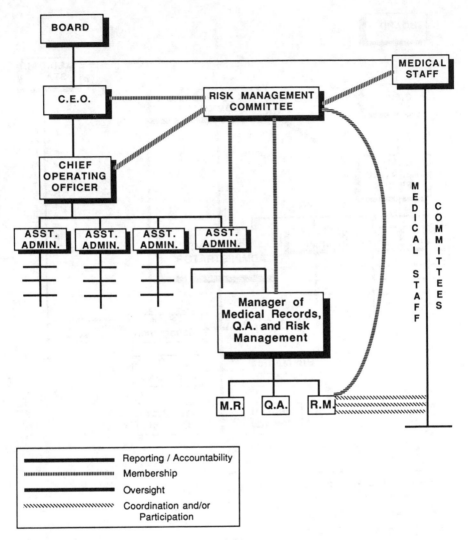

Figure 2-5 The line management model.

tion. Our experience indicates that the location of the office of risk management within a health care facility is most often as a department reporting to an assistant administrator or person of comparable rank within the organization. Note that the office is placed on an equal plane with other functions that are collateral to risk management.

In Figure 2-5 the office of risk management is a low-level line function which reports to a middle manager. This model is commonly used throughout the indus-

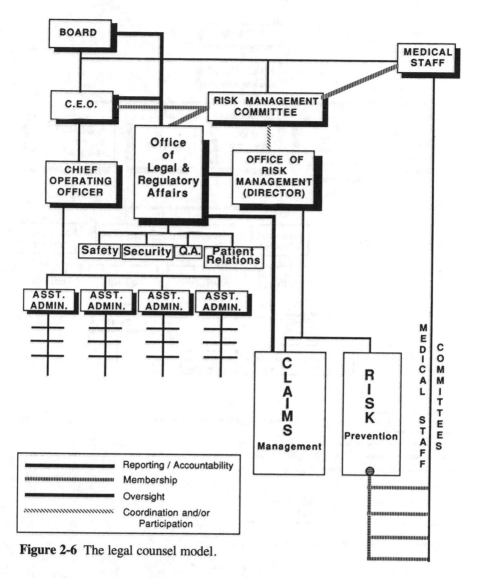

Figure 2-6 The legal counsel model.

try and usually denotes that the function is limited in scope and authority.

The legal counsel model, illustrated in Figure 2-6, appears to be increasing in use throughout the industry and is especially popular in organizations that have in-house legal counsel. Note that the office of legal counsel has line authority over risk management as well as over programs that are collateral to risk management, such as quality assurance, patient relations, safety, and security. This model gives the supervising attorney the opportunity to deal personally with or supervise the

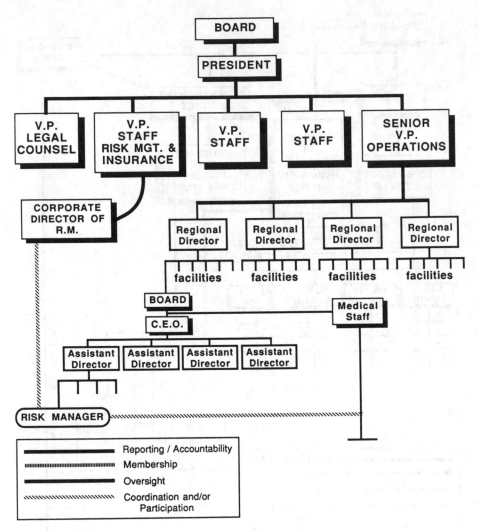

Figure 2-7 The multi-institutional model.

legal aspects of each function while delegating the nonlegal aspects of each function to specialists. (See the section on "Internal Office Organization" for an example of the internal organization of the risk management office.) Note that the legal office can report to either the board, the CEO, or both, with active involvement by a risk policy committee on which the medical staff is involved.

The last common model is that used primarily by multi-institutional organizations, particularly investor-owned hospital corporations (Figure 2-7). Note that each member institution has a resident risk manager who reports to that institution's administrator as well as having a direct line to the corporation's risk management director. The latter in turn reports to a high-ranking officer of the corporation, usually a vice-president or equivalent and often the CEO.

Besides the models illustrated above, there no doubt exist many variations. For example, the Geisinger Medical Center of Danville, Pennsylvania, uses a variation on the chief operating officer model (Figure 2-3). At Geisinger, the risk manager occupies the position of administrative assistant to the senior vice-president/medical director.[2] The rationale for placing the program under the medical director was to ensure that the program was in a prominent, visible position in the hospital structure.[3] When planning the program, it was decided that the risk control process and its functions would be placed under the medical director, but that the risk financing processes would fall within the purview of the chief financial officer.[4]

The organizational model for risk management that an institution chooses should be determined according to the functions, tasks, responsibilities, and authority that the board of directors expects to delegate to the office. Also, and most important, the model should reflect the importance and visibility that the administration places on risk management, and in particular on those processes associated with risk control.

Once these decisions have been made, the degree of training and skill desired in the risk manager can be determined. Given the total risk management processes described in Chapter 1, it is apparent that if the office of risk management is delegated the responsibility for carrying out most of the processes, then the board model or at least the CEO model must be chosen, with strong input by a risk policy committee with medical staff, administration, and board membership. On the other hand, if the office of risk management is to be merely a low-level staff position, without authority and with tasks and responsibilities limited to fact finding and data collection, then the line management model (Figure 2-5) would be appropriate. The point is that the location of the office of risk management within the chain of organization of the particular facility is determined by the importance and visibility the directors desire it to have.

Another important criterion when deciding what model to select is the economic one, particularly when the health care facility is small or has limited exposure, for example, a nursing home, a small hospital with fewer than 100 beds, or a free-standing health facility such as a surgical center or an ambulatory care clinic. In small facilities it may be wiser to consolidate risk management with collateral programs such as quality assurance to achieve economies of scale.

Interinstitutional Relationships

The success of a risk management program will depend to a great extent on the strength of its relationships with the departments, functions, committees, and activities within the health facility. The risk manager in a health care institution is primarily a coordinator and facilitator, whose principal task is to make the staff practice risk management techniques. Quite simply, he or she is a manager—one whose job it is to get work done by his or her subordinates. In the health facility all staff are subordinate to some risk management process.

The functional organizational chart illustrated in Figure 2-8 provides an example of how complex the interinstitutional relationships between the risk management office and the rest of the facility must be in order to carry out a comprehensive risk management program[5]. The risk management program, occupying the

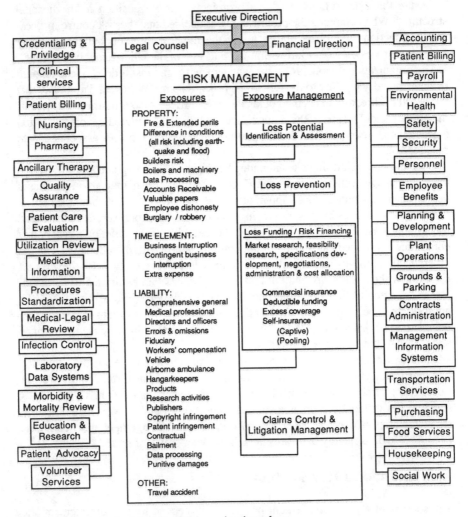

Figure 2-8 A typical functional organization chart.

Source: ASHRM

center rectangle of the illustration, is divided into exposures and exposure management processes. The exposures are subdivided into common areas found in most health care facilities, such as property, the time element, and liability. The management of the exposure areas is classified into four categories, which essentially represent the basic risk management processes explored in Chapter 1.

On the far left of Figure 2-8 we see a column of common activities associated with the professional care provided in an average hospital. On the far right is a column of common support services found in the typical hospital. The solid line leading from the risk management office indicates that this risk management program follows the assistant administrator model (Figure 2-4) of program organization. Note also, however, that the office of general counsel appears to have a coordinating and/or participatory role.

To establish, support, and enforce the interinstitutional relationships between risk management and the rest of the facility, a risk management plan must be established. The plan should be published and circulated throughout the organization in a risk management manual designed to provide the various departments, activities, and services of the institution with a description of their individual roles in the overall risk management program. The plan should begin with a policy statement provided by the board of directors and the CEO of the institution, to give the program the visibility and support necessary for its success. Within the risk management manual each of the departments, services, and activities indicated on the left and right columns of Figure 2-8 would find details of their specific involvement in the overall risk management plan. Also, each department, program, and activity would receive a copy of its own section of the manual. For example, the credentialing and privilege function of the medical staff would have its section of the total risk management plan clearly delineated and detailed. The plan should require the individual in charge of the credentialing and privileges process to provide the office of risk management with summaries of its activities on a timely basis. The timeliness of reports and information to be provided to the office of risk management obviously depends on the importance of each activity to the overall risk management process. The credentialing and privilege function may be such that information may need to be provided to the risk manager only a few times per year and when new individuals join or leave the institution or when a staff member's privileges have been increased or diminished. However, some activities, such as those of the medical records department dealing with requests for medical records by outside lawyers, would require almost daily contact. The risk management plan as it affects each function within the institution serves as a management tool for those individuals responsible for the operation of their specific activities.

Education is a necessary element in the overall risk management program as it pertains to the interrelationships of the various functions, services, departments, and activities of the institution. We are not referring here to the education associ-

In commitment to provide quality health care, and to assure the
continuing human, physical, and financial integrity to provide it, the
hospital has established a risk management program of activities to
minimize the adverse effects of loss through: identification and
assessment of loss potential, loss prevention, loss funding and risk
financing, and claims control.

The hospital has established a risk management office to direct,
supervise, and manage the program to oversee its effectiveness
throughout the institution.

An effective risk management program is a responsibility of all
managers of hospital resources and all staff members, in cooperation
with, and with direction and assistance from the risk management office.

It is the policy of the hospital to reduce, modify, eliminate, and
control conditions and practices that may cause loss. The safety and
well-being of patients, personnel and the public shall have the highest
priority.

It is the responsibility of the risk management office to manage the
identification and assessment of loss potential, to develop and assure
the effectiveness of loss prevention programs, to manage the development
and maintenance of adequate loss funding and risk financing programs,
and to contain losses that do occur through the development,
maintenance, and coordination of claims control activities.

Source: American Society for Hospital Risk Management. Reprinted by permission.

Exhibit 2-1 Sample risk management policy statement.

ated with the various aspects of risk prevention, but to the education necessary to inform other members of the institution of their role in risk management. Experience has shown that very few managers within health care facilities, from the executive director on down, have a clear understanding of the risk management process and their individual role in it. It only stands to reason that if individual department heads within an institution do not understand risk management, they will not comprehend their role and will be in a position to weaken the overall program by their lack of knowledge and commitment. Therefore, the risk management plan must incorporate routine in-service education for managers on a timely basis, so that their involvement in a changing field of risk management can be maintained.

The American Society for Hospital Risk Management has published a sample risk management policy statement, which is presented in Exhibit 2-1. A similar policy statement must be published and provided to every manager throughout the rank and file of the organization from the executive director to the lowest line manager. The policy statement will provide evidence of the commitment of the office of risk management and all divisions within the facility to the principles of risk management. The policy statement serves as the charge that supports the program and strengthens its interrelationships with other functions, services, departments, and activities of the enterprise.

Exhibit 2-2 presents an example of a section of the risk management plan for a specific activity within the department of medical records. The plan describes the involvement of the legal correspondence secretary with the office of risk management. Note the activity and purpose statement and the listing of specific information to be provided to the office of risk management and the time period required. Exhibit 2-2 is just an example of one page of the risk management plan for one section of one department within an institution. Each activity that has active risk management involvement must have its own detailed policy in writing so that the individuals within each section and the office of risk management itself know their involvement in the overall risk management program. As the reader can surmise, the risk management plan for an entire institution will become a sizeable document, requiring substantial work in keeping it current.

Risk Management and Quality Assurance

Risk management and quality assurance are much akin, yet there is so much misunderstanding throughout the health profession about their roles and functions that the subject deserves special attention.

The mission, role, objectives, and control of risk management and quality assurance have often been debated and written about. Unfortunately, much of the literature and the conversation centering around these two subjects is based on misunderstanding and lack of knowledge of the purposes of the two programs. In some circumstances, because of concerns by individuals over turf, risk management and quality assurance have been set at odds, and instead of complementing each other they have created polarization among the staffs of institutions. The primary reason for the misunderstanding stems from a lack of knowledge of the purpose, the derivation of the two concepts, and the interrelationships of members of the administration of the facility.

Studying the origin and the objectives of both risk management and quality assurance and reviewing the total risk management process as outlined in Figure 1-2 makes it quite obvious that quality assurance and risk management should complement one another. Figure 2-9 illustrates the relationship between risk management and quality assurance. The arrow leading out of the risk management circle and up indicates that the goal of risk management is to reduce unplanned financial loss to the institution. One obvious means of reducing financial loss is to prevent the adverse occurrences that give rise to claims and lawsuits and the expenses associated with them. At the far right of Figure 1-2, risk prevention is included as a major subsection of the risk process called risk control. Returning to Figure 2-9, an arrow leaving the quality assurance circle to the right and going down the diagram indicates that the goal of quality assurance is to improve the quality of patient care. It is obvious that if one can improve the quality of patient care, certain injuries will be prevented that otherwise could give rise to the claims

Department: Medical Records
Section: Legal Correspondence

Risk Management Activity and Purpose:

The office of legal correspondence has the responsibility of
providing patient medical information to individuals and
organizations for a variety of legal, insurance, and related
purposes. A patient, former patient, next-of-kin, or their
advocate may desire the medical record or parts thereof for many
reasons, one of which may be to use in litigation against the
hospital or a member of its medical or professional staff. It is
desirable for the institution to know as soon as possible that
there is a likelihood of litigation in order to investigate the
case, evaluate its position, and plan a strategy. Therefore, the
active involvement of the legal correspondence office is important
to the institution's overall risk management plan.

Risk Management Tasks:

1) The hospital legal correspondence secretary shall notify the
office of risk management of the names of all legal counsel,
patients, or advocates requesting copies of a medical record where
the purpose cannot be ascertained, or where the purpose is to
propose a claim or suit against the hospital, its medical staff,
or any of its employees.
2) The legal correspondence secretary shall provide the risk
manager with monthly reports on all correspondence activity
according to a format to be provided.
3) The legal correspondence secretary shall provide copies of the
medical records of any patient to counsel for the hospital or its
medical staff or its employees upon the request of the risk
manager. Charges for copies of records shall be determined by the
risk manager and may be waived at his/her discretion.
4) The legal correspondence secretary shall notify the risk
manager and/or the hospital legal counsel upon receipt of any
subpoena for medical records or other information for court
appearances and depositions.
5) The legal correspondence secretary shall notify the office of
the risk manager of any telephone request or personal appearance
by an attorney who appears to be an adversary against the interest
of the institution, its medical staff, or its employees.
6) The office of risk management shall provide the legal
correspondence secretary with a list of individuals who have
threatened suit or sustained a potential compensatory event while
a patient. Any request for the patient's record shall be
communicated to the office of risk management immediately.
7) The legal correspondence secretary shall maintain frequent
communications with the office of risk management, and any
activity out of the ordinary of a risk or legal nature shall be
communicated to the office of risk management as soon as possible.

Exhibit 2-2 Sample of part of a hospital's risk management plan.

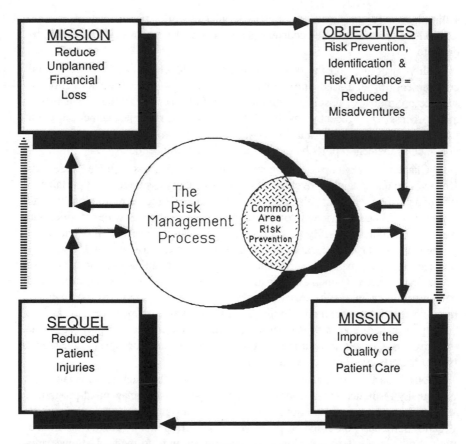

Figure 2-9 The risk management-quality assurance relationship.

and lawsuits that the risk manager attempts to prevent. This idea is represented by the arrow leading from quality assurance to risk management and from risk management back to quality assurance. In summary, if one accepts the total risk management processes as illustrated and discussed in Chapter 1, then it appears that the quality assurance is simply a part of the risk prevention process of risk management.

Why personnel involved in risk management and quality assurance feel that their activities should be separate seems a mystery, but it is probably a result of the origin of both programs, the emphasis given quality assurance by the Joint Commission on Accreditation of Hospitals (JCAH) and the individuals who direct each. The impetus for hospital risk management originated with the insurance industry. Risk management programs were in place in other industries long before they were adopted in the health field. It is understandable and logical that, besides

selling insurance, an insurance company would also offer risk management services to help prevent adverse occurrences and reduce the claims that they would be
liable to pay.

Quality assurance, on the other hand, has the JCAH as well as the federal
government (through Medicare) as its procursor. The JCAH requires quality assurance programs[7] of hospitals while giving only lip service to the risk management process. Only recently has the JCAH recognized risk management through
its accreditation process, primarily by suggesting that risk management information such as incident reports be used as a quality assurance too[8].

In Chapter 8, a synopsis of the risk prevention process will be presented.
However, to understand more clearly the role of quality assurance as it pertains to
risk management one must dissect the risk prevention process more closely. Risk
prevention can be subdivided into two major sections: preoccurrence activities and
postoccurrence activities. By preoccurrence we mean the prevention of the event
or incident that gives rise to the injury and the subsequent claim or lawsuit. By
postoccurrence we mean those activities carried out after an incident or an adverse
event occurs that are aimed at mitigating damages so that loss can be minimized
and perhaps a claim or suit averted. Remember that prevention in the risk management context means preventing both the adverse event, or misadventure as it is
sometimes called, and the financial loss, which is the mission or purpose of the
total process. Consequently, it is clear that quality assurance occupies a substantial
part of the process of preoccurrence risk prevention.

Another cause of misunderstanding and competition between risk management
and quality assurance arises from the organization of risk management programs.
As stated above, some institutions place the risk management program low on the
organization chart, on an equal plane with such programs as quality assurance,
patient relations, safety, security, infection control and bio-medical engineering.
All of these programs have overlapping risk prevention functions, and so the
competition between their directors is obvious and predictable. If the risk management tasks in a hospital are limited to risk prevention, and the risk manager carries
out few activities beyond this process, it is only natural that quality assurance and
risk management will compete, since they are both carrying out essentially the
same objectives under different names. Therefore, if the institution plans to limit
the risk management responsibility to prevention and to assign the other processes
of risk management discussed in Chapter 1 to other divisions of the institution—for
example, if the chief financial officer becomes responsible for risk financing, and
loss and claims investigation is carried out by representatives of the insurance
company or legal counsel—then it may be wise to merge the quality assurance and
risk management programs into one activity. Several authors have actively called
for the integration of risk management and quality assurance.[9] Their integration is
a practical matter in circumstances where the institution is small enough that the
risk prevention tasks can be carried out by one individual regardless of his or her

title. John F. Monagle, in his text *Risk Management: A Guide for Health Care Professionals,* incorporates a model for an integrated quality assurance and risk management activity.[10]

Many hospitals and other health care facilities have chosen to integrate risk management with quality assurance. The ASHRM survey reported that 66.1 percent (2,009) of respondents were employed within integrated programs. Of the total, 22.4 percent (451) managed the integrated program alone, 48.7 percent (977) did so along with a quality assurance professional, and 28.9 percent (581) shared management of the program with some other type of professional.[11] Programs with primary risk prevention responsibility can better achieve desired results by integrating quality assurance and risk management into one overall program, thus realizing better economy and coordination.

A strong risk management committee is essential to success. Membership on the committee should include the CEO, the chief of medical staff, and most senior officers. Representation by a member of the board of directors is also recommended.

If one desires to integrate risk management and quality assurance for any of the reasons discussed above, the example in Figure 2-10 is suggested. Note that the joint program uses the board model depicted in Figure 2-1, but the title of the committee has been expanded to give visibility to both functions. The title of the office should also incorporate the primary functions carried out—in this case, quality assurance and risk management. One could also integrate the legal counsel into this organization model by incorporating legal affairs in the title of the oversight committee and office. Figure 2-10 includes the office of legal affairs as an option, identified by the dotted lines.

In summary, there are very good reasons why risk management and quality assurance should be integrated and consolidated under one office. In small institutions, the function should be carried out by the same party. By merging the two programs, the institution could no doubt realize substantial savings, reduce unnecessary duplication of effort, and, most important, better guarantee that information collected by each function would be utilized.

A close analysis of Figure 2-10 indicates that the functions of quality assurance, infection control, safety, and patient relations (patient representative) all have some relationship to the risk management process, generally in the area of preoccurrence risk prevention, except for the patient relations function the involvement of which is usually postoccurrence prevention. Therefore, the grouping of these functions under a single director, so that each prevention-related management task can be closely coordinated, should have a substantial benefit to the facility by reducing unnecessary duplication of effort as well as better accomplishing the risk prevention process. The integration of quality assurance and risk management along with strengthening of networks with infection control, safety, and patient relations is therefore highly recommended.

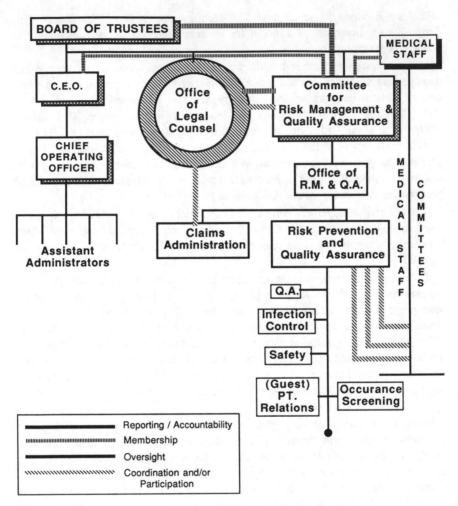

Figure 2-10 An integrated risk management-quality assurance program.

The Role of the Medical Record Department in Quality Assurance

The medical record as a quality assurance tool provides source information that may be screened according to prescribed explicit criteria designed to glean answers to questions posed by a particular focused study. The biggest problem with quality assurance is documentation.[12] Quality assurance is a basic part of hospital management. It monitors costs, quality, efficiency, utilization, and performance.

Quality assurance also affects productivity. Output minus poor quality output equals productivity, according to Spath. This section describes the quality assurance contributions made by both the medical record and its custodian.

Although medical record personnel do not deliver direct patient care, they do manage the records that document direct patient care. Raymond Goodman wrote that the role of the medical record cannot be overemphasized as a principal source for studies on medical care audit, and in particular on the quality of health care services as they relate to personnel services.[13] This is demonstrated, he wrote, by the fact that as long ago as January 1979 there were 63 organized national medical record associations throughout the world. One of the oldest is the American Medical Record Association, established in 1928.

Selected Studies

Fessel and Van Brunt wrote that outcomes which appear much more accurately to reflect the quality of care may be unrelated to the recorded process of care.[14] These authors studied patients with two common conditions, acute appendicitis and myocardial infarctions, and found that neither quantity, nor quality of recorded data was related to either condition's outcome. They concluded that unless outcomes are very unusual or statistically improbable, an individual's medical record cannot be evaluated. Quality can be assessed only by a comparison of groups of patients having the same condition who had similar initial severity indices, or were treated by different physicians, by different methods, or perhaps at different institutions. Other variables, such as length of stay, and numbers or types of postoperative complications, must be taken into consideration, as well as the patient's satisfaction with his or her management and its associated costs. The patient-physician relationship, an important intangible criterion for measuring quality, is not necessarily a part of the recorded process of care. It could be, however, if physicians would document their human interest procedures (office and bedside discussions with patients about the condition and its treatment course), but time constraints and a lack of perceived importance for this documentation often preclude such complete and thorough record keeping. In a subsequent study, Lyons and Payne found a statistically significant, although not perfect, relationship between good medical record documentation and good medical care.[15]

The problem-oriented medical record (POMR), according to Bronson et al.,[16] is seen by some as a method of combating this situation. Findings from the study by Fernow et al.,[17] revealed that although the POMR is not necessarily better than a well-kept traditional record, it does appear that it may be an invaluable adjunct to a poorly kept record.

Physician action, including patient education, is linked to a specific health problem in the POMR[12] according to Bronson, et al. Education becomes an integral part of treatment, not just an adjunct. In a rather bold, unusual move

Bronson and his associates began sharing records with their patients in order to enhance quality control. They felt that record sharing made patients more responsible for managing their own health care and increased their ability to use health care services intelligently and economically. Record sharing also enchanced patient-physician communication, a necessary step in reducing potential malpractice claims.

After treatment goals and plans had been formulated and the record had been compiled, a typewritten copy was sent to each patient with a covering letter, which explained how to read and "audit" the record. Patients were asked to check for the thoroughness and accuracy of the statements to be sure all health problems have been addressed. Finally, the patients examined the record for clarity of goals and plans and were encouraged to question them if unclear.

The physicians in the Bronson study found that the record sharing procedure forced them to write in clear, understandable lay language. This made them more adept at viewing the problems as they affect the whole patient, to say nothing of the improved patient-physician communication. A patient who participates in his or her own treatment plan is better equipped to understand the reasons for the medical actions taken. Records can be shared without invoking fear, and honesty between the patient and the physician enhances the patient's ability to deal more effectively with his or her problem.

Thirty-four hundred patients received their records and 665 responded to the request to review the record (19.6 percent). Patient responses were categorized into three groups: 1) information corrected, 2) progress reported in meeting goals, and 3) additional information supplied or questions asked. In all, only 8 percent of the responses led to changes in problem statements or plans. Bronson and his associates posited that there is only a small percentage of patients who may audit and use their records well, which could be explained by patient reluctance to question medical authority.

The Medical Record Professional's Role in Quality Assurance

Medical record professionals contribute to quality assurance through quality assurance activities related to the medical record itself. Complete and accurate coding of diagnoses and procedures, careful following of policies and procedures relating to confidentiality and release of patient information, and concurrent monitoring of records using screening criteria are just a few examples of these activities. If diagnoses and procedures are not accurately documented and coded, hospitals could be shortchanged monetarily under today's prospective payment system. Concurrent monitoring ensures that proper patient care is being delivered. There must be close work with the professionals responsible for record documentation to facilitate accurate coding.[18] More detailed charting by physicians, nurses, and clinical support personnel should be encouraged. Third-party payors review charts to make sure that the services billed are the services received. If these services are not documented, then as far as the payor is concerned they were not received, and therefore should not be reimbursed.

Miccio wrote that the "DRG creep" is more a myth than a reality. (A DRG creep is the unauthorized, unethical manipulation of data to obtain higher reimbursement under the prospective payment system in effect for Medicare patients. Optimal reimbursement does occur properly when the principal diagnoses and procedures are reported accurately.) However, some medical record practitioners relate stories of receiving directions from hospital administrators to report diagnoses and procedures in ways that would bring the highest amount of revenue to the hospital. This violates the coding principles that medical record professionals are instructed to follow and that originate from such authoritative entities as the U.S. Department of Health and Human Services, the American Hospital Association, and the American Medical Record Association. It is unethical for medical record practitioners to manipulate codes to maximize reimbursement in ways inconsistent with professional and regulatory guidelines.[19] Using the complete medical record as a source document, employing qualified coders, developing written coding policies that conform to proper professional guidelines, and developing quality control procedures to monitor coding consistency and completeness will ensure that poor-quality data can be minimized.

The medical record department's and the medical record practitioner's functions in and contributions to a hospital-wide, integrated quality assurance plan vary. An inverse relationship exists between the medical record department's or practitioner's quality assurance responsibilities and the size of the health care facility. As the size of the hospital decreases, that role increases and a more direct relationship exists between the medical record practitioner's abilities and his or her contributions to quality assurance.

The role of a quality assurance professional today is as a clinical information specialist actively involved in planning, data gathering, information dissemination and follow-up.[20] In 1984, the American Medical Record Association recognized the quality assurance expertise of its members and formed a quality assurance Section, which today boasts over 1,200 members throughout the world. The fact that medical record professionals rely on objective data as a framework for program decision making is an essential source of credibility for this allied health group. Medical record practitioners should be familiar with the Conditions of Participation for Hospitals (Medicare), the Joint Commission on Accreditation of Hospitals (JCAH) standards related to quality assurance activities, and the provisions of the latest Professional Review Organization (PRO) legislation in order to be knowledgeable participants.[21]

The following functions and guideline statements compiled by the American Medical Record Association best describe both the medical record department's and the medical record practitioner's role in quality assurance activities:[22]

A. A medical record practitioner's knowledge of federal and state regulations and licensing and accrediting agency requirements for quality assurance enables him or her to share this knowledge with administration, the medical staff, and other health professionals. By taking an active role in the institution's committees and functions, the medical record practitioner is able to recommend revisions to institutional policies and medical staff bylaws, rules, and regulations where appropriate.

B. The medical record practitioner identifies areas within the institution that allow for the department's participation in the integrated quality assurance program and expands the department's relationships with other health care practitioners enhancing these activities.

C. The medical record practitioner develops procedures for problem identification and data collection and display. In addition, there are policies and procedures within the medical record department for storing, using, and maintaining confidentiality of the quality assurance data. Accurate and timely reports of the findings are produced with subsequent follow-up.

D. Data collection activities promote reliability, reduce redundancy and duplication of work, and produce data consistent with institutional and external agency requirements. The source and reliability of data collected for quality assurance and utilization maintenance activities are documented and periodically reviewed.

E. A mechanism is established through the integrated quality assurance program whereby health record documentation and content are monitored. Appropriate follow-up is conducted when problems in the health record content and/or documentation are brought to the quality assurance program's attention. In turn, the quality assurance program lends its support when the medical record practitioner takes action to correct content and documentation problems.

F. The medical record professional is responsible for in-service education programs that describe the record's role in quality assurance not only to employees within the medical record department but also to administration, medical staff, and other health care professionals.

G. Finally, the medical record department assesses the costs and services provided by the quality assurance staff in an effort to maintain the most efficient and effective operations. In addition, it determines the sufficiency of quality assurance activities and documentation to meet institution and external agency requirements.

The list of skills a quality assurance coordinator must have resembles the curriculum followed in educational programs for medical record professionals:

1. Knowledge of data evaluation techniques
2. Knowledge of data management techniques
3. Skill in the organization and administration of health care facilities and departments
4. Communications skills
5. Knowledge of the legal aspects of health information management
6. Knowledge of health care legislation, standards, and regulations
7. Knowledge of medical terminology

In addition, medical record professionals have backgrounds in anatomy, physiology, and pathology. Yet quality assurance coordinators' positions often go to utilization review coordinators, risk managers, or associate and assistant administrators, most of whom are credentialed in other professional disciplines. The person to be appointed must be able to justify his or her candidacy by remedying deficiencies and on occasion learning new concepts. Traditionally, medical record professionals have been handicapped by their image as file clerks and librarians. Low visibility and other health care professionals' ignorance have contributed to this image, which does not reflect the wide range of knowledge and skills representative of the profession.[23]

The Medical Record Professional's Perceived Role in Quality Assurance

The role of medical record professionals in hospital quality assurance activities ranges from nonexistent to prominent. Some practitioners feel that medical record professionals can be more involved in quality assurance activities than they are, but additional skills such as financial management and leadership flexibility are needed.

Sixty-five selected medical record practitioners in the United States were surveyed to determine their perceived role in quality assurance and risk management activities. Forty-six (71 percent) responded to questions about the medical record department's or practitioner's position in the integrated quality assurance and risk management plan in their facilities; about the quality assurance/risk management tasks performed by these professionals; about whether these roles reflect the professionals' training, academic preparation, and capabilities; and about any recommended changes to enhance these roles.

Twenty-seven out of 46 respondents described the medical record department's or practitioner's authority in their health care facility's quality assurance plan as both line and staff in nature, and about 25 percent of these respondents said they performed staff functions only. The majority of the respondents reported that the tasks they perform in the quality assurance plan are as follows: 1) attending quality assurance committee meetings; 2) retrieving data, compiling statistics, and displaying data, 3) screening for and reporting discrepancies in documentation, and 4) serving as a quality assurance resource or advisor for other departments. Additional tasks mentioned were developing screening criteria, performing utilization review, performing the quality assurance studies themselves, preparing reports, maintaining follow-up on identified problems, and approving the design of forms. Several responded that they were responsible for the initial development of the quality assurance plan, and a few reported that their only activity was to pull charts for the reviewers. The respondents were not asked to indicate the size of the facility in which they were employed, but judging from the literature reviewed those medical record practitioners with the most responsibilities for quality assurance activities probably are employed in relatively small institutions.

Nearly 75 percent of the respondents felt that their expertise, knowledge, and academic preparation were reflected in these roles. However, five people responded that in their facility a medical record professional was either not necessary or for other reasons no longer contributed to the quality assurance program. Only a small percentage of respondents felt that their expertise, knowledge, and academic background were underutilized, and there were no real concrete suggestions for role enhancement except that some respondents felt the medical record professional should be more involved in the quality assurance program, while others suggested that practitioners needed additional skills in order to perform their functions.

From these responses it appears that medical record practitioners feel their contributions to the quality assurance activities are adequate, and there is little need to increase this involvement. For the most part, these reported activities conform to the professional practice standards described earlier. It is probably safe to assume that with the elevation of the medical record department's role in the financial health of the institution, medical record practitioners feel that additional responsibilities would detract from rather than enhance their contributions to quality assurance. This is particularly true since most of these professionals have had to adjust to reduced staffing patterns in their departments. However, with added skills and the fact that some practitioners have focused their continuing education on quality assurance activities, medical record professionals could play an even more influential role in these functions, although these survey results did not seem to support such a possibility.

In Chapter 9, we will explore in depth the medical record, the medical record department, and the medical record professional's role in risk management.

Internal Office Organization

Certain preexisting conditions will influence decisions regarding the internal organization and design of a risk management office. One consideration, of course, is the size of the institution. Small hospitals, nursing homes, and freestanding health facilities usually do not require complicated risk management programs, since most major decisions such as risk funding, risk avoidance, and claims management are made by administrative officers who are not given the title of risk manager. Large institutions, of course, have such a volume of activity that the office of risk management could require not only a director but several assistants with responsibility over certain related activities.

A second consideration is the functions and processes that will be delegated to the office. For example, will the office carry out the risk financing activities, or will they be delegated to another division of the institution, such as the chief financial officer? Another activity to consider is legal affairs. If the institution has an in-house legal counsel, this will influence the delegation of certain functions to the risk manager. A third consideration is the degree of integration and consolidation of risk prevention-related activities desired by the institution's administration, such as infection control, patient advocacy, quality assurance, safety and similar functions. Once these decisions have been made, one can organize the office in such a way as best to achieve the objectives of risk management.

Before we discuss a model internal functional organization of a risk management program, the reader should review Figure 2-8 and observe the way the sample functional organizational chart organizes the various tasks and activities in categories. The reader should specifically pay attention to those activities under property exposure and liability exposure.

The model functional organizational chart for the internal operation of a risk management program, illustrated in Figure 2-11, is designed after the board of directors model for risk management organization illustrated in Figure 2-1. This type of organization is designed for a large health care system, one that could include several hospitals and other related health activities. Also, this type of organization assumes that decisions regarding which functions and processes are to be carried out by the office of risk management have already been made, and that they include as many of the risk management processes as are optimal for a self-insured organization, including risk financing. Another assumption is that the institution has an internal legal affairs office. The third assumption of this model is that the hospital desires to achieve the maximum degree of integration and consolidation of risk-related activities.

Note that the oversight committee's title reflects most of the major activities to be carried out within the office. Note also that the office of legal counsel and the function of risk financing have been delineated with solid lines leading to the director. This simply means that these functions are controlled or perhaps even

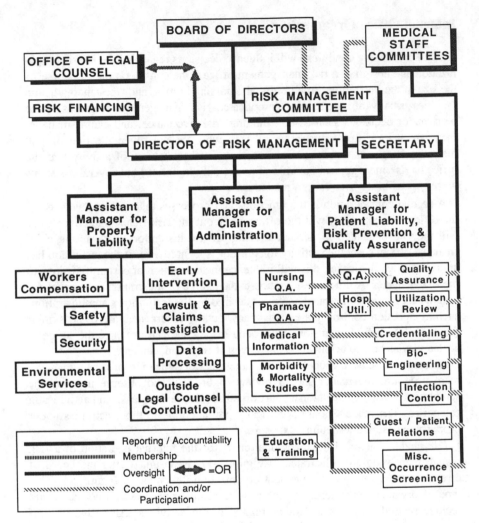

Figure 2-11 Internal organization of a risk management program.

carried out by the director, depending on whether a decision is made to have risk management supervised by an attorney or by an individual knowledgeable in risk financing such as an insurance expert.

The model is organized in three fundamental parts. The first part, labeled "Director of Patient Liability, Risk Prevention, and quality assurance," incorporates all basic risk prevention activities of a preoccurrence nature such as infection control, credentialing and privileges, nursing, pharmacy, quality assurance, patient care evaluation activities, utilization review, medical information, and morbidity and mortality studies. By placing these functions within this division, it is implied that the director either controls these activities through a line-staff relationship or coordinates their activities through indirect linkages.

The "Director of Claims Administration" deals with postoccurrence prevention activities such as early intervention. These activities can be carried out by the individual directly or by the patient relations representative, or both. This function also oversees claims and lawsuit management. It may require that the director of this division or the director of the overall risk management department be an attorney, or perhaps be the same individual. This decision will of course depend on the volume of activity. Implied in this division is that the legal department or the director, if he or she is an attorney, shall take active management of all lawsuits, particularly those assigned to outside law firms.

The third function, called the "Director of Property Liability," has the responsibility of overseeing directly, or indirectly through linkages, those activities that reflect on property and related liability. This includes workers' compensation, safety, security, environmental services, and other activities as indicated.

The director of the risk management program illustrated in Figure 2-11 has the responsibility of facilitating and coordinating risk management activities throughout the whole organization. Those activities for which the director has line management responsibility obviously will require close supervision, and the selection of assistants should be determined by the expertise needed to carry out the responsibilities. For example, claims administration may be carried out by the director, if he or she is an attorney or perhaps by an assistant who has a law or claims administration background. Patient liability, risk prevention, and quality assurance would probably be the responsibility of an individual from the health professions, such as a nurse with experience in quality assurance and those activities of a preventive nature. Property liability management might be assigned to an individual with a background in safety, workers' compensation, or related expertise associated with a physical plant, engineering, or similar background. Risk management is an activity that requires primarily the coordination and facilitation of others. It is therefore important that the risk manager maintain a staff that is balanced with respect to education and experience, so that they are not only competent to carry out their tasks but also have the ability to educate others within the institution.

The risk manager and his or her staff must have sufficient office space to carry out the functions required. Because risk management deals with extremely sensitive information, it is wise to provide the professional staff with a private office, so that they can meet and confer with members of the institution's medical, nursing, allied health and general staff in confidence. Besides the obvious secretarial support, which will be determined based on the number of assistant staff members, the office must have the necessary tools, including a personal computer. In Chapter 4 we will deal in detail with the necessity for an information system; at this time it is sufficient to state that a personal computer with at least 256K RAM memory is necessary as a support item. A computer of this size will provide the capacity to support a word processing function as well as to maintain files on incident reports and other information. One may even be able to justify the hiring of a computer operator if the institution desires a state-of-the-art information system. It would then be preferable for the office of risk management to have a computer with sufficient memory to keep all records associated with the department on easy-access file. For this a personal computer with a hard disk drive of at least 10 megabytes, such as the type that comes on the IBM XT personal computer, is recommended.

Because misadventures occur at all hours within health facilities, staff members of the risk management office must be available 24 hours a day. A paging system should therefore be provided.

The Risk Management Committee

Hospitals traditionally have been very "committee-oriented." In fact, some institutions have found that they have too many committees and have resorted to a committee on committees to resolve the situation.

In today's setting, hospitals are looking to avoid another committee whenever possible. Thus, there might be some resistance to the idea of a risk management committee, even when the organization's ability to prevent and/or minimize its liability risks would be enhanced by such a body. On the other hand, one should not assume that all hospitals require a risk management committee. For example, the JCAH has a standard calling for the existence of a safety committee at all institutions.[24]

In analyzing the need for and type of risk management committee, hospitals sometimes look to whether or not the functions and responsibilities can be undertaken by the quality assurance or safety committees. A popular example today is the trend toward a combined quality assurance/risk management committee, especially in a community hospital setting.

In theory, a risk management committee should oversee all activities of the institution aimed at protecting the financial assets of the hospital against the adverse effects of accidental loss. Obviously, the safety committee has traditionally provided the oversight for exposure to loss other than that resulting from patient or professional liability. However, when the malpractice crisis of the mid-1970s erupted, the issue of controlling professional liability exposures to loss became a priority. Unfortunately, the typical safety committee does not have the credibility or experience to deal with sensitive malpractice issues, especially those involving physician activities.

With the continued emphasis on quality assurance by the JCAH, hospitals have looked to their quality assurance programs to address their risk management concerns as well. Again, however, one cannot assume that a quality assurance committee automatically covers risk management issues, especially because the quality assurance focus is limited to patient care exposures and usually addresses concerns from a trend or pattern standpoint. Risk management's focus is usually on the single incident and its impact on the institution's financial assets.

Because risk funding or risk financing is part of the risk management equation also, we must look at this aspect when discussing the need for and scope of a risk management committee. In the typical setting, the risk funding aspects have been handled by the financial office of the institution, whereas the risk control (or risk management) issues have been the domain of the administrative office.

The type and size of the institution will also affect the existence, scope, and emphasis of the risk management committee. Smaller institutions might not have a separate committee, but rather use the safety or quality assurance committee (or others) to perform the functions. These smaller institutions are less likely to employ a full-time risk manager. Of course, one could argue that in a small hospital it should be easier to coordinate the functions and responsibilities of risk management.

The larger, more complex medical centers and university medical school institutions are more likely to have a risk management committee. In the latter case, there is the need to coordinate the risk management activities of the university with those of the hospital. A risk management committee can help this task tremendously. In the larger, non-medical-school setting, the committee helps ensure that the various risk management issues are communicated to and discussed with the right administrative and professional staff throughout the institution.

Still other variables affect the decision whether to establish a risk management committee. For example, the hospital's insurance carrier might dictate such a committee as part of its underwriting criteria. Also, an institution might self-insure a major portion of its professional liability risks and incorporate the need for a risk management committee in the statement of coverage of the self-funding plan.[25] However, in these two instances, care must be taken that the committee does not exist on paper only, with few meetings, weak agendas, and a perceived lack of importance.

The characteristics of the person serving as the institution's risk manager can also determine the existence or the type of committee. Risk managers in health care settings have varied backgrounds, experience, and credentials, including nursing, law, claims, insurance, medical records, quality assurance, utilization review, safety, hospital administration, and medicine. In any of these cases, the risk management committee's primary purpose might be to compensate for the gaps in the risk manager's capabilities. With health care risk management still a relatively young discipline, few risk managers have complete risk funding and risk control skills and experience.

Although risk management committees are affected by many variables, some key aspects of these committees need to be addressed regardless of the variables. These common denominators or ideal characteristics are outlined below.

Membership

Ideally, the risk management committee should include some individuals with policymaking authority and responsibility. Because risk management is primarily a staff function, there needs to be sufficient accountability for the program and its objectives. A strong risk management committee can perform this role very well, especially when the risk manager is not at a top administrative level in the organization.

In any setting, the membership of the risk management committee should include at least the following personnel:

- Administrator (or designate)
- President of the medical staff (or chief of staff)
- Medical director (if there is one)
- Representatives from the independent medical staff
- Chief financial officer (or designate)
- Risk manager
- Legal counsel (if there is one)
- Nursing director (optional)
- Board member (optional)
- Quality assurance coordinator or director (optional)
- Safety officer (optional)
- Others on an ad hoc basis

Scope

There is considerable variation in the scope of risk management committees' activities. As mentioned earlier, the risk management committee might be an expanded safety committee or quality assurance committee. The committee might also be either a working body or an oversight group.

With the increased emphasis on the malpractice crisis in the mid-1970s and again in the mid-1980s, risk management committees were developed primarily to address the prevention and minimization of professional liability claims and incidents. However, if one considers the global perspective, the risk management committee should oversee how the institution is addressing all its responses to loss among patients, visitors, employees, physical plant, and equipment. To date, we see the risk management committee dealing primarily with the most difficult and most sensitive issue, namely, professional liability. As hospitals become more sophisticated and involved with risk management, we should see more and more "umbrella" committees with the broader scope discussed above.

Reporting Channels

Variety is again the norm with respect to reporting channels. The umbrella committee could report to the CEO or possibly the board of directors. When the committee has both quality assurance and risk management responsibilities, the reporting line might also include the medical executive committee.

If the membership of the committee is appropriate from the standpoint of its ability to effect change either directly or through communication with the right administrative and professional staff, the reporting channel issue becomes secondary and maybe even just a formality (e.g., periodic reporting to the board). In another respect, the activities of the risk management committee need to be kept somewhat confidential, since discussion at meetings might include sensitive patient care issues.

Prevention Versus Minimization

Some risk management committees are in reality claims committees whose primary mission is to discuss the ins and outs of a malpractice claim or serious patient issue. We are not subordinating this function, since every hospital needs to evaluate its ability to put the lid on potentially volatile incidents and claims. But how do the lessons learned or problems identified through the claims process get back into the pipeline so that recurrence is not an issue? Ideally, the risk management committee will analyze the problem and suggest or recommend the necessary changes in protocols, policies, and procedures to prevent the problem or suit from happening again. Some hospitals have assigned the claim minimization function to a subgroup of a parent risk management committee. In this way, they are able to react quickly and appropriately as needed to specific incidents and claims. This subgroup is sometimes called a medical-legal committee.

Meetings

The type of and scope of the risk management committee will dictate how often the committee will convene. A working committee armed with the task of coordinating the institutional risk management program will probably meet monthly, as do other key administrative and professional committees. However, if the hospital has a large and active risk management staff that is able to effectively coordinate the program and communicate with the people who are in management positions, the oversight committee might meet only quarterly or bimonthly. For maximum results, the committee should have a standing agenda, and "old business" items should be carried forward until resolution is attained.

Alternative Delivery Systems and Settings

With recent major changes in the health care industry forcing hospitals to identify new, diversified activities and compete for patients and physicians, the risk management committee's role should take on an added dimension. Before an institution embarks on a new venture (surgicenter, off-site health center, health maintenance organization, management contract, etc.), the risks should be evaluated. The risk management committee offers the forum for discussing these new ventures to determine if any exposure to loss is created, and if this exposure can be handled appropriately (either retained or transferred). In this way, a hospital can prospectively deal with its risks rather than find out after the fact (usually after the problem develops) that the new venture contained some inherent exposures to loss.

The risk management committee should be a most effective tool for hospitals trying to control their exposures to loss, and not merely a "paper tool" required by an outside organization.

Summary

Risk management programs are located within health care facilities along the usual chain of organization and can be classified according to reporting location. Their power and influence frequently can be assessed by their location on the chain of command. Those programs reporting to high-ranking individuals or groups such as the chief executive officer or board of directors are usually the most influential and visible. The office of risk management most often reports to the chief executive officer and frequently the institution has an oversight body called the risk management committee responsible for setting policy and making key decisions for the program.

The risk management program must have well-established liaisons with other departments, sections, and units within the organization that also have a risk management role. The facility's administration can best achieve this by publishing a risk policy statement and providing each unit with a risk management plan.

Many authors suggest that serious consideration be given to integrating risk management with quality assurance. There could be advantages to combining the two functions in small institutions for economic reasons. In large organizations the two functions could be separate or they could be combined under the title of risk prevention and placed under the overall risk management department.

The medical records department should play a significant role in risk management and quality assurance, especially in the audit, monitoring, and data collection functions of risk prevention. Also, it can play an important role in education of the institution's staff in the documentation process. In small or specialized facilities, the medical records department could be responsible for risk management.

The risk management program should be organized according to the needs of the organization and must be provided with the necessary facilities, staff, tools, and budget necessary to carry out the process.

Chapter Exercise

You are the administrator of a 500-bed general hospital. You have purchased commercial insurance in the past, but beginning with the next fiscal year will become self-insured for professional liability, workers' compensation, and general liability. Your hospital operates one satellite clinic and a nursing home and plans to expand into nontraditional services.

The hospital has an in-house legal counsel, who primarily does corporate legal work associated with acquisitions, contracts, and labor law issues. Your institution has programs in quality assurance, infection control, safety, utilization review, biomedical engineering, and patient relations, as well as the usual professional services. The medical staff also has the typical mix of committees.

The hospital does have a risk manager, but it appears that the office serves only as a staff function to the various insurance companies, and the incumbent has expressed her desire to leave in the immediate future in order to marry.

Questions

1. Draw an organizational chart of the institution and incorporate the desired model for the operation of a risk management program.

2. Using the chart, design a functional organizational chart of the risk management program incorporating the networks, linkages, and lines of authority you will delegate to the office.

3. Explain each functional area, network, linkages, and those programs for which the risk manager will have line authority. Assign appropriate titles to committees and programs.

References

1. American Society for Hospital Risk Management, "Survey of Hospital Risk Management Responsibilities and Salaries—1983," (Spring 1984):3-23.

2. Richard E. Wright and Thomas S. Gaudiosi, "A Management-Oriented Program Implemented Through the Medical Director's Office," *QRB/Quality Review Bulletin* vol. 7, no. 7, (July 1981): 10.

3. *Idem.*

4. *Idem.*

5. Joan L. Isserman, (Unpublished presentation at the annual meeting of the American Academy of Hospital Attorneys, San Diego, June 1984), 4.

6. *Idem*, p. 5.

7. Joint Commission on Accreditation of Hospitals, *Accreditation Manual for Hospitals*, AMH 85 (Chicago: Joint Commission on Accreditation of Hospitals, 1985), 149-52.

8. Joint Commission on Accreditation of Hospitals, *"Back to Basics": An Introduction to Principles of Quality Assurance*, (Chicago, Joint Commission on Accreditation of Hospitals, 1982), I-9.

9. James E. Orlikoff and Gary B. Lanham, "Why Risk Management and Quality Assurance Should Be Integrated," *Hospitals* vol. 55, no. 11 (June 1, 1981): 54.

10. John F. Monagle, *Risk Management: A Guide for Health Care Professionals* (Rockville, Aspen Systems Corporation, 1985), 84.

11. American Society for Risk Management, "Survey," 15.

12. P. L. Spath, "The Education of QA Professionals," *QRB/Quality Review Bulletin* vol. 11, no. 7 (July 1985): 202-03.

13. R. D. Goodman, "Medical Care Audit—a Retrospective Review," *Topics in Health Record Management* vol. 1, no. 2 (December 1980): 84.

14. W. J. Fessel and E. E. Van Brunt, "Assessing Quality of Care from the Medical Record," *The New England Journal of Medicine*, 286 (January 20, 1972): 134-38.

15. T. F. Lyons and B. D. Payne, "The Relationship of Physicians' Medical Recording Performance to Their Medical Care Performance," *Medical Care* vol. 12, no. 8 (August 1974): 714-20.

16. D. L. Bronson, A. S. Rubin and H. M. Tufo, "Patient Education Through Record Sharing," *QRB/Quality Review Bulletin*, (special edition, (1978): 76-8.

17. L. C. Fernow, C. Mackie, I. McColl, and M. Rendall, "The Effect of Problem Oriented Medical Records on Clinical Management Controlled for Patient Risks," *Medical Care* vol. 16, no. 6 (June 1978): 476-87.

18. B. L. Miccio, "Lesson in Balancing Cost and Quality," *Topics in Health Record Management* vol. 5, no. 2 (December 1984): 70.

19. Rita Finnigan, *Coding for Prospective Payment* (Chicago: American Medical Record Association, 1984), 73.

20. Spath, 202-03.

21. Edna Huffman, *Medical Record Management* (Berwyn, IL: Physicians' Record Company, 440-447, 532-534.

22. American Medical Record Association, *Professional Practice Standards* (Chicago: American Medical Record Association, 1984.

23. L. A. Fox, "The Quality Assurance Administrator: Who Will It Be?" *Topics in Health Record Management* vol. 1, no. 2 (December 1980): 1-3.

24. Joint Commission on Accreditation of Hospitals, *Accreditation Manual for Hospitals*, 131.

25. University of Missouri, *Plan Document for Medical Professional Liability (Amended)*, (Columbia, MO: University of Missouri, 1979, unpublished), 2.

CHAPTER THREE

THE RISK MANAGER

Gary P. Kraus

This chapter previews the risk manager and the attributes that those who work in the profession of risk management exhibit. We will see that individuals who work as risk managers carry out a variety of tasks and are identified by many titles. They come from many educational programs and have degrees from many professions. A sample job description is provided as well as the results of surveys on various aspects of the profession. Also provided is information about professional societies and methods of credentialing risk managers.

Much of the information in this chapter comes from the 1983 Survey of Hospital Risk Management Responsibilities and Salaries conducted by the American Society of Hospital Risk Management (ASHRM).[1] Those tables in this and other sections of this book that present data from this survey are identified by the letters ASHRM-SRS. The survey was initiated in June 1983 by ASHRM in conjunction with the Department of Special Surveys of the American Hospital Association's Hospital Data Center. For more details regarding the survey, the reader should contact the Director, American Society for Hospital Risk Management, American Hospital Association, 840 North Lake Shore Drive, Chicago, Illinois 60611.

Role of the Risk Manager

The role that the risk manager plays within the health care facility must be determined by those functions and tasks that the administration of the institution has planned for the risk management department. Such major decisions as where the program will fit within the institution and other questions discussed in Chapter 2 must be resolved before specific activities can be assigned. Regardless of the specific tasks and functions assigned, it is a given that a risk manager within a health care facility will be fundamentally a coordinator and facilitator of all activities related to risk. We have seen in Chapters 1 and 2 that the risk management process is extremely broad, encompassing many details and activities, and consequently it would be impossible for the risk manager to carry out all the necessary activities alone.

Table 3-1 Titles of Professionals with Responsibility for Risk Management

Title	No. of Individuals	Percent
Senior Officer/Vice-President	844	27.7
Risk Management Coordinator/Director	492	16.2
Chief Executive Officer/President	451	14.8
Director of Risk Management and Quality Assurance	215	7.1
Quality Assurance Coordinator/Director	170	5.6
Personnel Officer	159	5.2
Administrative Assistant to CEO/Senior Officer	154	5.1
Chief of Engineering or Safety/Security	144	4.7
Financial Officer	107	3.5
Nursing Administrator/Director	86	2.8
Operations Officer	38	1.3
Medical Records Manager/Director	36	1.2
Legal Services Officer	35	1.2
Chief Medical Officer	25	0.8
Marketing/Public Relations Officer	17	0.6
Board of Trustees Member/President	2	0.1
Other	36	1.2
Missing responses	26	0.9
Total	3037	100.0

Source: ASHRM-SRS, p. 5.

Assuming, therefore, that the administration of the institution has carried out the necessary planning activities for the office of risk management, specific tasks can be assigned and the risk manager's role within the institution more accurately defined. Generally, hospital and health facility risk managers carry out a variety of supervisory and functional responsibilities and have authority over some specific activities. The 1983 ASHRM survey of risk managers has provided the profession with much insight into the role of the risk manager in health care facilities.

Table 3-1 lists some of the titles held by risk management professionals. Risk management functions and roles are carried out by individuals holding a variety of titles within health care facilities. In the largest percentage (27.7 percent of cases) risk management is the responsibility of an individual with the office of senior officer/vice-president. The second largest number go by the title of risk management coordinator/director, and it appears from the survey that in a substantial number of hospitals the management activities are carried out by individuals who do not incorporate the notion of risk management in their job titles.

The largest average number of personnel supervised directly by the respondents of the ASHRM survey was 3.45 professional staff members (Table 3-2). The largest average number of personnel supervised indirectly was 14.23 technical staff members.

Table 3-2 Average Number of Personnel Supervised Directly and Indirectly by Individuals with Responsibility for Risk Mangement[a]

Staff Category	Average No. of Personnel Supervised Directly	Average No. of Personnel Supervised Indirectly
Professional staff[b]	3.45	10.60
Technical staff[c]	1.71	14.23
Clerical staff[d]	1.63	7.83

[a]Figures based on an average of 2,949 responses.
[b]Positions normally requiring managerial judgments and decisions.
[c]Positions normally requiring analytical ability with some judgment and decision making.
[d]Positions normally requiring record-keeping and retrieval skills.
Source: ASHRM SRS, p. 9.

Table 3-3 Individuals Whose Risk Management Responsibilities Include Risk Financing

Extent of Responsibility for Risk Financing	No. of Individuals	Percent
Full	511	16.8
Limited	910	30.0
None	1553	51.1
Missing responses	63	2.1
Total	3037	100.0

Source: ASHRM SRS, p. 10.

Table 3-3 shows that full responsibility for the risk financing function was reportedly held by 16.8 percent (511) of the respondents, whereas 30 percent (910) reported that their risk financing responsibilities were limited.

Complete authority for selecting insurance brokers was held by 6.3 percent (191) of the respondents, as indicated in Table 3-4, whereas 18.8 percent (571) reported that they shared authority for this activity.

Table 3-5 indicates that 6.9 percent (210) of the respondents reported that they held complete authority for selecting insurance carriers, whereas 18.9 percent (574) reported that the authority for this activity was shared.

Table 3-6 presents data on comprehensive risk management program responsibilities. The ASHRM survey indicated that the risk identification/evaluation process was the most frequently reported risk management responsibility and was carried out by 94.3 percent (2,864) of the survey's respondents. The survey further indicated that loss prevention and safety administration were the second and third most frequently reported risk management responsibilities and were carried out by 87.8 percent (2,665) and 73.7 percent (2,239), respectively, of the respondents answering the survey.

Table 3-4 Individuals Whose Risk Management Responsibilities Include Authority for Selecting Insurance Brokers

Extent of Authority for Selecting Brokers	No. of Individuals	Percent
Complete	191	6.3
Shared	571	18.8
Consulting	544	17.9
No authority indicated	1731	57.0
Total	3037	100.0

Source: ASHRM-SRS, p. 11.

Table 3-5 Individuals Whose Risk Management Responsibilities Include Authority for Selecting Insurance Carriers

Extent of Authority for Selecting Carriers	No. of Individuals	Percent
Complete	210	6.9
Shared	574	18.9
Consulting	621	20.4
No authority indicated	1632	53.8
Total	3037	100.0

Source: ASHRM-SRS, p. 12.

Table 3-3 indicates that the responsibility for the risk financing process is not delegated to most of the members of the ASHRM survey who responded. It is significant that just over half (51.1 percent) of the respondents, or 1,553 individuals, indicated that they had no responsibility for risk financing. If these statistics hold true of hospital and other health facilities administrations in general, it appears that the risk financing process within the health industry is carried out by other members of the administration than the risk manager.

Another source of information regarding the role of the hospital risk manager is an article published by Grace C. Brantley[2] in the *Journal of the American Medical Record Association* in February 1982. Her study, which was limited to hospitals within the state of Ohio and included only 20 respondents, nevertheless constitutes a reasonable cross-section of risk managers in that state's hospital setting. Table 3-7 outlines the duties of the risk managers as extracted from the Brantley study.

Although a majority of individuals who hold the title of risk manager do not carry out risk financing activities, a large number of them do. Patricia Scully, in the October 22, 1984, issue of *Business Insurance*,[3] outlined a number of points that the individual responsible for risk financing must consider when evaluating the risk financing role.

Table 3-6 Individuals with Responsibility for Handling Individual Components of a Comprehensive Risk Management Program

Program Component	Respondents with Responsibility		Percentage of Individuals Whose Authority Is:			Average Percentage of Respondent's Time Spent
	Percent	Number	Complete	Shared	Consulting	
Risk identification/evaluation	94.3	2864	39.5	55.9	4.6	12.6
Loss prevention	87.8	2665	33.2	61.0	5.8	7.9
Safety administration	73.7	2239	34.4	53.5	12.1	6.1
Handling patient complaints	65.9	2001	24.3	66.1	9.6	4.3
Property/casualty claims	65.5	1989	40.6	52.2	7.2	4.8
Product liability claims	52.9	1607	38.1	51.3	10.6	1.8
Security	51.2	1554	39.8	43.5	16.7	3.2
Workers' compensation claims	45.2	1373	40.7	45.0	14.3	2.7
Conducting patient satisfaction surveys	40.6	1234	27.3	58.2	14.5	1.6
Other employee benefits design/administration	31.2	949	29.5	54.4	16.1	1.3
Premium forecasting/budgeting	30.2	916	35.8	49.2	15.0	0.9
Group insurance plan design/administration	29.2	888	31.0	53.0	16.0	1.3
Group insurance benefit claims	28.6	868	39.5	46.7	13.8	0.1
Insurance accounting	27.0	821	33.4	52.1	14.5	1.0
Management of department personnel (at least two)	25.6	778	66.6	28.4	5.0	3.4
Pension/retirement income payments	21.8	663	39.5	45.0	15.5	0.6
Family counseling	20.3	616	22.9	55.3	21.8	0.9

Source: ASHRM-SRS, p. 13.

1. Is each entity within a multi-institutional system adequately covered, and has each potential exposure been identified and protected?

2. When addressing all the major contracts of the institution or the adequacies of insurance, are there other risks that can be transferred?

3. When dealing with contracts, are indemnification agreements considered?

4. Has the adequacy of professional liability insurance been considered, specifically the need for tail coverage for claims-made type policies?

5. What are the role of and need for insurance for other health professionals such as nurses, midwives, and allied health practitioners?

6. Does the institution have copies of the insurance policies of independent contractors working within the facility, including construction project employees?

7. Do contracts that require employees to perform services in other institutions give the home institution the right to see information of a claims nature arising from incidents that may have occurred in other hospitals?

8. Are the services of the institution's insurance brokers, claims representatives, consultants, and actuaries clearly delineated?

9. Are the boundaries between professional liability and general liability insurance clearly delineated?

10. Should the institution consider insurance coverage for directors and officers, particularly given the number of lawsuits being filed by disgruntled medical staff members against the boards of their institutions?

11. Is the institution's insurance adequate to protect it from claims of negligent administration of employee benefit plans? Are the workers' compensation programs cost effective? Where employees are employed by contracting organizations, is the primary workers' compensation coverage clearly delineated in the contract?

12. Who coordinates the purchasing of all insurance or the carrying out of all risk financing responsibilities within the institution?

13. Are the property liability insurance areas of the institution clearly delineated and updated regarding costs of replacement?

14. Are the nature and extent of hospital-owned vehicles clearly delineated in hospital policies and procedures and reflected in the insurance policy?

15. Are the institution's bonding requirements adequate, particularly as they pertain to alcohol being used by the pharmacy?

16. Is there adequate protection for the hardware and software in the hospital's computer systems?

Table 3-7 Duties of Risk Managers

Duties	Hospitals[a]
Review incident reports	14
Prepare security reports	3
Develop programs for prevention of incidents	4
Act as liaison for defense council	7
Enlist staff support in area of legal-medical concerns	5
Conduct continuing education programs	5
Handle claims	10
Manage self-insurance trust fund	2
Supervise fire protection	1
Handle insurance and workers' compensation	6
Handle safety programs	6
Chair professional liability committee	1
Develop comprehensive risk management/quality assurance program	4
Act as special advisor in high-risk areas	1
Act as JCAH coordinator	1
Coordinate external surveys	3
Prepare statistics and maintain files	2

[a]Number of hospitals indicating this task as one performed by the individual responsible for risk management.

Source: Grace C. Brantley, "A Pilot Study of Risk Management," *Journal of the American Medical Records Association* (February 1982): 71.

The above issues indicate that the risk manager must have some adequate training in the area of insurance or consult with either internal or external insurance experts to adequately oversee the risk financing activities of the institution.

Education and Experience Prerequisites

Just as we have learned that the risk management processes are very broad and encompass many tasks, activities, functions, and programs, so too the backgrounds of individuals who are employed in risk management in various health care facilities vary greatly. The 1983 ASHRM survey of risk managers offers insight into the backgrounds of many of the individuals employed in risk management within the health care industry. Table 3-8 indicates that although the survey respondents had been employed in health care or a related field for an average of about 13.92 years, they had occupied their present positions for an average of only 4.28 years. This seems to indicate that many health care risk managers gravitated into their current positions, probably by making lateral moves from one position to another within the institution.

When one considers the broad spectrum of tasks and activities required of the risk manager, it is not surprising that the academic requirements for the position

Table 3-8   Years of Employment in Health Care Reported by Respondents

Employment Situation	Average No. of Years
Present position	4.28
Affiliated with present organization	8.06
Employed in health care or related field	13.92

Source: ASHRM-SRS, p. 17.

Table 3-9   Highest Level of Education Attained by Respondents

Educational Level	Number	Percent
Master's degree	1142	37.6
Bachelor's degree	963	31.7
Associate degree	245	8.1
High school diploma	175	5.8
Doctoral degree	167	5.5
Other[a]	319	10.4
Missing responses	26	0.9
Total	3037	100.0

[a]A 25 percent random sample suggests that this category includes approximately 190 diploma RNs, 38 LPNs, 26 accredited records technicians, 26 persons certified in health care administration, 13 who have completed some unspecified risk management training, 13 registered medical technologists, and 13 who have completed training in safety, security, and/or criminal justice.

Source: ASHRM-SRS, p. 18.

might be high. The ASHRM survey supports this proposition, and Table 3-9 points out that 37.6 percent of all incumbents hold master's degrees. Bachelor's and associate degrees were the second and third most frequently reported maximum education levels.

The survey also found that the most common academic subject area in which incumbent risk managers were prepared is health care administration. Table 3-10 indicates that 22.2 percent of the respondents held degrees in health care administration, with the second most frequent academic area being business administration. Nursing and nursing administration was third, with 12.7 percent of respondents. The balance of responses cover various areas of technical preparation. Although in the 1983 survey only 107 respondents identified law as their academic subject area, our experience suggests that this figure is probably substantially higher now, since during the last few years a large number of attorneys attending professional meetings have indicated risk management as their occupation.

Table 3-11 lists the most frequently reported professional disciplines in the ASHRM survey. According to the study, 45.6 percent of respondents (1,385) indicated hospital administration as the area in which their professional experience had been concentrated. Health care and personnel management were the second

Table 3-10   Subject Areas in Which Respondents Hold Academic Qualifications or Degrees

Subject Area	Number	Percent
Health care administration	674	22.2
Business administration	577	19.0
Nursing and nursing administration	385	12.7
Social sciences	141	4.6
Law	107	3.5
Allied health care (except nursing)	106	3.5
Accounting	98	3.2
Medical records	91	3.0
Public administration	73	2.4
Education	66	2.2
Humanitics	58	1.9
Biological and health sciences	54	1.8
Medicine (MD)	48	1.6
Personnel management	41	1.4
Physical sciences	26	0.9
Engineering	24	0.8
Risk management	13	0.4
Health care education	8	0.3
Industrial psychology	6	0.2
Other	241	7.9
Missing responses	200	6.5
Total	3037	100.0

Source: ASHRM-SRS, p. 19.

and third most frequently reported disciplines of professional concentration, respectively, with 19.0 percent (577) and 6.9 percent (209) of the respondents.

Table 3-12 lists the professional designations that the respondents of the ASHRM study identified themselves as having. The survey did not anticipate a wide range of possible responses, as evidenced by the substantial percentage of designations that fell within the category of "other." Registered nurse was the most frequently reported professional designation given, with 18.8 percent (569) of respondents.

The statistics in the above tables notwithstanding, it appears that the professional designation of the hospital or health care risk manager is a wide open field and that there is no clear-cut identifiable professional label uniformly applied. Because risk management is relatively new to the health industry, the future will determine how the profession designates risk managers and what academic or credentialing labels will apply. It may be safe to predict that the typical hospital risk manager will in the future have a label designating his or her primary educational background, such as R.N., J.D., R.R.A., coupled with a label gained by some form of certification in risk management.

Table 3-11   Discipline in Which Respondent's Professional Experience Has Been Concentrated

Discipline	Number	Percent
Hospital administration	1385	45.6
Health care	577	19.0
Personnel management	209	6.9
Medical records administration	134	4.4
Accounting	106	3.5
Law	99	3.3
Business	87	2.9
Insurance	61	2.0
Engineering	50	1.6
Claims handling	49	1.6
Other[a]	240	7.9
Missing responses	40	1.3
Total	3037	100.0

[a]A 25 percent random sample suggests that this category includes approximately 153 safety, security, and criminal justice professionals; 28 quality assurance professionals; 14 food service management personnel; 10 health planners; 10 public relations specialists; 10 program analysts/evaluation specialists; 10 biomedical engineers; and 5 patient representatives.
Source: ASHRM-SRS, p. 20.

For the health administrator, the decision regarding what attributes to seek in a risk manager, or for that matter a director of risk management services for the institution, may be a difficult one. To make an appropriate selection one must consider the tasks that will be assigned to the office. For example, if the office will carry out primarily risk prevention tasks, then the incumbent ought to have a background in and knowledge of the health care delivery system with specific, detailed knowledge of the areas in question. Consequently, the best background for the risk manager may be one in nursing, medicine, or the allied health professions. This is particularly true if there will be an integration of quality assurance with risk management. However, if the risk management office is to be given broad duties, with several subdivisions as indicated in Chapter 2, then an individual with strong management skills is required, and an individual from a master's-level program in health administration or law would be recommended. Regardless of background, the responsibilities of the risk manager are such that experience within the health care industry is absolutely essential. The nuances of health care facility practices and its specialized professional language preclude effective risk management communications by individuals from outside the health care industry.

In selecting a director of risk management, four specific attributes should be considered and should be demonstrated by the candidates. First, the candidate must understand what management is all about. Second, he or she must have some working knowledge of health care facilities and particularly of the technical as-

Table 3-12 Professional Designations Held by Respondents

Professional Designations	Number	Percentage
Registered Nurse	569	18.8
Attorney (J.D.)	100	3.3
Accredited Records Technician	79	2.6
Registered Record Administrator	70	2.3
Associate in Risk Management	53	1.7
Health Care Safety Professional	45	1.5
Physician (M.D.)	45	1.5
Certified Public Accountant	40	1.3
Chartered Property/Casualty Underwriter	13	0.4
Certified Safety Professional	13	0.4
Associate Safety Professional	8	0.3
Professional Engineer	8	0.3
Chartered Life Underwriter	5	0.2
Other[a]	668	22.0
Missing responses	1321	43.4
Total	3037	100.0

[a]A 25 percent random sample suggests that this category includes 187 fellows or members of the American College of Hospital Administrators, 53 licensed nursing home administrators, 53 licensed clinical social workers or masters in social work, 40 licensed practical nurses, 107 hospital ancillary service professionals (i.e., pharmacists, physical therapists, registered medical technologists, and registered dietitians), 80 hospital safety/security professionals (i.e., health care safety/security administrators, certified hospital engineers, certified protection professionals, and certified hazard control managers), 27 paralegals, 27 licensed insurance brokers, 27 certified personnel consultants, 27 masters in public health, 13 members of the American Society of Law and Medicine, and 27 who hold various other professional and membership designations.

Source: ASHRM-SRS, p. 21.

pects of health care delivery. The candidate must have a working knowledge of law, particularly those areas dealing with liability, contracts, and employment practices. Last, the candidate should demonstrate some knowledge of insurance and the insurance industry. An individual with balance in the above areas, regardless of his or her educational background, is essential for carrying out the wide range of activities required of a risk manager in a health care facility. Another important feature to look for is the ability to adapt readily to new ways of doing things and to accept the prospect of continuing education. The area of health care risk management is changing so fast and so frequently, that continuing education is an ongoing requirement of the risk manager. Candidates for this position should demonstrate their willingness and ability to comprehend this fact by their involvement in the ongoing activities of the profession. One should beware of individuals who pass themselves off as risk managers but who have not demonstrated participation in continuing education programs. Membership in the ASHRM as well as in the state chapter or regional association, if available, is a good indication that an applicant for a risk management position is truly involved in the profession. Beware of individuals who carry various labels and symbols behind their name, which by themselves are no indication of the quality and experience required. More will be said of the various professional societies and the credentialing available for risk managers later in this chapter. If the administration of the facility decides to fill the risk management position with an attorney, and if claims administration will be a major process of the office, then care must be taken to find an attorney who is not a die-hard litigant. Attorneys in the United States are trained under the adversary system and are expected to defend their clients vigorously and expect justice to come from the courts. A risk manager who is too adversarial cannot compromise when wisdom requires compromise. Therefore, those interested in selecting an attorney as risk manager should seek a candidate who has some training in or exposure to alternative dispute resolution. If the candidate has not had experience in alternative dispute resolution, he or she should at least be psychologically disposed to use it when necessary. Last, beware of candidates who are too patient oriented, for they will want to give away the assets of the organization unnecessarily. Thus, whoever is selected should demonstrate balance between these two extremes.

Job Descriptions and Compensation

The health care institution should preface a job description for the director of risk management position and for the directors of all major subdivisions within the program, if the program size requires them. Exhibit 3-1 is an example of a job description for a hospital risk manager.

Regardless of how the program is organized, the job descriptions of the risk manager position and the other major actors within the department must contain certain elements. Besides the job title, there should be a statement clearly delineating who manages the office and to whom the risk manager or the directors of the various divisions of the risk management office shall report. There should be evidence of a clear chain of command and authority. A second feature of all job descriptions must be a statement of the basic functions of the office and the incumbent. This statement will be broad but should contain as much specificity as is practical. Another important feature of the job description is a statement of the objectives that the incumbent is expected to achieve. A balance must be found between a statement that is so general as to be meaningless and one that is so specific that it becomes lost in endless detail. The next section of the job description generally describes the nature and scope of the office. This is usually the largest part of the job description and describes in detail many of the duties expected of the individual. Last, the job description should list the qualifications desired of the individual.

The compensation to be paid to the institutional risk manager and the directors

Sample job description for a risk manager

Title: Director of Risk Management

Immediate Supervisor: Chief Executive Officer and Chairman, Risk Management Committee

Job Function: As Director of Risk Management the incumbent has the responsibility of coordinating all tasks and activities associated with exposure identification, measurement, and handling for the medical center. The Director of Risk Management will work closely with all senior officers of the medical center administration and members of the medical staff in conducting the necessary activities of the position.

Objectives: Reduce unplanned financial loss to the medical center due to exposure hazards of the physical plant and those associated with visitors, employees, and patient treatment and safety. To enhance the quality of patient care by preventing accidents and other misadventures.

Activities:

1. Develop and implement a risk management plan for all medical center departments and units.

2. Coordinate a complete risk identification program for safety, patient care, and other operating units.

3. Coordinate risk measurement activities with insurers, consultants, and administrative financial officer.

4. Coordinate, place, and select all insurance plans with brokers, oversee bidding, carry out or coordinate self-financing program design.

5. Administer self-insurance trusts or other plans as needed.

6. Establish, manage, and/or coordinate loss prevention program for all exposure areas.

7. Establish an automated risk management information system and establish networks with quality assurance and other programs for data utilization.

8. Handle claims administration including reports to insurance companies.

9. Investigate cases covered under self-insurance programs and coordinate defense with legal counsel.

10. Coordinate insurance data with Director

Exhibit 3-1 Sample job description for a hospital risk manager.

```
                              of Finance when appropriate.

                              11.  Develop and review policies and pro-
                              cedures that affect risk management.  Coordi-
                              nate procedures with biomedical engineering,
                              patient relations, safety, and other de-
                              partments with a risk prevention mission.

                              12.  Supervise professional and support
                              staff.  Carry out routine administrative
                              tasks associated with office management.

                              13.  Monitor compliance with JCAH guidelines
                              and other regulatory agencies.

Education and Experience
Requirements:                 Bachelor's degree (master's preferred) in
                              health administration or related health area.
                              Law, business, or insurance degree will be
                              considered.

                              Experience in risk management, claims admin-
                              istration, or insurance.

                              Knowledge of health care delivery systems
                              mandatory.

                              Knowledge of the fundamentals of tort in-
                              surance and health law plus local and state
                              regulations and procedures.

                              Strong management skills including the
                              ability to coordinate work with others in-
                              cluding medical staff.
```

Exhibit 3-1 Cont'd.

of the major subdivisions of the risk management program will be determined by the importance and complexity of the tasks assigned to each office, as well as by the circumstances of the community environment. Internal circumstances will be determined by the place the risk management office maintains within the institution's chain of organization. For example, if the risk manager is placed at a low level with functions strictly related to risk prevention, then the salary paid must be commensurate with those of other individuals within the facility with similar education backgrounds and responsibilities. On the other hand, if the director of risk management reports high up on the organizational chain—for example, to the board of directors—and the office is expected to carry out most of the risk management process of the institution, then the institution must be prepared to pay a salary commensurate with the educational and experience requirements of such a position.

The 1983 ASHRM survey included a substantial number of questions regarding compensation. Table 3-13 provides an aggregate of salary ranges reported by the respondents of the 1983 survey. Although the data speak for themselves, it is

Table 3-13   Aggregate Salary Ranges of Risk Managers

Salary Range	Number	Percent
Under $15,000	87	2.9
$15,000–19,999	248	8.2
$20,000–24,999	452	14.8
$25,000–29,999	595	19.5
$30,000–34,999	515	17.0
$35,000–39,999	372	12.2
$40,000–44,999	297	9.8
$45,000–49,999	124	4.1
$50,000–54,999	86	2.8
$55,000–59,999	55	1.8
$60,000–64,999	38	1.3
$65,000–69,999	18	0.6
$70,000 or more	33	1.1
Missing responses	117	3.9
Total	3037	100.0

Source: ASHRM-SRS, p. 23.

significant that the average salaries of hospital risk managers appear to fall within the range of $25,000 to $35,000, with the most frequent being the $25,000-to-$39,999 category. The survey results contained many additional tables not included here, and the data were broken down by region and state. Of significance is the fact that the three most common salary ranges tended to include substantial percentages of respondents, regardless of hospital size or region.

Professional Societies and Credentialing

As discussed earlier, the growth and development of the position of risk manager in the health care setting have been noteworthy. Before the first malpractice crisis of the mid-1970s, hospitals had no desire or reason to designate either a full-time or even a part-time risk manager. When the malpractice crisis hit, health care institutions started to appoint risk managers, either of their own volition or because their state regulations or malpractice insurance carriers required it. The major question was what sort of person to hire in terms of education, experience, and areas of expertise. What we saw was a variety of people with a variety of skills being hired as risk managers, including safety and security officers, personnel staff, nurses, administrative staff, medical directors, finance staff, attorneys, quality assurance specialists, utilization review and medical records coordinators, insurance company personnel, and others. As time went on, the most noticeable trend was not the standardization of personnel and experience, but rather more and more institutions hiring and appointing full-time risk managers. As health care entered the mid-1980s, the malpractice crisis returned, but the variety among risk managers remained.

In 1980, the American Hospital Association (AHA) formed a national group dedicated to hospital risk management. This group, known as the American Society for Hospital Risk Management (ASHRM), has grown in membership to over 1,000. Even now, if one scans the ASHRM membership list, one can see the variety in backgrounds of the personnel acting as risk managers in their facilities.

A few years back, concern was expressed by the ASHRM leadership that the society was not promulgating minimum qualifications and continuing education requirements for risk managers. Most of the AHA's societies suggest or require specific types of personnel and levels of experience and education for membership status. At the 1985 ASHRM annual conference, draft categories of membership were published for the first time. There will probably be considerable discussion and modification of these before the final product is established. One of the difficulties is how to reorganize and distinguish members with such diverse backgrounds, experience, education, and job descriptions.

There is also great variety in the type and scope of risk management programs in hospitals today. The traditional safety model was forced to expand to address the suddenly volatile professional liability climate. Yet many programs today still keep malpractice risk control separate from (and sometimes not even coordinated with) the safety program. Another area of split function is between risk control activities and risk funding concerns. Here again we see numerous variations in coordination and segregation.

The degree to which an individual hospital was feeling the malpractice pressure, either in terms of claim volume or premium and funding levels, also had a bearing on the type and intensity of the risk management program it established. How does one set qualification and experience standards for individuals with a variety of backgrounds, skills, and in-house programs?

In the early 1980s another trend emerged, that of appointing attorneys as risk managers or as administrators for risk management in their capacity as legal counsel. The results and benefits of this approach need more time to be determined. Another emerging issue was the use of clinical personnel as risk managers, mostly registered nurses. A third noteworthy development was the coordinating of risk control (especially prevention) efforts with the quality assurance function. Despite all this, the bottom line in the mid-1980s is the need to have the medical staff, including the independent attending physicians, become involved with the hospital's risk management program. How does one fit this need with basic, minimum credentials and/or experience for risk managers?

Once the ASHRM was established, another trend developed. States, cities, and regions started to form their own hospital risk management societies and organizations. The major objectives were to promote sharing of information among risk managers and to provide an ongoing educational forum. Today, almost all states have formed societies and are in the process of becoming affiliated with the national organization. Again, as discussed earlier, a major challenge for these state and local groups has been to adequately address the needs and interests of their diverse members.

What is the likely future of the hospital risk manager position? We can see an interesting dilemma developing. At a time when the professional liability climate has greatly worsened and almost every hospital needs to pay attention to preventing and minimizing claims and incidents, there is great pressure on hospitals to reduce staffing due to prospective payment and the changing health care delivery system. The hope is that we can attain a "happy medium" whereby the hospitals can develop effective and efficient risk management using accepted minimum standards and requirements established by a joint effort among states, insurance companies, and hospitals themselves. As part of this, the issue of the risk manager should be addressed. Hopefully, the national group, along with the various state and local societies, can promote some uniformity among risk managers. This could be accomplished by establishing minimum credentials, experience, and continuing education requirements.

The following criteria have been published by ASHRM as the requirements for professional recognition.[4] Eligible participants are those persons who are members of the society or have been members for a minimum of five years. The Society has established two levels of achievement and recognition: the Fellow and the diplomate. The Fellow is designated for superior achievement and the Diplomate for outstanding achievement in risk management.

The professional achievement criteria required of applicants differ, depending on the level one is attempting to achieve. These criteria include academic credentials, continuing education, employment experience, and contributions to the field.

Academic Credentials

Applicants for Fellows must possess two of the following criteria, and applicants for Diplomate must possess three:

- Bachelor's degree
- Graduate or professional degree (master's, Ph.D., M.D., or J.D.)
- Certified Safety Professional (C.S.P.)
- Associate in risk management (A.R.M.)
- Chartered Property/Casualty Underwriter (C.P.C.U.)
- Associate in Claims (A.I.C.)
- Associate in Loss Control Management (A.L.C.M.)
- Advanced Safety Certificate (by the National Safety Council).

Continuing Education

Applicants for Fellows must provide evidence of at least 75 contact hours of risk management or related continuing education credits earned within 5 years prior to the date of application. Applicants for Diplomate must provide evidence of at least 150 hours of risk management continuing education credits earned within 10 years prior to the date of application.

Employment Experience

Applicants for Fellows must possess at least 5 years experience in a position with primary responsibility for risk management, and applicants for Diplomate must possess at least 10 years experience.

Contributions to the Field

Applicants for Fellows must meet all requirements in any two of the contribution categories, whereas applicants for Diplomate must meet all requirements in all three of the contribution categories of:

1. Leadership: Demonstration of service as a risk management organization officer, board member, or committee chairman.

2. Publishing: At least two articles published, within 5 years prior to the date of application, in journals or periodicals whose circulation exceeds 1,000 readers; articles published as a matter of routine job responsibilities will not be accepted. All articles submitted must bear the publication's name and date.

3. Lecturing: Documentation demonstrating participation as a faculty member in two risk management or related educational programs conducted within 5 years prior to the date of application. Lectures or presentations delivered as a matter of routine job responsibilities will not be accepted.

Those designated as Fellows or Diplomates must submit evidence that they have earned at least 25 risk management continuing education contact hours during the calendar year following the year of their designation and during each year thereafter in order to retain their rank.

Fellows may advance to Diplomate anytime by completing the requirements of the higher rank. Once achieving designation, individuals may place the letters F.A.S.H.R.M. or D.A.S.H.R.M. behind their names.

Summary

The role of the health care facility risk manager is primarily that of a coordinator and facilitator of risk management processes carried out by others. Most risk managers employed in hospitals and other types of health care organizations conduct activities that fall into the category of risk prevention and identification. Few risk managers in hospitals do risk financing. The screening of incident reports and claims administration are the two most frequently reported tasks according to the Brantley study.

Most health facilities risk managers report to the chief executive officer. Over 37 percent of risk managers have a master's degree; most have been in their present job less than 5 years but have been employed within the health industry an average of almost 14 years.

The ASHRM study indicates that hospital administration is the most frequent discipline in which risk managers have concentrated professional experience. Registered Nurse was the most often cited professional designation by respondents of the ASHRM survey. The most frequent quoted salary of risk managers was between $25,000 and $35,000 per year.

Although there is no required credentialing system in place for health facility risk managers, ASHRM has announced criteria for professional recognition. The society has established two levels, the Fellow and the Diplomate, both of which require substantial education, experience, and contribution to the field in order to qualify.

Chapter Exercises

1. Using the facts and scenario from the exercise in Chapter 2, plan the role for a risk manager to fill the soon-to-be-vacant position.
2. If assistants to the risk manager are needed, plan the roles for them.
3. Draft a job description for each person in questions 1 and 2 above.
4. Explain the training and education you desire in each person whose job description you have designed.

References

1. American Society of Hospital Risk Management, "Summary Report Survey of Hospital Risk Management Responsibilities and Salaries—1983," (Spring, 1984): 3-23.

2. Grace C. Brantley, "A Pilot Study of Risk Management," *Journal of the American Medical Records Association* (February 1982): 71.

3. Patricia Scully, "Checklist Shows the Role of a Hospital Risk Manager," *Business Insurance* (October 22, 1984).

4. *American Society for Hospital Risk Management Professional Recognition Program.* (Chicago: American Hospital Association, 1985).

CHAPTER FOUR

THE RISK MANAGEMENT INFORMATION SYSTEM

Gary P. Kraus

As a coordinator and facilitator, the health care risk manager is involved in the information processing business. The success or failure of the risk management program will hinge on how well information flows through the facility or multi-institutional system to the risk management office, and how the information is massaged and flows back to all programs in the system. Subsequently, administrators must be cognizant of the fundamentals of good communications and the sources of important data. They must know how to construct efficient conduits of information and protect sensitive material from adverse parties. The large volume of data will require modern computerized information systems, and the health care administrator must realize the value of data for quality assurance and risk management purposes.

Risk Management Communications

Rapid, accurate, and timely communications are essential for a successful risk management program. The risk manager must be one of the best-informed individuals within the institution and must receive timely and accurate data in order to support a program of loss prevention. This will be especially true if the United States implements a no-fault malpractice liability program such as that provided by the Alternative Medical Liability Act introduced by Congressmen Gephardt and Moore in 1984.[1] Early intervention with aggrieved parties requires that dispute resolution commence as soon after the misadventure occurred as is practical, and for this a reliable and rapid information system is necessary.

The gathering of risk management information will require formal and informal communication links with virtually all departments and personnel, but especially those shown in Figure 4-1. Formal communications are those established by the organization's policies and procedures and generally follow the chain of command. They may require either oral or, more frequently, written communication, usually by use of an established form, the incident report or its equivalent being the most

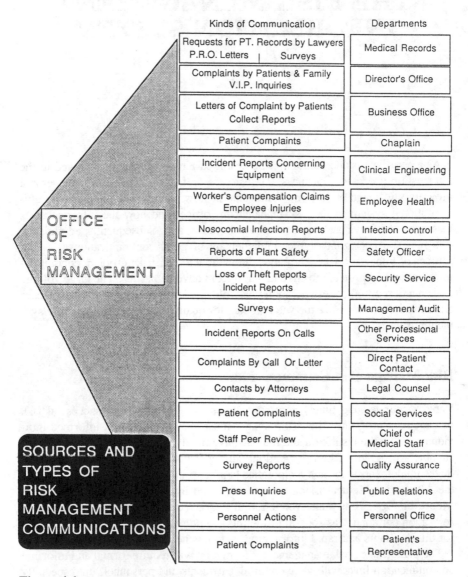

Kinds of Communication	Departments
Requests for PT. Records by Lawyers P.R.O. Letters | Surveys	Medical Records
Complaints by Patients & Family V.I.P. Inquiries	Director's Office
Letters of Complaint by Patients Collect Reports	Business Office
Patient Complaints	Chaplain
Incident Reports Concerning Equipment	Clinical Engineering
Worker's Compensation Claims Employee Injuries	Employee Health
Nosocomial Infection Reports	Infection Control
Reports of Plant Safety	Safety Officer
Loss or Theft Reports Incident Reports	Security Service
Surveys	Management Audit
Incident Reports On Calls	Other Professional Services
Complaints By Call Or Letter	Direct Patient Contact
Contacts by Attorneys	Legal Counsel
Patient Complaints	Social Services
Staff Peer Review	Chief of Medical Staff
Survey Reports	Quality Assurance
Press Inquiries	Public Relations
Personnel Actions	Personnel Office
Patient Complaints	Patient's Representative

OFFICE OF RISK MANAGEMENT

SOURCES AND TYPES OF RISK MANAGEMENT COMMUNICATIONS

Figure 4-1 Sources and types of risk management communications.

common. The formal communication system must be closely analyzed to prevent unnecessary delays in forwarding data to the risk manager.

If the institution uses an in-house generic screening system, information generated therefrom should also be communicated to the risk manager and used as a source of valuable data.[2] The communications system between line departments and the risk manager should not include all links in the chain of command, because the result will be unacceptable delays and data filtration. Communication with the risk manager involves transferring information that is sensitive and often accusatory in nature. It may imply shortcomings in personal behavior, procedures, or methods. This can have a negative impact on responsible middle or upper managers, who may attempt to lessen the perceived impact by sanitizing records or reports. The risk manager need only know that an adverse event occurred, who the parties involved were, and the current status of the case. The risk manager should complete all necessary follow-up and orchestrate events thereafter. Also, local case or statutory law may require that incident reports be sent directly to a risk manager, who may serve as a representative of the institution's attorney or insurer, to protect the information from discovery during litigation. In some states, if incident reports are circulated around an institution and used as a quality assurance or risk management tool, they could be deemed business records subject to discovery. However, records sent directly to insurers or legal counsel, who unlike the risk manager are not considered as staff persons, are usually deemed "reports made in anticipation of ligitation" and are privileged from discovery.[3]

Informal communication networks are perhaps the most important sources of risk management information. They usually produce news that is very timely but often fragmented. The most frequent form is a telephone call to the risk manager alerting him or her to a misadventure. These linkages should be well cultivated since they can elicit valuable information in a nonintimidating fashion. The identity of the caller is not always essential unless he or she is a party to the occurrence. The risk manager must also tap into the organization's grapevine, because informal communications usually follow not the established lines of authority, but person-to-person relationships, which are a source of important information.

It is absolutely essential that the risk manager's information system, whether informal or formal, be supported by the institution's administration. The risk manager must not be perceived as an extension of the management structure for purposes of retribution, but should have the independence to conduct his or her task objectively. If the rank and file believe that contacts with the risk manager will result in an immediate barrage of management activity, confidence in the office will erode and communication cease. The facility administration may have to exercise restraint and wait until after risk management strategies have been implemented before taking action in sensitive cases. Some of the best-laid settlement strategies have been upset by well-intentioned administrators who failed to coordinate their actions with the risk manager. Such acts as attempting to collect a bill or disciplining an injured patient's favorite nurse could antagonize the patient to the point that the patient visits an attorney.

Conditions or situations requiring change should be reported to the risk management committee to prevent future events of the same nature. Support for the change can then filter from the committee to the appropriate manager for action.

Although the incident report is the most common form of formal communication with the risk manager, many such reports contain only benign information, relating minor infractions of management standards rather than serious misadventures. Serious occurrences are often communicated by telephone or in person; however, in many institutions the incident report is used in these circumstances as well.

The term *incident report* is rapidly losing its appeal because it connotes to laypersons a serious event, when in fact the report writer may be communicating only a minor deviation from a management standard. Such terms as *variance report* or *occurrence report* are replacing the older term. Incident reports vary in size, scope, and degree of comprehensiveness but usually include identification of the patient or victim and a description of the event with any resulting injury and outcome data. Exhibits 4-1 and 4-2 are examples of two basic types of incident reports. Exhibit 4-1 represents the more traditional style, which is designed to capture identification data and the substantive information about the event, with outcome and follow-up left to the writer to supply in a narrative format. The traditional style is less efficient since it takes longer to complete and to read. The reader is left at the mercy of the writer not only to provide the necessary information but to do so in a legible and comprehensible manner. The traditional form is also hard to computerize since the reader must take time to judge which data are significant. Risk managers and their secretaries also find the style troublesome because the writer often uses medical terminology and jargon, which may be impossible to translate without a good command of clinical language and symbols.

The form shown in Exhibit 4-2 represents a more modern approach to data collection and is becoming more prevalent among hospitals, especially those with automated risk management information systems. This form is designed to capture rapidly all relevant data about the patient or victim and the event. The writer can simply circle the correct field; however, space is also available for narrative and follow-up remarks. Most important, the form asks all the necessary questions and does not leave the choice to the writer. If the risk manager utilizes such a form, software such as A.R.M.I.S.[4] can be easily programmed with corresponding field numbers and codes for quick data entry.

To this point we have used the terms *incident* and *occurrence* synonymously to identify events that are negative in nature and could lead to grave consequences. Although both terms are frequently used by members of the health professions to mean the same thing, the reader should now attempt to reprogram his or her vocabulary to take account of the fact that the terms have slightly different conno-

07980

PATIENT INCIDENT REPORT

INSTRUCTIONS: This form is used to report an incident, which is any happening not consistent with the routine care of a particular patient. This includes accidents and situations which could result in accidents. Incidents occurring anywhere within or on the property of the University of Missouri-Columbia Medical Center are reported on this form. This form is also used to report damage to personal property of a patient, but it shall NOT be used to report an incident occurring during a therapeutic or diagnostic procedure.

This form is submitted by:
   (1) the physician whose name appears in Item 9, or if not applicable,
   (2) the employee who witnessed or was first advised of the incident.
One LEGIBLE copy of this form is signed by the person submitting the report and forwarded immediately to the Risk Manager. DO NOT PLACE THIS FORM IN THE PATIENT CHART OR SEND TO MEDICAL RECORDS. Incident reports are submitted and maintained at the direction of the University's General Counsel for the purpose of preparing to defend against possible litigation. This report is CONFIDENTIAL and it is NOT TO BE COPIED.

NAME :
PATIENT #:
ROOM #:
D.O.B :
MARITAL STATUS: S   M   D   W
SEX: M   F

1. Cause for hospitalization or treatment:

2. Patient's mental condition *before* incident: ☐ Normal   ☐ Sedated   ☐ Disoriented   ☐   Other_____

3. Date, Time & Place of Incident: /   /   ____ hrs.

4. Describe details of the occurrence - what happened, how it occurred, patient's comments following; if an injury state part of body injured, describe property or equipment damaged, if applicable.

5. Name of witnesses:

6. Date & Time of Report: /   /   ____hrs.   *Bedrails:*   Up   Down   N/A

7. Was physician notified: Yes   No   Did physician see patient after incident?   Yes   No

   If yes, name of physician & date/time seen: /   /   ____ hrs.

8. Name of Responsible Resident:

   Name of Attending Physician:

9. Findings of Examining Physician:

Physician's Signature

10. Name & title of person submitting report:

ROUTING OF REPORT		DATE & TIME RECEIVED	DISPOSITION		DATE SENT
Supervisor _____	RN		Insurance_____		
Director _____	RN		General Counsel_____		
Risk Manager _____			Administration_____		

Exhibit 4-1A Traditional patient incident report form.

TO BE ANSWERED BY PERSON COMPLETING REPORT ONLY

DO NOT USE

11. In your opinion, what caused this occurrence?

12. In your opinion, what can be done to prevent similar occurrences in the future?

TO BE COMPLETED BY SUPERVISOR ONLY

DO NOT USE

13. Plans for followup:

Individual Counseling _____

Referral to Staff Development _____

Other corrective action (describe)_____

TO BE COMPLETED BY RISK MANAGER ONLY

14. Action Taken: ☐ None   ☐ Followup Investigation

15. Individuals Contacted:

16. Investigative findings:

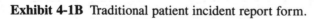

Exhibit 4-1B Traditional patient incident report form.

	UNIVERSITY OF MISSOURI VARIANCE/INCIDENT REPORT (see reverse side for instructions)	1 ADDRESSOGRAPH:

FORM NUMBER

Patient Name:

2 TIME OF INCIDENT

Address:

DATE:_____/_____/_____

3 STATUS

I - Inpatient
O - Outpatient
V - Visitor
X - Other_____

DOB:

TIME:_____
use 2400 clock

Pt. Number:

4 SEX	**5 DIAGNOSIS**
M - Male	
F - Female	

NOTE: Space for details or additional information on back of form in space 18 and/or 23

6 LOCATION OF INCIDENT (circle one and fill in as needed)

1 Patient Room
2 Bathroom in Patient Room
3 Hall_____
4 Bathroom in Hall
5 Day Room on Unit
6 Treatment Area
7 Waiting Area
8 Nursing Station_____
9 OR/L&D Suite
10 Pharmacy
11 Radiology
12 OPD_____
13 Emergency Room
14 ASU
15 Path. Laboratory_____
16 Other Laboratory_____
17 Other Location_____

7 STAFF MOST CLOSELY INVOLVED (circle one)

1 Attending Physician/Surgeon
2 Resident/Intern
3 Medical Student
4 Nurse Practitioner/PA
5 RN/Graduate Nurse
6 LPN
7 Nursing Technician
8 Nursing Student
9 Dietitian
10 Food Service Worker
11 Housekeeping Staff_____
12 Engineering Staff_____
13 Clerical
14 Volunteer
15 Pharmacy Staff_____
16 Laboratory Staff_____
17 Radiology Staff_____
18 Physical Therapy Staff_____
19 Respiratory Therapy Staff_____
20 OT/Other Rehab Staff_____
21 Other_____

8 PATIENT FACTORS PRIOR TO INCIDENT (circle all that apply)

a Alert/Normal
b Agitated
c Unconscious
d Refuses to Cooperate
e Confused
f Senile
g Depressed
h Suicidal
i Sedated
j Anesthetized
k Substance Abuse

l Intoxicated
m Handicapped
n Mentally Retarded
o Neurological Impairment
p Language Barrier
q BR Restrictions
r Bed Restraints
s BRP Restrictions
t Up with Help
u Other_____

9 PATIENT OR FAMILY ATTITUDE AFTER INCIDENT (circle one)

1 Unaware
2 Understanding
3 Cooperative

4 Belligerent
5 Angry
6 Threats of Suit

DESCRIPTION OF THE EVENT

10 PATIENT FALL (circle one)

1 Ambulating
2 From Bed
3 From Chair
4 From Commode
5 From Stretcher/Gurney
6 From Support Equipment
7 From Wheelchair
8 From Crib/Isolette
9 From Exam Table
10 Other_____

(circle all that apply)

a Rails on Bed Up
b Call Light Not Available
c Call Light On
d Call Light Malfunction
e Floor Slippery
f Struck by Equipment
g Patient Unattended
h Struck by Another Person
i Other_____

11 MEDICATION VARIANCE (circle one)

1 Medication Missing
2 Adverse Side Effects
3 Medication Given but Not Charted
4 Medication Omitted
5 Duplication/Extra Dose
6 Time Variance
7 Wrong Routing
8 Wrong Dose
9 Wrong Med Administered
10 Rx Filled Wrong
11 Rx Compounded Wrong
12 Wrong Patient

13 IV Compounded Wrong
14 IV Not Checked Properly
15 IV at Wrong Rate
16 Check here if IMED used:_____
17 Other_____

12 PROCEDURAL VARIANCE (circle one)

1 Performed on Wrong Patient
2 Improper Preparation of Patient
3 Lost Specimen
4 Spoiled Specimen
5 Patient Did Not Arrive As Scheduled
6 Staff Did Not Arrive As Scheduled
7 Omission of Procedure
8 Performed Wrong
9 Performance Delayed
10 Radiation Exposure
11 NPO Violated
12 Other_____
13 Blood/Blood By-Products Problem (explain)_____

13 EQUIPMENT VARIANCE (circle one)

1 Electrical Problem
2 Electrical Shock
3 Equipment Not Available
4 Improper Use
5 Mechanical Problem
6 Operator Unqualified
7 Other Malfunction/Defect
8 Wrong Equipment
9 Other_____

16 SECURITY VARIANCE (circle one)

1 Damage/Loss of Property (explain on reverse)
2 Code Red
3 Security Problem
4 Drug Count Variance
5 Drug Tampering
6 Drug Keys Variance
7 Other_____

14 OR/ER/L&D EVENT (circle one)

1 Consent Problem
2 Break in Sterile Technique
3 Anesthesia Problem
4 Count Discrepancy
5 Foreign Body Left In Patient
6 Unexpected Death
7 Precipitous Delivery
8 Return to OR Same Day
9 Surgical/L&D Procedure Delayed
10 Trauma to Healthy Tissue
11 Unexpected Complications
12 Other_____

15 MISCELLANEOUS EVENT (circle one)

1 Fight Among Patients
2 Patient Attacked Staff
3 Patient Abused by Staff
4 Left Without Notice
5 Burn
6 Cardiac Arrest/Code Blue
7 Cross Infection/Code Yellow
8 Diet Problem
9 Patient Left AMA; Refused to Sign AMA Form
10 Threats of Suit
11 Suicide Attempt
12 Patient Denied Treatment
13 Other_____

UMUW FORM 192 (REV JUN 82)   ● CONTINUE ON REVERSE SIDE ●   c Copyright UM 1982

Exhibit 4-2 Coded variance/incident report form.

tations. Generally, the term *incident* refers to an event that could lead to grave consequences. However, the word *consequences* has no particular meaning when coupled with the term *incident* and could mean physical consequences, such as a patient sustaining an injury, management consequences, such as the person who caused the incident being disciplined, or legal consequences, such as the person who committed the error or caused the incident being sued. The incidents that the reports communicate often range from minor events of no consequence from a legal perspective to major events that could evoke disastrous financial and legal consequences. *Occurrences,* on the other hand, are events or incidents, if one desires to use the terms synonymously, that could lead to grave consequences of a legal nature.

In some areas there is movement away from use of the term *incident* because it is simply too broad. To the medical community it includes all types of events, the outcome of some of which may be benign, whereas to the lay public and the legal profession the term connotes a very bad event. Also, the multiple use of the reported data can create legal questions regarding the discovery of the information during litigation. Therefore, to better take advantage of the law, it is recommended that health care institutions separate events by severity and report them differently.

At the University of Missouri Hospital and Clinics, the use of the term *incident* is discouraged, and the incident reporting system has been bifurcated into two reports. The former incident report has been changed to a "management variance report" for minor events in which the patient has sustained no noticeable injury or legal damages, and an "occurrence report" is used for events that are serious with possible sequelae. The management variance report is used primarily as a quality assurance tool and is circulated throughout the management chain of command so that those who need to know about the event will have an opportunity to see it. In Missouri, the management variance report would be subject to discovery. The occurrence report is not written on a preprinted form but is simply a narrative, either handwritten or typed, that is produced by the person responsible for the occurrence and sent directly to the risk manager. It is considered a "report made in anticipation of litigation" and often labeled as such; it is therefore not subject to discovery. Exhibit 4-3 is an example of a management variance report, which evolved from the "incident/variance report" shown in Exhibit 4-2. The term was selected because the event or incident usually results from a deviation from management standards. Because the act giving rise to the event was a variance from acceptable practice, the title of the form is very descriptive of its purpose. The form was well received by the nursing and medical staffs; however, substantial in-service education was required to teach the staff the difference between the two reporting formats.

Regardless of whether an institution uses a single reporting format called an incident report, or bifurcates the reporting format into variance reports and occurrence reports, all reports should communicate certain common information:

UNIVERSITY OF MISSOURI **MANAGEMENT VARIANCE REPORT** (see reverse side for instructions)			1 **Addressograph:**

FORM NUMBER

2 **Time of Incident**	3 **Sex** (circle one)	4 **Status** (circle one)
Date: _____ _____ _____	Male	1 - Inpatient 2 - Outpatient
Time: _____ use 2400 clock	Female	3 - Visitor 4 - Other _____

Patient Name:

Address:

DOB:

Pt. Number:

NOTE: Space for details or additional information on back of this form

5 Diagnosis (circle all that apply)
1 Disease or Disorder of the Nervous System
2 Disease or Disorder of the Eye
3 Disease or Disorder of the Ear, Nose, or Throat
4 Disease or Disorder of the Respiratory System
5 Disease or Disorder of the Circulatory System
6 Disease or Disorder of the Digestive System
7 Disease or Disorder of the Hepatobiliary System or Pancreas
8 Disease of the Musculoskeletal System or Connective Tissue
9 Disease of the Skin, Subcutaneous Tissue or Breast
10 Endocrine, Nutritional, or Metabolic Disease
11 Disease or Disorder of the Kidney or Urinary Tract
12 Disease or Disorder of the Male Reproductive System
13 Disease or Disorder of the Female Reproductive System
14 Pregnancy, Childbirth, or the Puerperium
15 Neonate with Certain Conditions of the Perinatal Period
16 Disease or Disorder of Blood or Blood-Forming Organ or Immunity
17 Certain Neoplasms (Not Elsewhere Classified)
18 Infectious or Parasitic Disease (Systemic)
19 Mental Disorder
20 Substance Use Disorder or Substance Induced Organic Disorder
21 Injury, Poisoning, or Toxic Effect of Drugs
22 Burn
23 Other _____

6 **Location of incident** (circle one and fill in as needed)	7 **Staff Most Closely Involved** (circle one)
1 Patient Room No. _____ 2 Bathroom in Patient Room _____ 3 Hall _____ 4 Bathroom in Hall _____ 5 I.C.U. _____ 6 Treatment Area _____ 7 Waiting Area _____ 8 Nursing Station _____ 9 OR L&D Suite 10 Pharmacy 11 Radiology 12 Clinic _____ 13 Emergency Room 14 ASU 15 Path Laboratory _____ 16 Helicopter _____ 17 Other Location _____	1 Attending Physician/Surgeon 2 Resident Intern 3 Medical Student 4 Nurse Practitioner PA 5 RN Graduate Nurse 6 LPN 7 Nursing Technician 8 Nursing Student 9 Dietitian 10 Food Service Worker 11 Housekeeping Staff _____ 12 Engineering Staff _____ 13 Clerical 14 Volunteer 15 Pharmacy Staff _____ 16 Laboratory Staff _____ 17 Radiology Staff _____ 18 Physical Therapy Staff _____ 19 Respiratory Therapy Staff _____ 20 OT Other Rehab Staff _____

8 Patient Condition Prior to Variance (circle one)
1 Alert Normal
2 Agitated
3 Unconscious
4 Refuses to Cooperate
5 Confused
6 Senile
7 Depressed
8 Suicidal
9 Sedated
10 Anesthetized
11 Substance Abuse
12 Intoxicated
13 Handicapped
14 Mentally Retarded
15 Neurological Impaired
16 Language Barrier

9 Patient or Family Attitude After Variance (circle one)
Unaware (1)   Cooperative (3)   Angry (5)   Threats of Suit (6)

Circle the Event that Best Describes the Variances

10 Patient Fall (circle one)	**11 Medication Variance** (circle one)	**12 Procedural Variance** (circle one)
1 Ambulating 2 From Bed 3 From Chair 4 From Commode 5 From Stretcher Gurney 6 From Support Equipment 7 From Wheelchair 8 From Crib Isolette 9 From Exam Table 10 Other _____ (circle all that apply) a Rails on Bed Up b Call Light Not Available c Call Light On d Call Light Malfunction e Floor Slippery f Struck by Equipment g Patient Unattended h Struck by Another Person i Other _____	1 Medication Missing 2 Adverse Side Effects 3 Medication Given but Not Charted 4 Medication Omitted 5 Duplication Extra Dose 6 Time Variance 7 Wrong Routing 8 Wrong Dose 9 Wrong Med Administered 10 Rx Filled Wrong 11 Rx Compounded Wrong 12 Wrong Patient I.V. VARIANCES 13 IV Compounded Wrong 14 IV Not Checked Properly 15 IV at Wrong Rate 16 Infiltration	1 Performed on Wrong Patient 2 Improper Preparation of Patient 3 Lost Specimen 4 Spoiled Specimen 5 Patient Did Not Arrive As Scheduled 6 Staff Did Not Arrive As Scheduled 7 Omission of Procedure 8 Performed Wrong 9 Performance Delayed 10 Radiation Exposure 11 NPO Violated 12 Misdiagnosis 13 Blood Blood By-Products Problem (explain) _____

13 EQUIPMENT VARIANCE (circle one)	**14 OR/ER/L&D Event** (circle one)	**15 Miscellaneous Event** (circle one)
1 Electrical Problem 2 Electrical Shock 3 Equipment Not Available 4 Improper Use 5 Mechanical Problem 6 Operator Unqualified 7 Other Malfunction Defect 8 Wrong Equipment 9 Other _____ **16 Security Variance** (circle one) 1 Damage/Loss of Property (explain on reverse) 2 Code Red 3 Security Problem 4 Drug Count Variance 5 Drug Tampering 6 Drug Keys Variance 7 Other _____	1 Consent Problem 2 Break in Sterile Technique 3 Anesthesia Problem 4 Count Discrepancy 5 Foreign Body Left In Patient 6 Unexpected Death 7 Precipitous Delivery 8 Return to OR Same Day 9 Surgical L&D Procedure Delayed 10 Trauma to Healthy Tissue 11 Unexpected Complications 12 Other _____	1 Fight Among Patients 2 Patient Attacked Staff 3 Patient Abused by Staff 4 Left Without Notice 5 Burn 6 Cardiac Arrest Code Blue 7 Cross Infection Code Yellow 8 Diet Problem 9 Patient Left AMA: Refused to Sign AMA Form 10 Trauma to Healthy Tissue 11 Suicide Attempt 12 Patient Denied Treatment 13 Other _____

UMUW FORM 192 (REV JAN 85)   • CONTINUE ON REVERSE SIDE •   Copyright UM 1985

Exhibit 4-3 Management variance report form.

1. Name and identification of the patient, visitor, or other person sustaining the injury or accident involved in the event, including date of birth, sex, and address

2. Date, time, and location of the event

3. Name of the person completing the report and the date the report was completed

4. Name of the person who caused the event, if known

5. Names and addresses of witnesses to the event

6. Conditions of individuals involved in the event before and after

7. Description of the event

8. Any account given by an individual involved.

A close analysis of Exhibits 4-2 and 4-3 will provide guides to the information that should be communicated. Regardless of whether an automated format, such as the forms in Exhibits 4-2 and 4-3 is used, or a narrative format as shown in Exhibit 4-1, there should be some space for parties to write extemporaneously. However, the use of extemporaneous narrative should be not used in jurisdictions where incident reports are not protected from discovery or legal compulsion.

For a good discussion of incident reports and their legal significance, the reader can consult such authors as Clemon W. Williams[5] and William H. Roach,[6] among others.

Incident Screening

One of the primary skills necessary in a risk manager is the ability to separate benign incidents from the potential compensable event (PCE; see Figure 4-2). Most incident reports will communicate variances from management standards, most of which never result in litigation, rather than serious occurrences. Although these incidents lack a necessary ingredient to create a PCE, collectively they represent a valuable source of data for quality assurance and management follow-up. Unfortunately, most institutions still do not tap this valuable source of data. Later in this book, the use of risk management data will be discussed and examples of management reports illustrated. Experience at the University of Missouri indicates that approximately 95 percent of all incident reports received are management variances, and only 5 percent are classified as PCEs.

Figure 4-1, which indicates the source and types of risk management communication, also helps to illustrate the beginning of the screening process. Since any contact with the office of risk management could involve communicating facts about an event that could result in a claim or lawsuit, each contact should be taken seriously and screened.

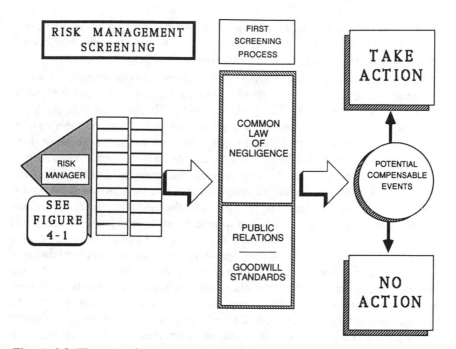

Figure 4-2 The screening process in risk management communications.

A PCE is generally defined as any adverse occurrence that has the necessary ingredients to cause a financial loss to the hospital or its insurer. The term should not be applied narrowly to only those cases in which claims or lawsuits are likely to be filed, but must be broad in its application, regardless of how remote the chances for litigation. If one dissects this definition, a clearer meaning of the term can be obtained. Since the purpose of a hospital is to provide health services to patients, even the deviation of such resources as money, employee time, and services to the investigation and management of an adverse event already represents a loss, because had the event not occurred these resources could have been utilized in pursuit of their intended purpose. Whether an event is adverse or not depends on whether the patient has sustained a real or perceived injury. Real injuries are easy to prove, and therefore we need not dwell on them. However, perceived injuries are almost impossible to deal with because judgment must be based on the person's own value system. What might be trivial to one person could be serious to another. Because one cannot judge perceived injuries accurately, one must watch for other signs to determine whether the alleged injury should be taken seriously. Some of the common signs are anger shown by the patient, threats by the patient to sue or to contact an important person such as an elected official, leaving against medical advice, and refusal to pay the hospital bill even though the patient has the means to do so. These and other signs coupled with an event are usually enough to confirm an adverse occurrence, and one can be reasonably sure that the person has experienced a perceived injury or sustained perceived damages.

Once the risk manager has determined that a person has experienced a real or perceived injury, additional tests should be applied to complete the screening of PCEs from occurrences, incidents, and variances. The first test to apply is the common law test of negligence. For a plaintiff to prove a prima facie case of negligence—that is, a case that can be legally submitted to a jury—one must show that the hospital or one of its staff owed the plaintiff a duty of reasonable care. It must further be proved that the duty of care was breached, which essentially means that the caregiver performed below the standard established by the profession for the activity involved. The plaintiff must also show that there was a direct causal relationship between the failure to practice at the acceptable standard and the injury received. Last, the plaintiff must show that the injury resulted in legal damages. If the four elements of duty, breach of duty, cause-in-fact, and damages are present, then at least a technical case of negligence exists. At this point in the case analysis, one may wish to label the event a PCE and conclude the screening; otherwise a closer review of the damage issue may be made to determine if the technical case is not in fact a realistic case of negligence. The difference between a technical case and a realistic case is one of common sense and economics and usually centers around two issues: First, are the damages sufficient to sue over? and second, can the case be proven? Although the second issue used to be the determining factor, it is rapidly losing its significance because of the increasing availability of the expert witness. However, the economics of hiring experts might still be considered. The first issue, that of the degree of damages, is now the primary factor. The high cost of litigation generally requires that claimants must have incurred substantial damages, usually physical or mental impairments that are long-lasting or permanent; otherwise the expense of prosecuting the case is not equal to the damages that are legally recoverable. Therefore, in many PCEs the damages will be too little to sue over regardless of the merits of the case. If experience shows that the amount of damages is high enough, then it is likely that a claim will result, and the case is definitely a PCE.

In the event that the facts, whether communicated on an incident report form, or orally, or by some other means, fail the test of negligence, the risk manager should then apply a second test based on public relations or goodwill standards. The risk manager should ask himself or herself, "Does this patient have a legitimate complaint from the viewpoint of fundamental fairness?" In other words, from the consumer's perspective, did the patient receive the services that he or she was entitled to receive? Cases such as these usually are easily identifiable because the patient or the patient's family is angry and upset over the failure of the hospital staff or its system to fulfill their own expectations of reasonable care. Examples of situations when reasonable expectations are not met are confrontations with rude staff, problems with meals, lost test results resulting in delays or repetition of uncomfortable procedures, lack of attention by staff, and sloppy nursing care. Although the patient may not have a realistic cause of action for a lawsuit, sometimes these events, if left to fester, can result in insidious losses. This is particularly true when the situation involves a public hospital that looks to the state or some governmental entity for funding. A person who is very angry over the treatment he or she or a family member received may lodge complaints that will result in inquiries. If the inquiries come from an important or powerful member of the community or from a family member of such a person, the risk manager should show very real concern. An example of such a case is the state representative who lodges a protest with the university trustees over an event that occurred at the university hospital and threatens to hold up or reduce appropriations if something is not done. Cases of this type are very real PCEs and require close attention.

Once the tests described above have been applied to the various forms of risk management communications, most PCEs will have been screened out. The screening process will not, of course, catch all PCEs, since no system is foolproof and some cases will go unreported. The frivolous case will usually not be identified, because by definition such a case lacks merit and fails the screening tests. Such cases are often revealed only when an attorney begins making inquiries and asks for a copy of the claimant's medical record, or when a claim or lawsuit is actually filed.

The treatment of PCEs is the subject of another chapter and will not be considered until the student has gained some fundamental understanding of the law, and specifically the area of negligence, which is discussed in Chapter 5. All risk managers should develop skill at screening risk management communications so that PCEs can be identified and dealt with effectively. The institution's insurance contract may require all that all PCEs be identified and notice be given. The hospital therefore, has a real economic interest in screening all communications, because the insurer usually sets reserves for each PCE, which could have an impact on future premium levels. Some companies offer incident report services and even provide the forms to be used. This service should not be used as a substitute for the vital process of risk management communications screening, but only as a parallel service. The early detection of an adverse event is paramount if the institution has a program of early dispute resolution and early settlement is to be successful. Also, the hospital administration should find out about problem areas on its own rather than have outside organizations identify them.

Computerized Filing and Report Systems

Risk management data constitute one of the greatest sources of untapped information in many hospitals and other health care facilities. The reason this information is underutilized is that risk management contacts flow to the office not as part of an organized system, but rather in one-way communications channels. This information is frequently reviewed, screened for PCEs, and then stored in files until someone decides that the forms are no longer needed. Thus, in the offices of many risk managers and the storerooms of many health care facilities it is not uncommon to find boxes of old reports gathering dust and just adding to storage costs.

However, with the development of specialized risk management software and less costly personal computers, things are changing. As a result of a series of recently published articles[7] and papers read at meetings of the American Society for Hospital Risk Management,[8] many health facilities' risk managers are putting their data to work and creating valuable quality assurance and risk management tools in the form of follow-up reports, trend analyses, and other forms of management information. No doubt the greater emphasis provided by the Joint Commission on Accreditation of Hospitals will stimulate the use of risk management information. Health facilities still have a long way to go before the practice of using risk management information as a prevention and quality assurance tool becomes universally accepted.

With the commitment of approximately $5,000, a facility can purchase the necessary ingredients to develop a reasonably sophisticated computerized information system. A stripped-down system could be designed for less. These costs would include the cost of a personal computer with two floppy disk drives or one floppy and one hard disk drive, such as an Apple II, IBM PC or XT, Compaq, or one of any number of available desktop machines with printer, monitor, and disk drives, as well as one of the many databased management software packages available, such as Visifile, dBase II, or Lotus. The computer should have at least 256K of memory. There are also available a number of canned software packages (such as the A.R.M.I.S. program) that can be immediately loaded into one of the above computers, providing the user with an instant automated data collection and processing format. All that is needed is for the user to design the system to integrate the risk manager's automated data processing capabilities. Therein lies the most difficult task, for it may take a substantial amount of time and management skill to have the nursing and allied health departments and services change their data collection habits and accept a new format. After the collection and processing parts of the system are functioning, and new and revealing reports are being generated, the last and most difficult aspect of the system must be accomplished, that of getting the members of the administration to accept and use the reports and other information generated. This task could be made simpler with the support of an involved and dedicated risk management committee.

A computerized risk management information system has five distinct parts: 1) data collection; 2) data screening, review, and coding; 3) data processing; 4) report generation; and 5) information analysis and feedback. If the five parts are effectively tied together, a complete management loop has been created. Figure 4-

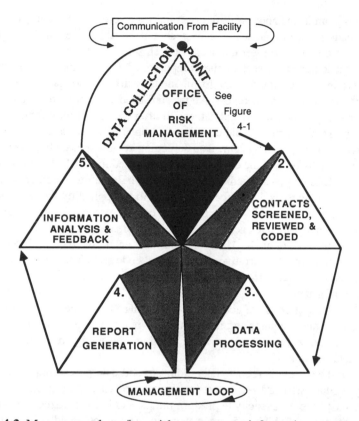

Figure 4-3 Management loop for a risk management information system.

3 illustrates a management loop of a risk management information system using a computerized format.

Part 1 of the system requires that data collection be accomplished in a format that makes data capture fast and accurate. The use of an incident report or management variance report form similar to those displayed in Exhibits 4-2 and 4-3 is necessary. The form should have the capability of being coded so that the computer can be programmed to process the coded information. Better yet, one should select or write the software first and design the form to fit the software requirements necessary to produce the information desired. You will see that in Exhibits 4-2 and 4-3 every piece of data has a corresponding code number, which pertains to a particular field of information. For example, in Exhibit 4-3, field 5, pertaining to diagnosis, has 23 subcodes. The individual feeding data into the computer has only to type in the code 5-05, for example, and the software will file the information in the diagnosis field under "disease or disorder of the circulatory system." When retrieval is desired, one has only to call up the correct codes. If the system program is designed well, the possibilities of cross-referencing and indexing are endless. Consequently, the user should be able to create a variety of individualized reports to meet the needs of each staff member.

The most important aspect of the computerized form is that the information desired is already preprinted on the form, and the staff does not have to guess what information to include in the report. All the staff need do is circle the relevant field or supply a few needed words and names. To offer the opportunity for extemporaneous remarks, the forms should contain some lined blank spaces.

The second part of the system, data screening review and coding, consists of review by an individual of the communication obtained in part 1. The purpose is to screen for PCEs so that immediate attention can be given to them. In some less sophisticated systems, code numbers may have to be applied by the risk manager, and regardless of how good the information capture procedures are, many staff members will not complete each field or will provide the information desired in a narrative format or not at all. The individual who enters the data in the computer will have to translate the narrative into a desired code and place it in the appropriate field, and may have to contact the reporting unit or individual and request additional information.

Part 3 of the system is the actual data processing. This aspect of the system is carried out by the computer and its software. It makes use of all of the functions contained in the software such as filing, editing, retrieving, reporting, storing, backup, and printing.

Part 4 of the system is report generation. A good data processing system must not only produce standardized reports on a periodic basis, as illustrated in Exhibit 4-4, but must have the capacity to produce unique and individualized reports, such as that depicted in Exhibit 4-5, upon demand, easily and rapidly. The program must also be able to produce the individualized report with little programming effort. Exhibit 4-4, is not specific with respect to the data it shows, but is simply a printout of all files for a given period of time. Exhibit 4-5, however, is a printout of a specific event for specific units of a hospital. The report deals with only one desired event for a stated period of time, which in this case is what the requesting manager desired. In this example, the requesting manager wanted to study medication errors. The advantages of a flexible report generating system are obvious.

The last part of the system is analysis and feedback of the information produced. This activity is usually completed by the risk manager and those members of the health facility administration furnished with the data. The successful feedback of risk management information could very well be the most difficult part of the system, because it requires the facility administration to confront and accept the significance of the data. As anyone familiar with military intelligence knows, the most difficult aspect of the process is not discovering the secret, but getting your own superiors to believe it.

RISK MANAGEMENT DEPARTMENT
PCE FILE

PAGE 2

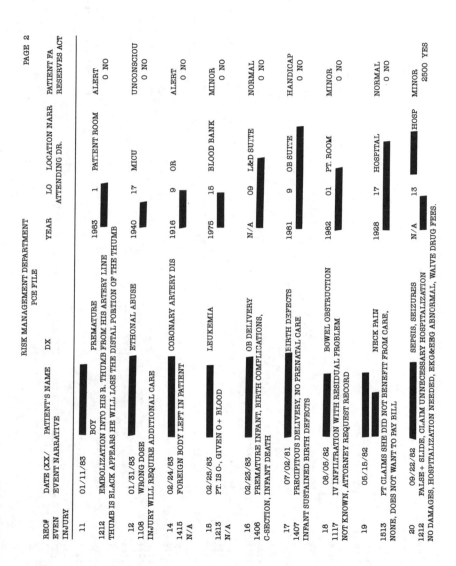

REC# / EVEN / INJURY	DATE (XX/ / PATIENT'S NAME / EVENT NARRATIVE	DX	YEAR	LO ATTENDING DR.	LOCATION NARR	PATIENT FA / RESERVES ACT
11 / 1212	01/11/83 BOY — EMBOLIZATION INTO HIS R. THUMB FROM HIS ARTERY LINE THUMB IS BLACK APPEARS HE WILL LOSE THE DISTAL PORTION OF THE THUMB	PREMATURE	1983	1	PATIENT ROOM	ALERT / 0 NO
12 / 1108	01/31/83 — WRONG DOSE INJURY WILL REQUIRE ADDITIONAL CARE	ETHONAL ABUSE	1940	17	MICU	UNCONSCIOU / 0 NO
14 / 1415 / N/A	02/24/83 — FOREIGN BODY LEFT IN PATIENT	CORONARY ARTERY DIS	1916	9	OR	ALERT / 0 NO
15 / 1213 / N/A	02/25/83 — PT. IS O-, GIVEN O+ BLOOD	LEUKEMIA	1975	15	BLOOD BANK	MINOR / 0 NO
16 / 1406	02/23/83 — PREMATURE INFANT, BIRTH COMPLICATIONS, C-SECTION, INFANT DEATH	OB DELIVERY	N/A	09	L&D SUITE	NORMAL / 0 NO
17 / 1407	07/02/81 — PRECIPITOUS DELIVERY, NO PRENATAL CARE INFANT SUSTAINED BIRTH DEFECTS	BIRTH DEFECTS	1981	9	OB SUITE	HANDICAP / 0 NO
18 / 1117	08/05/82 — IV INFILTRATION WITH RESIDUAL PROBLEM NOT KNOWN, ATTORNEY REQUEST RECORD	BOWEL OBSTRUCTION	1982	01	PT. ROOM	MINOR / 0 NO
19 / 1513	05/15/82 — PT CLAIMS SHE DID NOT BENEFIT FROM CARE, NONE, DOES NOT WANT TO PAY BILL	NECK PAIN	1928	17	HOSPITAL	NORMAL / 0 NO
20 / 1212	09/22/82 — FALSE + SLIDE, CLAIM UNNECESSARY HOSPITALIZATION NO DAMAGES, HOSPITALIZATION NEEDED, EKG&EEG ABNORMAL, WAIVE DRUG FEES.	SEPSIS, SEIZURES	N/A	13	HOSP	MINOR / 2500 YES

A.R.M.I.S.

July 1, 1985 Medications Errors from Intensive Care Units 1st Quarter 1985

Number	Date of Event	Unit	Time	Pt's Name	Pt's Number	Event Code	Event	Sequel
1312	1/12/85	BICU	0900	Charles	00-65-81-32-1	11-2	adverse side effect	none
1323	1/14/85	CCU	2115	Mary	00-66-82-33-2	11-4	omitted	none
1339	1/22/85	NICU	0130	Baby Boy	00-43-65-81-1	11-14	I.V not checked properly	Skin sluff may require plastic surgery to cover
1355	1/25/85	CCU	1100	Robert	00-78-43-54-2	11-6	Time variance	none
1361	1/28/85	SICU	1755	Joan	00-42-55-98-3	11-5	Duplication/extra dose	none
1375	1/30/85	TICU	2245	Stephen	00-51-78-41-1	11-9	wrong meds administered	Pt. expired, question cause
1380	1/30/85	BICU	0215	George	00-87-33-21-1	11-4	medications omitted	none
1386	2/02/85	TICU	0630	T.J.	00-34-31-66-1	11-16	I.V. infiltration	arm swollen
1391	2/03/85	NICU	2330	Baby Girl	00-84-63-88-2	11-16	I.V. infiltration	none
1402	2/04/85	SICU	1100	Tirone	00-12-54-37-1	11-7	wrong routing	none
1415	2/07/85	CCU	2045	Betty	00-58-32-77-1	11-8	wrong dose	cardiac arrest, code called pt. recovered, extra stay

Exhibit 4-5 Printout of specific medication errors for specific units of a hospital.

Summary

Risk management communications should include formal and informal links with virtually every service and key individual in the health care facility. Timely notice of serious misadventures is essential, especially if the facility has or desires to set up an early dispute resolution program. The administration of the institution must support the communication system and not take actions that could upset risk management strategy.

The most common form of risk management communication is the incident report or its equivalent. Incident reports should be designed for the fast and accurate capture of desired information in a format that will lend itself to computerization. risk managers must be familiar with the rules of discovery within their jurisdiction in order to protect sensitive information and incident reports.

Incident screening is the process of filtering from the universe of risk management communications those serious incidents that could result in a claim or lawsuit. Serious misadventures are called potential compensatory events, because they contain all the necessary ingredients of a prima facie case of negligence. A prima facie case requires that the plaintiff prove the existence of a duty, breach of that duty, causation, and damages on the part of the defendant. The damages must be substantial enough to elicit the interest of a trial attorney.

A modern health care facility should establish an automated risk management information system and use risk management data as both a quality assurance tool and a claims administration control device. A system can be designed and implemented for less than $5,000 by purchasing a personal computer with about 256K of memory and either two floppy disk drives or one floppy and one hard disk drive. A printer and a monitor are also required, with support software. A system can be individually designed and programmed, or canned software is available, such as A.R.M.I.S. The system should have the ability to create a variety of individualized reports besides routine filing and retrieval functions.

The institution should plan its total computerized risk management information system before purchasing the computer and software, since each part must interface effectively with every other part. There are five parts to the system: data collection; data screening, review, and coding; data processing; report generation; and information analysis and feedback. An effective and efficient system will create a closed management loop using the computer for speed and convenience.

Chapter Exercises

1. Discuss in detail which pieces of information you would require in a formal risk management communication form.

2. When screening for potential compensable events, what elements would you be most alert for? Explain why in detail.

3. In your own words, explain a closed management loop for a risk management information system.

References

1. H.R. 5400, 98th Cong. 2d sess. (1984).

2. "Generic Screening Effective in Problem Identification," *Hospital Peer Review* vol. 6, No. 11 (November 1981): 1.

3. *St. Louis Little Rock Hospital, Inc. v. Gaertner* (Mo. App. 1984), No. 48899 11/27/84.

4. "Automated Risk Management Information System" computer software program, University Associates in Health Services Management, Columbia, Missouri 1984.

5. Clemon W. Williams, "Guide to Hospital Incident Reports," *Health Care Management Review,* (Winter 1985): 19-25.

6. William H. Roach, "Legal Review," *Topics in Health Record Management* 2 (December 1981): 86-89.

7. Tzvi Raz, Jay Goldman, and Gary P. Kraus, "Computer Is Key Factor in Risk Studies," *Modern Healthcare,* Vol. 13, No. 6 (June 1983): 98-102.

8. Annette M. Delany, "In-House Computer Applications for Hospital Risk Management Programs." Paper delivered at the 5th Annual Educational Conference of The American Society for Hospital Risk Management, Boston, MA, 1 September 1983.

CHAPTER FIVE

A SUMMARY OF HEALTH PROVIDER LIABILITY LAW

Gary P. Kraus and Phyllis S. Solomon

A risk manager in a health care environment must be familiar with some fundamental principles of law, since they serve as the guidelines by which risk management decisions are made. In this chapter are presented the basics of those areas of law that most often affect risk management. It is not the objective of this chapter to teach the reader to be a junior lawyer, but simply to acquaint the reader with enough law to begin developing the expertise needed to distinguish serious problems from less significant matters.

Fundamentals of Liability Law

The law of torts (civil wrongs) holds persons liable for certain behavior. The purpose of tort law is to compensate those who have suffered unreasonable harm at the hands of others. Courts generally measure the "unreasonableness" of harmful behavior by viewing its social utility. In other words, courts will balance the harm against the benefits gained by the harmful behavior to determine whether the harmful behavior was reasonable under the circumstances.

Torts fall into three basic categories, which relate to the wrongdoer's conduct. The categories are:

1. Intentional torts
2. Negligence
3. Torts in which the wrongdoer is "strictly liable" because of the nature of his or her harmful conduct.

It is important to distinguish among these three types of torts. Not only will the classification affect the wrongdoer's liability, but it also will determine the amount and type of damages the court will assess.

Intentional Torts

To prove the wrongdoer liable for an intentional tort, the wronged party generally must prove that the wrongdoer intended to cause him or her some sort of physical or mental harm. The wronged party is not required to prove *subjective* intent. Instead, the wronged party must prove *objective* intent—that is, whether a "reasonable person" conducting himself or herself in the same manner would have done so because he or she desired to harm the other person or, at least, was substantially certain that harm would result from such conduct. Tort cases are usually tried before a jury, and it is presumed that the individual jurors' ideas and experiences will merge so that their opinion represents that of a "reasonable person."

Whereas those acting negligently are held liable only for foreseeable consequences, those who act intentionally are held liable for almost every result stemming directly (or even slightly indirectly) from their conduct, no matter how unlikely such results might have seemed at the time of the wrongful conduct.

An example of an intentional tort is battery, the intentional infliction of a harmful or offensive touching. *Mohr v. Williams*[1] is one of many cases in which a physician has been held liable for battery. In that case, a woman saw an ear doctor about a problem with her right ear and consented to surgery on that ear. The physician discovered during the operation that the left ear actually needed surgery, and performed the procedure on that ear instead. The court found the doctor liable for an unauthorized, offensive touching (battery), even though the surgery was in no way detrimental to the patient's health.

The wrongdoer can plead defenses in his or her lawsuit to show why he or she should not be considered liable for the actions. The courts and legislatures have established such defenses as self-defense through cases and statutes. One defense that is often used is the consent defense, in which it is claimed that the wronged party (the plaintiff in the lawsuit) consented to the invasion of his or her interests. This consent may be expressed, but it need not be. Instead, consent may be implied from the circumstances surrounding the action. An example is the case of *O'Brien v. Cunard S.S. Co.*[2] Passengers preparing to leave a ship discovered they could not enter the United States without a certificate showing they had been vaccinated. They also learned that the ship's doctor could vaccinate anyone who so desired. The plaintiff stood in line with other passengers waiting to be vaccinated, but she told the doctor she had already been vaccinated. The doctor told her she should be vaccinated again, since there was no visible mark. The plaintiff did not say anything, but held up her arm. The doctor vaccinated her, and she later sued for battery. The court concluded that a reasonable person would have thought her conduct meant that she consented, and therefore she was deemed to have consented, regardless of her actual thoughts.

There are circumstances, however, in which persons are considered incapable of giving consent (for instance, when intoxicated or unconscious). In such cases, objective manifestations of consent are ineffective. On the other hand, consent is implied by law if all of the following are true:

- The patient is incapacitated.
- Immediate treatment is needed to save the patient's life or prevent permanent harm.
- There is no indication that the patient would withhold consent if able to do so.
- A reasonable person in the patient's circumstances would consent.

Even if all of the above appear to be true, a physician may be required to seek substitute consent of a close relative if one is available.

If a person actually consents to allow another to invade his or her interest, that other person will not be privileged to exceed the scope of the consent. An example is again provided by *Mohr v. Williams,*[3] in which the patient consented to surgery on the right ear but awoke to find the surgeon had operated on the left ear instead. It is irrelevant that the surgery on the left ear was desirable from a medical standpoint. An exception would be if the surgery performed were an emergency. The court would take this into consideration and weigh the risk of waiting to bring the patient back to consciousness to obtain consent, against the risk from the additional surgery.

Most surgery performed in hospitals today is pursuant to such general consent forms that the scope of consent presents no serious problems. As will be discussed later, however, it is important that the form not be too vague. If it is, it may not hold up in court.

Even when the patient does not sign a hospital consent form, the court may interpret the patient's consent to surgery as being quite broad. This is especially true in cases where the physician cannot make a diagnosis until he or she has explored inside the body. In the case of *Kennedy v. Parrott,*[4] the court said that a surgeon may extend an operation to remedy any abnormal condition in the area of the original incision, if he or she determines, in the exercise of sound professional judgment, that correct surgical procedure would require such extension.

Negligence

Whereas the wrongdoer's mental state is of prime importance in cases of intentional torts, it is insignificant when he or she stands accused of negligence. The essence of a negligence suit is that the wrongdoer imposed an unreasonable risk of harm upon the wronged party, which resulted in injury.

Legal negligence is not mere carelessness. The plaintiff must prove the following:

1. Duty
2. Breach of duty
3. Causation (both causation in fact and proximate cause)
4. Actual damages
5. In some jurisdictions, lack of contributory negligence.

Duty Duty here refers to legal duty, a citizen's responsibility to act so as to minimize unreasonable risks to others. Generally, one has the duty to exercise such care as a reasonable person would exercise. The jury in a lawsuit is responsible for deciding whether a reasonable person exercising ordinary care would have acted in a like manner were he or she in the defendant's shoes. There are, however, some exceptions to the reasonable person standard. For example, severely retarded persons usually are exempt, as it is thought that they cannot be negligent since they cannot even understand that danger exists. Children, too, are excepted from the rule. The Restatement (Second) of Torts says that a child must act as a "reasonable person of like age, intelligence, and experience under like circumstances."[5] An exception to this exception occurs, however, when a child engages in a potentially dangerous activity normally limited to adults—for example, driving a car.

Generally, one may not be held liable for nonfeasance (failure to take action), but only for misfeasance (an affirmative action that harms the plaintiff). There are cases, however, in which nonfeasance renders the party liable because of a special relationship tying together plaintiff and defendant in the lawsuit. For example, some courts require that businesses warn their clients of hazards and assist business visitors, regardless of the source of danger. The same has been held to apply to employers aiding employees injured in the course of employment. A second exception is that one has a duty to warn and assist if his or her own conduct (or an instrument under his or her control) endangers the plaintiff. Still another exception comes about if one voluntarily begins to render assistance although under no duty to do so. Once a person assumes a duty, he or she must proceed with reasonable care. In other words, one must not unreasonably aggravate the injured person's condition or abandon the injured person. Courts usually rely on the supposition that, once a person voluntarily begins to aid an injured person, third parties will believe the injured person is in good hands and decline to offer aid themselves.

Furthermore, courts have held that a custom of giving warnings or assistance may constitute an undertaking to assist—at least where the plaintiff is aware of the custom. Even a promise to give aid may constitute assumption of risk.[6] In the case of *O'Neill v. Montefiore Hospital,* an ill man came to the hospital. Personnel refused to treat him but asked that he return later to see a physician. The man died of a heart attack before he could return. The court interpreted the advice that he return as an undertaking to give aid.

There are still other ways in which duty may arise in nonfeasance cases. For instance, the defendant may have such a relationship with a third party that the defendant has a duty to prevent that third party from harming the plaintiff. A famous case is *Tarasoff v. Regents of the University of California*,[7] wherein the defendant psychotherapists were treating a man who told them of his plans to kill the plaintiff's daughter. The court held that, because of the doctor-patient relationship, the doctors had a duty to warn the daughter of the plot. A state statute granted the doctors immunity from a duty to institutionalize the man.

A comment to the Restatement (Second) of Torts further illustrates:

> A operates a private hospital for contagious diseases. Through the negligence of the medical staff, B, who is suffering from scarlet fever, is permitted to leave the hospital with the assurance that he is entirely recovered, although his disease is still in an infectious stage. Through the negligence of a guard employed by A, C, a delirious smallpox patient, is permitted to escape. B and C communicate the scarlet fever and smallpox to D and E respectively. A is subject to liability to D and E.[8]

Because of the misfeasance/nonfeasance distinction, a physician withholding emergency aid would have no liability while one giving aid would leave himself open to a malpractice charge (especially since proper equipment generally is unavailable when an emergency arises). To protect physicians, most states have passed "Good Samaritan" statutes, which relieve a physician from all liability other than, perhaps, gross negligence when providing assistance in an emergency.

Breach of Duty To demonstrate breach of duty, the plaintiff must show that the defendant failed to act as a reasonable person would given like circumstances. This test requires that the plaintiff show the standard of care expected of the defendant and show that the defendant fell below the standard. The standard of care can be established by such guidelines as statutes, accrediting standards, professional credentialing requirements or state rules and regulations, association bylaws that the defendant is supposed to follow, or the policies and procedures of an institution. Generally, these published standards lack specificity. The plaintiff, therefore, must establish the standard of care by the use of expert witnesses.

Causation The plaintiff must show that the defendant's breach of duty caused the plaintiff's harm. Causation is divided into two components: causation in fact and proximate cause.

Causation in Fact The plaintiff must show that if it were not for the defendant's actions, the plaintiff probably would not have suffered those injuries he or she sustained. This principle encompasses a broad range of actions, and in any given situation there may be several causes in fact. For example, if a car driven by the defendant hits the plaintiff, who is walking along the shoulder of the road, one might say that but for the defendant's driving the car too far over to the right shoulder, he probably would not have hit the plaintiff. One also could say, however, that but for the plaintiff's walking with the flow of traffic, at night, and wearing dark clothes, he probably would not have been hit by the defendant's car.

Sometimes an expert witness will be required to prove causation in fact, especially in malpractice cases, where the lay jury would have insufficient knowledge as to whether a doctor's treatment could have caused the plaintiff's injury.

Proximate Cause The courts require that the plaintiff prove that the defendant "proximately caused" his or her injury so that the defendant's liability will be limited to those damages resulting most directly from his conduct. Each jurisdiction has its own method for determining proximate cause.

Some courts view proximate cause in terms of foreseeability. The courts ask the jury to decide whether a reasonable person could have foreseen that the defendant's conduct would harm another person. If so, the defendant is said to have proximately caused injury to the plaintiff. Once proximate cause is found, the defendant is held liable for any additional unforeseen consequences (provided these do not stem from such unlikely intervening causes that liability is superseded). This principle is referred to as the "thin skull rule" or the "eggshell skull theory," because it often is illustrated by a hypothetical case involving a plaintiff who, unknown to the defendant, has a skull of eggshell thinness. If the defendant negligently inflicts a minor injury on the skull, but the plaintiff dies from this injury because of the hidden defect, the defendant may be held liable for the plaintiff's death. The rationale is that since some amount of physical harm was foreseeable, the defendant proximately caused harm to the plaintiff, and the court should not have to specify just how much harm the defendant caused.

Other courts use a hindsight test to determine proximate cause. This test dictates that the defendant proximately caused the plaintiff's harm if, in retrospect, it is not extraordinary that such harm resulted from the defendant's conduct.

The final test upon which some jurisdictions rely is the direct results test. Courts subscribing to this theory hold the defendant liable for direct results of his or her negligence, no matter how unforeseeable.

Even if the court finds, under one of the three tests, that the defendant proximately caused the plaintiff's injury, it may release the defendant from liability because of a "superseding cause." This is a cause that comes about after the defendant's negligent act, which contributes so strongly toward the injury that it prevents the defendant's negligence from being considered the proximate cause of the damage. Whether a particular cause is considered as superseding is, in part, determined by its foreseeability. If the defendant should have foreseen the intervening cause, or the kind of harm resulting from that cause, and if the defendant's conduct increased the risk to the plaintiff, then the defendant is considered to have proximately caused the harm despite the intervening cause. If, however, the event or harmful result were unforeseeable, the intervening cause is said to supersede the defendant's liability.

A situation illustrating this concept is one involving physical injury to the plaintiff. It is foreseeable that if a person is injured, others will try to offer aid. Suppose the defendant runs into a pedestrian, knocking him onto the edge of a cliff. If a rescuer slips on the edge and breaks a leg, the plaintiff will be liable for the rescuer's injuries, because they are a foreseeable result of the pedestrian's injuries. In addition, the defendant will be held liable to the plaintiff for any additional injuries inflicted during the rescue, unless the rescuer was grossly negligent in rendering aid. This includes medical malpractice, which generally is not considered a superseding cause unless the physician is grossly negligent in treating the patient.

Actual Damages The defendant may not be held liable for his or her negligent action unless the plaintiff suffers actual damages. Realistically, the damages sustained must be substantial enough to elicit the interest of legal counsel. Damages are measured in dollars, since money is the only medium that can be used to repay the plaintiff for his or her loss. Common damages awarded are current and future medical expenses and care needed by the injured party, lost wages from employment, loss of consortium, pain and suffering, and other related expenses.

Freedom From Contributory Negligence In some jurisdictions, the plaintiff must show that he was not contributorily negligent. Usually, however, the plaintiff need not bring the subject up unless the defendant pleads contributory negligence as a defense to liability.

Negligence Per Se Although in many cases the jury decides whether the defendant was negligent because of conduct unbecoming a reasonable person, situations arise for which the legislature has defined reasonable conduct. When lawmakers enact a statute to protect society, violations of that statute that proximately cause injury to another constitute negligence per se. For conduct to be classified as negligent per se, the defendant must:

1. harm a member of the class of persons whom the statute was designed to protect; and

2. Cause the type of harm that the statute was designed to prevent.

There are defenses that a defendant may plead against a charge of negligence per se:

- That he or she made a reasonable attempt to obey the law
- That his or her conduct was in response to an emergency (which the defendant had not brought about)
- That compliance with the law would have caused even greater harm to the plaintiff.

If the defendant can show one of the above, he or she may be excused from liability.

Res Ipsa Loquitur Literally translated, the phrase *res ipsa loquitur* means "the thing speaks for itself." This doctrine was designed to aid plaintiffs who cannot prove whose conduct was negligent. It lets the plaintiff prove that he or she suffered injuries and infer that the defendant probably was negligent and probably caused the plaintiff's injuries and therefore should be held liable. For example, suppose the plaintiff enters a hospital for surgery, but the postoperative pain does not subside after several months. The plaintiff goes back for an examination, and x-rays indicate that an instrument was left in his body when the surgeon closed the wound. Since the defendant was unconscious during the operation, he cannot say from firsthand knowledge whose fault it is that the instrument was left behind. The doctrine of *res ipsa loquitur* enables him to sue the surgeon nonetheless, because normally instruments would not be left inside unless someone was negligent, and because the surgeon carried out the procedure, he probably was the negligent party.

Defenses in Negligence Actions There are several defenses that, if argued successfully, can relieve the defendant of liability.

Contributory Negligence If the defendant can show that the plaintiff's negligence was a proximate cause of the plaintiff's own injuries, the defendant usually will be relieved of any liability.

Comparative Negligence If the defendant can show that the plaintiff, too, was negligent, and that the plaintiff's negligence was a proximate cause of his or her own injuries, the court will apportion damages between defendant and plaintiff according to their relative degrees of fault. A state may recognize either this defense or contributory negligence, but not both.

Assumption of Risk If the defendant can show that the plaintiff voluntarily assumed the risk of the harm that occurred, the defendant usually will be relieved of liability. A plaintiff may assume risk expressly, or assumption of risk may be implied from his or her actions.

Statute of Limitations The statute of limitations is the legal time period within which a plaintiff must file his or her action. If the statute of limitations prescribed by law has expired on a claim, then the plaintiff is barred from recovery, even if it can be proven that the defendant's negligence caused his or her injuries.

This defense presents some problems in medical malpractice cases. An example is the hypothetical case above in which a surgical instrument was left in the patient following surgery. The issue is, when did the statute of limitations begin to run—when the surgery occurred, or when the instrument was discovered? The answer depends on the jurisdiction. Historically, the statute was considered to begin to run as soon as the act was committed. Many courts, however, have said that this is not fair, because in some cases a patient could not reasonably be expected to discover that malpractice occurred until after the statute had run. These courts adopted one of the following modern views:

1. The statute begins to run when the doctor-patient relationship ends. Although the plaintiff still may not have discovered the injury by this time, he or she at least gets the benefit of some extra time.

2. The statute begins to run at the time the plaintiff discovers (or reasonably should discover) that a negligent action occurred and caused injury.

3. The statute begins to run at the date of the last treatment for the injury that gave rise to the malpractice claim.

Malpractice Although in most cases the defendant has a duty to respond to a situation as would a reasonable person, a different set of rules applies in cases involving medical malpractice. Physicians must practice at the level of skill "ordinarily possessed and employed by members of the profession in good standing."[9] This standard applies even to new interns. A specialist must practice within an even higher standard—he or she will be held to the minimum standards of the specialty. This does not mean that the specialist must guarantee successful treatment, but merely that he or she must act as would any other competent physician in the specialty. When there is more than one school of thought, the physician should be judged in accordance with the school he or she follows. Osteopaths and chiropractors, therefore, generally are not judged by the same standards as M.D.s.

Medical negligence usually must be shown through expert testimony, because an expert is usually needed to inform the jury about standard medical practice. Without such knowledge, it would be impossible for the jury to determine that the defendant departed from such practice. There are situations, however, in which negligence is obvious even to a layperson. If the judge determines that a physician's negligence was blatant, the judge may dispense with the expert testimony requirement.

Until recently, physicians almost always had to practice according to the standards prevailing in their own communities. Since medical schools across the country have become more uniform, however, most courts have abolished the local standards rule. This makes the plaintiff's case easier, because he or she can call experts from outside the community to testify, rather than have to rely on the defendant's local colleagues.

A few cases have held that professional standards themselves are negligent and that the defendant should be held liable for following them. For example, in *Harris v. Browne,* a Tennessee court held that the hospital had a duty to count instruments, even though this was not common practice at the time in the hospital industry.[10]

Strict Liability

There are some situations in which the nature of the defendant's activity renders him or her strictly liable for all injurious consequences. For example, dynamite blasting required for building expansion entails a high risk of serious harm that even due care could not eliminate.

The plaintiff's contributory negligence is never a defense to a strict liability claim. However, a plaintiff who voluntarily and unreasonably subjected himself or herself to the danger may be barred from recovery. The plaintiff also may not recover if harm would not have resulted but for the plaintiff's abnormal sensitivity to the defendant's conduct.

Corporate Negligence

Historically, health care facilities as corporations have had two major responsibilities, which in recent decades have expanded. First, the institution has a duty to its patients and invited visitors to exercise reasonable care in maintaining the building and grounds. To recover damages, a plaintiff must prove that the operators of the facility either created a dangerous condition or knew (or should have known) the condition existed but failed to correct it. The plaintiff generally will not recover damages if the condition was readily apparent, because everyone has a duty to exercise ordinary care for his or her own safety.

Second, the institution has a responsibility to exercise reasonable care in selecting equipment suitable for a given purpose and in maintaining that equipment. A doctor who uses defective equipment is not personally liable unless the defect could have been found by mere observation as well as by proper maintenance. The mere fact that newer equipment is available on the market usually does not create corporate liability for failure to acquire such equipment.[11] However, once a substantial number of facilities use the new equipment, they create a new standard of acceptability, and a duty to update equipment to meet that standard can arise. A few courts have said that "there are precautions so imperative that even their universal disregard will not excuse their omission."[12] Liability may not be avoided through service agreements with independent contractors, because corporate duties may not be delegated.[13]

Before 1965, the above duties represented the extent of health care corporations' responsibilities. However, the *Darling v. Charleston Community Memorial Hospital*[14] case extended the duties that facilities must fulfill under the law of corporate negligence. In the much-touted *Darling* case, the Illinois Supreme Court upheld a jury verdict against the hospital, on the grounds that the hospital did not have enough qualified nurses to bring a patient's worsening condition to the attention of the administration or medical staff so that adequate medical consultation could be obtained, and that the hospital did not review the patient's treatment and acquire needed consultation. The Illinois court focused on the hospital's obligation to control its standard of practice.

Liability has been extended to cases in which a hospital has inadequate facilities, staff, and equipment to treat a particular patient but does not transfer that patient to another facility. In *Carrasco v. Bankoff*,[15] the court said the hospital had a duty to transfer the patient to another hospital since it lacked the equipment reasonably necessary for the patient's treatment but had held itself out as being able to care for the patient's particular needs.

The *Darling* theory has expanded even further the responsibility of health care corporations for the quality of care provided. Now included is the duty to exercise reasonable care in selecting and retaining staff. It is not enough that a physician applicant has a valid, current license to practice medicine. In *Johnson v. Misericordia Community Hospital*,[16] the court said that a hospital must exercise the same degree of care in selecting its staff as would an average hospital. In this case, a doctor grossly misrepresented his credentials, and the hospital failed to make even a cursory check. The court said that hospitals should:

> (1) solicit information from the applicant's peers, including those not refer-
> enced in his application, who are knowledgeable about his education, train-
> ing, experience, health, competence and ethical character; (2) determine if
> the applicant is currently licensed to practice in this state and if his licen-
> sure or registration has been or is currently being challenged; and (3) in-
> quire whether the applicant has been involved in any adverse malpractice
> action and whether he has experienced a loss of medical organization
> membership or medical privileges or membership at any other hospital.
> The investigating committee must also evaluate the information gained
> through its inquiries and make a reasonable judgment as to the approval or
> denial of each application for staff privileges.[17]

Under the doctrine of corporate negligence, a hospital may be liable for a staff physician's negligence if it knew (or should have known) the physician was incompetent to perform a procedure and therefore should have restricted or revoked staff privileges. The hospital is not responsible for the doctor's malpractice; rather, it is liable for breach of its own duty to provide quality patient care and retain only competent staff physicians.

The rule of law established by the *Darling* case and expanded by the *Johnson* case has resulted in more restrictive requirements for Joint Commission on Accreditation of Hospitals[18] and Medicare[19] conditions of participation. The failure of an institution to carefully select and periodically review the performance of its professional staff could result in liability being imposed.

Respondeat Superior

The doctrine of vicarious liability allows one person's wrongful act to be imputed to another because of some special relationship between them. Thus, a completely blameless person may be held liable for another person's conduct.

The most common scenario in which courts find a party vicariously liable for another's acts involves the employer-employee relationship. Under the doctrine of *respondeat superior,* an employer will be held liable for any tort an employee commits during the period of his or her employment. Literally translated, *respondeat superior* means "let the person higher up answer." The reason for the rule is that the employer generally has more resources for payment of damages than does the employee.

To determine whether the employer should be responsible for an employee's conduct, one must look at 1) whether the employee is subject to the employer's control and 2) whether the employee acted with an intent to further his or her employer's business purpose.

Independent contractors usually are not considered employees for purposes of this doctrine, since they are not subject to the control of the person hiring them. Where staff doctors have only the privilege of treating private patients who are hospitalized at a health care institution, they usually are considered independent contractors. Thus, the hospital is not liable for their actions. If, however, the doctors are paid by the hospital (as in the case of interns and residents), the hospital usually is liable for their malpractice or other wrongful acts.

Generally courts do not hold an employer responsible for an employee's torts that occur while that employee is traveling between the workplace and home, because employers have no control over their employees during this period. Similarly, courts will not hold an employer liable for torts occurring when an employee deviates from an intended route or purpose while on a business trip, unless the deviation was so minor as to have been reasonably foreseeable to the employer, because major deviations are thought to have taken the employee away from his or her business purpose.

An employer may be liable for an employee's wrongful act even if the employer has expressly forbidden such act, provided it was done in furtherance of employment. On the other hand, the fact that the employer has forbidden a particular act may be evidence that the employee was acting contrary to the boss' business purpose.

Although an employer usually is not held liable for an employee's intentional torts stemming from personal motives (for example, if an employee gets angry and hits a visitor), the employer will be held liable if he or she has a duty to protect the victim (for instance, because the employer assumed care for that person). In addition, some courts consider the employer to be liable for employees' torts arising from personal motives, if they are foreseeable.

If the employer entrusts an employee with a dangerous instrumentality, some courts will hold the employer liable even if the employee uses it for his or her own purposes. The employer is also liable for his own direct negligence, and therefore will be held responsible when an incompetent employee harms another person if a reasonable employer would have realized that the employee was unfit for the job and thus would not have hired that employee.

The Borrowed Servant Rule

In some jurisdictions, physicians are held vicariously liable for the acts of nurses and others who are under their direction with regard to patient care. Such liability is based on the "borrowed servant rule." This rule was established when hospitals were given immunity from lawsuits as charitable organizations. Because of such immunity, the doctor often was the only solvent defendant whom an injured party could sue. The rule enabled hospital staff members to become temporary employees of the physician. This also became known as the "captain of the ship" doctrine, because the doctor was regarded as the "captain" of all those assisting him or her and therefore became liable for the torts committed by the "crew."

Charitable immunity for hospitals has gradually faded; this fact, combined with the recognition that members of the hospital staff have specialized functions over which the physician has no control, has led to substantial modifications of the borrowed servant rule. Recent cases, for example, have indicated that a doctor who prescribes medication does not become the temporary employer of the nurse carrying out his or her order.[20] To assert otherwise would be unfair, because the doctor is not physically present when the drugs are given and has no real ability to control their administration.

Apparent Agency

Even if a physician is an independent contractor, and therefore not an employee of the hospital for purposes of *respondeat superior,* the hospital may be held liable if the doctor is an apparent agent of the hospital, that is, if representations were made such that the patient reasonably believed the physician was acting as an agent of the hospital. In *Mduba v. Benedictine Hospital,*[21] a hospital was held vicariously liable for the negligence of its emergency room physicians, despite the fact that those physicians were independent contractors, because the hospital advertised that it provided emergency services. In *Stewart v. Midani,*[22] the court said that a hospital could avoid liability by placing a notice in the emergency room that it was under the control of independent contractors. To make a successful claim for hospital liability based on an apparent agency theory, a plaintiff must show 1) that the principal represented another to be his or her servant or agent, 2) that the representation caused the plaintiff to rely on the care or skill of the apparent agent, and 3) that the reliance was justifiable.[23]

Informed Consent

"Every human being of adult years and sound mind has the right to determine what shall be done with his own body; and a surgeon who performs an operation without his patient's consent commits an assault, for which he is liable in damages."[24] So said Judge Cardozo in *Schloendorff v. Society of New York Hospital.* This often-quoted portion of his opinion may well be where the issue of consent got its start. It has expanded, however, to encompass the more stringent doctrine of informed consent. This doctrine requires that the patient (or the person authorized to consent for him or her) be conscious, be legally capable of giving consent, and be competent to do so. In addition, the person must possess knowledge and understanding about the pending medical treatment. The physician can be held liable for failure to obtain informed consent if:

1. The patient did not understand enough about the treatment to give effective consent;

2. The doctor did not give the patient the same information that other patients generally receive in similar circumstances;

3. The patient would not have consented to treatment if he had received the proper amount of information; or

4. The doctor did not warn the patient about a complication that subsequently occurred.[25]

Even if he or she did not give informed consent, the patient may collect only the actual damages that accrue. A procedure that does not harm the patient physically will not support a monetary award.

Litigation stemming from failure of informed consent may involve any of the above deficiencies. Most cases revolve around the patient's claim that the doctor either misrepresented some material aspect of the medical procedure or neglected to tell the patient about a foreseeable risk.

Two kinds of misrepresentation crop up in consent lawsuits: affirmative misrepresentation and misrepresentation by silence. An example of the former occurred in the case of *Corn v. French.*[26] Before consenting to a "test" for cancer, the patient asked if the doctor planned to remove her breast. He replied that he had no such plans, whereupon she signed a consent form agreeing to a mastectomy, not knowing what the word meant. The doctor was held liable.

Similarly, a signed consent form did not protect the physician from liability in the case of *Rogers v. Lumberman's Mutual Casualty Co.*[27] In this case, however, the form did not name the surgical procedure to be performed. This is an example of misrepresentation by silence.

Physicians have a duty to disclose all inevitable risks and foreseeable collateral risks. In *Bang v. Charles T. Miller Hospital,*[28] the patient consented to surgery but was not told that the surgery would inevitably render him sterile. The doctor was held liable. Similarly, the physician was held liable in *Mitchell v. Robinson*,[29] for failing to tell a patient undergoing electroshock and insulin therapy that up to 25 percent of patients suffer convulsive fractures as a result of such treatment. Whether a physician has a duty to inform the patient of merely possible consequences could depend upon the generally accepted standards of practice in the medical profession. In such cases, expert witness testimony would be required to establish for the jury a deviation from such standards. Of course, expert testimony requirements place a burden on the plaintiff of finding an expert willing to testify against a colleague. It also lets physicians establish their own standards for disclosure of information regarding risks. The modern trend, therefore, is for courts not to require that information conform to medical standards, but instead to require that the physician exercise reasonable care under the circumstances. As the judge stated in *Scaria v. St. Paul Fire & Marine Insurance Co.*:

> The need of a particular patient for competent expert information should not necessarily be limited to a self-created custom of the profession. The disclosures which would be made by doctors of good standing, under the same or similar circumstances, are certainly relevant and material and we surmise would be adequate to fulfill the doctor's duty of disclosure in most instances. However, the duty to disclose or inform cannot be summarily limited to a professional standard that may be nonexistent or inadequate to meet the informational needs of a patient.[30]

The judge ruled further, that:

> In short, the duty of the doctor is to make such disclosures as appear reasonably necessary under circumstances then existing to enable a reasonable person under the same or similar circumstances confronting the patient at the time of disclosure to intelligently exercise his right to consent or to refuse the treatment or procedure proposed.[31]

Who May Consent?

A physician may not obtain consent from just anyone—it must be from the proper person. Only the patient or a properly authorized agent may consent to treatment of an adult patient. It is best to obtain consent directly from the patient, provided the patient is capable of understanding the need for treatment and the significance of his or her consent. A patient probably will not be considered competent if under the influence of mind-altering medication. Conversely, an emotionally disturbed patient may be considered competent if he or she understands the ramifications of his or her consent. The physician should decide in his or her professional judgment whether a patient is mentally competent to consent. If the patient is determined incompetent, the physician should refer the matter to court for legal determination and appointment of a guardian.

If the patient is competent to consent to a procedure, the spouse will not be considered an authorized agent, even in cases involving unborn children. This means, for example, that a husband may not sue a physician for performing a consented-to hysterectomy or abortion on his wife. It also means that a hospital insisting on spousal consent may face legal problems. A requirement of spousal consent could be considered discriminatory and per se illegal. The doctor could be held liable for entering into a doctor-patient relationship and then withholding care pending spousal consent, if that delay caused harm to the patient. The patient could sue the doctor for invasion of privacy and breach of confidentiality for discussing the patient's care with another person without the patient's permission.

Because the courts and lawmakers have imposed rules for obtaining only the patient's consent, they have protected physicians who comply. For instance, in *Murray v. Vandevander,*[32] in which the husband did not consent to his wife's hysterectomy, the court said the husband had no cause of action for loss of consortium. It said the wife has a right to health, and her consent based upon a doctor's professional advice was all that was needed.

If an adult patient is legally incompetent, and if waiting for a court order likely would harm the patient, the spouse probably is authorized to consent. In fact, in *Pratt v. Davis,*[33] a doctor was held liable for performing surgery on an incompetent woman without her husband's consent. If incompetence stems merely from the use of mind-altering drugs, however, the doctor may have a duty to try to obtain consent from the patient before such drugs are used. In *Gravis v. Physicians' and Surgeons' Hospital of Alice,*[34] the spouse's consent to surgery did not protect the physician from liability because the doctor could have obtained the patient's consent before administering sedatives to her.

Whenever a spouse, parent, or other person is declared to be a properly authorized agent to grant consent, he or she is considered to have stepped into the patient's shoes and may assert certain other rights for the patient. The agent does not have a legal right to bar treatment if an emergency exists. In such cases the law presumes that the patient would choose life, and the need for consent is obviated. The agent may, however, assert the patient's right of privacy on his or her behalf (under the doctrine of substituted judgment) if the patient is incompetent and therefore unable to assert that right for himself or herself.

A famous case dealing with this issue is *In re Quinlan.*[35] This case involved a young woman who suffered severe brain damage and was comatose for several months. The New Jersey Supreme Court allowed her father, acting as her guardian, to assert her constitutional right of privacy—her right to refuse treatment. The court pointed out that, although a state may intervene in a patient's personal decision to withhold consent if it has a compelling interest to protect life, such compelling interest arguably did not exist in this case because Quinlan's prognosis for life was considered dim. The court discussed the importance of the guardian, the attending physician, and the hospital ethics committee concurring in the decision to withdraw life support. It did not specify, however, what it classified as life support subject to withdrawal. As a protection, the court said that the state's power to punish citizens for murder does not extend to doctors terminating medical treatment pursuant to a patient's right of privacy.

The right of consent to a minor's care rests with the parents or guardians. At common law, the age of majority for consent was 21. Statutes in some jurisdictions reduced the age of adulthood for consent purposes to 18. Some states consider men and women to be adults for purposes of consent as soon as they marry.

Unless emergency care is indicated, a hospital must try to find a parent or someone else authorized to consent to a minor's care. If it cannot locate anyone, it should apply for a court order authorizing care until it can locate a proper person. If the child was deserted, the hospital should also notify child welfare.

Laws in most states let minors consent to their own care under certain circumstances. These laws vary but usually include treatment for contagious diseases (including venereal diseases), drug abuse, and pregnancy. The United States Supreme Court has authorized abortions for minors without parental consent, but many private hospitals refuse to provide such services. These hospitals must take care not to harm a minor by refusing a therapeutically necessary abortion. In any case, unless state law specifically requires informing the minor's parents, there is no basis for violating the confidential nature of the doctor-patient relationship. Minors have the same right of privacy as adults. In fact, in *Poe v. Gerstein*,[36] a Florida statute requiring that a guardian's written consent be obtained for abortions performed on unmarried women less than 18 years old was declared unconstitutional.

Courts are mixed as to whether a parent or guardian may consent to surgery on a minor or an adult incompetent when that surgery is for another person's benefit (for example, removal of a kidney for transplant to a sibling). Even those courts that allow minors capable of understanding consent to give their own informed consent often will distinguish those cases involving surgery for another's benefit and not allow the minor to consent in such circumstances.

Refusal of Consent

If a parent or guardian consents to treatment of the minor, but the mature and understanding minor refuses consent, the hospital faces a dilemma. Generally, it is best not to do anything. Conversely, if the parent or guardian withholds consent but the mature and understanding minor consents, it is often best to proceed with treatment. Invading the rights or interests of a parent entails less legal risk than invasion of a patient's interest. In most states, child welfare laws make it a violation to deny a child medical care. Health care personnel, therefore, have a duty to help children obtain care. Such laws grant immunity from liability to the person treating the child but subject the person to a penalty if he or she does not help the child.

A different, though equally serious problem arises if the parent of an immature minor refuses consent and the child needs immediate treatment. In an emergency, it is best to proceed without consent. The courts tend to be lenient in cases where parents sue physicians for saving their child's life.

If the treatment is necessary but not emergent, it is best to obtain a court order to proceed. Some courts will allow the parents' refusal to prevail, whereas others have said that the parents' refusal constitutes neglect. Although constitutional issues, such as religious freedom, will be considered, such issues are not conclusive:

> The right to practice religion freely does not include liberty to expose . . . the child . . . to ill health or death. . . . Parents may be free to become martyrs themselves. But it does not follow they are free, in identical circumstances, to make martyrs of their children before they have reached the age of full and legal discretion when they can make that choice for themselves.[37]

In *State v. Perricone*,[38] the New Jersey Supreme Court ordered a blood transfusion to be administered to the infant child of parents who were Jehovah's Witnesses:

> Respondent concedes that appellants evidenced sincere parental concern and affection for their child. But those are not the controlling factors. Thus, courts have held that the refusal of parents, on religious grounds, to submit their infant child to a blood transfusion necessary to save its life or mental health amounted to statutory neglect, and therefore it was proper to appoint a guardian and to award custody to him for the limited purpose of authorizing transfusions.[39]

Competent adult patients have the right to refuse care for themselves, however. If a patient refuses to consent or withdraws consent, the physician should obtain a written release of liability. It is best to take the matter to court for a ruling, so that the doctor cannot be subjected to an "abandonment of care" charge later. It is important to note that, although a patient may withdraw consent for care, the right to control one's own body does not allow one to consent to euthanasia (affirmative mercy killing).

Although physicians have no legal duty or right to save patients from themselves, they do have a duty to warn patients of the consequences of refusing care. If the doctors, or a patient's family, want to fight the patient's refusal of care, they should petition the court for appointment of a guardian to consent for the patient.

To make such an appointment, the court would have to interfere with two protected freedoms: the freedom to control one's own body, and the freedom of religion.

If a court does choose to intervene, its legal basis probably will be society's compelling interest in the preservation and sanctity of human life. The court may justify such intervention, even if refusal was based on religious beliefs, by saying that the patient's religious convictions are not violated if he or she is not responsible for the decision.

Implied Consent

There are circumstances in which treatment without consent is justified. The physician must show that it was impossible at the time of the procedure to obtain authorized consent, and that there was an immediate threat to the patient's life (or threat of permanent impairment of health). Some courts have liberalized this to allow immediate treatment without consent when needed to alleviate extreme pain and suffering. The doctor must show by a preponderance of the evidence that an emergency existed.

This privilege to render emergency medical care without the patient's consent is based on a theory of implied consent. It is assumed that an unconscious patient would consent to emergency care if he or she were conscious and able to consent. This theory applies only if the patient has not let the physician know in advance that he or she refuses care. Implied consent may never override explicit rejection of care.

The theory of implied consent may extend to situations that call for expansion of the scope of consent. For example, during surgery a surgeon may encounter an unanticipated condition that must be corrected immediately to prevent an immediate threat to life or a permanent impairment of health. The surgeon must justify his or her action by showing that express consent would have been granted if legally possible, and by showing that the extended operation did not involve a substantially different risk or new incision.

Another situation in which the theory of implied consent comes up is that in which police ask hospital personnel to draw blood, take a urine sample, or perform a breath analysis test on a person in police custody, to determine whether that person is under the influence of drugs or alcohol. Such tests would constitute assault and battery if consent were lacking. For this reason, many jurisdictions have enacted implied consent laws that provide that anyone driving a motor vehicle on a public highway implicitly consents to the administration of such tests if arrested and charged with driving under the influence. If the person also is granted a statutory right of refusal, however, the hospital should not perform the test if the person expressly refuses. Hospital personnel must be sure that the person was formally arrested and charged, if that is required by the statute. Additional problems arise if the driver is dead or unconscious, because any information learned could have an adverse effect on the estate of the decedent or on the criminal or insurance status of the unconscious individual. Since the driver cannot then exercise his or her right of refusal, the test probably should not be administered unless a statute dictates otherwise.

Hospital personnel must keep in mind that an alleged criminal also has the right to informed consent. A problem arose in *Graves v. Beto,*[40] in which a suspect consented to giving a blood sample at the request of police, who indicated that they wanted the sample to determine whether he was intoxicated. Actually, they wanted to ascertain his blood type in relation to a rape investigation. Since they misrepresented the procedure's need and purpose, the court held the consent to be ineffective.

Sometimes a competent person suspected of driving while intoxicated will request a test to provide evidence of his or her innocence. Hospitals, especially if federally or state operated, should arrange for such tests, because failure to do so may constitute deprivation of the suspect's right to due process of law.

Form of Consent

If possible, consent should be obtained in writing. It should specify the attending physician and the proposed treatment. The date, the patient's signature, and the signature of a witness should appear. The more risks and alternatives to the pending procedure are named, the less chance of a successful suit based on failure of consent.

Only a physician is qualified to see that the patient is well informed; therefore, the physician should be the one to obtain the patient's signature. The doctor is privileged to withhold information from the patient if there are sound therapeutic reasons for doing so.[41] The doctor should document these reasons in the medical record. If the facts indicate that a competent and rational patient would have declined treatment had he or she received the withheld information, this defense will not hold up in court.

If a patient cannot read English but speaks English, a witness should attest that the consent form was read to the patient and that the patient signed the form after it was read and explained. The same applies if a Braille form is unavailable for a blind person. A deaf patient should have an interpreter to help with his or her questions, and the interpreter, too, should sign the consent form. A non-English-speaking patient requires similar interpretation.

Hospitals are advised to use two different consent forms. One, signed upon admission, obtains consent to routine hospital care, nursing services, and diagnostic procedures. This form should name the attending physician and recognize that nurses and laboratory technicians also will touch the patient during hospitalization.

It should state that the physician makes no guarantee of a cure. This consent form is of lesser legal importance than subsequent consent forms because the patient is assumed to have consented to such care by being present in the hospital. Nevertheless, it could be essential if the patient later claims that treatment was rendered against his or her will (e.g., because he or she was a committed psychiatric patient or was originally admitted while unconscious).

The second type of consent form should be filled out whenever surgery, anesthesia, radium or x-ray therapy, or special diagnostic procedures are pending. It should name the physician, authorize him or her to select assistants, list the procedures, state that the patient understands them, and state the patient's consent to administration of anesthesia under the supervision of a named doctor or nurse. It should also recognize that unforeseen conditions arising during surgery may dictate additional procedures and state that the patient consents to such of these as may, in the professional judgment of the physician, be advisable.

Such written consent forms are designed for the health care professional's protection. Oral consent is equally valid, but the physician has the burden of proving it. Even written consent forms will not be valid legally if the information in the forms was not explained (especially if the forms are long and involve medical jargon). The requirement that consent be informed is important so that the patient will not arrive at an unreasonable expectation of inevitable cure.

Statutes in some states have specified requirements for consent forms. In Ohio,[42] for example, if the patient or his or her agent signs a statutory consent form, or if the form meets statutory requirements, it is presumed to be valid. No evidence indicating otherwise is admissible in a subsequent lawsuit except where a preponderance of evidence proves that the doctor did not act in good faith, that he or she induced the patient to sign the form through fraudulent misrepresentation of material facts, or that the person signing the form was unable to understand the language in which it was written.

This is in agreement with the general rule that, even if the patient would not have consented except for the fact that he or she is mistaken about some material aspect of the situation, such a mistake by itself is not enough to render the consent ineffective, unless medical personnel knew of the patient's mistaken belief. Such knowledge would vitiate consent if the mistake were related to an aspect of the invasion that made it harmful or offensive.

A physician's duty to obtain informed consent arises only when he or she formally orders or actually performs a procedure or conducts a course of treatment. Therefore, in *Halley v. Birbiglia,*[43] a doctor who examined a child and recommended a test was not held liable when the test caused injury to the child, because the doctor did not formally order the test. Conversely, a doctor who prescribed a procedure that was performed by another was held liable in *Berkey v. Anderson.*[44]

Privacy and Confidentiality

All that may come to my knowledge in the exercise of my profession or outside of my profession or in daily commerce with men, which ought not to be spread abroad, I will keep secret and will never reveal. If I keep this oath faithfully, may I enjoy my life and practice my art, respected by all men and in all times; but if I swerve from it or violate it, may the reverse be my lot.[45]

So say thousands each year, as they take the Hippocratic Oath and embark on medical careers. There are exceptions, however, to a physician's duty to protect his or her patients' privacy and confidentiality. Both legislators and the courts have established these exceptions, with the general result that a patient has a legal right to privacy only when a potential recipient of "private" information has no interest in it.

First, the patient may request that someone of his or her choice be allowed to inspect or copy his or her records. Although the doctor owns any records in his or her office and the hospital owns hospital records, the patient generally has a right to the information in those records. Most health care professionals will allow the patient to obtain a copy upon signing a form authorizing their release.

Employees of the physician or hospital may also review patient records, but they, too, are bound to keep private the contents of such records. Hospital staff usually may use medical records for research, education, peer review, and quality assurance programs. There are exceptions, however, such as the case of *Estate of Berthiaume v. Pratt*,[46] in which the court said that photographing a terminally ill patient without his consent invaded his right of privacy, even though the doctor intended only to place the photo in the patient's medical file. Although physicians usually may use photographs for scientific or research purposes if they preserve the patient's anonymity, it is important to obtain prior consent whenever possible.

It is also important to obtain consent before allowing medical students and other nonprofessionals to watch medical procedures. In *De May v. Roberts*,[47] a doctor was held liable for letting a lay friend watch him deliver a baby in the mother's home. The torts of breach of privacy and breach of confidentiality not only can result in civil damages; they can also lead to criminal charges and revocation of the doctor's license. License revocation is an especially likely result if the doctor breached a state licensing statute or association rule providing for confidentiality.

There are situations in which the doctor and the hospital are relieved from tort liability because of a special privilege to disclose ordinarily confidential information. Doctors have a duty to comply with statutory reporting requirements, for example, and therefore may disclose the contents of a patient's medical record without the patient's consent if:

• the patient has a contagious disease (such as venereal disease) that must be reported to a public health department;

- the patient has suffered a violent injury (such as a stab wound) that must be reported to police; or

- the patient appears to be a victim of child abuse.

Insurance companies are privileged to obtain records whenever a patient makes a workers' compensation claim. They are not, however, privileged to check a patient's records before insuring the patient or paying a claim unless the patient has signed a release as part of the policy or claim form.

A doctor may release information from medical records when called as a witness in a lawsuit where the patient's health is an issue, or when the court subpoenas the records themselves. Some states have enacted privileged communication statutes, however, which prohibit doctors from making such disclosures in judicial proceedings unless the patient has waived the right of confidentiality or consented to disclosure. Generally a doctor-patient relationship must exist as a condition precedent to such a privilege. In *State v. Kuljis*,[48] for example, the results of a blood test for alcohol content were admissible in a criminal trial because the doctor did not take the test for the purpose of treating the patient and did not mislead the patient as to the test's purpose.

Congress has enacted special legislation regarding drug and alcohol records. For example, in the Comprehensive Drug Abuse Prevention and Control Act of 1970,[49] it imposed rules for maintaining the confidentiality of a patient's participation in drug and alcohol abuse research programs. Under this act, all hospitals and other health care providers that receive federal funds are prohibited from releasing medical information to anyone not connected with their research program. Even courts are denied access to such records.

Conversely, the Drug Abuse Office and Treatment Act of 1972[50] lets hospitals release records of patients undergoing alcohol or drug abuse treatment upon receipt of a court order showing good cause.

Although doctors and hospitals may escape tort liability by defending on the basis of "privilege to disclose," they may not escape liability if the patient sues on a contractual basis. In *Doe v. Roe*,[51] the New York Supreme Court held that doctors, in agreeing to provide medical care, implicitly promise not to reveal a patient's personal medical information. The court said that unlawful disclosure of such information gives the patient cause to sue for breach of contract.

Additionally, the doctor-patient relationship is such that the physician stands in a fiduciary capacity with respect to the patient. The physician has an obligation, therefore, to provide total patient care. For example, in *Alexander v. Knight*,[52] the court said that a physician is bound not to disclose medical information that would aid the adverse party in a lawsuit involving the patient.

Antitrust Law

Section 1 of the Sherman Act reads in part as follows:

> Every contract, combination in the form of trust or otherwise, or conspir-
> acy, in restraint of trade or commerce among the several States, or with
> foreign nations, is declared to be illegal. Every person who shall make any
> contract or engage in any combination or conspiracy hereby declared to be
> illegal shall be deemed guilty of a felony. . . .[53]

There are three prerequisites to a Sherman Act claim. The plaintiff must "(1)
identify a relevant channel of interstate commerce (2) substantially and directly
affected (3) by the allegedly improper activities of defendants."[54]

Until the mid-1970s, health care facilities were rarely sued for alleged Antitrust
Act violations. The change came about in 1976, when the United States Supreme
Court held, in *Hospital Building Co. v. Trustees of Rex Hospital*,[55] that hospitals
may have a substantial effect on interstate commerce and thus are susceptible to
antitrust claims. Although the court recognized the apparent local nature of a
hospital's business, it focused on the facts that hospitals receive a great deal of
revenue from the federal government and out-of-state insurance companies, and
that a lot of medicine and supplies come from out-of-state sources (in the case at
bar, $100,000 worth). The court also noted that Rex Hospital paid management
service fees to its out-of-state parent company and planned an expansion to be
financed by out-of-state lenders.

The Supreme Court has since identified specific practices that, because of their
inherently anticompetitive nature, are per se illegal. It is presumed that these
particular restraints on trade are unreasonable and that no justification exists to
excuse such practices.

Per Se Violations

Agreements Related to Price

Competitors sometimes agree to fix prices so as to maintain control over their
market. These so-called horizontal price agreements are per se illegal, even if the
prices the competitors establish are reasonable. The United States Supreme Court
held in *Arizona v. Maricopa County Medical Society*[56] that the health care industry,
like other industries, must comply with per se rules against price-fixing. In that
case, doctors from two medical foundations established a maximum fee schedule
which dictated the amount they could collect for serving policyholders. The court
held this to be a violation of antitrust laws.

Any agreements that indirectly hamper competitive pricing may also be illegal.
In *American Medical Association v. Federal Trade Commission*,[57] for instance, the
Supreme Court affirmed the Commission's finding that the Association's "Princi-

ples of Medical Ethics" unreasonably restrained trade by restricting advertising by doctors. It was thought that doctors would have less need to compete with others' prices if their fees were not made public.

Agreements regulating minimum and maximum prices, credit terms, or discounts are per se illegal. The same holds true for agreements to limit supply or production, to refrain from competitive bidding, or to raise and lower prices together.

Group Boycotts Individual buyers and sellers of goods or services may choose with whom they would like to deal. It is unlawful, however, for groups of buyers or sellers to combine in concerted refusals to deal. In *Robinson v. Magovern*,[58] for example, the plaintiff alleged that the hospital and its staff engaged in a per se illegal group boycott of his services. In this case the court held for the hospital, but only because the plaintiff had not proven that his request for privileges was denied in response to third parties' demands.

Market Divisions Competitors may not divide and allocate markets so as to avoid competition, as such divisions are per se violations of the Sherman Act. The rule applies both to agreements allocating geographic areas and to those providing for division of product markets.

Tying Arrangements Tying arrangements occur when a seller refuses to sell a good or service ("tying" product) unless the buyer purchases another good or service ("tied" product). For an antitrust claim based on the tying theory to succeed, it must be shown that the seller exploited "its control over the tying product to force the buyer into the purchase of a tied product that the buyer either did not want at all, or might have preferred to purchase elsewhere on different terms."[59] *Portland Retail Druggists Association v. Kaiser Foundation Health Plan*[60] illustrates an alleged tying. In that case, certain health maintenance organizations allegedly required customers to buy their drug plan in order to obtain their health plan.

Rule of Reason

Although the above practices are considered per se illegal, courts otherwise do not interpret the Sherman Act literally. To do so would be to declare all contracts illegal, since all contractual agreements restrain the parties in some way. Instead, most courts apply the Rule of Reason test, whereby only unreasonable trade restraints are found to violate the Sherman Act.

> The true test of legality is whether the restraint imposed is such as merely regulates and perhaps thereby promotes competition or whether it is such as may suppress or even destroy competition. To determine that question

the court must ordinarily consider the facts peculiar to the business to which the restraint is applied; its condition before and after the restraint was imposed; the nature of the restraint and its effect, actual or probable.[61]

Exclusive Contracts for Hospital-Based Services Courts generally hold exclusive contracts for hospital-based services to be legal, because of procompetitive benefits that outweigh their anticompetitive effects. The court applied the rule of reason in *Mays v. Hospital Authority*[62] to find that a contract between a hospital and a radiology firm did not violate the Sherman Act. The court pointed out that

where patients at the hospital formerly had the choice of only one radiologist, they now can choose among the six radiologists of [the group]. . . . There are at least two other hospitals offering hospital and radiological services. One of these hospitals has an open staff policy with regard to radiologists. . . . The Plaintiff has not shown an adverse effect on quality, price or availability of radiological services in any of these markets.[63]

Exclusive service contracts nonetheless are a source of many antitrust lawsuits.

Monopolies The Sherman Act provides, in section 2, that "Every person who shall monopolize, or attempt to monopolize, or combine or conspire with any other person or persons, to monopolize any part of the trade or commerce among the several States, or with foreign nations, shall be deemed guilty of a felony. . . ."[64]

A federal court summed up the guidelines for determining when a monopoly has occurred:

The offense of monopolization is established if (1) relevant product and geographic markets have been established, (2) the Defendants had the power to control prices in or exclude competitors from the relevant market, (3) the Defendants unreasonably used such power to exclude Plaintiff [from the market] . . . and (4) Plaintiff [was] . . . injured in [his] . . . businesses or property as a result of the Defendants' conduct.[65]

Mergers Mergers are covered by the Clayton Act, which states that

No person engaged in commerce or in any activity affecting commerce shall acquire, directly or indirectly, the whole or any part of the stock or other share capital and no person subject to the jurisdiction of the Federal Trade Commission shall acquire the whole or any part of the assets of another person engaged also in commerce or in any activity affecting commerce, where in any line of commerce or in any activity affecting commerce in any section of the country, the effect of such acquisition may be substantially to lessen competition, or to tend to create a monopoly.[66]

There are two types of mergers: horizontal and vertical. An example of a horizontal merger is one between two health care facilities operating in the same area. Its legality depends on such factors as the degree of market concentration (that is, the number and size of their remaining competitors), the nature of their product, and the barriers to entry in their particular market. Vertical mergers are those between firms standing in a supplier-purchaser relationship (for example, a hospital and a drug company).

Price Discrimination The Robinson-Patman Price Discrimination Act forbids discrimination with respect to prices and other sales terms, services, or facilities:

> It shall be unlawful for any person engaged in commerce, in the course of such commerce, either directly or indirectly, to discriminate in price between different purchasers of commodities of like grade and quality, where either or any of the purchases involved in such discrimination are in commerce . . . and where the effect of such discrimination may be substantially to lessen competition or tend to create a monopoly in any line of commerce, or to injure, destroy, or prevent competition with any person who either grants or knowingly receives the benefit of such discrimination, or with customers of either of them.[67]

This act does not apply to mere offers to sell commodities.

The defendant in a Robinson-Patman lawsuit may rebut the plaintiff's allegations by showing a cost justification for selling like commodities at different prices. If the seller can show that the disparate pricing reflected cost differences, the plaintiff will not succeed in court. The seller also may defend his or her actions by showing that the price was adjusted in a "good faith" effort to match a competitor's price.

State Action Doctrine

Under the state action doctrine, government actions, or those undertaken in an effort to comply with established public policy, are exempt from antitrust laws. Thus, certain state policies may protect certain health care practices from antitrust scrutiny. For example, if a state mandates hospital peer-review procedures, those involved cannot be held liable for denying a physician hospital privileges for good cause. Such immunity is limited, however, to specific conduct mandated by state law. It is not enough that the state regulate the health care industry as a whole.[68]

Labor and Personnel Issues

Title VII of the Civil Rights Act of 1964[69] prohibits discrimination on the basis of race, color, sex, religion, or national origin in all employment-related activity. The act also provides for an Equal Employment Opportunity Commission (EEOC) to enforce the regulations against discrimination. Title VII applies to all state and municipal governments, labor organizations engaged in an industry affecting commerce, and private employers with 15 or more employees engaged in an industry affecting commerce. Amendments to Title VII have enlarged it to encompass discrimination with regard to pregnancy and childbirth policies. Employers now must include pregnancy as a covered disability in any disability benefits plan it provides for employees.

Employees who wish to prosecute for Title VII violations must file discrimination charges with the EEOC first. If the alleged unlawful employment practice occurred in a state with a local law covering such practices, the employee must bring state charges before filing a charge with the EEOC. There are ways to sidestep the EEOC, however. For example, since employers and employees have a contractual relationship, the employee may sue under the Civil Rights Act of 1866.[70] This act guarantees citizens the right to make and enforce contracts, and "affords a federal remedy against discrimination in private employment. . . ."[71]

State or local government employees may file a discrimination claim under the 14th Amendment to the United States Constitution,[72] which says that states may not deprive citizens of equal protection under the law. Federal employees may pursue similar claims under the 5th Amendment's due process clause.[73]

An individual who chooses to bring a claim to court under Title VII must show the following in order to have the case get past the EEOC to a jury:

1. That the individual applied and was qualified for a job or promotion for which the employer sought applicants,

2. That the employer rejected the applicant, and

3. That the position remained open and the employer continued seeking applications from others with the same qualifications.[74]

To refute the discrimination allegation, the employer may show that his or her workforce has the same racial balance as the surrounding community. Alternatively, the employer may show that there was a legitimate business reason for acting as he or she did. If the employer defends his or her actions by showing a legitimate business purpose, however, the employee must be given a chance to prove that the employer's business reason was merely pretextual, and that the true motive was discriminatory.

Sometimes employment policies that appear fair on the surface actually have an adverse impact on a particular group. For example, certain weight requirements may discriminate against women or men. To determine whether such seemingly fair policies in fact are discriminatory, the EEOC will compare the percentage of minority or female applicants hired with the percentage of nonminority or male applicants hired. It will also compare the ratio of employees allegedly discriminated against with the ratio of the same group in the surrounding community's total work force. If the EEOC finds the employment policy has a disparate impact on a particular group, it will presume that the employer violated Title VII unless the employer is able to prove otherwise (for example, by showing that the disparate practice was necessary for some reason related to job performance). The EEOC may presume a Title VII violation even if there is no apparent intent to discriminate.

An example of an employment practice that often has a disparate impact is the requirement that applicants take a test. The employer must be able to justify its use, otherwise the EEOC will presume it was used unlawfully to filter out certain classes of citizens.[75]

Federal statutes do not require employers to establish affirmative action programs under which they are obligated to maintain quotas of certain classes of workers. Such programs are mostly voluntary, with the exception of those ordered by courts to remedy an employer's proven discrimination, and those required of all employers who contract for work with the federal government. Nevertheless, they may be necessary for an employer to overcome significant racial imbalances so as to avoid scrutiny by the EEOC for disparate employment policies. Any employer who sets up an affirmative action program must do so carefully—since Title VII protects all classes of people, employers who discriminate against nonminorities may set themselves up for reverse discrimination suits.[76]

Employers may not engage in employment discrimination based on sex. The Equal Pay Act of 1963[77] prohibits paying workers of one sex at a different rate from workers of the opposite sex who do the same type of work. The act says that any employer found to do so must raise the pay of the lesser-paid employee. The EEOC will enforce this act, but if the aggrieved party wishes, he or she may sue the employer directly rather than take the case to the EEOC.

Title VII also protects employees who are segregated into occupational categories that pay less and have less opportunity for advancement. The EEOC must investigate such situations to determine whether discrimination or a legitimate business purpose accounts for the segregation.

The EEOC has developed guidelines to deal with sexual harassment in employment.[78] These guidelines define sexual harassment as including:

Unwelcome sexual advances, requests for sexual favors, and other verbal or physical conduct of a sexual nature . . . when

(1) submission to such conduct is made either explicitly or implicitly a term or condition of an individual's employment,

(2) submission to or rejection of such conduct by an individual is used as the basis for employment decisions affecting such individual, or

(3) such conduct has the purpose or effect of unreasonably interfering

with an individual's work performance or creating an intimidating, hostile, or offensive working environment.[79]

Employers are held liable for acts of their agents and supervisors when sexual harassment is found.[80] Employers also may be held liable for harassment by rank-and-file employees[81] or even such nonemployees as patients,[82] if the employer knew or should have known about the conduct. In addition, EEOC guidelines create employer liability to third parties who lose an employment opportunity or benefit to another who cooperated with unlawful sexual advances.[83] An employer not only must put a stop to sexual harassment in the workplace; he or she also has a duty to inform employees of their right to sue the company for such harassment under Title VII.[84] An employee who sues will recover back pay if termination or loss of promotion is involved and may recover other monetary damages in addition.[85]

The Age Discrimination in Employment Act of 1967[86] prohibits discrimination in terms, conditions, and privileges of employment against persons 40 to 70 years old. It also prohibits compulsory retirement before age 70 except for certain employees who are in executive or high policymaking positions. The act applies to all private employers with 20 or more employees and to government entities. Aggrieved parties may seek redress in court but first must file charges with the EEOC.

Several pieces of legislation seek to prohibit employment discrimination against handicapped persons. The Vietnam Era Veterans' Readjustment Assistance Act of 1974[87] provides for affirmative action with regard to qualified disabled veterans and veterans of the Vietnam era. It also gives military personnel the right to return to their former jobs without losing their prior status.[88]

The Rehabilitation Act of 1973[89] prohibits employment discrimination based on a person's handicap. It applies to all programs and activities receiving federal funding,[90] and to federal contractors and subcontractors.[91] The act says that an employer may not deny an applicant employment solely because of his or her handicap if the applicant is capable of performing the essential functions of the job with reasonable accommodation to the handicap.[92] "Reasonable accommodation" includes such things as physical modification of facilities, provision of readers for the blind, and changes in work schedules[93]—in other words, any accommodation that would not impose undue hardship on the employer's business.[94] The applicant need not be able to perform *all* the functions that a nonhandicapped person could perform.

In 1980, the EEOC issued revised guidelines for handling religious discrimination.[95] They require that an employer take reasonable steps to accommodate an employee's practice of any "moral or ethical beliefs as to what is right and wrong which are sincerely held with the strength of traditional religious views."[96] Reasonable steps are those that do not impose "undue hardship on the conduct of [the employer's] . . . business."[97] EEOC guidelines indicate, for example, that it would not be unreasonable for an employer to pay administrative costs incurred in rearranging work schedules or arranging substitutions.[98]

According to the EEOC, an employer may be guilty of religious discrimination if he or she asks an applicant whether the applicant would work normal hours if hired, if the question is directed toward determining unavailability for religious reasons.[99] EEOC guidelines recommend the following procedure: The employer should inform the applicant as to the normal work hours for the job. Then, after clarifying that the applicant is not required to disclose his or her need for religious absences during scheduled work hours, the employer may ask whether the applicant otherwise is available to work during those hours. Finally, after the employer offers the applicant a job but before hiring the applicant, the employer can ask if the applicant would need religious accommodation. If so, and if this would create undue hardship, the employer may be able to revoke the offer.[100]

Section 7 of the National Labor Relations Act (NLRA)[101] gives employees the right to organize into labor unions and to bargain through representatives of their choice. It also gives employees the right not to organize, should they not wish to form unions. Any employer who interferes with such rights commits an unfair labor practice.[102]

This law does not mean that the employer must allow a union to come in and take over. The employer lawfully may prohibit certain union activity that interferes with his or her right to operate a business. For example, an employer may refuse to let union organizers solicit on the premises if they are distracting employees from their work and have adequate opportunity to contact employees elsewhere. Conversely, health care facilities must let unions solicit employees and distribute union information in nonwork areas during employee breaks, if this can be accomplished without disturbing patients or health care operations.[103]

In some cases, an employer will have a legitimate business reason for wanting to prevent union activity but will also want to keep the union out because he or she dislikes unions. The National Labor Relations Board (NLRB) adopted a procedure for dealing with such "dual-motive" cases in *Wright Line, Inc.*[104] In that case, the NLRB's general counsel alleged that the company discharged an employee for his union involvement. The employer claimed he had done so for legitimate business reasons. The NLRB said that, in such cases, its general counsel must produce some evidence that the employee's union activity was a motivating factor in the employer's action. Once it has done so, the employer must step forward and prove that he would have taken that action regardless of the worker's union activity.

Union activity is not the only employee activity protected by the NLRA. A health care facility may be committing an unfair labor practice if it disciplines nonunion employees for engaging in any protected conduct, such as an economically-motivated strike.

Unions may commit unfair labor practices as well. For example, in 1974 some hospital amendments were added to the NLRA. One requires unions to give 10 days written notice to health care institutions and the Federal Mediation and Conciliation Service before any strike, picket, or other concerted refusal to work.[105] Although the NLRA protects workers who strike for economic reasons or to protest employer unfair labor practices, hospital workers who do not give the required notice lose their protected status. The employer may fire them immediately.

Although the NLRA requires only labor unions to give the 10 days' notice, nonunion employees will lose their NLRA protection against employer discipline for striking without notice if:

1. The strike's timing or unexpectedness creates great danger (if, for example, emergency department personnel leave the department unstaffed),[106]

2. The workers' employment contracts require them to give advance notice before striking,[107] or

3. They previously told the hospital, in response to a survey of employees following union notice of an upcoming strike, that they planned to cross the picket lines.[108]

The United States Supreme Court has ruled that employees have a right to have their union representative present at any meeting with their employer, if the employees reasonably fear disciplinary actions may result from that meeting. This Supreme Court ruling is known as the Weingarten doctrine.[109]

The NLRB limited the Weingarten doctrine in *Baton Rouge Water Works Co.*[110] It said that an employer need not let the representative attend if the meeting's sole purpose is to inform the employee of a disciplinary decision already made.

Health care facilities and employees sometimes will agree to submit their grievances to arbitrators. Either the American Arbitration Association will grant an impartial arbitrator, or each side can select one and the two chosen will appoint an impartial third. The arbitrators will let each side present its case, and then will make a binding decision. The benefits are that arbitration is faster and less expensive than litigation. One possible drawback is its unpredictability—arbitrators need not follow legal precedent; they merely do what is "fair" in a given situation.

Medical Staff Issues

In addition to its other duties, a hospital's governing board is responsible for the selection and review of its medical staff. As mentioned before, a hospital will be held liable if it lets unqualified physicians practice as a result of inadequate screening and peer review.[111] Although the governing board may delegate its review functions to a medical committee (and probably should, since physicians are best qualified to judge other physicians' capabilities), the board may not delegate its responsibility for ensuing decisions. To protect itself, the board must verify the applicant's professional license and determine the authenticity of his or her letters of reference and resume.

It is important that the hospital establish guidelines for hiring staff members. This will help assure that the hiring committee does not violate any laws inadvertently. For example, no hospital that receives federal funds (including Medicare reimbursements) may discriminate in medical staff appointments on the basis of race, color, religion, sex, or national origin.[112]

Courts give private hospitals more discretion in hiring and retaining staff than they give public hospitals. For example, in *Group Health Cooperative v. King County Medical Society*,[113] the court said it was unreasonable for a public hospital to hold a particular physician ineligible for staff membership. The same court, however, refused to get involved when a private hospital denied the same doctor staff privileges.

In *Sosa v. Board of Managers*, a federal court of appeals said that:

in exercising its broad discretion the board must refuse staff applicants only for those matters which are reasonably related to the operation of the hospital. Arbitrariness and false standards are to be eschewed. Moreover, procedural due process must be afforded the applicant so that he may explain or show to be untrue those matters which might lead the board to reject his application. (citations omitted)[114]

As espoused in the Sosa case, professional staff bylaws should specify a method of affording due process through a hearing, whenever an applicant for privileges is turned down or receives more restrictive privileges than requested. A hearing also is in order whenever renewal of privileges is denied or is more limited than what the doctor requested.

Hospitals must have reasonable house staff requirements. The courts already have determined a number of requirements to be unreasonable. In *Foster v. Mobile County Hospital Board*, a federal appeals court held it was unreasonable for a hospital to require that its staff doctors belong to the county medical society and have their employment applications signed by at least two active staff members acquainted with them.[115] A state appellate court held unreasonable a hospital's requirement that all applicants for staff first have completed satisfactorily a one-year internship at an approved hospital.[116]

Some requirements' reasonableness depends on the jurisdiction in which those requirements are imposed. In *Stribling v. Jolley*,[117] the court said that a hospital's ability to reject osteopathic physicians depends on whether the state's laws equate doctors of osteopathy with medical doctors. If so, osteopaths must get the same opportunities as other equally qualified physicians.

Still other prerequisites for employment are considered reasonable only for certain kinds of hospitals. So said an appeals court in *Dillard v. Rowland*,[118] when it stated that a private hospital affiliated with a university medical school could confine the hospital staff to only those doctors who also hold a university faculty appointment. The court said this was reasonably necessary for the successful operation of a teaching institution.

In addition to establishing hiring guidelines, the governing board has an ongoing duty to monitor physicians and control the quality of care. If a patient's safety and health are threatened, an immediate suspension or restriction of staff privileges is in order. If the hospital is public or receives any governmental funding whatsoever, it must comply with the due process requirement that a hearing be held within a reasonable time to determine whether such disciplinary action should continue.[119] In addition to the hearing requirement, the staff member has a right to receive adequate notice of the charges and pending hearing a right to introduce evidence in his or her favor, and a right to cross-examine witnesses.[120]

Health-impaired professionals present special problems. Some doctors are unable to practice medicine in a reasonably safe or skillful manner because of physical or mental illness, deterioration through the aging process, or excessive alcohol or drug use. The hospital not only runs a risk that the impaired professional will mistreat patients, it also could be held liable if the professional sues on allegations that it responded improperly to his or her alleged impairment. It is best, therefore, to rehabilitate that person rather than use disciplinary tactics, unless this would endanger the health and safety of patients.

Some states have enacted statutes to deal with the problem. In Florida, for example, a doctor may be compelled to submit to a mental or physical examination upon a showing of probable cause that his or her faculties are impaired.[121] Failure to submit to the exam is deemed an admission of the allegations, unless the failure was due to circumstances beyond the physician's control. The statute requires that physicians determined to be impaired be afforded an opportunity, at reasonable intervals, to demonstrate that they are once again competent.

Once a physician is deemed to be impaired, the statute sets forth a number of alternative penalties. Licensure may be revoked or suspended, or the physician's practice may be restricted. The physician may be fined up to $1,000 for each offense and may be required to submit to treatment.[122]

If the physician believes the hospital is withholding privileges unfairly, there are several theories upon which to base a lawsuit. These include malicious interference with the right to practice his or her profession, defamation, failure to afford due process, and violation of antitrust laws.

Malicious interference with the fundamental right to practice one's profession constitutes cause for a suit.[123] If a doctor can prove, for example, that the review board was motivated by its own financial interests in preventing him or her from obtaining staff privileges, he or she can sue the hospital and its review and governing boards.[124]

The physician may sue for defamation, or injury to his or her reputation by publication of false statements. The Restatement (Second) of Torts says that "one who publishes a slander that ascribes to another conduct, characteristics or a condition that would adversely affect his fitness for the proper conduct of his lawful business, trade or profession . . . is subject to liability. . . ."[125] Generally the hospital and its governing and review boards incur no liability, however, because they can successfully plead a defense to the action. One defense is that the injurious statement was true. This is a complete bar to recovery in a defamation suit. A second defense is that the physician consented to the publication of defamatory matter concerning him. If the doctor signed a form upon obtaining staff privileges, in which he or she agreed to undergo periodic review, the doctor may be barred from recovery.

Anyone who is required by law to publish defamatory material is absolutely privileged to do so and therefore incurs no liability. In Florida, for example, a statute requires that the Department of Professional Regulation be notified whenever a physician is disciplined by a licensed hospital or its medical staff for violation of any medical practice law.[126]

Finally, the review board may defend its action by showing that it was conditionally privileged to publish the defamatory matter so as to protect the interests of the hospital and its patients, as well as the reputation of other physicians working in the hospital. The board will lose its conditional privilege, however, if it knows the matter to be false, acts in reckless disregard of its truth or falsity, or publishes the information for a purpose other than that of furthering the public interest. It also may be held liable if it publishes a rumor that it states to be fact or discloses defamatory matter to someone not privileged to receive such information.

The physician may sue the hospital for withholding privileges if it failed to provide those safeguards required for procedural due process: adequate notice, a hearing, a right to introduce favorable evidence, and a right to cross-examine the hospital's witnessess.[127] The physician may also claim that the hospital's withholding of privileges was unreasonable or arbitrary and therefore in violation of substantive due process requirements.[128]

Finally, the physician may base his or her suit on an antitrust theory. In *Jefferson Parish Hospital District No. 2 v. Hyde*,[129] a doctor sued because the hospital would not allow him on its staff. The reason was that the hospital had an exclusive contract with an anesthesiological firm, which required that all anesthesiological services in the hospital be performed by members of that firm. As Justice O'Connor stated in her concurring opinion,

> Exclusive dealing is an unreasonable restraint on trade only when a significant fraction of buyers or sellers are frozen out of a market by the exclusive deal. . . . When the sellers of services are numerous and mobile, and the number of buyers is large, exclusive dealing arrangements of narrow scope pose no threat of adverse economic consequences. (citation omitted)[130]

Although the Supreme Court held that the exclusive agreement in Hyde did not violate the Sherman Act,[131] it is important to note the facts on which the court based its decision. The hospital was one of at least 20 in the New Orleans metropolitan area, and therefore the plaintiff was unable to show that the contractual agreement unreasonably restrained competition in the market by closing off any possibility of penetration by competitors of the anesthesiology group. Indeed, only about one third of the patients (and potential anesthesiology customers) living in Jefferson Parish used that particular hospital. Dr. Hyde, it would seem, had ample opportunity to practice his trade elsewhere in the community.

Medical students create special liability problems for health care facilities. They are not licensed to practice medicine, yet they often have significant leeway in making important medical decisions. State laws generally permit this, provided a licensed physician supervises the student. These laws protect the student only from a suit for the unauthorized practice of medicine; they do not prevent prosecution for malpractice or fraud.

A lawsuit for fraud may result if the patient initially believes the student is a licensed doctor. The patient may recover damages for any injuries resulting from his or her belief that the medical student is a physician. These include both physical injuries and emotional trauma resulting from the knowledge that confidential information was disclosed to a layperson.

To prevent potential confusion, students must be introduced to patients as students and must correct patients who refer to them as "Doctor."

Lawsuits also may arise if the students are left unsupervised. It is important that a licensed physician cosign all students' orders, especially those involving the administration of medication.

Workers' Compensation Law

Workers' compensation is a name commonly used to designate the methods and means created by the various state statutes for giving protection and security for workers and their dependents resulting from injury or death which occur in the course of employment. Workers' compensation should not be confused with health insurance, which is designed to compensate individuals for sickness and illness regardless of how it is incurred.

The origins of workers' compensation laws in the United States and other industrialized nations go back to the last century. With the Industrial Revolution in Western Europe and the United States, complex machinery began to replace various crafts, resulting in mass-produced products. As a natural result of the use of this machinery, workers sustained injuries and death. Consequently, society through its governments made demands on employers to compensate the victims or their dependents for injuries that resulted in death or handicap, for the loss of future income.

Germany was the first nation to implement workers' compensation programs in the middle and late nineteenth century.[132] By the early 1900s Germany had developed and refined its industrial accident laws to the point that injured workers recovered a scheduled amount of compensation regardless of the issue of fault. Other European countries, including England,[133] developed liberal compensation laws, and this concept spread to the United States and other industrial nations. In 1908 the United States passed a form of workers' compensation law to cover government employees, to be followed by New York in 1910.[134] By 1921, all but a handful of states had passed similar workers' compensation legislation. Today all states of the union have workers' compensation statutes.[135]

The risk manager must be thoroughly acquainted with the workers' compensation statute of his or her state. Each state has provisions in its law that may not be applicable in other states. Generally, all workers' compensation statutes have similar features. For example, they all eliminate fault as a requirement of recovery. The impact of this feature is what makes workers' compensation different from other liability laws. Under workers' compensation law, the employee is covered even if he or she was the sole cause of the injury and the employer did nothing at all to cause the misadventure. In tort law, as we have learned, the burden of proof is on the plaintiff to prove that the defendant caused the injury. No such requirement is necessary under workers' compensation statutes.

A second common feature is that the process of filing claims is designed to speed up recovery for the employee or his or her dependents. Generally, workers' compensation programs begin to compensate the victim or the dependents very soon after the incident. An employee can begin to receive workers' compensation benefits immediately after the injury if the employer authorizes the physician or other health care provider to treat the individual and guarantees payment. Other benefits begin to accrue and be disbursed as they become due. For example, employees who have a genuine work-related injury can frequently expect compensation for lost time within a matter of days or a few weeks after the incident; consequently they often do not feel the hardships of lost income.

A third feature of workers' compensation programs is guaranteed recovery for employees' lost time and medical expenses, and compensation for permanent or partial disabilities. Generally, this element of the statutes is very mechanical and is approved in advance by accepted payment schedules based on the degree of injury and the expenses incurred. (Exhibit 5-1 is an example of a permanent/partial disability schedule for the State of Missouri).

The last noteworthy feature of workers' compensation statutes is that they include the burden of loss in the cost of producing goods and services and insulate employees from that loss. In essence, throughout the United States the cost of producing goods and delivering services incorporates workers' compensation expenses as a cost of doing business.

An element of the workers' compensation law of the State of Missouri that may

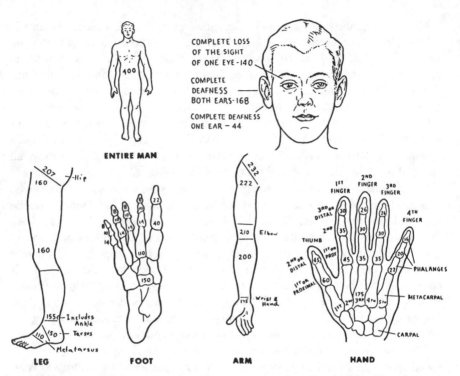

Exhibit 5-1A Permanent Partial Disability Schedule. Visual Chart Showing Number of Weeks of Compensation Payable for Permanent Partial Disabilities under the Missouri Workmen's Compensation Law. When there is complete loss of a member—either by severance or loss of use—the number of weeks indicated on this chart for such member(s) is increased by ten (10) percent (eye injuries being specifically exempted from such increase).

not be applicable in other states is that it covers only employers who have five or more employees[136] or who buy a workers' compensation insurance policy. Because the law applies to the employer who has five or more employees, even if the employer is not insured, the importance of adequate risk financing is self-evident. Risk managers must also know which employees the statute covers. It is obvious that the statute covers regular employees; however, state laws may differ as to whether they cover borrowed employees, independent contractors, volunteers, or other individuals.

Workers' compensation statutes are generally classified as a form of strict liability for the employer if they apply, but they are not without legal questions. An example of some of the issues that are frequently litigated in unclear cases is whether or not an employer-employee relationship exists. Under Missouri law the employee or the claimant has the burden of bringing himself or herself within the

	175 Hand			210 Elbow			232 Shoulder	
5%	8.75 =	1193.50		10.5 =	1432.20		11.6 =	1582.24
10%	17.5 =	2387.00		21.0 =	2864.40		23.2 =	3164.48
15%	26.25 =	3580.50		31.5 =	4296.60		34.8 =	4746.72
20%	35.0 =	4774.00		42.0 =	5728.80		46.4 =	6328.96
25%	43.75 =	5967.50		52.5 =	7161.00		58.0 =	7911.20

	155 Ankle			160 Knee			207 Hip	
5%	7.75 =	1057.10		8.0 =	1091.20		10.35 =	1411.74
10%	15.5 =	2114.20		16.0 =	2182.40		20.70 =	2823.48
15%	23.25 =	3171.30		24.0 =	3273.60		41.40 =	4235.22
20%	31.0 =	4228.40		32.0 =	4364.80		62.10 =	5646.96
25%	38.75 =	5285.50		40.0 =	5456.00		82.80 =	7058.70

	400 Body as a Whole	
5%	20.0 =	2,728.00
10%	40.0 =	5,456.00
15%	60.0 =	8,184.00
20%	80.0 =	10,912.00
25%	100.0 =	13,640.00

Exhibit 5-1B Permanent Partial Disability Settlement Values. These figures are for illustration only. The actual amount an employee may receive could be greater or less. Many factors can be involved in determining the value of an injury that cannot be generally illustrated. In computing these figures a rate of $136.40 per week was used. While it is useful for a doctor to have a general understanding of what a rating will involve in terms of financial gain it is not recommended that the doctor ever discuss the monetary value of a case with the patient.

provisions of the statute and must establish that he or she is an employee or the dependent of an employee in the service of the employer.[137] If this requirement becomes an issue of dispute, then certain other aspects of the case are considered. Among them are the voluntary condition of services by the employee to the employer, the acceptance of such service by the employer and the right to direct and control the employee. Under Missouri law, the fact that the individual was an unpaid employee is not relevant.[138] Other activities that affect the employee-employer relationship are the payment of wages, the furnishing of equipment, the right of discharge, and various provisions of an employee contract. The issue of an employee-employer relationship can become very cloudy and the subject of much debate in situations where an independent contractor is involved. Each state has cases that have litigated the issue and defined who are independent contractors and who are not; however, some factors should be considered. Generally an independent contractor is one who exercises independent employment, contracts to do a piece of work, and does it according to his or her own methods without being subject to the control of the employer.

Another common requirement is that the employee sustained a personal injury, illness, or death, and that it resulted from an accident or an occupational disease. In many states, a large number of cases have litigated the issue of what is an accident or an occupational disease. Generally the former must be a sudden, unexpected, traumatic event that is not a result of normal or everyday work activities. For example, under Missouri law, if a person's job were to empty a wastebasket and the person strained his or her back by carrying out this work, it would not necessarily meet the test of an accident unless the employee incurred the injury as a result of some sudden twisting or slipping that is unexpected, violent, or out of the ordinary.

Occupational diseases are easy to classify in some industries and difficult in others. The most common occupational disease in coal mining, for example, is black lung disease, whereas in the health care environment one could argue that any disease that a patient brings to the institution and that the employee is in a position to catch should be classified as an occupational disease. However, there is much litigation around this issue. A common occupational disease in the health care industry is hepatitis caused by exposure to blood and blood products such as needle sticks.

The last element that must be present for an occupational injury or illness to be compensable in most states is that the event must arise out of employment and in the course of employment. These key words are usually statutorily interpreted in each state, and numerous cases have been decided on the issue of whether an accident or occupational disease arose out of and in the course of employment. The test usually contains two parts, which must be met by the employee in order to sustain a claim. The employee must prove that the event arose out of employment and, separately, in the course of employment. If one of the requirements is met and the other fails, then the claim will fail.[139]

An accident and resultant injury arise out of employment when there is a direct causal connection between the injury and the employment. It is not necessary that the exact accident or injury sustained by the employee have been anticipated. However, it must have been a rational consequence of some hazard connected with the employment.[140]

An accident is said to have arisen in the course of employment when it occurs within the period of employment at a place where an employee might reasonably be and while the employee is reasonably fulfilling the duties of his or her employment or is engaged in the performance of some task incidental thereto.[141] It is beyond the scope of this text to define in detail the words "arising out of employment and in the course of employment" since each state has had many cases that have been litigated over the issue of the definition as it pertains to particular facts. Nevertheless it is incumbent upon the risk manager to be familiar with his or her state's definition of these key phrases.

The benefits available to an injured or occupationally ill employee will also be determined by each state's statute. However, most statutes have common elements that include medical treatment expenses and temporary total disability, which usually is a percentage of the total salary the individual was making, subject to a statutorily-mandated maximum amount. Permanent partial disability is also generally awarded and represents the degree of disability expressed in terms of a percentage of disability times the maximum rate as set by statute. The employee can also expect to be reimbursed for necessary expenses associated with treatment, such as mileage, housing, and rehabilitation expenses, if required. In situations where the person can no longer seek employment, he or she can claim permanent total disability. Once again, the states usually mandate these amounts by statute, according to formulas. Death benefits are also available to the dependents of employees, as well as funeral expenses and other miscellaneous costs pertaining to the death of an employee. Also, an employee can be compensated a certain amount in some states for disfigurement. Lastly, prosthetic expenses are compensable for individuals who have lost limbs or vital organs that are replaceable by such devices.

Another important feature of most state workers' compensation laws deals with procedures. The statutes generally go into great detail about how claims are to be processed, how data are to be collected and how hearings, appeals, and settlements are to proceed. Because workers' compensation is a no-fault system, many of the procedures become very mechanical and are conducted on standardized forms provided by the state (see Exhibits 5-2 and 5-3). Generally the process begins when an employee or dependent files a report of injury with the employer. The employer may be required to send a notice report to the state agency such as the State Labor and Industrial Relations Commission or some other similar organization as required by statute.142 Standardized forms such as the surgeon's report in Exhibit 5-3 are usually used to verify treatment. If the case is not disputed, the state agency may carry out routine audits to determine whether employers are meeting the requirements of the law; otherwise the case may go to an administrative law judge, who will oversee the claim's administration. If the employer takes issue with a claim, or in cases where the employee does not accept a determination by an employer, the statutes usually contain all the details for processing and hearing the dispute. An administrative law judge, sometimes called a hearing officer, conducts the proceedings for workers' compensation claims administration.

In Missouri, if a party takes issue with the decision of the administrative law judge, the case is appealed to the Industrial Commission. Generally the Industrial Commission operates under the rules of administrative law and has certain powers delineated by the workers' compensation statute or the state administrative law statutes. Appeals are made from the Commission within the State of Missouri or an equivalent body outside the state to either a circuit court or an appellate court. In Missouri the law was recently amended so that appeals from the Industrial

FORM 1 (Sixth Revision)		ISSUED BY DIVISION OF WORKMEN'S COMPENSATION

Insurer's No._____

Employee's Case No._____

Division of Workmen's Compensation
DEPARTMENT OF LABOR AND INDUSTRIAL RELATIONS
OF MISSOURI
JEFFERSON CITY, MISSOURI

Report of Injury

This form is both the notice and the report of the injury as required by Section 287.380 RSMo 1969. Do not report any occurrence unless it causes personal injury serious enough to require medical aid. This report must be sent in whether or not the employer is under the Law. If not under it, no further reports are required unless requested. Mail to the Division of Workmen's Compensation, Jefferson City, Missouri. Do not accompany by letter.

AN ANSWER SHOULD BE MADE TO EVERY QUESTION

DO NOT FILL IN

Injury No._____

Rec. Ack. Form _____

Under Law _____

Compensable _____

Disability _____

Checked By _____

1. NAME OF EMPLOYER: THE CURATORS OF THE UNIVERSITY OF MISSOURI	2. MAILING ADDRESS (NO. & STREET) (CITY) (STATE) (ZIP CODE) ATTN. BUSINESS & INDUSTRIAL SRCS., WORKERS' COMPENSATION COORDINATOR, #1 HOSPITAL DRIVE, COLUMBIA, MO 65212		DO NOT USE
3. LOCATION OF ESTABLISHMENT IF DIFFERENT FROM MAILING ADDRESS SAME AS ITEM 2	4. MISSOURI U.I. ACCOUNT NO. 300508-0-000-8221		5.
5. NATURE OF BUSINESS & SPECIFIC PRODUCT EDUCATIONAL INSTITUTION	6. PHONE NUMBER (314) 882-1586		
7. INSURANCE CARRIER AND ADDRESS SELF INSURED			11.
8. DAYS PER YEAR BUSINESS OPERATES 365	9. NUMBER OF EMPLOYEES Approximately 21,000		12.
10. DATE OF ACCIDENT OR INCIDENT OF DISEASE	11. TIME A.M. P.M.	12. PLACE OF ACCIDENT (STREET, CITY, COUNTY, STATE)	19.
13. NAME (FIRST, MIDDLE, LAST)		14. SOCIAL SECURITY NUMBER	22.
15. HOME ADDRESS (NO. & STREET) (CITY OR TOWN) (STATE) (ZIP CODE) (PHONE NUMBER)	15a. DATE OF BIRTH	16. AGE	23.
17. SEX	18. MARITAL STATUS ☐ MARRIED ☐ SINGLE	19. YEARS EMPLOYED 20. REGULAR OCCUPATION 21. REGULAR DEPARTMENT	28.
22. OCCUPATION WHEN INJURED	23. HOW LONG AT CURRENT OCCUPATION? 24. WORK DAYS PER WEEK? 25. WEEKLY WAGE?		29.
26. WAS ACCIDENT OR EXPOSURE ON EMPLOYER'S PREMISES?	27. TIME WORK BEGAN FOR EMPLOYEE ON INJURY DATE		30.
28. HOW DID THE ACCIDENT OCCUR? (DESCRIBE FULLY)			31.
29. WHAT WAS EMPLOYEE DOING WHEN INJURED? (BE SPECIFIC)			32. CODE
30. NAME THE OBJECT OR SUBSTANCE WHICH DIRECTLY INJURED THE EMPLOYEE			CAMPUS HOSPITAL AND CLINICS
31. DESCRIBE THE INJURY OR ILLNESS IN DETAIL AND INDICATE THE PART OF THE BODY AFFECTED			11.
32. DID INJURY RESULT IN DEATH? ☐ YES ☐ NO IF SO, ANSWER QUESTIONS 47 & 48 ON REVERSE SIDE HEREOF			16.
33. WAS THERE ANY DISMEMBERMENT, DISFIGUREMENT, OR OTHER PERMANENT DISABILITY? ☐ Yes ☐ No IF SO, STATE NATURE			17.
34. HAS EMPLOYEE RETURNED TO WORK? ☐ Yes ☐ No	35. DATE	36. AT WHAT WEEKLY WAGE?	21.
37. WHEN DID TEMPORARY DISABILITY BEGIN?	38. END?		
39. NAME AND ADDRESS OF ATTENDING PHYSICIAN			28.
40. NAME AND ADDRESS OF HOSPITAL			30.
41. ACTUAL OR ESTIMATED COST OF MEDICAL AID	42. IS FURTHER MEDICAL AID REQUIRED? ☐ YES ☐ NO		31A.
43. NAME AND ADDRESS OF INDIVIDUAL TO WHOM COMMUNICATIONS SHOULD BE ADDRESSED SAME AS #2			31B
44. DATE OF REPORT	45. REPORT COMPLETED BY (SIGNATURE)	46. TITLE WORKERS' COMPENSATION COORDINATOR	ACT / COND

SEE BACK FOR INSTRUCTIONS   (OVER)   UMUW FORM 3 (SEPT 85)

Left margin labels: EMPLOYER / INJURED EMPLOYEE / OCCURRENCE OF INJURY / NATURE OF INJURY / OTHER

Exhibit 5-2 A standardized workers' compensation injury report form.

Commission go directly to the state appellate court that has jurisdiction. The last appeal from the circuit or the appellate court to the state supreme court will depend on the rules of the particular state. Exhibits 5-4 and 5-5 are examples of preprinted required forms used in workers' compensation litigation in Missouri. Many states

FORM 9 (REVISED)

STANDARD FORM FOR

SURGEON'S REPORT

Issued by the

Division of Workers' Compensation

Department of Labor and Industrial
Relations of Missouri

State's	File:
Number	Carrier:
For:	Employer:

Carrier's File No.

The Patient

1. Name of Injured Person: .... Age: .... Sex: ....
2. Address: No. and St. .... City or Town .... State ....
3. Name and Address of Employer: ....

The Accident

4. Date of Accident: .... Hour .... M. Date disability began ....
5. State in patient's own words where and how accident occurred: ....

The Injury

6. Give accurate description of nature and extent of injury and state your objective findings: ....

7. Will the injury result in (a) Permanent defect? .... If so, what? ....
   (b) Disfigurement of normally exposed parts of body? ....

8. Is accident above referred to the only cause of patient's condition? .... If not, state contributing causes: ....

9. Is patient suffering from any disease of the heart, lungs, brain, kidneys, blood, vascular system or any other disabling condition not due to this accident? .... Give particulars: ....

10. Has patient any physical impairment due to previous accident or disease? .... Give particulars: ....

11. Has normal recovery been delayed for any reason? .... Give particulars: ....

Treatment

12. Date of your first treatment: .... Who engaged your services? ....
13. Describe treatment given by you: ....

14. Were X-Rays taken? .... By whom? .... When? ....
    (Name and Address)
15. X-Ray diagnosis: ....
16. Was patient treated by anyone else? .... By whom? .... When? ....
    (Name and Address)
17. Was patient hospitalized? .... Name and address of hospital: ....
18. Date of admission to hospital: .... Date of discharge: ....
19. Is further treatment needed? .... For how long? ....

Disability

20. Patient was/will be able to resume regular work on: ....
21. Patient was/will be able to resume light work on: ....
22. If death ensued, give date: ....

REMARKS: (Give any information of value not included above) ....

I am a duly licensed physician in the State of ....
I was graduated from .... Medical School in .... Year ....
Date of this report: .... (Signed) ....
This report must be signed personally by physician. Address: .... Telephone ....
Cost of Medical aid: $ ....

Exhibit 5-3 A standardized surgeon's report form used in workers' compensation cases.

require that such standardized forms be used in workers' compensation cases, and thus the procedure leaves little opportunity for legal innovation. In Missouri and many other states even lawyers' fees are limited by statute; for example, in Missouri the limit is 25% of the amount awarded.

The importance of workers' compensation to the worker, the employer, and particularly the risk manager cannot be overstated. The workers' compensation

Issued by DIVISION OF WORKMEN'S COMPENSATION   (Revised) Form 21

BEFORE THE

Division of Workmen's Compensation
Department of Labor and Industrial Relations of Missouri
JEFFERSON CITY, MISSOURI

Claim for Compensation

(To be sent to the Division at Jefferson City, Missouri, within one year after
the injury or death, or from the date of the last payment of Compensation.)

DO NOT FILL IN

Injury No. _____

Rec. Ack. Form_____
County _____
Place of Hearing_____

Checked by _____

NOTE: Send two copies for the Division and one copy for each employer and insurer.

Use only when employer or insurer finally refuses or neglects to pay compensation.

GIVE HOUSE NUMBER, STREET, CITY AND STATE IN ALL ADDRESSES

1. Claim is hereby made as follows for compensation as provided in the Missouri Workmen's Compensation Law, for personal injury (or death) of the employee by accident or occupational disease arising out of and in the course of his employment, both employer and employee having elected to accept said Law before and at the time of the accident.

2. Names and addresses of all claimants_____

3. Names and addresses of all employers_____

4. Names and addresses of all employers' insurers_____

☐ Check here and fill in reverse side of this form if Second Injury Fund is involved.

5. Injured employee's name_____   6. Average weekly wages, $_____

7. Date of { accident
            { incidence of occupational disease } _____ (Month) _____ (Day), 19___ (Year)   8. Hour _____M.

9. Place: ___(Number or Location)___ (Street) ___ (City) ___ (County) ___ (State)

10. Did injury result in death _____ If so, answer questions 24 and 25 on the reverse side hereof.

11. Parts of body injured_____

12. Weeks of temporary disability to date_____   13. Weeks of probable future temporary disability_____

14. Exact nature of any permanent injury_____

15. How injury occurred, cause, and work employee was doing for employer at the time _____

16. Additional statements. (See reverse side hereof.)

17 Total compensation paid to date, $_____   18. Total value compensation claimed, $_____

19. Dated _____   20. Claimant's Signature _____

22. Claimant's Attorney _____   21. By _____

23. Address _____

NOTE: Line 20 MUST BE SIGNED—NOT TYPED

Exhibit 5-4 A standardized workers' compensation claims form.

program is often the only medical insurance program to which the employee may look for payment of medical expenses and lost wages, particularly in small organizations that do not offer health care benefits. It is often the only compensation for permanent or partial disability. From the employer's point of view, workers' compensation is both a burden and a benefit. It is a burden because it is another

Issued by DIVISION OF WORKMEN'S COMPENSATION   (Revised) Form 22

BEFORE THE

Division of Workmen's Compensation

Department of Labor and Industrial Relations of Missouri

JEFFERSON CITY, MISSOURI

Answer to Claim for Compensation

(To be sent to the Division at Jefferson City, Missouri, within fifteen (15) days of receipt of copy of Claim for Compensation. Send one copy for the Division, one copy for each claimant, and one copy for each claimant's attorney.)

STATE FACTS AND NOT CONCLUSIONS

Injury No. ....

(DO NOT FILL IN)

Rec. Ack Form ....

County ....

Place of Hearing ....

Checked by ....

1. Claimants ....

2. Names and addresses of Employers ....

3. Names and addresses of Insurers ....

4. Injured Employee ....

5. Date of Accident .... 6. Place ....
                                                                        (City)   (State)

7. All of the statements in the Claim for Compensation are admitted except the following:

Here should be separately set forth the question number of each disputed statement in the Claim for Compensation, the reason why disputed, and the facts in regard thereto. Also any other facts tending to defeat the Claim.)

(If additional space is needed, use reverse side)

19. Dated .... 20. Employer's
                                                                          Signature ....

24. Employer and/or Insurer's Attorney   21.   By ....

.... 22. Insurer's

                                                                          Signature ....

25. Address .... 23.   By ....

Exhibit 5-5 A standardized form used in replying to a workers' compensation claim.

cost of doing business in a highly competitive world. However, insurance is usually readily available, and this expense can be funded through nonaffiliated insurance organizations or, as some large institutions do, through self-insurance mechanisms. Generally the cost of workers' compensation can be passed on to the customer and the expense incorporated with the cost of the product or service.

Another expense the employer must consider is the administration and recordkeeping required. Lastly, the employer should put substantial effort into reducing employee injuries through a viable safety program incorporating education and other loss prevention mechanisms.

A major benefit of workers' compensation, however, is that the system is generally rapid, and compensation is fair based on the degree of loss and expenses incurred. It is also ethically and morally proper. In a highly litigious society such as the United States, without workers' compensation it would be fair to assume that many employers would be bogged down in costly litigation, which could result in outrageous losses sufficient to cause the demise of the corporation.

Although workers' compensation claims can usually be handled in a routine fashion, the risk manager must keep a close watch over this exposure area. In many environments it is not unusual for workers' compensation to be the most significant loss center associated with the risk management program. Health care facilities are particularly vulnerable to certain expensive losses, particularly those related to back injuries associated with the lifting and transportation of patients. It is not unusual for a workers' compensation program to result in higher losses to the institution than those associated with medical malpractice and general liability.

As an example of the magnitude of the problem in one state, in Missouri in 1979 there were 147,343 reported work-related injuries and 6,421 reported occupational diseases, of which 116 resulted in deaths, for a total figure of 153,388 cases. Payments made to or on behalf of these employees equaled $92,534,625, of which more than $33,000,000 was paid in the form of medical care.[143] The workers' compensation program of each state is therefore an important facet of the job of the risk manager with which he or she must be familiar. The money that changes hands through workers' compensation programs is important to the professions of law and medicine as well as to other health professions.

Summary

Some knowledge of the fundamentals of law is essential for a risk manager since he or she must judge the behavior of others in order to determine if it deviates from community or professional standards. This is necessary to determine if the organization or person is potentially liable.

The law in this chapter is basically an overview of the major legal areas important for the risk manager to understand. This does not mean that risk managers must be experts, but that they can adequately recognize unacceptable conduct and seek legal counsel. The risk manager must know the difference between intentional torts, negligence, and strict liability torts. Also, some knowledge of common defenses is important, as well as the measure of damages for torts, antitrust, and other actions.

Risk managers must likewise know the rules of informed consent. Members of the staff will often refer questions regarding consent issues to the risk manager and often ask questions about privacy and confidentiality. Issues associated with personnel and hiring practices as well as medical staff questions are also often asked of the risk manager. Lastly, some knowledge of workers' compensation law is essential.

Risk managers who are not lawyers must maintain a close relationship with legal counsel throughout their careers and should follow changes in the law.

Chapter Exercises

1. Your state requires all hospitals and doctors to retain patient records for 7 years. Mrs. Smith was operated on by Dr. Cutquick for an emergency appendectomy on July 10, 1978. While jogging last week, Mrs. Smith felt a sharp pain in her side that would not go away. She consulted Dr. Doright, who x-rayed her and discovered a hemostat in her abdominal cavity. During the operation to remove the hemostat, Dr. Doright discovered that Mrs. Smith's Fallopian tubes had been resected. On hearing about the surgery, Dr. Cutquick destroyed his records on Mrs. Smith and cancelled his membership in the Zero-Population Association. He then called his friend Mr. Banker, who was on the board of directors of the local hospital where both surgeries were performed, and said, "You had better get rid of Mrs. Smith's records and Dr. Doright." Mr. Banker told the hospital administrator to destroy Mrs. Smith's records and to write a letter to Dr. Doright saying that his privileges would not be renewed after they expired next month because the hospital had too many surgeons, he did not carry enough malpractice insurance, and he was not a member of the local medical society.

A. What liability issues are raised in this scenario?

B. Assume that Mrs. Smith sues and her attorney pleads *res ipsa loquitur*. What necessary elements must she show?

C. List any other legal issue.

2. While reading your mail recently, you came across a letter addressed to you as Risk Manager of Coal City Hospital. The letter reads as follows:

To Whom It May Concern:

Six weeks ago I was in your hospital. I had to go into the hospital because one of the doctors in your office building messed up my private parts, when I asked him to fix me so I cannot have anymore kids. When I was in the hospital they took me to the operating room to stop my bleeding and fix me proper. Now, I get these letters saying I should pay up or you are going to take me to court. I got news for you S.0.B.'s my cousin's boy, Leroy, is a lawyer down here and he's just itchin to take you on. I ain't the same man I was and it's your fault and I ain't paying you nothing.

Signed
George Johnson

A review of Mr. Johnson's medical records indicates that Mr. Johnson is 63 years old and was admitted by Dr. Klang at 5:00 p.m. for control of bleeding associated with a vasectomy performed at 8:00 a.m. on that same day of admission in Dr. Klang's office, which is located in the Coal City Medical Office Building adjacent and attached to the hospital. The office building is owned by the hospital, and space is leased to doctors. The building also contains a laboratory, a pharmacy, and a family planning clinic. A pathology report dated the same day of the procedure at 9:00 a.m. indicates the tissue sample to be a section of blood vessels. Subsequent lab reports reveal sections of the vas canal. Mr. Johnson was in the hospital 3 days and received a unit of blood and the usual care and treatment. The follow-up surgery was performed by a urologist, and his bill was $1,000. Hospital charges equal $4,400. Dr. Klang is a general practitioner and does not enjoy surgery privileges at the hospital because of opposition from the hospital's chief of surgery for reasons unknown to you. It is common knowledge that Dr. Klang does outpatient surgery in his office. He is also medical director of the family planning clinic, which is part of the hospital. The record also indicates that Mr. Johnson lives on his 100-acre farm in the Ozarks, his wife is 32 years old, and he has six children. He has a small insurance policy that pays about 35% of all charges.

A. Are there any issues of agency in this scenario?

B. What about the liability of the hospital, its board, etc.? List the legal issues.

References

1. *Mohr v. Williams,* 104 N.W. 12 (Minn. 1905).

2. *O'Brien v. Cunard S.S. Co.,* 28 N.E. 266 (Mass. 1891).

3. *Mohr v. Williams,* 104 N.W. 12 (Minn. 1905).

4. *Kennedy v. Parrott,* 243 N.C. 355, 90 S.E.2d 754 (1956).

5. Restatement (Second) of Torts, Section 283A (1965).

6. *O'Neill v. Montefiore Hosp.,* 11 A.D.2d 132, 202 N.Y.S.2d 436 (1960).

7. *Tarasoff v. Regents of the Univ. of Cal.,* 118 Cal. Rptr. 129, 529 P.2d 553 (1974) (en banc).

8. Restatement (Second) of Torts, Section 319 comment a, illustration 1 (1965).

9. W. Keeton, D. Dobbs, R. Keeton, and D. Owen, *Prosser and Keeton on Torts,* (5th ed. 1984), 187.

10. Geoffrey Segar, *Hospital Liability Issues* 18-19, citing *Harris v. Browne* (Tenn. App. 1971).

11. *Emory Univ. v. Porter,* 103 Ga. App. 752, 120 S.E.2d 668 (1961); *Lauro v. Travelers Ins. Co.,* 261 So. 2d 261, 50 A.L.R. 3d 1130 (La. App. 1972).

12. *The T. J. Hooper,* 60 F.2d 737, 740 (2d Cir. 1932), cert. denied, 287 U.S. 662 (1932).

13. *Hill v. James Walker Memorial Hosp.*, 407 F.2d 1036 (4th Cir. 1969).

14. *Darling v. Charleston Community Memorial Hosp.*, 33 Ill.2d 326, 211 N.E.2d 253, 14 A.L.R. 3d 860 (1965), cert. denied, 383 U.S. 946 (1966).

15. *Carrasco v. Bunkoff*, 220 Cal. App. 2d 230, 33 Cal. Rptr. 673, 97 A.L.R. 2d 464 (1963).

16. *Johnson v. Misericordia Community Hosp.*, 99 Wis. 2d 708, 301 N.W.2d 156 (1981).

17. Ibid., 174-175.

18. Joint Commission on Accreditation of Hospitals, *Accreditation Manual for Hospitals* (Chicago: Joint Commission on Accreditation of Hospitals, 1983), 99.

19. 42 C.F.R., Section 405.1023(d)(2) (1984).

20. *Burns v. Owens*, 459 S.W.2d 303 (Mo. 1970); *Bernardi v. Community Hosp. Ass'n*, 166 Colo. 280, 443 P.2d 708 (1968) (en banc); *Honeywell v. Rogers*, 251 F. Supp. 841 (W.D. Pa. 1966).

21. *Mduba v. Benedictine Hosp.*, 52 A.D.2d 450, 384 N.Y.S.2d 527 (1976).

22. *Stewart v. Midani*, 525 F. Supp. 843 (N.D. Ga. 1981).

23. Restatement (Second) of Agency, Section 267 (1958).

24. *Schloendorff v. Society of N.Y. Hosp.*, 211 N.Y. 125, 105 N.E. 92, 93 (Ct. App. 1914).

25. E. Richards III and K. Rathbun, *Medical Risk Management* (Rockville, MD: Aspen Systems Corporation, 1983), 250.

26. *Corn v. French*, 71 Nev. 280, 289 P.2d 173 (1955).

27. *Rogers v. Lumberman's Mut. Casualty Co.*, 119 So. 2d 649 (La. App. 1960).

28. *Bang v. Charles T. Miller Hosp.*, 251 Minn. 427, 88 N.W.2d 186 (1958).

29. *Mitchell v. Robinson*, 334 S.W.2d 11, 79 A.L.R. 2d 1017 (Mo. 1960).

30. *Scaria v. St. Paul Fire & Marine Ins. Co.*, 227 N.W.2d 647, 653 (Wis. 1975).

31. Ibid., 654.

32. *Murray v. Vandevander*, 522 P.2d 302 (Okla. Ct. App. 1974).

33. *Pratt v. Davis*, 224 Ill. 300, 79 N.E. 562 (1906).

34. *Gravis v. Physicians' and Surgeons' Hosp. of Alice*, 427 S.W.2d 310 (Tex. 1968).

35. *In re Quinlan*, 70 N.J. 10, 355 A.2d 647 (1976).

36. *Poe v. Gerstein*, 517 F.2d 787 (5th Cir. 1975).

37. *Prince v. Massachusetts*, 321 U.S. 158, 166-167, 170 (1944).

38. *State v. Perricone*, 37 N.J. 463, 181 A.2d 751 (1962), cert. denied, 371 U.S. 890 (1962).

39. Ibid., 477, 181 A.2d at 759.

40. *Graves v. Beto*, 424 F.2d 524 (5th Cir. 1970), cert. denied, 400 U.S. 960 (1970).

41. *Stanes v. Taylor*, 272 N.C. 386, 158 S.E.2d 339 (1968); *Roberts v. Wood*, 206 F. Supp. 579 (Ala. 1962).

42. Ohio Rev. Code Ann., Section 2317.54 (Page 1981).

43. *Halley v. Birbiglia*, 390 Mass. 540, 458 N.E.2d 710 (1983).

44. *Berkey v. Anderson*, 1 Cal. App. 3d 790, 82 Cal. Rptr. 67 (1969).

45. *Dorland's Illustrated Medical Dictionary*, 25th ed. (Philadelphia: W. B. Saunders, 1974), 715.

46. *Estate of Berthiaume v. Pratt*, 365 A.2d 792, 86 A.L.R.3d 365 (Me. 1976).

47. *De May v. Roberts*, 46 Mich. 160, 9 N.W. 146 (1881).

48. *State v. Kuljis*, 70 Wash. 2d 168, 422 P.2d 480 (1967).

49. 42 U.S.C., Section 242a (1982).

50. 21 U.S.C., Section 1175(b)(2)(C) (1982).

51. *Doe v. Roe*, 93 Misc. 2d 201, 400 N.Y.S.2d 668 (N.Y. Sup. Ct. 1977).

52. *Alexander v. Knight*, 197 Pa. Super. 79, 177 A.2d 142 (1962).

53. 15 U.S.C., Section 1 (1982).

54. *Cardio-Medical Ass'n v. Crozer-Chester Medical Center*, 536 F. Supp. 1065, 1076 (E.D. Pa. 1982).

55. *Hospital Bldg. Co. v. Trustees of Rex Hosp.*, 425 U.S. 738 (1976).

56. *Arizona v. Maricopa County Medical Soc'y*, 457 U.S. 332 (1982).

57. *American Medical Ass'n v. Federal Trade Comm'n*, 638 F.2d 443 (2d Cir. 1980), aff'd, 455 U.S. 676 (1982).

58. *Robinson v. Magovern*, 521 F. Supp. 842 (W.D. Pa. 1981), aff'd, 688 F.2d 824 (3d Cir. 1982), cert. denied, 459 U.S. 971 (1982).

59. *Jefferson Parish Hosp. Dist. No. 2 v. Hyde*, No. 82-1031, Slip op. at 9 (U.S. Mar. 27, 1984).

60. *Portland Retail Druggists Ass'n v. Kaiser Found. Health Plan*, 662 F.2d 641 (9th Cir. 1981), cert. denied, 105 S. Ct. 1230 (1985).

61. *Board of Trade v. United States*, 246 U.S. 231, 238 (1918).

62. *Mays v. Hospital Auth.*, 596 F. Supp. 120 (N.D. Ga. 1984).

63. Ibid., 122.

64. 15 U.S.C., Section 2 (1982).

65. *Weiss v. York Hosp.*, 548 F. Supp. 1048, 1055 (M.D. Pa. 1982), cert. denied, 105 S. Ct. 1777 (1985); See also, *Pontius v. Children's Hosp.*, 552 F. Supp. 1352 (W.D. Pa. 1982).

66. 15 U.S.C., Section 18 (1982).

67. 15 U.S.C., Section 13 (1982).

68. *Cantor v. Detroit Edison Co.*, 428 U.S. 579 (1976); *Retail Liquor Dealers' Ass'n v. Midcal Aluminum Inc.*, 445 U.S. 97 (1980).

69. 42 U.S.C., Section 2000e-2 (1982).

70. 42 U.S.C., Section 1981 (1982).

71. *Johnson v. Railway Express Agency*, 421 U.S. 454, 460 (1975); See also, *McDonald v. Sante Fe Trail Transp. Co.*, 427 U.S. 273, 296 (1976).

72. U.S. Const. amend. XIV,, Section 1.

73. *U.S. Const. amend* V. See also, *Washington v. Davis*, 426 U.S. 229, 239 (1976); *Bolling v. Sharpe*, 347 U.S. 497 (1954).

74. *McDonnell Douglas Corp. v. Green*, 411 U.S. 792, 802 (1973); See also, *McDonald v. Sante Fe Trail Transp. Co.*, 427 U.S. 273, 278-285 (1976).

75. *EEOC Uniform Guidelines on Employee Selection Procedures*, 29 C.F.R., Section 1607.3 (1985).

76. *Regents of the Univ. of Cal. v. Bakke*, 438 U.S. 265 (1978).

77. 29 U.S.C., Section 206(d) (1982).

78. *Guidelines on Discrimination Because of Sex*, 29 C.F.R., Section 1604 (1985).

79. 29 C.F.R., Section 1604.11(a).

80. 29 C.F.R., Section 1604.11(c).

81. 29 C.F.R., Section 1605.11(d).

82. 29 C.F.R., Section 1604.11(e).

83. 29 C.F.R., Section 1604.11(g).

84. 29 C.F.R., Section 1604.11(f).

85. *Heelan v. Johns-Manville Corp.*, 451 F. Supp. 1382 (D. Colo. 1978).

86. 29 U.S.C., Section 621, et. seq. (1982).

87. 38 U.S.C., Section 2014 (1982).

88. 38 U.S.C., Section 2021 (1982).

89. 29 U.S.C., Section 701, et. seq. (1982).

90. 29 U.S.C., Section 794 (1982).

91. 29 U.S.C., Section 793 (1982).

92. 29 C.F.R., Section 32.3 (1985).

93. Ibid.

94. 29 C.F.R., Section 32.13 (1985).

95. 29 C.F.R., Section 1605 (1985).

96. 29 C.F.R., Section 1605.1 (1985).

97. 29 C.F.R., Section 1605.2 (1985); See also, *Trans World Airlines, Inc. v. Hardison*, 432 U.S. 63 (1977).

98. 29 C.F.R., Section 1605.2 (1985).

99. 29 C.F.R., Section 1605.3 (1985).

100. Ibid.

101. 29 U.S.C., Section 157 (1982).

102. 29 U.S.C., Section 158(a)(1) (1982).

103. *Beth Israel Hosp. v. NLRB*, 437 U.S. 483 (1978).

104. *Wright Line*, 251 NLRB 1083 (1980), enforced, 662 F.2d 899 (1st Cir. 1981).

105. 29 U.S.C., Section 158(g) (1982).

106. *Montefiore Hosp. & Medical Center v. NLRB*, 621 F.2d 510, 515-516 (2d Cir. 1980).

107. Ibid., 516.

108. Ibid.

109. *NLRB v. J. Weingarten, Inc.*, 420 U.S. 251 (1975).

110. *Baton Rouge Water Works Co.*, 246 NLRB 995 (1979).

111. *Darling v. Charleston Community Memorial Hosp.*, 211 N.E.2d 253 (Ill. 1965), cert. denied, 383 U.S. 946 (1966).

112. 42 U.S.C., Section 2000e-2(a) (1982).

113. *Group Health Coop. v. King County Medical Soc'y*, 39 Wash. 2d 586, 237 P.2d 737 (1951).

114. *Sosa v. Bd. of Managers*, 437 F.2d 173, 176-177 (5th Cir. 1971).

115. *Foster v. Mobile County Hosp. Bd.*, 398 F.2d 227, 37 A.L.R.3d 637 (5th Cir. 1968).

116. *Porter Memorial Hosp. v. Harvey*, 151 Ind. App. 299, 279 N.E.2d 583 (1972).

117. *Stribling v. Jolley*, 241 Mo. App. 1123, 253 S.W.2d 519 (1952).

118. *Dillard v. Rowland*, 520 S.W.2d 81 (Mo. Ct. App. 1974).

119. *Storrs v. Lutheran Hosps & Homes Soc'y of Am.*, 609 P.2d 24 (Alaska 1980).

120. *Branch v. Hempstead County Memorial Hosp.*, 539 F. Supp. 908 (W.D. Ark. 1982).

121. Fla. Stat. Ann., Section 458.331(1)(s) (West 1981).

122. Ibid. Section 458.331(2) (West 1981).

123. *Raymond v. Cregar*, 38 N.J. 472, 185 A.2d 856 (1962).

124. *Cowan v. Gibson*, 392 S.W.2d 307 (Mo. 1965).

125. Restatement (Second) of Torts, Section 573 (1977).

126. Fla. Stat. Ann., Section 458.337(1)(b) (West 1981).

127. *Silver v. Castle Memorial Hosp. Inc.*, 53 Hawaii 475, 497 P.2d 564 (1972), cert. denied, 409 U.S. 1048 (1972).

128. *Miller v. Eisenhower Medical Center*, 27 Cal. 3d 614, 614 P.2d 258, 166 Cal. Rptr. 826 (1980) (en banc).

129. *Jefferson Parish Hosp. Dist. No. 2 v. Hyde*, No. 82-1031 (U.S. Mar. 27, 1984).

130. Ibid., Slip op. at 14 (O'Connor, J., concurring).

131. 15 U.S.C., Section 1 (1982).

132. John D. Steele, "History, Administration and Jurisdiction," *Missouri Workers' Compensation Law,* (MOBARCLE, the Missouri Bar Association, 1982): 1-2

133. Ibid.

134. William F. Prosser, *Law of Torts,* 4th Ed. St. Paul, Minn. West Publishing Co. 1971, 530.

135. Ibid.

136. Mo. Rev. Stat., Section 287.030, 1(3).

137. *Shireman v. Rainer Home Furnishers, Inc.*, 402 S.W. 2d 64 (Mo. App. 1966).

138. *Orphant v. St. Louis State Hosp.*, 441 S.W. 2d 355, (Mo. 1969).

139. *Evard v. Woman's Home Companion Reading Club*, 234 Mo. App. 760, 122 S.W. 2d 51,54 (1938).

140. Adrian DeYong, "Arising Out of and In the Course of Employment," *Missouri Workers' Compensation Law*, Mo. Bar CLE, the Missouri Bar Association, 1982, 5-4.

141. Ibid, 5-20.

142. Rex R. Redhair and Bart E. Eisfelder, "Procedures and Proceedings," *Missouri Workers' Compensation Law*, Mo. Bar CLE, the Missouri Bar Association 1982, 8-3.

143. "Update on Missouri: Workers' Compensation Law," Daniel K. Atwill, Paper delivered at the Missouri Workers' Compensation Law Seminar, Columbia, Missouri, 1983.

CHAPTER SIX

ADVERSE OCCURRENCE SCREENING AND INVESTIGATION

Gary P. Kraus, Nancy J. Sublette, and David Tapp

In the medical malpractice or professional liability defense field, the risk manager is a key player in the investigative process. The risk manager functions as the advocate of the health facility, and his or her position within the organization provides a unique posture in the area of investigation. The risk manager has the ability to build bridges between different departments and to establish lines of communication and alliances that will stand outside any interdepartmental jealousies or rivalries. The effective risk manager has already built bridges to the medical staff, to employees, and to the administration as well as to all other affiliated branches of the institution in order to facilitate his or her work, particularly during the investigation process. The risk manager is an insider, and therefore can conduct a more candid investigation than anyone from the outside. It is extremely important in the investigation that the risk manager get candid reviews and candid appraisals from people who are involved in the potential compensable event (PCE). An outside investigator is always an outsider and will not have the candid rapport with the employees of the institution that the risk manager should have.

The risk manager should assume a leading role in the investigation, even if the institution is insured by a commercial insurance carrier. Experience has shown that even when an attorney is involved and suit has been filed by the plaintiff, the risk manager should be on hand with the attorney, to show the involved employees that the institution is behind them and is looking after their best interest. Only in this manner will the involved employee be completely relaxed and able to give a complete, accurate, and candid recount of the facts that led to the incident giving rise to the lawsuit or claim. Without this candid approach, the institution or its insurer will be unable to make a valid decision supported by documentation regarding whether any actual legal liability attaches to the event. Without such a review, one will not be able to judge accurately whether the case should be one for settlement or for defense.

The investigation process should lead eventually to such a decision. Without a complete and accurate investigation, however, no one is in a position to make an informed judgment. It is usually very unpleasant for the institution or its insurance carrier to have surprises occur later in the case that should have been discovered early on had the investigation been completed properly and comprehensively. Decisions are often based on the investigation by the risk manager and/or the investigator for the insurance company, and a defense strategy is often based on this investigation as well. The investigation process is also the mechanism for the beginning of discovery in the event the claim turns into a lawsuit at a later date. If an incomplete or inaccurate investigation results, the claim may lead the attorney down false paths, which wastes the time of the defense as well as the money of the defendant. It is entirely proper for the defense attorney to charge for the investigation time necessary to accurately and thoroughly assess the case. The attorney defending the institution, either on behalf of the self-insured facility or on behalf of the insurance carrier, charges for his or her time by the hour. Therefore an early and thorough investigation will point the attorney in the direction that needs to be followed and will ultimately save defense dollars for the institution or its insurance company.

Many insurance companies will request that the risk manager turn over all case information and not become further involved with the investigation, except on a request basis by either the company or its counsel. We take issue with this position and feel that the risk manager, who is more familiar with the operations of the institution than any outside investigator, must of necessity be intimately involved in the total investigation process from beginning to end. The risk manager should be thoroughly acquainted with the policies and procedures manual of the institution and can thereby save an outside investigator many hours of work reviewing the manual. The risk manager is also acquainted with or has access to the work schedules of any employees who may need to be interviewed, and is therefore much more capable than an outside investigator of arranging the schedule of the employees so as not to interfere with their jobs. The outside investigator may be an expert in the field of professional or other forms of liability claims management as they relate to health facilities, but that investigator may not be thoroughly familiar with procedures that are followed in the institution that he or she is investigating. The risk manager who is involved in the investigating process is much more attuned to the local nuances and should be an invaluable help to the independent investigator.

There is another reason the risk manager needs to be involved in the investigative process even when the insurance company is involved: The risk manager is usually aware of the total picture of PCEs and is therefore able to give guidance to the employees and management of the institution in preventing a repeat of the event that precipitated the claim or suit. It reflects negatively on the risk management function when several PCEs of the same type reoccur on a rather frequent basis. The risk manager should be able to recognize the PCE and devise preventive methods, so that repeat performances do not occur.

Risk managers must be aware of the law in their state regarding comparative fault. For example, in Missouri, *Gustafson v. Benda*[1] was the case where the State Supreme Court did away with contributory negligence and adopted comparative fault. Risk managers must make themselves aware of the changes in the law of their jurisdiction, since this will have a direct bearing on the investigation. A person considering comparative fault in the investigative process should always keep in mind during interviews and when examining records that, if they are able to show that there was negligence on the part of the plaintiff or another outside defendant, it could potentially reduce the award if at a later trial judgment is rendered against the facility. In some states, contributory negligence is still the law, and this should also be kept in mind during an investigation, because by establishing this defense, the defendant may be able to defeat the plaintiff's case or at least reduce any potential damages. The application of legal principles to the investigation process may also reduce the evaluation of the settlement value of a claim or lawsuit. In the event the risk manager or the investigator is able to develop defenses in these areas, the matter should be taken to legal counsel for their evaluation and possible direction of further investigation before making a firm decision either to defend or to settle that claim.

The Potential Compensable Event

A potential compensable event (PCE) is an unplanned situation associated with an exposure area that has or is perceived to have an unfavorable or an unacceptable consequence sufficient to warrant compensation or other financial consideration. Others define a PCE as a "disability caused by health care management."[2] Numerous terms are used in the industry to describe situations that may or may not be the same as a PCE. For example, the terms *incident, adverse event, misadventure,* and *occurrence* are frequently used. Therefore, it is important to understand that to determine a PCE requires the application of a test or one's experience to the facts in order to determine whether the situation is one in which the risk manager should take action or simply observe. The common law test of negligence (i.e., duty, breach of duty, causation, and damages) is the obvious application of a rule of law, which if present creates a prima facie case. Situations where these elements are present are obvious PCE's, particularly, if damages are significant. When the risk manager may have to allocate resources and perhaps even defend a case, regardless of whether the test of negligence fails or is questionable, a PCE also exists. Therefore, PCEs include not only obvious and serious misadventures, but also those actions perceived by the patient or the patient's family to be substandard to the degree that they personally or through a representative raise a question of negligence, bad outcome, or general dissatisfaction.

In the mind of the patient or family member, an event is compensable if the patient sustains an outcome that is attributable to institutional or professional performance below the standard that is commonly expected. Consequently, a PCE is also an event that, in the patient's opinion, creates an unfavorable situation. Examples of easily recognizable PCEs are 1) unplanned removal, injury, or repair of an organ during surgery, 2) neurological deficit present at discharge that was not present on admission; 3) falls from beds resulting in fractures; 4) unexpected deaths, particularly of children. There are other events that may not be perceived as PCEs by a risk manager but probably should be classified as such, because they are perceived by patients as substandard care. Examples of only a few are 1) failure to explain complications such as infections as well as other issues associated with informed consent; 2) common accidents sustained by children, but occurring within the health care environment, such as falling from a chair and receiving a minor laceration; 3) administrative problems that raise questions about the physician's or provider's commitment to a patient's care, such as the unexplained absence of the primary physician with care being provided by a colleague unknown to the patient.

A situation often becomes a PCE if the patient or family members feel that wrong has been done or something is owed them. This happens more frequently in situations where doctor-patient communications are not strong. For example, a case in which a patient must return to the operating room for bleeding is usually an obvious PCE, but it may not be one unless the patient or family perceives an error rather than merely a possible, expectable complication. These cases demonstrate the importance of positive communication between the physician and the patient or family on medical-legal issues. A return to the operating room to remove a forgotten sponge has a much greater chance of resulting in a claim or litigation, despite the physician-patient relationship. In such cases, early intervention, for example, agreeing to cancel charges or offering other consideration often can prevent a claim or suit. An event should also be classified as a PCE if the person committing the act both views the result as a bad outcome and is critical of his or her own performance.

Frequently, PCEs do not become known until long after the fact, because the client involved was hesitant to criticize his or her care during hospitalization, but once the patient is at home and feeling better, the "injustice" becomes paramount. PCEs, therefore, should be identified at the time of the incident, or when perceived and reported by physicians and staff, or when the patient's dissatisfaction with a bad outcome is perceived, so that early intervention can take place. More than dollars can be involved in a claim against an institution. When the case is evaluated through the eyes of a juror, loss can occur in terms of reputation and goodwill as well as the resources needed to defend the provider, even if the case is viewed as frivolous.

When a contact is made through the risk manager's office regarding a situation, whether it is referred to as an incident, an occurrence, a misadventure, an adverse event, a management variance, or by some other name, a screening must take place to determine its significance. One should attempt to screen out all situations that do not meet any of the above tests for a PCE. This generally should eliminate a very large percentage of contacts which one may wish to label as management variances. Our experience has shown that only about 5 percent of all contacts with the risk management office regarding patient care are PCEs, the balance being benign events with no sequel. The majority of contacts that are not PCEs are nevertheless important sources of quality assurance information and should be saved for risk management information purposes as described in Chapter 4. The identification and disposition of PCEs are what separates the role of risk management from that of quality assurance.

The 1976 California Medical Insurance Feasibility Study[3] found that 4.65 percent of all hospitalized patients experienced temporary or permanent disability as a result of their health care management. These events were further reviewed by a physicians' attorney group, and it was determined that 17 percent of admitted patients might have won compensation if the cases had been brought to litigation.[4]

For those events labeled PCEs by the risk manager, decisions must be made whether any action should be taken to investigate the situation. In some cases, the risk manager will have lost the initiative for early intervention due to delay or other circumstances. Usually, in such cases the only option left is to wait and see whether the patient or his or her representative recontacts the institution with a complaint. In those cases reported soon enough for early intervention, the risk manager has an opportunity to attempt to mitigate the damages sustained, if they are real, or to attempt to placate the patient or the patient's family if there is only a perceived wrong or maltreatment. These can be collectively referred to as "action cases." Those cases in which the risk manager determines that some action should be taken, but no claims have been made by an attorney, perhaps can be disposed of through early intervention, with an agreement being reached with the patient, family, or representative to waive charges or even make a cash settlement. Other PCEs for which action is necessary are those in which claims have been filed on behalf of the injured party by a representative, usually an attorney, in the form of a claim or lawsuit.

The institution may also have a clause in its insurance contract requiring that the insurance company be notified about certain events. The types of cases that must be reported should be clearly understood and may well be the same events described above as PCEs. However, insurance companies generally only desire to be notified of PCEs that are serious, as judged either by the outcome or by an overt gesture on the part of the patient or his or her representative.

PCEs and Occurrence Screening

PCEs usually come to the attention of the risk manager through persons who were associated with the misadventure. However, there are other paths for identifying them. One such method is by occurrence screening, which is the generic screening of medical records for a variety of reasons, including the search for cases with potential liability. Occurrence screening is becoming popular, with emphasis being placed on "preventive litigation," and is utilized by a number of medical centers. Occurrence screening can be carried out while the patient is in the facility (concurrent screening) or retrospectively. Concurrent screening is more desirable for both patient care and risk management purposes because it provides the opportunity to alter treatment and perhaps prevent a worse outcome. It also permits early intervention if a bad outcome results, provided the facility has an active early resolution program. Occurrence screening is simply a method of screening to identify problems associated with quality assurance and risk management; when conducted concurrently with inpatient admission, it is used for preventing and mitigating iatrogenic misadventures.

Many institutions are duplicating manpower and physicians' time in reviewing the same record for different reasons. Some of the purposes for reviewing charts are 1) utilization review, which is designed to look for inappropriate admissions or to monitor the length of stay; 2) infection control, which is the monitoring of the incidence of nosocomial infections; 3) morbidity and mortality review, for determining the cause and outcome of medical care. Occurrence screening can serve all of these functions if the criteria are well outlined and the staff appropriately trained.

One hospital that uses occurrence screening is Good Samaritan Medical Center in Phoenix, Arizona.[5] Good Samaritan's Medical Management Analysis System is a comprehensive, systematic approach to hospital quality assurance, utilization, and risk management. The screening criteria for this program are adapted from those developed for the California Medical Insurance Feasibility Study.[6] At Good Samaritan, all patient charts are reviewed by six nurses with utilization review experience at the time the patient is admitted, every 4 days thereafter, and after discharge.[7]

Implementation of a screening process involves a systems approach. After the screening tool is developed, criteria for review, selection and training of reviewer, reporting of findings, and subsequent activities must be defined. Quality assurance customarily coordinates this activity, which also involves the peer review, utilization review, medical records, pharmacy, safety, and infection control committees, and any other committees that resolve systems problems once identified. The medical staff needs to be included in all stages of the process to ensure that the systems' objectives are met.

Standard screening forms are available from many sources, such as the American Hospital Association, Division of Quality Control Management. Many institutions and medical staffs choose to create their own screening format. Because of geographic, population, and personal circumstances, the kinds of occurrences may vary. Occurrence screening tools center around high-risk departments, frequently performed procedures with associated risk, and any other activities or places where screening is deemed necessary (see Chapter 8).

Various sources provide criteria to be used in monitoring patients, and some are offered through proprietary consulting firms. One such set of criteria for patient monitoring, from the American Hospital Association, is listed below.[8]

1. Hospitalization at this or any other acute care hospital, prior to this admission: patient age 65 years to 6 months.

2. Hospital incurred trauma.

3. Adverse drug reaction while patient in hospital.

4. Patient transferred from general care to special care or isolation unit, e.g., ICU, CCU isolation.

5. Patient transferred to another acute care facility.

6. Patient returned to operating room on this admission.

7. Patient surgery for repair of a laceration, perforation, tear or puncture of an organ subsequent to the performance of an invasive procedure.

8. Unplanned removal or repair of an organ or part of an organ during an operative procedure.

9. Acute myocardial infarction and surgical procedure on the same day.

10. Wound infection present on last full day prior to or day of discharge.

11. Neurological deficit (not present at admission or prior to surgery) on last full day prior to and/or day of discharge.

12. Death (if patient died, don't screen for Criteria 13-17).

13. Cardiac or respiratory arrest.

14. Discharge with indwelling urinary catheter.

15. Patients with temperatures greater or equal to 101° F (38.3° C) a full day prior to and on day of discharge.

16. Parenteral analgesics last full day prior to and/on the day of discharge.

17. Instructions to patient undocumented.

18. Transfusions.

19. Other complications.

Any one of these criteria could reveal a PCE that needs to be brought to the risk manager's attention. Exceptions to these criteria generally involve planned rather than unplanned events. How the risk manager is apprised of the screening information depends on the system and the organization structure; however, the risk manager or his or her designee should sort through the objective data collected by the screener to identify PCEs and should classify incidents into action and no-action categories. Often a PCE will be identified, but there will be no claim or dissatisfaction expressed by the patient or family. The problem can then be objectively evaluated and resolved before a repeat incident occurs, thus preventing future PCEs. Examples of such events are provided below:

1. A patient sustains a 1-centimeter superficial electrical burn on the back during surgery. The burn is noticed by nursing that evening. Investigation reveals a faulty ground plate which is replaced.

2. A patient returns to the hospital with nausea and vomiting after having been discharged the day before. During the investigation it is discovered that a new physician discharged the patient after receiving a letter from utilization review indicating that, unless there was a major complication, insurance would not cover continued hospitalization. The new physician is educated about the utilization review process.

A generic screening tool will indicate problems in the health care system by identifying specific areas that need closer monitoring and or specific screening tools. Operating rooms, the emergency department, obstetrics, and intensive care units are generally recognized as common high-risk areas. Screening tools specific to these departments will surface PCEs that are not apparent in generic screens. Generic screening in a hospital may reveal a high number of quality issues on a particular medical service or nursing ward. This pattern would be more closely monitored with the aid of a screening tool. A screening tool specific to an area should outline what could happen that needs to be brought to the attention of the risk manager and/or the quality assurance coordinator. An example of an occurrence screening tool for the operating and recovery rooms was published by *Occurrence,* the risk management newsletter of the Chicago Hospital Risk Pooling Programs and appears below:[9]

1. Wrong patient operated upon.

2. Wrong procedure performed.

3. No written consent or improper consent (exceptions).

4. Unplanned removal or repair of organ or body parts not in consent.

5. Patient injured during transfer to and from operating room and/or recovery room.

6. Patient burned from equipment.

7. Unplanned disconnection of equipment where there is potential for injury.

8. Incorrect needle, sponge, or instrument count.

9. Instrument breakage.

10. Foreign object or material found.

11. Break in sterile technique.

12. Patient operated on for repair of laceration, perforation,tear or puncture of organ subsequent to invasive procedure.

13. Return to surgery for repair or removal of organ or body part damaged in surgery.

14. Adverse results of anesthesia.

15. Intubations resulting in injury (including teeth).

16. Post-op nerve damage.

17. Cardiac arrest.

18. Respiratory arrest.

19. Acute MI during or following surgery.

20. Death.

21. Any untoward patient reaction in the operating or recovery room.

Concurrent collection of this data enables the risk manager to take some preemptive measures to negate the possibility of a claim. A retrospective screen only alerts the risk manager to the occurrence of a PCE, allowing only classification of the case as one for action versus no action. Collecting and trending the results of screening will alert the risk manager to patterns. Obvious patterns place the institution at high risk, and profiling these patterns will raise quality-of-care issues that must be addressed. Prevention of PCEs is a direct result of occurrence screening for risk management. What appear on the surface to be unrelated events may have a commonality of personnel which trending will identify.

The advantages of occurrence screening in a health care facility are numerous. Efficiency in reviewing charts is an initial gain. A decreasing number of events discussed in peer review conferences should occur, since these issues are being dealt with through quality assurance. Occurrence screening has the potential to reduce the number of claims made against the hospital. The risk manager is in a better position to deal with PCEs if he or she is aware of the incident, particularly if this awareness occurs at a time when resolution of the incident is possible to avoid a claim or litigation.

Record and Evidence Preservation

Generally the first action to be taken in the event of a dispute is preservation of the medical record of the potential plaintiff. The medical record should be complete, it should be signed by the attending physician, and it should be preserved in its original state. Once a PCE has been identified, the patient's medical record should be segregated from other medical records and kept in a separate location in the medical records area. It is usually devastating to a defendant if the plaintiff is able to show that the medical record has been amended, tampered with, or in some manner changed after the patient has been discharged from the hospital.

Any changes in the medical record or correction of errors should be noted at the time, and the error should be lined out only once so that the original wording is still legible. A brief explanation of why the record is in error and any additional notations should be made beside the correction or immediately after if space is available. The medical record should be kept in its original state, and it should not be reduced to microfilm or destroyed so long as there is a potential for legal action involving that chart. Destruction of a medical record is always frustrating and is sometimes unexplainable to a jury when the record is to be used as evidence in a court of law. The original record kept in its original state is probably the best tool that defendants have. Many plaintiffs' attorneys will request copies of the medical record as soon as they have been hired by the plaintiff. They will at some later date before the trial compare their photocopies with the original record to see if changes have been made in the original after they received their copies. Obviously, if changes have been made, the plaintiff's attorney will exploit this fact to full advantage before a jury. If the plaintiff's counsel is able to establish that the medical record has been sanitized, there is real danger that a jury will disregard the substance of the dispute and punish the defendant for fraud and deceit.

Physicians' office records are important to the defense of any claim or lawsuit. The risk manager should obtain the office records of the treating physician both before and after hospitalization. The risk manager should obtain a medical authorization from the potential plaintiff allowing access to any and all medical information regarding his or her care and treatment. It is not suggested that the risk manager attempt to acquire physicians' office records without the plaintiff's medical authorization form. To do so could result in the record being excluded as evidence. It is important to examine the physician's office records to see if the complaints of the potential plaintiff are consistent with the complaints with which the patient was hospitalized. It is also important to examine the physician's office records after the patient's hospitalization to determine if the patient has made a complete recovery from the occurrence that gave rise to the PCE. If the office records show a complete recovery with no subsequent disabilities, the plaintiff's attorney will not be able to establish large damages resulting from the event that occurred in the hospital.

Frequently there are outpatient records that involve the potential plaintiff. During the investigation process, one should check with the outpatient office of the facility and with the emergency department for other records that may be important in defending a claim or lawsuit. One such area is evidence of prior complaints by the same patient of the same nature as the injury or damages that are now the subject of the claim or lawsuit. In other words, was the patient complaining of the same problem before hospitalization that is now being alleged to be a result of the hospitalization?

Another area that must be considered is the personnel records of employees involved in the PCEs. These records will in most cases be subpoenaed by the plaintiff's attorney. Whether or not these records can be obtained will depend upon the law of the state in which the facility is located. The risk manager needs to know immediately upon the occurrence of a PCE whether there are adverse comments in the personnel records of the employees involved. It could have a devastating effect if the employee had been counseled previously regarding the same activity that precipitated the present claim or lawsuit.

The risk manager should advise all allied departments to sequester all records of patients who have sustained a PCE. Specifically, the risk manager should notify the radiology department that all original x-rays should be retained in the department and not released to any outside source. It is very embarrassing when the plaintiff has the original x-ray records and the defending institution must try to obtain copies of its own records. Hospital policy should address this issue and prohibit original x-rays from being allowed outside the institution. Copies can be provided to any party who has legal access or legitimate medical need for the records, but only copies should be provided and originals must be kept within the department. Even when there is no lawsuit pending, it is embarrassing to a facility not to be able to provide x-rays to medical personnel involved in the patient's subsequent treatment. X-rays given in their original state to outside sources are always subject to disappearance or loss.

The laboratory should also be advised to preserve test results, tissue samples, and related information regarding a potential litigant against the facility. As a defendant, one does not prejudice one's position in any manner by refusing to supply original x-rays, lab results, tissue samples, and the like to an outside source. Copies of these things can be provided at cost to the plaintiff, and therefore the originals should never leave the facility absent a court order.

Incident, variance, or occurrence reports of PCEs should be preserved in their original state but must be protected from discovery. In the self-insured institution, consultation with legal counsel before litigation should provide guidance as to the laws of the state regarding discovery and how to protect these records from the plaintiff and his or her attorney. As stated in Chapter 4, the incident report is very important to the risk manager, since the first notice of a PCE should be contained in the record as well as other information made at or near the time of the misadventure. The record could be used to support the investigation to be undertaken by the risk manager.

Inquiry Procedures

The risk manager who is undertaking the investigation of a PCE must become familiar with the procedures necessary to preserve the evidence that he or she has been able to develop. All risk managers should be prepared to tape-record conversations of persons involved in the PCE, including potential plaintiffs and employees and perhaps even physicians. If tape recording is not possible or it is too intimidating to the patient or witness, then handwritten statements must be obtained. After the medical records have been reviewed, these statements are the backbone of the investigation. Statements are the best way of preserving the recollection of the actors involved in the PCE and should be made as soon as possible after the incident. Every statement, whether tape recorded or handwritten, should contain several elements. It should state the identity and the employment status of the person being interviewed. It should state the marital status, number of children, and all relevant family information regarding a potential plaintiff. It should contain a complete description of the situation that led to the misadventure and all the information regarding the event itself. It should also list the measures taken to alleviate the condition after the event occurred. The statement should also reflect the knowledge and consent of the individual being interviewed, and the individual's signature should be obtained if it is a handwritten statement. The statement will not necessarily be admissible as evidence in a court of law; its purpose rather is for finding the facts surrounding the event and possibly impeaching the plaintiff at a later deposition, should the suit proceed to that stage.

The risk manager or the insurance investigator should make contact with the potential claimant as quickly as possible after notification of the claim. Experience has shown that the faster the contact is made with the potential claimant, the better the results of the contact. It usually works to the advantage of the facility if contact is made with potential plaintiffs before their leaving the hospital, provided notification has reached the risk management office in time. It is not necessary that settlement be made at that time, but only that the matter be looked into and the patient assured that he or she will be contacted when the investigation is complete. This tactic has on many occasions defused a potentially explosive situation and maintained a line of communication with the potential plaintiff. So long as negotiations continue and lines of communication are maintained, the chances of the potential plaintiff seeking legal counsel are reduced. During the first meeting with the potential plaintiff, a short but accurate statement of the misadventure should be obtained. In that initial interview, it is important to know some of the potential plaintiff's ideas regarding where he or she perceives liability to lie. The potential plaintiff should be asked to express what he or she feels was wrong, or what caused the event, and also what injuries were sustained. The potential plaintiff should be encouraged to express details about his or her injuries, since this may tend to limit the damages alleged at a future date.

Contact with involved employees is essential to the inquiry procedure. Statements from the involved employees taken on or near the date of the event are the best method of preserving recollection of the facts associated with the PCE. The employees' statements should contain everything that they can recall regarding the patient. They should contain their recollection of the event itself, the damages sustained by the patient that were caused by the incident, and all steps taken to limit the damage or alleviate the problem. Often it is several years after the event before the employees' depositions will be taken in a lawsuit. The statement taken at or near the time of the event will be very helpful in refreshing an employee's memory of the patient and other activities that were going on at the time. All employees from whom depositions are to be taken should review the medical chart of the plaintiff. However, years after the event most employees will have no clear recollection of the details of the case, much less of any relevant facts surrounding the case that may have precipitated the lawsuit.

The recollections of any physicians involved in the care of the plaintiff are important and must be included in the investigative process. Statements from the involved physicians would be nice to have; however, in the real world few physicians are willing to make statements regarding the treatment of one of their patients who is now a plaintiff, unless they feel they themselves are not at risk of being named a defendant. The risk manager should have previously built bridges to the medical staff, so that he or she can approach the physician on an informal basis and obtain valuable information. If an extemporaneous meeting does occur with the physician, the risk manager should immediately write a memo for the file, recording the significant information gained from the conversation.

Witness statements are essential to the investigation of a PCE. They should be taken as near to the time of the incident as possible. However, without an efficient information system much time often passes before witnesses are identified and contacted. The names and addresses of witnesses should always be listed on the report that is forwarded to the risk manager. One of the essential parts of of a witness statement is the witness's recollection of what the involved employees did to alleviate the problem. Another important part is the witness's recollection of whether or not the potential plaintiff followed the instructions of the nursing staff and physicians. The classic example is the patient who falls and fractures a hip after the physician and the nursing staff have ordered the patient to be on bed rest and all precautions have been taken to keep the patient in bed. Does the witness have a recollection of the nursing staff advising the patient not to be out of bed without assistance? Does the witness recall the location of the call light? Was the call light attached to the pillow within easy reach of the patient, and did the patient attempt to summon the nursing staff before getting out of bed? If the patient did not follow the instructions of the nursing staff and physicians, there may be an element of comparative negligence to consider, since the patient contributed to his or her own injury.

Physicians who were not involved in the care of the patient but are respected members of the medical staff should be contacted on an informal basis for an opinion as to whether or not the care was proper. Again, if the risk manager has built bridges to the medical staff and has established good interpersonal relations, the informal approach can elicit valuable informal opinions. The informal opinions of physicians not involved can keep the risk manager from going off on irrelevant tangents and spending many hours of fruitless time investigating areas that are not important. Often, informal contacts with physicians who are not involved in the affair will assist the risk manager in finding the expert witnesses necessary in defending against the claim or lawsuit.

Medical authorization forms should be obtained at the first contact with the potential plaintiff. The forms should be dated, signed, and kept in the risk manager's file. The medical record request form should be photocopied and the copy sent to the medical facility or physician from whom records are being requested . One should always advise the person from whom medical records are being requested that the costs will be borne by the requesting institution.

In cases where the claim is very serious, with the potential for large losses, the risk manager should try to obtain authorization to acquire the potential plaintiff's employment records. Frequently, however, the plaintiff's counsel will resist, especially if the records contain facts that reflect negatively on the claim or lawsuit.

These inquiry procedures are designed to help reach conclusions regarding legal liability that are necessary to determine whether the case is defensible or not. The risk manager who has completed the proper inquiry procedures should have sufficient data from which to make decisions regarding the issue of liability. The data available should not only reflect on whether or not the institution is at risk, but also on the risk status of all other parties who could be jointly liable with the institution. The data should also cover all the other necessary elements of the case so that the trial lawyer will have little investigative work to do.

Witness and Actor Interviews

In the preceding section the content of statements taken from people who had contact with the PCE—employees, the potential plaintiff, and witnesses—was discussed. This section provides more detail about the elements of the statements to be taken from the parties. The statement taken from the potential plaintiff should include the following:

1. Identification (name, address, etc.) of the person giving the statement

2. Identification of the person as the potential plaintiff

3. What the person saw or knows by some other means regarding the PCE

4. Any special knowledge the person has, whether medical or related to some other aspect of the event

5. Any information about the person's employment in the health field or any

other type of background that gives the person special knowledge of the medical industry

6. The cause of the hospitalization or the diagnosis

7. Prior hospitalizations, their locations, and the names of treating physicians

8. What injuries the potential plaintiff is claiming and how the potential plaintiff feels he or she was injured

9. Whether any corrective treatments were provided for the real or perceived injuries

10. Whether the potential plaintiff lost work because of the injury

11. Whether the potential plaintiff has filed any prior claims or there are any current claims or lawsuits pending

12. Any special knowledge of witnesses or other plaintiffs to the event

13. Any ideas about how the injury occurred and how it might have been prevented.

A witness will of course have less knowledge about background information than the potential plaintiff or an employee involved in the PCE. Witness statements should contain the following:

1. Identification of the person giving the statement

2. Identification of how the witness is involved, and whether the witness is any relation to the potential claimant

3. What the witness saw or knows about the event

4. Any special knowledge the witness has by being in some way associated with the medical field

5. The witness's place of employment, particularly if employed in the medical industry

6. Knowledge of the witness about the event and where the witness was when the event occurred

7. Whether the witness has any ideas as to how the injury occurred and how it could have been prevented.

By following these guidelines the investigator should be able to obtain a grasp of the facts that caused the PCE and any steps that were taken to minimize the damages. The investigator and the attorney for the defendants should use this information in connection with other data uncovered in the investigation, so that an accurate decision regarding legal liability and damages can be made.

Case Verification

In all reports of PCEs, the risk manager, as the investigator, should be in a position to verify that the event actually took place. An incident report identifying a PCE is the starting place, although one will not gain a full appreciation of the event strictly from the report. In many settings, the incident report will identify an event that took place, but it will not show the damages that occurred. In many instances, for example, the original incident report will show that the patient fell while going from the bed to the bathroom. It may not be until a day or two later that x-rays taken after the fall show that the patient has suffered a fractured hip or some other injury. The medical records would show that a qualified physician made the diagnosis, which verifies that the injury the patient complained of did actually occur. It is usually possible to get a complete diagnosis from the medical records; therefore, if the investigator follows up by checking the medical records and finds that there is a report from a qualified radiologist that states that the patient has a fracture, and if the x-ray was taken immediately following a fall, it can be surmised that the fall was the cause of the fracture.

Once the above tasks have been completed, the investigator, whether the risk manager or an outside insurance investigator, can decide if the event actually took place and the injury did result therefrom. It is then appropriate to make contact with the injured patient. It is suggested that during this first contact one be as noncommital as possible about whether or not payment will be made. The investigator should advise the patient or the patient's family that an investigation is being conducted and that a follow-up visit will be made either in person or by phone. It is wise for the investigator making the contact to request a definite appointment time and follow up at the appointed time. To make an indefinite appointment to talk with the potential plaintiff or his or her family at some time in the future does not put the potential plaintiff at ease as does a definite time for the investigator to make contact. If the investigator feels that it will take 5 days to complete the necessary investigation, he or she should promise to contact the potential plaintiff immediately thereafter, set an appointment for a specific time, and make sure that it is kept. Even if the investigator has not completed the investigation and will require further time, the appointment should be kept and the potential plaintiff advised the person at that time that further investigation is necessary. The investigator should then set a future appointment and be sure that it too is kept.

In case verification, the investigator should always follow up with records of subsequent treatment. These treatments may be recorded in the original medical records, they may be late follow-up visits to the doctor's office, or they may be new admissions to the hospital. The investigator should have obtained the medical authorization on his or her first contact and should follow up by ordering records of the later treatments. Subsequent treatment records will establish the extent of the injury and will also show the results of treatments needed to alleviate problems caused by the injury. The injured individual may have sustained some permanent disability, but it will be impossible to establish this fact without follow-up medical records. Sometimes one finds in later medical records that the treatment was successful and that the potential plaintiff has no disability relative to the event.

It is important to obtain professional opinions on an informal basis regarding the care given before and at the time of the PCE as well as during follow-up treatment. In the example in which the patient fell and fractured a hip while going from the bed to the bathroom, it would be important to obtain a professional opinion from an orthopedist as to the extent of the injury and the possibility of resulting disability. Another step in case verification would be to check with a specialist about the physician's orders before the event that caused the problem, to see if they were appropriate to the condition of the patient before the event. Again using the example of the patient who fell going from bed to bathroom, one desires to know if in the informal opinion of the expert, the treating physician gave appropriate orders for bathroom privileges. One should also be alert in reviewing records to whether the staff has followed the orders of the physician as they were written in the chart.

Once these tasks have been completed and the information is ready, placed in the file, and summarized, the investigation is finished and the risk manager is ready to answer the ultimate question: "Does legal liability exist?" When this conclusion is reached, the risk manager is then in a position to decide whether the claim should be settled or defended. Once that decision has been made, one can then move on to the next step, the evaluation of the case.

Case Evaluation and Decision Making

The ultimate authority of a health care institution rests with its board of directors. The medical staff possess certain responsibilities, and the administration is charged with the day-to-day operation of the hospital, but the total operating authority is derived from the board. In the insured institution, the insurance company is usually the party that makes the decision whether or not the claim will be settled or defended, although this can be done with the advice and consent of the board.

In the self-insured medical center with an active and skilled investigation program, the risk manager reports directly to the board of directors or to a risk management committee, if the facility uses a board model as discussed in Chapter 2. The risk manager, after consultation with the facility administration, will be able to answer questions regarding the facility's liability and the decision whether to settle or defend the case. In some self-insured organizations, the board of directors will create a claims management subcommittee with authority to make these decisions. This committee is usually small, with an average size of three members. The risk manager usually has developed a strong relationship with the claims subcommittee because of its small size and their mutual interest and purpose. Frequently, the claims subcommittee can reach its decision over the telephone in minor cases.

If the case is one in which investigation reveals some legal liability to exist, certain elements should be considered when evaluating the dollar value of the case. The risk manager should always be aware that cases will have different values at different points in time. The earlier a settlement is made the more likely it is that a reasonable settlement can be made. Below are outlined certain costs and considerations that the risk manager must factor into a settlement offer:

1. Medical cost for treatment to correct or alleviate the condition

2. Dollar cost estimate of future medical care resulting from the event

3. Loss of income already suffered by the injured individual and his or her family

4. Future loss of income

5. Loss of consortium suffered by the spouse of the injured individual

6. Costs of legal defense.

There is no magic formula for reaching a figure after one has put the above costs on paper. It then becomes a question of judgment, to be shared by risk management, defense counsel, the administration, and the board of directors, as to how much the claim is actually worth at this time.

Decision making is easy to accomplish in cases where liability clearly exists on the part of the institution; however, when one is not sure or when one can argue that both plaintiff and defendant were jointly responsible to some degree, decision making is difficult. In close cases of liability in which the risk manager feels that there is some liability, but settlement is still preferred, it should be made clear to the injured party that, because it is a close case, the full degree of damages must be partially mitigated. Therefore, a settlement offer must take into consideration the fact that the claim is not worth as much as it would be if liability rested completely with the institution. For example, if liability were complete and the case value were $10,000, then the same case where liability was close might have only $5,000 as its settlement value.

When negotiating with the opposite party over a close case, the weaknesses of the potential plaintiff's position are the leverage factor that the risk manager must use to diminish the value of the case. Very seldom is there a case in which some element of plaintiff contribution to liability cannot be argued. Keeping this point in mind, the risk manager should develop these strengths to the institution's advantage. If, for example, the potential plaintiff did not follow the physician's orders while in the hospital, this fact must be made clear, so that the plaintiff realizes it will be used as a defense if negotiations are not successful and litigation results. By combining defenses with the specific settlement offer, one can emphasize the point that the potential plaintiff has something real to lose. If the defense's position is placed before the opposite party without the offer, or the offer without the defense, the potential plaintiff may feel that his or her case is stronger than it really is and reject the offer or demand substantially more.

Always in the area of hospital claims handling one must realize that cases that involve financial decisions will also have an effect on public relations. In most cases it is not in the best interest of the facility for the case to be made public, because of the negative impact it may have. Even though a case may be completely and totally defensible with regard to legal liability, the potential public relations impact may be such that one might wish to offer some type of consideration to keep the matter from becoming public. Public relations settlements should never be large, but should be made according to the same strategy used to handle nuisance claims, which often are settled to preclude high defense costs associated with the case and to prevent adverse publicity.

One should always be aware of the case that has high jury sympathy. Recently there has been much publicity about damaged infants whose parents are filing claims against their physicians and hospitals. There have been tremendous settlements and very high court awards across the country. Often the infant was not damaged by any negligence on the part of the physician or the hospital but simply suffered from congenital defects or other natural causes. A problem to consider is that, without liability on the part of the medical practitioners, the injured baby will receive no money and be completely unable to care for itself for its lifetime. The risk manager must recognize that the plaintiff's attorney is going to make the most of the jury's sympathy that comes with these cases; therefore, the case with high jury sympathy has some value. During the decision-making process, one should be guided by the advice of counsel, since they should have a good grasp of what juries in the locality are likely to do. The jury sympathy case ought to be evaluated with great care and skill. It may be wise to seek advice from the board, the administration, the insurer, and the defense team so that a true picture of the case can be drawn.

There will be times when the risk manager is faced with the problem of a staff doctor being a potential codefendant along with the institution. The risk manager must consider the possibility that finger pointing at the physician will result in a loss of goodwill on the part of that physician and perhaps the whole medical staff. There may well be more risk to the institution from lost goodwill of the medical staff than from the potential plaintiff. If the medical staff feels that the institution is unjustly trying to place blame on the doctors, they may become disgruntled and begin sending their patients to competing institutions, thus resulting in a serious and insured loss of revenue.

Although the risk manager must attempt to develop all possible defenses, he or she must nevertheless factor the involvement of a staff doctor and the potential for lost medical staff support and goodwill into the decision-making process. It may require that the doctor's involvement in the case not be emphasized by the risk manager. It is very vexing to the negotiator to know something that could help the institution's position yet not be able to use the information because good sense or politics so dictates. Nevertheless, this attribute is one of the virtues that separates the professional risk manager from the amateur. Generally, the decision to avoid mentioning the codefendant staff doctor is not as difficult for the self-insured institution as it is for those that are commercially insured. The obvious reason is that the self-insured institution can weigh the loss associated with the case against the potential loss from reduced revenue brought about from the loss of a doctor's referrals. Also, the self-insured institution is dealing with its own funds, and they make the decision. Not so with the commercially insured. Most insurance contracts provide for the insurer to make all settlement and strategy decisions, including the selection of defense counsel. Consequently, the insurance company is primarily interested in reducing its losses, because it is their money, and lost goodwill probably has little or no bearing on defense strategy. This is particularly true in states with comparative negligence laws, where fault can be apportioned among codefendants.

Summary

The investigation process will be conducted by the risk manager or an investigator from a commercial insurer whenever a claim or lawsuit has been filed and, ideally, whenever a serious potential compensable event (PCE) is reported. An institution that is self-insured should establish a system of early intervention to help negotiate damages, preserve evidence, and perhaps prevent lawsuits. Therefore, an investigation program should be established and utilized whenever a PCE is reported. As an insider, the institution's risk manager is in a position to perform a valuable service to both outside insurance investigators and the facility itself, because the risk manager is more knowledgeable about the operation and nuances of the institution. Also, relationships with the medical staff have probably been established that can be used to save time and money as well as elicit important informal assistance.

The purpose of the investigative process is basically to gain knowledge so that the fundamental question regarding liability can be answered. Essentially, the risk manager must decide, on the basis of the findings, if liability exists on the part of the institution, its employees, the medical staff, or other outside parties. If liability is determined to rest with the institution, then a decision must be made either to settle or to defend the case, on the basis of such factors as cost, goodwill, and adverse publicity, balanced against the risk of gaining a reputation as an easy mark for unjust suitors and unnecessarily wasting the assets of the institution.

Chapter Exercise

You are the risk manager of a self-insured hospital with a risk management program based on the board model. The risk management committee has a claims handling subcommittee consisting of three persons; a board member, the chief of staff, and the hospital administrator. You and the institution's legal counsel are staff members to the subcommittee.

You have been notified that an elderly patient (over 75) was administered an overdose of drugs, which may have contributed to his recent death.

Questions

1. Sketch out a list of tasks that you will carry out, in the order in which you will proceed.
2. List the parties whom you will contact. Assume for the balance of the questions that the overdose did contribute to the patient's demise.
3. List what questions you may wish to be answered and by whom.
4. List what decisions you would reach in the case if question 3 establishes certain facts.
5. Determine the value of the case, and list some information that you have fabricated that was used in reaching the amount.

References

1. *Gustafson v. Benda,* 661 SW2d 11, (M.Sup. Ct. en Banc 1983).

2. California Medical Association and California Hospital Association. *California Medical Insurance Feasibility Study.* San Francisco, Sutter Publications, 1977. Quoted in "Lawsuits, Doctors and Hospitals." American Society for Hospital Risk Management, Chicago. Typescript.

3. Ibid.

4. Ibid.

5. Ibid.

6. Craddick, Joyce. "Medical Management Analysis: An Innovative System for Hospital Quality Assurance," *Medical Management Analysis International* (1985): 3.

7. Ibid., p. 8.

8. Chicago Hospital Risk Pooling Program, *Occurrence* 1 (January-February 1981).

9. Ibid.

CHAPTER SEVEN

STRATEGY, SETTLEMENT TECHNIQUES, AND LITIGATION DEFENSE

Gary P. Kraus, Herb Squire, and David Tapp

We have seen in Chapter 6 that the risk manager is often the person who should conduct the investigation of general or professional liability claims. The risk manager by definition should also be the focal point for the settlement of the claim or lawsuit and the consolidation of all the elements that go into both the investigation and the settlement of the dispute. The risk manager must be a strong personality who can negotiate with both potential litigants and their attorneys on an equal footing. A risk manager who is nothing more than a conduit through which monies are paid is soon known throughout the legal community as an easy touch. Such an individual will soon find that nonmeritorious claims are being made against the facility on a regular basis, with the understanding that some amount will be paid. Conversely, the risk manager who is obstinate and refuses to pay anything will soon become inundated with lawsuits, with no prior offers to negotiate or notice having been received. It is therefore important that the risk manager maintain balance by being neither too obstinate in refusing to negotiate nor too generous in making settlements. This kind of balanced approach will only develop in an individual through experience.

Strategy and settlement techniques in the defense of professional liability claims contain an element of listening. The ability to listen, not to the words but to the underlying reasons for the claim, is elementary to being a good negotiator. Most often the potential litigant will voice many complaints and many problems, but only one is truly relevant. As a result, one may have to listen to many scenarios before one understands the real substance of the complaint, although such an understanding is necessary before settlement of the matter can be attempted. The development of a claim usually is provoked by a single action, which acts as the straw that breaks the camel's back. However, other elements go into the final making of a claim by a former patient and potential litigant. The task of the negotiator then becomes one of sifting through the collateral elements and getting to the heart of the matter, the final blow that caused the patient to decide that someone was going to pay for what happened.

The risk manager must be able to operate in this element, and of course the role varies depending upon how the institution finances its exposure. In the preceding chapter we discussed the screening of adverse occurrences and the investigative process that precede the settlement of a dispute. We now assume that the investigative process has reached the point where the risk manager and the others responsible for making such decisions have evaluated the case and have reached a conclusion about what to do with a particular claim or lawsuit. In the next section we discuss the methods by which the risk manager handles cases and the housekeeping chores necessary to keep control over pending claims and lawsuits.

Lawsuit and Claims Management Filing System

For institutions insured by commercial carriers, the claim and lawsuit management filing system may be more elementary than in situations where the facility is self-insured or has a large deductible. The risk manager nevertheless should take the lead in the negotiation of claims for facilities that are self-insured or commercially insured with large deductibles.

Both the commercially insured facility and the self-insured facility must of necessity have some system by which claims and lawsuits and their disposition are accounted for. In the commercially insured facility, it may be only necessary that the risk manager number the filing system and keep an ongoing record of cases and the dispositions made by the insurance company. The risk manager should be responsive to requests for information by the insurance company investigator. Involved in this are the bookkeeping processes that go into the keeping of records for internal purposes regarding settlements of claims and lawsuits and the amounts. A diary system that alerts the risk manager to timely review of files is also necessary. It may be that the diary system will alert the risk manager to some task that needs to be completed but has not been noticed by the insurance company representative.

A filing system becomes extremely important for self-insured health facilities and those with a large deductible; here most claims and lawsuits will be controlled by the risk manager. The process starts with the initial notification about the potential claim or lawsuit, and generally this begins with the incident report that is filed by an employee of the institution. Occasionally the risk manager will be given notice of a suit by the receipt of a summons from a circuit court. In these circumstances the risk manager is working under a time limit, generally 30 days, and must assign the case to a defense attorney so that proper defensive pleadings, such as an answer to the petition, can be filed with the court and with plaintiff's counsel. Once notified of the event by whatever method, the risk manager should establish a case file and should number the file corresponding to its position on the claims register. An example of a claims register is presented in Exhibit 7-1. Once the claim is placed in the claims register, the risk manager must determine whether the case is a professional or a general liability claim, and decide whether it should

CLAIM REGISTER

NAME OF CLAIMANT		DATE RECD	DATE OF EVENT	M or GL	BI or PD	MAJOR MINOR	Date Closed	V	AMOUNT RESERVE	AMOUNT PAID	DESCRIPTION OF ACCIDENT & INJURY
LAST	FIRST										

Exhibit 7-1 Claims register form.

```
                              File Folder Insert


Claimant's
Name:        Last, First, Initial    Date  Date  Date  Kind  How    Reopened
                                     of    Rec'd Set         Re-
                                     Event       Up          ported


Location in Hospital                 Age   Reason for Admission


Major_____

Minor_____      Date_____    BI_____   PD_____    Exp_____


                              RESERVE CHANGES

                  Date_____    BI_____   PD_____    Exp_____

                  Date_____    BI_____   PD_____    Exp_____

                  Date_____    BI_____   PD_____    Exp_____

                  Date_____    BI_____   PD_____    Exp_____

                  Date_____    BI_____   PD_____    Exp_____

Description of accident or injury:_____
_____
_____
_____
_____
```

Exhibit 7-2 File folder insert.

be classified as major or minor. This decision depends on the risk manager's assumption as to what the claim will eventually be worth. It is obvious that some claims initially thought to be minor eventually turn into major claims, and therefore the file should be changed appropriately when this happens. Besides the claims registry, one should establish a file folder with an insert providing pertinent information regarding the date and time the event took place, the time the risk manager was notified, and the method by which the risk manager was notified. Also included is the designation as to whether the case is considered a major or a minor claim (see Exhibit 7-2). At the same time, a calendar filing system should be established; this may consist of small index cards, on which pertinent information is recorded such as the name of the potential claimant, the file number, the date of the event, and the date the file was begun. The index files should be fixed according to a calendar where, for example, every 30 days the file will be pulled by index card and a review made. The calendar file card should then be used to review the cases on a periodic basis, whether it be 30, 60, or 90 days. We prefer a 30-day report, setting out the initial investigation and evaluation, followed by a 90-day report, which will contain more detail and provide updated information on the claim. The system prevents files from being lost, and a large folder with all reports and evidence can then be placed in a locked cabinet without the need to review each and every document in order to familiarize oneself with each case.

Risk managers who promise potential litigants that they will return calls, or will talk with the potential litigant at a certain time, may find that their system will not work without a calendar filing system. Failure to keep these appointments can further antagonize a potential claimant and make a bad situation worse. However, such a filing system will assure that every case is evaluated from time to time, from when it is opened until its closing, be it through a settlement, denial, or a judgment from a court.

A separate accounting system should be established for keeping track of legal and other fees paid to attorneys who defend the facility. This system can be as elaborate as the risk manager wishes to make it; however, a simple bookkeeping sheet in a loose-leaf binder setting out the names of the claimant and the defense attorney, the complaint, and a listing of the dates and amount of payments and to whom they were made is usually sufficient. Keeping account of legal fees gives accurate data regarding the cost of defense of professional and general liability claims. When the facility is anticipating purchasing insurance, potential insurers are quite interested in knowing the buyer's experience regarding legal fees. A good accounting of legal fees is impressive to an insurance underwriter and may very well result in lower premiums if one decides to become commercially insured for primary or excess insurance, or for insurance above a self-insured retention. If the facility is self-insured, an actuarial study at the end of the calendar or fiscal year is essential for the proper funding of the self-insurance trust fund. All actuaries want information on claims and the cost of legal fees. The above system is a quick and easy way to provide actuarial companies with information on the total amount spent on legal fees during the year.

The above methods have been described in traditional record keeping and accounting formats and can easily be computerized for the same reasons other office systems have been automated. Automated risk management information systems, discussed in Chapter 4, can be adopted to include accounting and calendar notice functions. The decision to automate should be based on cost effectiveness, caseload, and related factors.

Relationships With the Insurance Company

There are several situations in which commercial insurance companies will be involved in the strategy for settlement and defense of litigation. In the first-dollar-insured hospital (i.e., one whose insurance policy contains no deductible), the insurance company takes the lead and is responsible for the settlement or defense of all claims and litigation against the insured facility. The insurance company will dictate what the responsibilities of the risk manager are in regard to reporting events, providing information, and participating in negotiations. The insured hospital's risk manager should be aware of all the reporting requirements of the policy. Specifically, the risk manager must report all claims in a timely manner. This is critical in claims-made-type policies. There is usually a requirement in the policy that the hospital will report any claim as quickly as possible. There are also certain requirements for the reporting of particular types of potential compensable events (PCEs). These matters will all be contained in the professional and general liability policy, and they should be reviewed by the risk manager and be known and understood in detail. Specific requirements for the reporting of particular types of events, such as the loss of a limb, the loss of an eye, an event with significant neurological deficit, death, and other serious outcomes, might be required. Note that there is a difference between these reports and a claim—the insurance company is requiring notification as soon as the event occurs regardless of whether or not a claim is made. Failure to report these serious events in a timely manner may void the policy and the requirement that the insurance company provide a defense if at a later time a claim is received alleging professional negligence. Note also that the insurance company requires that the insured facility cooperate in the investigation and settlement of the claim. The risk manager must understand that the insurance company could invoke a noncooperation exclusion in the policy, if there are requests by the insurance company that are ignored by the risk manager.

The risk manager should have complete knowledge of all policy exclusions. The insurance company has the right to refuse to handle a claim if it falls within the policy exclusion, or to handle it only under a reservation-of-rights letter not waiving any defense that the insurance company has under the policy.

Failure to follow the terms of the policy can void coverage and leave the institution believing it is insured, when in fact it is self-insured or bare. In such a situation the institution has an unfunded liability, which may have to be funded from operating capital and not paid by the insurance company. Any question that the risk manager has regarding the policy terms and conditions should be addressed in writing to the insurance company, with the answers received in writing. Through this mechanism, if there are questions regarding the terms or conditions of a policy, they can be set out more specifically by the insurance company, and the risk manager will have documented evidence and does not run the risk of voiding coverage.

The risk manager should participate in all matters involving claims under the policy. This participation may take many forms, and the insurance company and the risk manager should work these matters out at the inception of the policy term if it is a new company. Ideally, the risk manager should have obtained written guidelines from the insurance company or a letter of understanding as to the role the risk manager will play in the investigation and settlement of claims made under that policy. We suggest that in the letter of understanding the insurance company advise the risk manager if there are certain claims that the risk manager can handle alone without prior commitment from the insurance company. This aspect of the policy is important in the situation where the cancelling of part of or all hospital charges would be all that is necessary to dispose of the matter. The risk manager who uses this strategy without the authorization of the insurer runs the risk of not being reimbursed. If the risk manager has a letter of understanding from the company that allows him or her to handle small claims by this tactic, the insurance company will then reimburse the insured facility for sums waived or cancelled. Another danger in handling small claims without a letter of understanding from the insurer concerns the forgiveness of a bill without receiving a release. If later the claimant files a lawsuit or makes further claims, the insurance company at this point will probably claim no responsibility either to settle or to defend the insured facility, since the company was not privy to the original negotiations and settlement.

Other standards and rules may apply to the self-insured institution that buys excess or umbrella liability coverage to cover large claims or lawsuits. Excess insurance is insurance that covers losses above a certain level. Excess insurance in the professional and general liability exposure area provides that in the event a claim or lawsuit exceeds the institution's self-insured retention level, the excess insurance company will step in and will pay on behalf of the insured facility the sum that the company is legally required to pay. Umbrella liability insurance pertains to the overall operations of the insured facility. It is insurance for all types of claims arising from the operation of the institution. The umbrella liability policy will define all coverages and will act as excess above those expressed levels in each underlying exposure area. The umbrella liability policy will apply in any claims above the retention level related to professional and general liability, transportation fleet liability, directors' and officers' liability, and any other programs listed in the umbrella liability policy. The self-insured institution should have more latitude in handling claims and meeting reporting requirements than the facility that has a small deductible or first-dollar coverage. For excess or umbrella liability coverage, the risk manager should be as aware of the requirements for reporting events as the risk manager who has first-dollar coverage. The requirements are usually less stringent, but they must be thoroughly understood, and letters of understanding or guidelines should be provided in writing from the insurance company. Most excess and umbrella liability policies will include the reporting requirements as an integral part of the contract, and they should be adhered to religiously.

To sum up the relationship between the insured institution and the insurance company, neither side should dictate to the other what will and will not be done. The situation should be one of mutual cooperation and respect which, it is hoped, will result in benefits to both parties. The insured health facility that finds it cannot relate on an interpersonal basis with the insurance company representative should request that the individual be reassigned and a different contact person be provided. Otherwise the facility should consider changing insurers. Ultimately, the health care organization should strive to find an insurer it can work with on a cooperative basis. Cooperation is essential to both parties, and failure to cooperate works to the detriment of both the insurer and the insured.

Prelitigation Strategy

Early awareness of serious misadventures is essential to a successful prelitigation strategy. A well-designed and well-implemented information system will help keep the risk manager apprised of events, and intervention can take place while the patient is still within the facility, so that the first steps toward mitigation of the problem can be taken. As stated previously, early notification of misadventure is one of the results of having built bridges to the medical and hospital staff.

Once a report has been made, the risk manager must decide if immediate contact with the patient or the family is warranted. Most times such contact is appropriate. If the decision has been made that contact with the patient should be established, this action is the first step in the procedure. After having established contact, the decisions will then flow from the course of the subsequent investigation, and a promise should be made to maintain communication with the patient or family once the investigation is completed.

The demeanor of the risk manager and his or her interaction with the potential litigants during the first contact is of vital importance. An attempt to create an atmosphere of trust between the potential litigant and the risk manager is essential. Trust is necessary in order to continue negotiations with the objective of settling a claim once it is established that there is liability. The first meeting between the parties is not the time to state any concrete opinions regarding the substance of the event; the objective should rather be to communicate the fact that a fair and equitable investigation will be conducted and the patient or family will be apprised of the conclusions. Rarely will a risk manager want to obligate the health facility to some type of settlement or financial arrangement during the initial contact. However, this is not to say that such an arrangement does not sometimes occur or that it is never appropriate.

During the first contact, the risk manager is walking a very narrow line between the necessity of winning the trust of the potential litigant and that of protecting the institution. Once mutual trust and lines of communication have been established, the primary objective of keeping the potential litigant out of the hands of a plaintiff's attorney may have been achieved. There are situations in which the potential litigant will nonetheless seek the services of legal counsel, but usually this is not for the purpose of commencing litigation, but for advice regarding the substance of the settlement offer.

Another important purpose of early intervention is to give potential litigants a forum to vent their disappointment or anger over the misadventure or poor care that precipitated the claim. Often the opportunity to vent anger or frustration will defuse the situation, so that a more reasonable understanding can be reached.

Once it is decided what the disposition will be regarding the claim, the risk manager must again contact the opposite party and communicate the findings. If it is decided that the claim will be denied, the reasons for the denial should be clearly explained. Simply to state that the claim is denied and no financial consideration will be made may exacerbate the situation instead of defusing it. If the risk manager delivers the decision with a clear explanation of the reason, often the potential litigant will accept the answer and not seek legal counsel. One should not, however, expect that all claimants will accept the negative decision gracefully or conclusively. The above strategy works some of the time but by no means all the time.

If the decision is made that the claim has merit, or there are other compelling reasons to settle the matter and make some offer of compensation or other financial consideration, then the negotiation procedures necessary to achieve acceptance and settlement, which are discussed in the section on "Settlement Techniques," are recommended.

In situations where an attorney has become involved before the first contact or shortly thereafter, some adjustments in strategy are necessary. It is considered unethical and inappropriate to make contact directly with potential litigants once it has been verified that they have representation by counsel. The involvement of an attorney does not necessarily mean that the strategy has failed, since most attorneys are more interested in settlement than in filing a lawsuit. Attorneys are in business to make money, and they can achieve this objective more often and faster by settlement than by long drawn-out litigation and trial.

With or without the involvement of an attorney, the assessment of liability explained in Chapter 6 should be completed. After a decision has been reached, negotiations should proceed as recommended in the section "Settlement Techniques."

Many insurance companies and some risk managers take the position that the mere fact that an attorney is now representing the claimant does not increase the value of that claim. We take issue with that assumption. It stands to reason that, although the claim itself may not have any more value, the attorney's representation requires the potential litigant to incur legal fees. Therefore, the attorney will have to inflate the value of the case in order to cover the cost of legal fees and expenses, so that the claimant's share of a settlement will be equal to or greater than the original value. The involvement of an attorney will also likely result in an increase in the value of most claims because lawyers are more knowledgeable of tort law and theories of liability and damages. They can usually find issues to exploit that laypersons do not realize exist, such as loss of consortium for the spouse of the injured patient. Since attorneys will generally not settle a case unless a fee can be earned, they have no recourse but to file a suit or withdraw as counsel if no settlement is reached.

When negotiating with an attorney regarding a prelitigation claim, it is essential to maintain communications. So long as communications are kept open there usually is little likelihood that an impasse will be reached. Discussions between the risk manager and the attorney should be conducted in a businesslike manner, with care taken to avoid making statements that cannot be substantiated. Of particular importance is the fact that the risk manager is an agent of the institution (principal), and therefore if an offer is made above or outside of authorized limits, the principal could be legally bound by it. The attorney has the right to rely on what is told him or her, and therefore the risk manager should be careful not to obligate the institution to an offer that cannot be met. It is wise not to close the door on any offers, however, because the attorney may feel that there is no manuevering room left and that the only alternative is to sue. A good tactic that will keep a line of communication open is to state that an offer or request is beyond granted authority and will have to be taken to a superior. However, one should be certain to give a specific time when a response can be expected.

Plaintiff Strategy

It is an oversimplification to say that the plaintiff's strategy in tort litigation is to win, or receive financial remuneration. Obtaining money is one mission or objective of the plaintiff or claimant and his or her legal counsel, and strategy is the plan or methods used to achieve the mission. A second objective of the plaintiff, but generally not of the attorney, may be revenge. Some plaintiffs want to get even for what they perceive as inappropriate behavior on the part of the defendant.

The Prospective Defendant

Once the plaintiff's attorney is satisfied that his or her client has a viable cause of action, he or she must decide whom to name as a defendant. Of course there are the obvious individuals or organizations who are responsible for the specific act or acts that resulted in the misadventure, such as the primary physician or the hospital. They can expect to be named. However, an experienced attorney will carefully consider the possibility of naming others, to increase the potential for success. By naming multiple defendants the plaintiff hopes to bring all of the actors into the action, regardless of how small the role they played. This also means there usually are multiple insurers or funds to pay the claim or judgment.

Significant and dramatic changes have taken place in medicine and health care delivery in the past decade, and the courts have likewise changed their attitude about accountability. (The reader may wish to refer to the section in Chapter 5 on "Corporate Negligence" for a review of relevant law.) In general, health facilities have become more than the doctor's workshop; they are a part of the major advances in medical science and technology. Many hospitals have become health care providers in their own right, furnishing a broad range of diagnostic and outpatient services, home health care assistance, and specialized treatment programs. This has prompted the public to rely on these institutions to provide the care that they want and need. Thus, the patient relies upon this projected image of the modern medical center as a "highly integrated system."[1] One court has stated:

> The conception that the hospital does not undertake to treat the patient, does not undertake to act through its doctors and nurses, but undertakes simply to procure them to act upon their own responsibility, no longer reflects the fact. Present day hospitals, as their manner of operation plainly demonstrates, do far more than furnish facilities for treatment . . . Certainly, the person who avails himself of "hospital facilities" expects that the hospital will attempt to cure him, not that its nurses or other employees will act on their own responsibility.[2]

Plaintiffs' attorneys not only accept but expound the above opinion and therefore will look for those individuals who collectively made up the health care team associated with the adverse event and bring them, their employer, or both into the litigation. Counsel for the plaintiff will sift through what information has been obtained from the medical record of the health facility or the physician's office or other sources, including medical texts, journals, and other documents, hoping to find evidence to support the position that the standard of care was not met by the defendants. Counsel may also make contact with the manufacturers of medical products or devices, depending on the nature of the case.

In the search for defendants, the plaintiff's counsel will also consider, and likely include, any legal entity owned or associated with the parties such as professional corporations or partners. Consulting physicians of various specialties, if involved, also are at risk of being named defendants. For example, suppose a patient is in some way harmed by a consulting physician either by failure to diagnose, by misdiagnosis or by performing a procedure negligently, which resulted in the patient's alleged injury and damages. Certainly there is then an independent duty owed by the consulting physician just as by the attending or primary physician. However, there is another strong possibility that the plaintiff's counsel may expand the duty of the primary physician and allege that he or she owed a duty to the patient to ensure that any consulting physician chosen was competent to perform the service that the patient required, just as the hospital has the like duty to its patients to determine the competence of its medical staff.[3] This could be even more of an issue if the consulting physician (radiologist, cardiologist, pathologist, etc.) were under an exclusive contract to provide such services for the facility's patients. There may be an issue of establishing the agency relationship, which would tie the institution to the alleged theory of negligence, and trying to prove that the corporation breached its duty to the patient.

If the misadventure involved the failure of a medical device or product, plaintiff's counsel will usually consider bringing the manufacturer of the device into the litigation as well as all those organizations in the chain of distribution. Counsel could recharacterize the case as one of product liability or add a count to the negligence petition using the same theory. The problem extends beyond the manufacturer, and there is a chance that the defending hospital or doctor will be drawn further into the lawsuit by allegations that they failed to determine the device's safety or misused the product.

Once the plaintiff's attorney has filed the suit, even if only the primary or attending physician or the health facility is named, others can be found through normal means of discovery. Interrogatories and depositions are always designed to learn the names and involvement of all persons who are even remotely connected with the case. A common strategy is to name some members of the health care team who were slightly associated with the event that gave rise to the injury and later offer to dismiss them from the litigation in exchange for their testimony against the primary defendant. One must seriously question the ethics of this tactic, since it is bound to further polarize employees of the health facility against the medical staff.

Besides the strategy of naming defendants who have ample insurance or other resources that could pay for a loss, the plaintiff's counsel will name all persons believed to be involved in the misadventure in order to avoid a situation at trial where a phantom defendant is blamed for the plaintiff's injury. A phantom defendant is a person who was involved in the event but not named and thus is not a party defendant. If the plaintiff's counsel fails to name a key actor who was responsible for the injured party's damages, and this becomes apparent to a judge or jury at trial, there is a real danger that the trier of fact will exonerate the defendant or diminish the amount of damages requested.

In states where joint and several liability is the law, a plaintiff can recover 100 percent of a judgment against one or all of the defendants even if a defendant was only partially to blame. This is especially important if the primary defendant has no insurance or assets.

The forum in which a case will be litigated is an important factor in tort law, since the size of jury awards is usually dependent on community attitudes. Kansas City juries, for example, have recently acquired a reputation for awarding large judgments in liability cases.[4] Therefore, a plaintiff's counsel will attempt to file the suit in a court where large judgments are routinely awarded, provided a legal nexus can be found that affords jurisdiction and the attorney is familiar with the surroundings. In most states, jurisdiction lies in the county where either the injury occurred or one of the defendants resides. Therefore, if the event occurred in a county where awards are generally low, or there is a history of reluctance to make awards against certain community institutions such as a popular hospital, then the plaintiff's counsel will investigate the residences of all potential defendants in hopes of finding one residing in a more favorable jurisdiction.

Ethical, Legal, and Administrative Considerations

One of the cornerstones of Anglo-American jurisprudence is the principle that conflicts between an injured party and those responsible for the injury can be properly resolved only within the confines of the legal system. On this basis, the legal profession and others have been critical of risk management, whose purpose, as they see it, is to prevent potential plaintiffs from turning into actual plaintiffs. Conduct such as waiving hospital bills after an iatrogenic incident in return for the patient signing a hold-harmless agreement, or offering settlement compensation to a party not represented by legal counsel, as well as other early intervention techniques are viewed as unethical since they presumably deprive injured parties of access to the tort system and their concurrent rights to adequate compensation and retribution.

It can be argued that the question of whether access to the tort system should be the measure of ethical risk management depends on the extent to which the legal system has itself been ethical and fair to the plaintiff. The fact that only about 25 percent of patients who sue ever win makes the system resemble a lottery,[5] and seems to indicate that access to the court system as the measure of what is ethical is simply not right. It would appear that what is ethical or moral should be based on whether a person recovers financially for his or her loss, not on how this eventuality is brought about.

On the positive side, tort law has created the doctrine of informed consent and has made hospitals liable for negligently appointing and retaining unqualified physicians. In addition, the health care system has responded to increased litigation with increased emphasis on quality of care (if only for financial, not moral reasons).

On the negative side, however, malpractice is still occurring. It is estimated that 4.7 percent of all patients who are admitted to the hospital experience some iatrogenic incident; however, only a small percentage of these incidents result in a claim.[6] Although the increase in litigation has resulted in increased interest in quality of care in some sectors, it has also encouraged the practice of defensive medicine, and therefore additional exposure to iatrogenesis. Once a suit is filed, resolution can take as long as 5 years. Even if liability is found, the injured party goes without compensation for as long as the process takes. O'Connell has calculated that only 28 cents of every dollar of jury awards goes to the victim.[7] Furthermore, some plaintiffs' attorneys will not take a case, even where the liability is clear, if the potential award is insufficient to cover the cost of discovery and provide an adequate fee. No attorney will take a case if the target defendants have no insurance or other assets.

Although the tort system itself has not adequately served the needs of individual plaintiffs or the public, it is the system under which we presently operate. How then, does a risk manager operate ethically within the system (until a better method is implemented) to best serve the potentially conflicting needs of the patient and the hospital? The answer simply is to assure that patients' rights are consistently upheld in every aspect of the risk management program. Since violation of patients' rights often leads to provider liability, protecting patients' rights also means protecting the health care institution and physicians.[8] In practice, therefore, the risk manager must:

- Always do what is in the patient's best medical interest
- Keep the patient apprised of any iatrogenic incident and what is being done to remedy it
- Never place the patient in an unequal bargaining position, but be up front about suggesting that the patient obtain legal representation if he or she does not understand or feels uncomfortable about a claim, despite resolution, and do not push the patient to the point of harrassment to agree to a settlement
- Offer a fair and reasonable compensation for injuries incurred.

Patients who are ill often cannot advocate on their own behalf. Ideally, there should be someone present to advocate for them who is not salaried by the hospital and does not have a vested interest in the system.[9] Until such a day arrives, if it ever does, it is the risk manager's ethical, legal, and administrative responsibility to see that patients' rights are upheld.

Another problem faced by risk managers centers around the issue of joint defendants. We have learned that hospitals and other health care providers are often dragged into litigation, not because they are the real cause of the problem, but because they have the so-called "deep pocket." Suing a defendant with no assets or insurance is an exercise in futility, and therefore plaintiff's counsel will take great care to bring into the litigation a party who has insurance, regardless of how small that party's role was in the misadventure. The issue that risk managers and their attorneys must face is whether to name as party defendants the physicians and others who did in fact contribute to the event but were overlooked or ignored by the plaintiff. Although one can argue that it is only just that the true tort-feasor be named and be made to compensate the victim, the truth of the matter is that the question is often one of politics and business, not ethics and morality.

Risk management is management, and managers must balance interests. Filing a cross claim against a member of one's medical staff or a referring physician could so alienate them as to destroy the support necessary to keep the facility financially viable. If this issue should arise, the risk manager should submit this question to the organization's risk management committee for decision.

Settlement Techniques

Let us assume that a claimant has sustained an actionable injury and that a decision has been reached that there is some merit to the case and that an attempt should be made to make an offer in hopes of settling the matter. If the claim was properly evaluated, then the amount the institution will pay to obtain a release has also been decided. In facilities insured by nonaffiliated companies, the risk manager may have had some input in evaluating the claim, but the insurance representative will probably have taken the lead in the negotiations and the final disposition of the case.

The opposite assumption may be true for self-insured institutions or those with a large deductible. The negotiator may be the risk manager, who may also assist in the decision about final disposition, after review by a risk policy committee. Below are some guidelines for those involved in the negotiation of a claim that they desire to settle.

Always be a good listener. Most claims will be settled, but one cannot settle without knowing what the other side wants. During negotiation of a claim with a potential litigant in a hospital environment, one may find that the forum available to the individual is the same facility about which he or she is voicing the complaint. The forum will give the potential litigant an opportunity to vent his or her feelings about every aspect of care perceived as an irritation while a patient. Listening through all the complaints and the long list of criticisms is essential to finding the one issue that is the real basis of the problem which caused the individual to become a potential litigant. A good negotiator will be able to identify the one act that the individual may feel was the legal wrong which, if mitigated, will settle the matter. One may, for example, have to sit through a long dissertation about the hard bed, bad food, noise, and other complaints. After the long tirade, one frequently can identify the specific event or person whose action precipitated the patient's decision to file a claim. Listening closely to the claimant will often provide the key to what it might take to open negotiations. In some cases, a claimant will drop the matter if a simple apology or explanation by the provider is made in a sincere and caring manner.

During the period of negotiation, it is strategically important for the defense negotiator to elicit from the other side what they really want. Two things have been accomplished when the other side has stated their desires. First, the real problem has been found, and second, a dollar amount has been stated that serves as the upper limit of the value they place on the claim. Unless one learns this amount, no limit is available for negotiations, and one is in a situation of bidding against oneself. By forcing the other side to make the first offer, one has found what the opposite side feels is the realistic value of the claim. If the demand is too high, one should not jump to conclusions by stating that the person is completely out of range, but simply state that they have evaluated the case higher than the provider's experience dictates. After having heard the claimant's position and taken a reasonable amount of time to analyze it, the potential defendant is then in a position to make a first offer. Experience shows that the first offer is generally not accepted; therefore one should calculate the offer to be somewhat lower than the amount for which the claim is actually valued. However, one should not make the offer so low as to anger the claimant, who then feels that he or she is not being dealt with fairly. The claimant may stop talking and hire an attorney. For example, if the case is valued by the facility at $10,000, and the claimant has suggested $20,000, then the opening offer might be $5,000. This gives the potential defendant the opportunity to increase the ante to a figure close to the case value, provided the claimant will cut his or her demand in half. During negotiations, the argument that the defendants have increased their offer by 100 percent, and therefore the claimant ought to decrease his or her offer accordingly should be clearly stated.

If the first offer is refused, one should communicate the point that it is only the first offer, and since there is considerable distance between the two figures there is opportunity for further discussions once the defendants have had a chance to discuss the matter and increase their authorized negotiating limits. By all means, one should never close the door to future negotiations unless this is the deliberate objective.

At this point, the risk manager must realize that negotiations are centered around the economic basis of the event. In negotiating with the potential plaintiff, one should elaborate on the points of defense and attempt to establish that the provider is not 100 percent liable. If the point can be made that the defendant is only 50 percent liable for the event, then the defendant can attempt to match the reduced liability with an equal reduction of the demand. Therefore, if the claimant desires $20,000 and the point is made that the defendant is 50 percent at fault, then half the demanded amount appears reasonable. It is also the value of the case and the target settlement amount. However, one should be very cautious when using this tactic and should be able to support the statement with arguments in one's defense.

If the negotiator fails to effectively back up the points of defense, he or she has in effect told the other side that their value is correct. The points of defense should therefore be well thought out and should be used to support the evaluation of the claim. Also remember that there are points on both sides, and listening is very important to keeping lines of communication open. By keeping communication channels open, one is effectively continuing to negotiate. The negotiating process is sometimes short with agreement reached quickly, but other times it is a long process, and open communication is essential.

There will be a time when the negotiations will end. One hopes the negotiations will come to an end through offers and counteroffers until an agreement has been reached. This is not always possible, and there will be times when an agreement cannot be reached. Good strategy dictates ending negotiations when one's limit has been reached. Unwise negotiators who expend their limits early in the process effectively preclude going further into the negotiations. One should remember to keep a little something back, so that when an agreement is near in the negotiations, settlement can be achieved by adding the little bit more that is sufficient to reach a final conclusion of the matter. Once the negotiator has expended the authority granted on a case, there is nothing further to negotiate. At this point it will be necessary to seek further limits from the committee or person that grants the authority to settle claims. It can be embarrassing to have evaluated a claim, started negotiations, spent one's authority early, and failed to reach an agreement with the potential litigant or his or her attorney who is willing to settle. Recourse at that point is to reevaluate the value of the case and go back for authority to grant more money and try to settle the claim. An accurate conclusion should already have been reached through the investigation process that would have led to a realistic evaluation of the claim. It sometimes happens, however, that claims are not realistically evaluated through no fault of the risk manager or the committee to which he or she reports. New developments about a case that one was not aware of may be discovered later and will add value to a potential claim. In such a situation, it is prudent to advise the opposite party that the facts stated are new and that time is needed to reevaluate the case based upon the new information that has been disclosed. It is important that the reevaluation be based on the new facts; if appropriate, one should revalue the claim and state the reasons for doing so. Reevaluation during negotiation will sometimes help reach a bargaining position that is agreeable to both sides.

Finally, the negotiator with the money is in a better position than the person who wants that money. If the other side wants to settle, and they do if they are negotiating, then the case can be settled. Settlement cannot be reached, absent a lawsuit, unless the negotiator for the defense agrees to pay money. This is probably the most important bargaining chip in the negotiating process. The checkbook is still the final authority in the negotiating process, and as the negotiator for the defense has the checkbook, he or she should use it wisely.

Risk Management and Defense Counsel

The choice of and interaction with defense counsel is a relevant issue to the facility that is basically self-insured or has a large deductible. If the facility is first-dollar insured, the insurance company will select the defense counsel that will represent the institution.

Most health facility risk managers involved with a self-insured retention or a large deductible will find it necessary to employ defense counsel. It is essential that the risk manager and defense counsel have a good working relationship based on mutual respect and ability. The novice risk manager who has little knowledge of court law will find that the defense counsel will take control and direct matters involving the lawsuit. The risk manager should become aware of and knowledgeable in this area so that his or her abilities will not be diluted by defense counsel. It is not necessary that the risk manager be aware of the workings of the law and the intricacies of the lawsuit and its strategy, but only that he or she have a broad, general acquaintance with these issues. One should leave procedural details to the attorney, who will be well versed in the intricacies of courtroom and related matters. In selecting a defense counsel the risk manager should consider the following:

1. Select an attorney with malpractice experience from a good-sized firm with the resources to conduct the necessary research. Visit the firm and check its library.

2. Avoid attorneys who wish to substitute enthusiasm for experience. These attorneys will charge the client for their learning experience.

3. Select an attorney who is familiar with complex litigation where there are multiple defendants with different counsel. The attorney should be able to work well with other counsel and not attempt to place blame on colleagues.

4. The risk manager and the trial attorney must understand and respect each other's position. Do not select counsel who attempt to usurp the authority to settle cases or establish strategy. These tasks belong to the defendant and the risk manager. Counsel should provide their assessment of the case and of the chances of winning at trial; however, the decision to settle or try the case rests with the defendant.

5. Select a trial counsel who can work well and communicate with the risk manager.

6. Select a counsel who is accessible. Some attorneys are so busy that they will not give you the time of day. Trial counsel must be reachable by telephone when necessary, since new information is frequently found during the discovery phase of the litigation.

7. Select an attorney who will permit the risk manager to be present during depositions and trial preparation as well as at the trial itself.

8. Select a firm on the basis of ability, not on hourly rates. Fees charged by an attorney are usually based on overhead and competition in the community. If increases in fees are anticipated, they should be decided before the attorney is hired.

9. Decide in advance on the method of payment. Fees are often paid monthly, quarterly, or at the conclusion of the case.

10. Select an attorney who is willing to provide some free, "off the record" advice. An attorney who charges for every phone call often is more interested in money than in providing service. There should be a mutual balance.

11. Evaluate counsel after each case to see if the case was unnecessarily prolonged, when it becomes obvious early on in the litigation that it could be settled.

12. Suggest that trial counsel provide a special rate in return for all or a large percentage of the defendant's business.

13. Compare legal fees and the cost of litigation with other risk managers to see if costs are within the range paid by other institutions.

Eventually, the health care provider and its risk manager should settle on an attorney or law firm or firms that they feel comfortable with. It may take a few cases to decide the matter, and from time to time one may wish to engage the service of new counsel.

Releases and Related Instruments

Risk managers are often faced with the question of whether or not to accept releases or some type of legal instrument that will protect their facility from future claims involving the same incident. This is particularly true for the self-insured institution or the facility that has a large deductible and the claim falls within the deductible of the insurance policy. Of course, the institution that is insured from the first dollar will have these questions decided by the insurance company, which will determine whether or not to take a release on the insured facility's behalf. Therefore, this section will deal with the self-insured hospital or the insured hospital with a deductible. The risk manager should make a determination at some point as to the advisability of a release being taken. When there is a possibility of a later claim, some disability is likely, or there is a serious injury or death, the risk manager should take a release. It is generally recommended that if the risk manager is paying any amount of money above the waiver of a hospital charge or a doctor's fee, the person receiving the money should not have any difficulty in executing a release to close the claim. A risk manager may be throwing money away if payment is made to an injured patient above the cost of services and no release is requested.

Risk managers should adhere to the advice of defense counsel in formulating the release. A release that is appropriate in one state may not be appropriate in

```
          RELEASE OF ALL CLAIMS AND INDEMNITY AGREEMENT

     FOR AND IN CONSIDERATION of the payment to me/us at this time of
the sum of _____ Dollars ($_____), the
receipt of which is hereby acknowledged, I/we, being or _____
its successors, agents, servants, and employees and all other persons,
firms or corporations liable or who might be claimed to be liable from
any and all liability now accrued or hereafter to accrue on account of
any and all claims, demands or causes of action whatsoever which the
undersigned now has/have or may hereafter have in any way arising from
any and all injuries, losses and damages to person and or property now
or hereafter sustained or received on account of any acts or omissions
to act at any time prior to the signing of this Release and Indemnity
Agreement including those received on or about the _____ day of
_____, 19 ___ through an occurrence at _____.
     I/we hereby declare that I/we fully understand the terms of the
settlement and that I/we voluntarily accept said sum for the purpose of
making a full and final compromise, adjustment and settlement of all
injuries, losses, consequences and damages as a result of the above
mentioned incident, said sum being accepted in full accord and
satisfaction thereof.
     In further consideration of the above payment, I/we, the
undersigned, hereby agree to hold harmless and indemnify the said
_____ its agents, servants, and employees of any
and all payments, expenses and legal fees of any kind whatsoever arising
because of any claim or lawsuit which may hereafter be presented by me
or any person on my behalf or who might have to assert a claim for
damages or personal injury as a result of the above mentioned occurrence
or because of any claim or cause of action asserted by any alleged
tortfeasor growing out of the above mentioned occurrence.
     It is also understood and agreed that the payment of the above sum
is only for the purpose of a compromise and is not in any way to be
construed as an admission of liability on the part of_____
_____ or its agents, servants, or employees.

Witness my/our hand(s) this _____ day of _____, 19___ at
_____.

Witnesses:

_____    _____ (SEAL)

_____    _____ (SEAL)

Before me _____ a Notary Public for an within the
County of _____ and the State of _____,
personally appeared the above mentioned _____
_____
to me known to be the person(s) who executed the foregoing release claim
and indemnity agreement and acknowledged that _____
executed same as _____ free act and deed for the uses and
purposes therein set forth.

                    NOTARY PUBLIC _____
```

Exhibit 7-3 A standardized release indemnification form.

another. Exhibit 7-3 is a release indemnification form that would be sufficient for legal purposes in the state of Missouri. The instrument is designed for the purposes of final and total closing of a claim against the facility identified therein. The form provides an indemnifaction clause that grants a contractual right of indemnification to the facility in the event that someone challenges the instrument at a later date. A challenge to a release form can be very expensive to the party defending it in court. In negotiating claims with married claimants or plaintiffs one must include the spouse so that claims such as loss of consortium are also extinguished. Both husband and wife must sign.

Special care should always be given to claims involving minors. Minors cannot execute a release on their own behalf, since they have no legal contractual rights. Therefore, any time a claim is generated by a minor and there is no legal representation, the court should be asked to approve the release for the claim. If one is dealing with a small claim that appears to have only a limited possibility of becoming a large claim at a later date, then one may consider taking a release and trust agreement signed by the parents of the minor. If the parents are not available, then the legal guardian of the minor should be the person who signs the release and trust agreement. A release and trust agreement operates as a bar to recovery by the parents or the legal guardian of the minor and requires them to hold any monies in trust in the event the minor at a later date wishes to question the release. The facility must be contractually able to seek a remedy against the signers of the release and trust agreement for indemnification (see Exhibit 7-4).

In some instances one may wish to make some type of settlement with a claimant in which the claimant refuses to sign a release. If it is a minor case and one does not anticipate further problems with the claimant, consideration should be given to accepting only a receipt for payment. The decision to accept a receipt should be determined by whether or not the receipt could be defended in the event of a subsequent claim. A receipt signed by the individual would prove that payment was made to the person prior to filing the claim, and would be used as a setoff against the eventual settlement or judgment in the case. A receipt for payment can be drafted by simply stating the date of the occurrence and the date and the amount of money received. It should contain the signature of the person receiving the money. The receipt with a cancelled check generally is sufficient to show that the patient or potential litigant actually received payment, which can be then used to show the case was mitigated.

Some states permit settlements by one joint tort-feasor and not others. Most states encourage settlement rather than litigation, and therefore laws have been passed to make the process easier. For cases in which settlement occurs before litigation, one uses an instrument called a covenant not to sue. This is a contract wherein the claimant agrees not to sue the facility or doctor in exchange for a specified amount of money. Care should always be used in these matters, since the potential litigant is not barred from filing suit against another joint tort-feasor

PARENTS RELEASE, INDEMNITY AND TRUST AGREEMENT

     FOR AND IN CONSIDERATION of the payment to me/us at this time the
sum of _____ Dollars
($_____),which shall be held in trust for the benefit of the minor
child named below, the receipt of which is hereby acknowledged, I/we,
the undersigned, father and mother and/or guardian of _____
_____, a minor born _____
                                   Month   Day   Year
do forever release, acquit, discharge and covenant to hold harmless
_____, _____ heirs, successors,
and assigns of and from any and all actions, causes of action, claims,
demands, damages, costs, loss of services, expenses and compensation, on
account of, or in any way growing out of, any and all known and unknown
personal injuries and property damage which we may now or hereafter have
as the parents and/or guardian of said minor, and also all claims or
rights of action for damages which the said minor has or may hereafter
have, either before of after . . . he has reached his/her majority,
resulting or to result from a certain accident which occurred on or
about the _____ day of _____, 19___, at or near
_____
_____
_____

     I/we further promise to bind myself/ourselves jointly and
severally, my/our heirs, administrators and assigns to repay to the said
releasees, heirs, executors, administrators and assigns any sum of
money, except the sum above mentioned, that he/she/they may hereafter be
compelled to pay because of injuries or damage sustained by the said
minor as a result of this accident.
     It is further understood and agreed that this settlement is the
compromise of a doubtful and disputed claim, and that this payment is
not to be construed as an admission of liability on the part of the
persons, firms, and corporations hereby released, by whom liability is
expressly denied.
     I/we further state that I/we have carefully read the foregoing
release and know the contents thereof, we are over 18 years of age, and
I/we sign the same as my/our own free act.

     WITNESS_____ hand and seal this _____ day of _____ 19___

WITNESSES

_____)
Address _____)
_____)
Address _____)   _____

Exhibit 7-4 A standardized release and trust agreement form.

involved in the case (Exhibit 7-5). If one decides to use this tactic, one should realize that a third-party action may be initiated against the facility by the code-fendant. It is suggested that risk managers double-check with legal counsel in the state in which they are doing business regarding the appropriateness of all instruments to be used in the negotiation and settlement of claims.

Structured Settlements

A structured settlement is a negotiated settlement of a claim, either before a lawsuit is filed, during litigation or trial, or even after a verdict is rendered, whereby the defendant agrees to make payments both as a lump sum and periodically. Structured settlements have become popular recently because of the number of huge awards and because they have become mandated by reform legislation in California, Illinois, and other states. A structured settlement is not just an annuity; it may involve any of several methods of payment, and annuities are frequently the method of making the periodic payment portion of the agreement.

Considering the advantages against the disadvantages, representatives of health providers generally prefer structured settlements to lump-sum payments, particularly when the organization is self-insured or has a large retention. Listed below are some of the benefits associated with structured settlements:

- They frequently serve to overcome an impasse during negotiation when the issue is the dollar amount.
- Structured settlement brokers can assist in the negotiations.
- The plaintiff can receive more money over the long run, while the defendant pays less up front.
- They prevent the question of the economic value of a case from having to be litigated, which can produce surprises.
- They protect beneficiaries of lump-sum payments from squandering their money and later having to be supported by the state (insurance statistics show that the average "widow" spends the insurance proceeds within 18 months[10]).
- Lump-sum payments cannot accurately gauge a person's worth, whereas a structured settlement that provides sufficient monies over time to meet living needs is more precise.
- They can be tailor-made to meet the needs of each individual case, by balancing up-front cash requirements with long-term payments.
- They provide a better hedge against inflation.
- They prevent the need for professional money management and thus save brokers' fees.

COVENANT

FOR THE SOLE CONSIDERATION OF, _____ Dollars,
the receipt and sufficiency whereof is hereby acknowledged, the
undersigned do hereby covenant and undertake with _____
_____ heirs, executors,
administrators, agents and assigns, to forever refrain and desist from
instituting or asserting against any claim, demand, action or suit of
whatever kind or nature, either directly or indirectly, for injuries or
damage, to person or property, resulting or to result from an accident
which occurred on or about the _____ day of _____ 19___, at
or near _____
_____

It is understood that the said _____ expressly
denies any negligence on _____ part causing or contributing to said
accident and any liability therefor, and that this agreement is entered
into for the purpose of avoiding litigation and shall not be construed
as an admission of liability on _____ part, and that undersigned
hereby expressly reserves the right to sue any other person or persons
against whom _____ may have or assert any claim on account of damages
arising out of the above described accident.

It is further expressly understood and agreed that as against
undersigned, _____ heirs, executors, administrators and assigns, this
instrument may be pleaded as a defense in bar or abatement of any action
of any kind whatsoever, brought, instituted or taken by or on behalf of
the undersigned on account of said supposed claim or claims against said
_____.

IN WITNESS WHEREOF, _____ have hereunto set
_____ hand _____ and seal _____ this _____ day of
_____ 19 ___

_____

_____

In presence of

_____

_____

Exhibit 7-5 A standardized form for a covenant not to sue.

- Payments are free of federal income tax.
- They protect the family against premature death.
- They offer the plaintiff's attorney the opportunity to defer fees, saving taxes and perhaps serving as a retirement fund.
- The periodic payments can be made into a variety of funds for education, medical care, retirement, custodial care, rehabilitation, Keogh/IRA, and so on.
- They eliminate potential malpractice suits claiming unsound financial advice to clients.
- They reduce the need for massive cash reserves for defendant institutions.
- They save court costs and other defense expenses.
- They reduce negotiation time.
- They reduce overall claims costs.
- They protect minors, incompetents, and disabled persons from unauthorized use by parents or guardians of the money awarded them.
- They protect the injured party from risks in the investment market, since the annuity is generally placed with high-rated firms and frequently is insured.

There is debate over when a structured settlement should be considered. Some authorities state that unless the case exceeds $100,000[11] it is not worth the effort to attempt a structured settlement. Others say that cases can be effectively structured for amounts as low as $50,000.[12]

The structured settlement is a formal contract between the parties to a dispute wherein the defendant agrees to perform certain financial acts and the plaintiff agrees to release the claim. Generally, structured settlements have two basic parts—the up-front or immediate payments, and the periodic financial arrangements—but this is not necessary in all cases. It is hypothetically possible that the first part could be absent in a structured settlement, if, for example, both the plaintiff and the plaintiff's attorney agree to accept all money and legal fees over a period of years. This, however, is usually not the case.

The cost of the periodic portion of the structure will fluctuate depending on the interest rate at the time of purchase. Since an annuity is a repayment of principal and interest over time, after deducting the fees and profit of the insurance companies, the annuity company, and the settlement brokers, the size of periodic payments will depend on the interest rate that the annuity company can get through long-term investments at the time they quote the settlement broker the cost. Therein lies the one risk with a structured settlement. If interest rates fall over a period of years, the periodic payments will represent a return over and above the amount that could be earned had the plaintiffs received a lump sum and invested it

Table 7-1   Initial Offer of a Structured Settlement*

Terms of Offer	Cost (to Defendants)	Benefit
Section I		
$450,000 immediately	$450,000	$450,000
Section II		
Monthly payments of $3,750 per month for life		
with 30 years certain	200,000	900,000
Section III		
Medical annuity: $500 per month for 10 years		
certain	40,000	120,000
Section IV		
Future lump sums:		
In 5 years	9,000	15,000
In 10 years	7,000	20,000
In 15 years	6,000	25,000
In 20 years	4,000	34,000
Total	$716,000	$1,564,000

*Figures are hypothetical and not necessarily actuarially sound.

themselves. However, if the structured settlement is placed during a time of relatively low interest, and interest rates rise substantially, then plaintiffs could realize a greater return by managing the funds themselves, assuming they knew how. However, considering the risk associated with the investment business, the average citizen is better off accepting annuity payments than attempting to manage the fund,[13] especially when one considers brokers' fees, taxes, and other factors. (The U.S. Bureau of Statistics reports that only 2 out of every 100 college graduates reaching age 65 in 1977 could provide for their own retirement.)

Risk managers who desire to use this technique have an advantage in that some firms[14] will offer to take over negotiation once an agreement is made to accept a structured settlement. Structured settlement experts should be prepared to offer both sides a variety of plans that they can settle upon. Table 7-1 is an example of such an offer.

As in every business, there are people who are good and others who are not. The risk manager should beware of so-called structured settlement experts who simply place an annuity with an insurance company and perform little else. They are primarily interested in a brokerage fee and will frequently sacrifice quality for quantity. A good expert in the field will spend substantial time arranging both parts to the structure and searching for an annuity that will provide maximum benefit with little risk. Risk managers must be wary of experts who place annuities with only one firm, because they may be doing so because they receive a better commission. Also, an expert who places the annuity with a parent insurance company may not be serving the client well. Experience has shown that experts in structured settlement should not engage in other businesses and should be independent professionals or employees of independent firms. They must be knowledgeable about the insurance industry, relevant tax law, and changes in the investment market.

Structured settlement experts can assist in the negotiation of claims related to all types of liability cases such as professional malpractice, wrongful death, workers' compensation, product liability, and antitrust, as well as any claim for money damages.

An important point to remember is that the cost of the structured settlement must be confidential and known only to the defendant. The plaintiff is usually told only of the benefits to be received. The plaintiff's counsel may wish to find out the cost of the settlement for two reasons; first, to determine the legal fee, and second, to determine their negotiating success. Most attorneys sign a contract to take a liability case on a contingency basis, for example, one third, 40 percent, or more. Since the total value of a structured settlement over a long period of time is high compared to the cost to the defendant, a legal fee based on the total benefits could be greater than the cost to the defendant. Therefore, the rule for attorneys' fees of structured settlements is that the percentage fee is based on the cost of the structure, not the benefits. By and large, the attorney's fee will be built into the structure and be negotiated along with other elements.

Suppose a 50-year-old married father of two children suffered blindness due to a medical error. Continuing medical payments are foreseen plus loss of income. Plaintiff's counsel offers to settle the case for a lump sum of $1,250,000 (see Table 7-1.)

In the Table 7-1 settlement figures, the total cost to the defendant is $716,000. Since the attorney's fees is one third the total cost, $238,428 of the immediate payment of $450,000 goes to the attorney. The balance of $211,572 will go to the victim. In the above hypothetical case, the defendant had to pay less than half the amount requested by the plaintiff, and the plaintiff received considerably more than he would have received in a lump sum, since the attorney would have received $416,250, leaving the claimant $833,750. Thus, the structured settlement method can benefit all sides to a dispute.

Summary

The health facility risk manager must be actively involved in all aspects of strategy, settlement and litigation of claims, and lawsuits filed against the organization or its employees. An adequate filing system will be necessary to maintain administrative control over cases, since each will have tasks and activities that must be completed on a timely basis. A filing system can be established either manually or by computer.

Risk managers of organizations who have first-dollar coverage from commercial insurance companies can expect to serve as support staff to the representative firms. The company must be notified of claims and suits according to the terms of the contract, and perhaps even PCEs will have to be reported. The company usually reserves the right to select defense counsel and to settle or defend a case.

Prompt notification of a misadventure is essential for early dispute resolution. It is important to be trustworthy and forthright when talking with a potential plaintiff, and open communications must be maintained if success is to be achieved. The plaintiff's strategy is not only to win, but to include as many defendants as possible to improve the chance for success.

Early intervention by risk managers raises ethical issues that should be considered. Honesty and willingness to meet with an advocate of the patient are essential to prevent allegations of unfairness. Also, the naming of a codefendant who is a member of the medical staff or a frequent referer of patients to a defendant health facility has the risk of creating administrative and political problems which must be considered.

Settlement techniques will depend on how the institution is insured and the methods preferred by the company or the risk manager. Generally, one begins with offers lower than the value assigned to the case. The defense counsel and the risk manager must work well together and respect each other's role.

Releases and other instruments used to settle cases must be reviewed by legal counsel to meet legal requirements. The form may vary with local law. Structured settlements usually contain two parts, the up-front cash payment and the periodic payment, which generally takes the form of an annuity. Frequently, a structured settlement will benefit both sides of a dispute by providing more benefits over time to the plaintiff for less cost to the defendant.

Chapter Exercises

1. Explain the purposes of a calendar claims filing card system.

2. Who generally takes the lead in negotiations over claims and lawsuits for health institutions insured by nonaffiliated companies? Explain the role of the insured health institution's risk manager in such negotiations.

3. Explain the role of the self-insured health facility risk management committee in negotiations over claims and lawsuits.

4. What is an essential element in an early intervention risk management claim administration program?

5. When should a risk manager first raise the question of financial settlement?

6. What is a common plaintiff's attorney's strategy when organizing a case for litigation?

7. Discuss ethical arguments against early intervention in cases in which patients have sustained an iatrogenic injury. Discuss the counterarguments.

8. What percentage of the plaintiff's first demand should be offered by the defendant?

9. What is the most important criterion for selecting a defense counsel?

10. Discuss an advantage for the plaintiff, the defendant, and society of using a structured settlement to resolve a dispute.

References

1. *Moore v. Board of Trustees of Carson-Tahoe Hospital.*, 88 Nev. 207 at 212, 495 P.2d 605 at 608, *cert. denied,* 409 U.S. 879 (1972).

2. *Bing v. Thunig,* 2 N.Y. 2d 656 at 666, 163 N.Y.S. 2d 3 at 8, 143 N.E. 2d 3 at 11 (1957).

3. *Purcell v. Zimbelman,* 18 Ariz. App. 75, 500 P.2d 335 (1972).

4. "The Crisis in Missouri." In *Case Study Medical Malpractice Insurance.* Jefferson City, MO: Missouri Hospital Association, 1985, p. 6.

5. Wallace, Cynthia. "Risk Management." *Modern Healthcare* (April 1984): 72.

6. Ibid.

7. Ibid.

8. Richards, Edward P. III, and Katharine C. Rathbun. *Medical Risk Management.* Rockville, Md.: Aspen Systems Corp., 1983, pp. 275-299.

9. Annas, George. *The Rights of Hospital Patients:* New York: Avon Books, 1978.

10. Gehring, Roy. "Everyone Can Win With Structured Settlements," *Risk Management* (July 1981): 18.

11. Welo, Tobias V., and James W. McDonnell. "Structured Settlements Give Both Sides a Time Option," *Risk Management* (February 1983): 42.

12. Ibid.

13. Gehring, p. 42.

14. Ibid. p. 42.

CHAPTER EIGHT

DEVELOPING AND IMPLEMENTING A COMPREHENSIVE RISK PREVENTION PROGRAM

Jacquelyn Goldberg and Gary P. Kraus

The previous chapters of this book have emphasized the identification of potential compensable events (PCEs) and claims management as key elements of a risk management program. Although early identification and management of claims are central to any risk management program, and in fact constitute the full extent of risk management activities in some hospitals, these activities alone are insufficient. Without a risk prevention component, claims identification and management activities amount to nothing more than crisis management. This chapter provides the basic information necessary for developing and implementing a comprehensive risk management program—one that emphasizes the importance of risk prevention as well as claims intervention and management. The chapter briefly defines the scope of risk prevention activities, then focuses extensively on high-risk areas and how to integrate numerous departments and staff into a comprehensive risk management program.

Defining Risk Prevention Activities

The goal of a risk management program that emphasizes risk prevention is to identify how and why claims occur in a particular institution and to initiate actions that will prevent further claims from occurring. For example, the most obvious reason for patients filing suits is that they have been injured (regardless of whether or not there has been actual medical negligence). Risk prevention activities must, therefore, attempt to identify both the kinds of injuries that occur and how they can be prevented.

Risk prevention activities should also address the subtleties of why patients sue. Acute dissatisfaction with the manner in which the staff treated the patient appears to be a major factor in motivating a lawsuit.[1] Consequently, patient relations is a function of risk management.

Finally, risk prevention activities must be facility-wide. It is not necessary and is probably impossible for a risk manager to be fully involved in all risk prevention activities. It is necessary, however, for the administration and staff in every department to practice risk prevention in order for risk prevention to work.

A facility-wide risk prevention program typically involves identifying occurrences and claims through audits and other information sources and responding to the audit results by appropriate changes in administrative policy and/or clinical practice. The specific components of risk prevention include:

1. Activities related to patient care
   - Initial and ongoing audits of occurrence and claims data; determining high-risk areas
   - Risk management follow-up and program development based on audit information,
     Staff education programs
     Skills assessment/monitoring
     Revising policies and procedures
   - Linkage with quality assurance committees
   - Patient relations
   - Interdepartmental communication
   - Credentialing of physicians and allied health professionals
   - Information clearing house/troubleshooting
2. Activities not directly related to patient care
   - Safety and security
   - Environmental impairment
   - Maintenance of equipment
   - Administrative activities
     Developing policies and procedures
     Organizing educational activities
     Monitoring and evaluating risk prevention activities.

Setting Institutional Priorities

High-Risk Areas

Given the myriad variety of incidents that can occur in hospitals which injure patients and which give rise, at least theoretically, to potential liability, the risk manager must set priorities. The most logical way to set priorities is for the risk manager to identify the high-risk areas in the institution and concentrate efforts in those areas. High-risk areas are those departments (or procedures, treatments, and locations) with the greatest potential risk of severe injury to patients and of significant liability to the hospital and/or its physicians. Whether or not a department is considered high-risk is measured by the frequency and severity of previous claims. For example, patient falls occur with relative frequency in hospitals and skilled nursing facilities but do not ordinarily result in injuries severe enough to produce large dollar losses in the aggregate.

The same is true of medication errors. Claims that arise in obstetrics, the emergency department, and surgery, on the other hand, are relatively frequent and severe enough to result in large dollar losses, and consequently are considered high-risk. Most risk managers consider radiology and anesthesia to be high-risk areas as well because injuries in these areas, although infrequent, can be catastrophic and may result in large settlements or awards.

The first step in identifying the high-risk areas in an institution involves building a database using the hospital's claims history, quality assurance audits, and occurrence screens (see Chapters 4 and 6). While this process of statistical data gathering and analysis is taking place, it is also useful to conduct detailed surveys of departments identified as high-risk in most institutions, since in all likelihood a data system will eventually identify these areas as high-risk areas in one's own facility. The advantage of the survey approach is that it may pick up significant occurrences or claims waiting to happen (prospectively) rather than rely solely on retrospective data such as audits or claims history. In addition, the survey gives a new risk manager an entree into a department, and a way to both identify the concerns of staff and introduce staff to risk prevention concepts.

Using the elements of a risk prevention program listed above, examples of a survey mechanism for the initial assessment of three high-risk areas—obstetrics, the emergency department, and radiology—with a brief discussion of surgery and anesthesia, are presented in the following sections. Each survey is prefaced by an introduction profiling relevant risk management issues in that high-risk area. The surveys are based on numerous sources of data, which have identified problems that commonly arise in each area.

The data currently available in risk management are not extensive. Only one major study of closed claims has been complete by the National Association of Insurance Commissioners. The NAIC national study published some 70,000 claims that were closed between 1975 and 1978[2]. The identification of obstetrics, surgery, the emergency department, radiology, and anesthesiology as high-risk areas is based on the NAIC study.

Although it can be presumed that many organizations have extensive internal databases, little of the information is made public, and therefore little is available for comparison purposes. St. Paul Fire and Marine Insurance Company is one of the few organizations that regularly publishes summaries of its claims data.

In addition to a basic lack of extensive data, there is a tendency to utilize the data inappropriately. The terms *average* and *typical,* and *verdict* and *settlement,* are often used interchangeably. Samples may be biased, and dollar figures may or may not be adjusted for inflation. The term *most frequent allegations* may include all allegations regardless of outcome or only those allegations in which there was a judgment for the plaintiff. Thus, whenever possible, it is important to clarify the precise nature of the data being collected or analyzed[3].

As will be evident, risk management, more than any other aspect of hospital administration, demands some working knowledge of clinical medicine. Since instruction in the basics of clinical medicine is beyond the scope of this book, the reader should refer to an appropriate text.

Obstetrics During the past 10 years the average dollar amounts awarded in lawsuits involving obstetrics have increased at a rate much greater than for other specialties. A 1981 nationwide study by Jury Verdict Research, Inc., indicated that the average award for infant deaths or injuries immediately preceding, during, or following delivery was $1,046,000, whereas the average award for other types of alleged malpractice (improper treatment, surgical maloccurrences, misdiagnosis) was approximately $300,000.[4] Recent verdicts for similar birth injuries in areas of the country known for particularly high awards commonly reach multimillion dollar levels.

According to a survey sponsored by the American College of Obstetricians and Gynecologists (ACOG), the malpractice crisis in obstetrics has had a significant impact on the way physicians in this specialty practice medicine. More than half of the physicians surveyed had increased their use of tests and other diagnostic procedures—in other words, were practicing defensive medicine. The frequency of consultations, referrals, providing written patient information, and obtaining written consent has increased. In response to the rise in the cost of malpractice insurance premiums, 50 percent of those surveyed passed some of that cost on to their patients in the form of increased fees, whereas 30 percent restricted their practice in some way, by either no longer practicing obstetrics or by reducing the amount of services.[5]

Why is the malpractice crisis so much more acute in obstetrics than in other areas? Numerous reasons have been suggested. It has been argued, for instance, that the recent explosion of medical technology and scientific knowledge in obstetrics means that the state of the art is constantly changing, and consequently the standard of care is often open to question.[6] Electronic fetal monitoring is a case in point. Required use of the monitors seems to have attained a legitimacy in the courts that it has yet to attain in the practice of medicine.[7] It is also said that high technology has encouraged high consumer expectations.[8] Childbirth is no longer seen as a quasi-illness with even the slightest potential for injury and even death. Yet when injuries do occur they can be catastrophic, involving severe retardation requiring institutionalization, often for a lifetime. Jury awards, mixing sympathy and fair compensation, are commensurately high. Finally, there remains the specter of actual malpractice. In spite of constant technological advances, the standard of care-in many aspects of obstetrical practice does not fall within a gray area but is clearly articulated in professional publications,[9] yet in too many instances this standard is still not being met.

In reviewing obstetrical cases, the same problems are seen again and again. The most frequently encountered problems (not in any particular order) include:[10]

1. Delay or failure to perform cesarean section, resulting in infant injury
2. Failure to monitor the infant, electronically or otherwise
3. Problems caused by drug-induced (oxytocin) labor
4. Failure to diagnose problems
5. Failure to identify and appropriately treat the high-risk mother
6. Failure to determine gestational age
7. Improper resuscitation of the newborn
8. Inadequate documentation in the medical record.

Many of these problems overlap and may arise in the context of a single case. Most of these problems can also be traced to failure to follow the standards set forth in the ACOG's Guidelines for Perinatal Care.[11] The following survey, which has expanded on these eight problem areas and utilizes the ACOG guidelines, will enable a risk manager to begin to determine the nature of the risks in his or her obstetrics department.

Patient Care Issues

Have audits been conducted for claims or occurrences involving delay or failure to perform cesarean section resulting in infant injury, failure to monitor the infant, oxytocin-induced labor, failure to diagnose, improper newborn resuscitation, and failure to identify (and therefore appropriately respond to) the high-risk patient and postmaturity?

Emergency Cesarean Sections

Does the hospital's obstetrical team meet the ACOG standard for emergency cesarean sections, which requires a start-up time of within 30 minutes? If not, what can be done to ensure that the hospital meets the standard?

Electronic Fetal Monitoring

Is the electronic monitor used for all high-risk deliveries? Are all physicians and nurses who are responsible for interpretation of electronic fetal monitoring strips sufficiently trained in interpreting the strips? Are their skill levels assessed periodically?

Oxytocin Administration

Is oxytocin (Pitocin) used only when appropriate, and is it properly administered? For example:

- Are totally elective inductions proscribed?
- Can staff physicians diagnose the contraindications to oxytocin use, such as cephalopelvic disproportion?
- Is a constant-infusion pump used to administer oxytocin?
- Is the rate of flow recorded every 10 to 15 minutes?
- Is an electronic fetal heart monitor used continuously during oxytocin administration? Are fetal heart rates charted every 15 to 30 minutes during stage I and every 5 minutes during other stages?

Miscellaneous

- Is a sonogram performed whenever there is a question of length of gestation?
- Is the assessment of maternal risk factors and of the hospital's corresponding capabilities to handle them done before or early in labor?
- Is the use of high forceps proscribed?
- Are indications of Erb's palsy responded to with prompt physical therapy?

Equipment

- Are monitors functioning properly? Are they checked regularly and repaired if necessary? Are checks and repairs documented?
- Are temporary difficulties adequately documented in the medical record and on the monitor strips?
- Are there monitors in the delivery room?

Staffing

- Do the physicians practicing obstetrics (obstetricians and family practitioners) have adequate clinical skills in labor and delivery?
- Are obstetricians being evaluated and reevaluated at intervals to assess and document their maintaining a level of competency?
- If audits and other evidence reveal that a physician is practicing below the standard of care, are his or her privileges restricted?
- Do the physicians arrive on time when called?
- Is a pediatrician or neonatologist who is skilled in neonatal resuscitation present in every case of fetal distress?
- What are the criteria for requesting a pediatrician or neonatologist at delivery?

- Is nursing communication between shifts adequate?

- Are emergency department nurses cross-trained in obstetrics?

- Is there 24-hour anesthesia coverage in labor and delivery? If not, can the on-call anesthesiologist be in the delivery room within 15 minutes?

- What is the resuscitation training for labor and delivery and nursery nurses? Is it being reinforced at intervals through in-service programs, and are evaluation and performance levels documented? Are the most qualified staff or anesthesiology personnel summoned in the event of problems in delivery when pediatric assistance is not available?

Documentation[12]

- Is the physician record on prenatal care complete? Does it contain at least the following: detailed obstetrical history, general and social history, identification of any high-risk factors, physical examination, laboratory test results, and description of subsequent visits?

- Is the record available to nursing and house staff upon admission of the patient?

- Is the hospital admission note complete? Does it include information such as time of arrival, time seen by physician, onset of contractions, status of membranes, use of any medication, blood group, Rh type, and any high-risk factors?

- During labor, is the fetal heart rate recorded every 30 minutes in the first stage of labor and every 15 minutes in the second stage?

- Does documentation during labor always include exact times of checks, pulse and temperature every 4 hours, maternal blood pressure every hour and before delivery, cervical dilation, effacement, station, frequency, and fetal heart rate immediately after membranes rupture?

- Is documentation in accordance with written hospital policies?

- Does delivery room documentation include type of presentation, description of placenta and cord, number of vessels, cord blood obtained and disposition, episiotomy and type, laceration and type or degree, anesthesia administered by whom, medications and times?

- If the delivery is by cesarean section, does the documentation include sponge counts, anesthesia record, etc.? Is the presence of a pediatrician or neonatologist recorded (since cesarean section is a high-risk procedure)?

- Are Apgar scores recorded at 1 minute and 5 minutes? Are other infant data recorded, such as respiration status and resuscitation methods, if used, and by whom?

- Is the patient adequately monitored in the recovery room, with checking of vital signs every 15 minutes for the first hour?
- Are meconium staining, head and chest circumferences, organomegaly, and other stigmata of congenital infections or malformations documented when they occur?
- Have special charting forms been developed for obstetrics to make documentation easier and more accurate?
- Are incident reports being utilized as a tool to inform administration and risk management of incidents where staffing, outcome, or other important factors were not optimal or of other problems that could lead to litigation?

Administrative Responsibilities

- Are all electronic fetal monitoring strips stored in case they need to be referred to in defending against litigation?
- Is there a system in place for transferring high-risk mothers and infants (who appear early in labor) if the hospital cannot provide proper care?
- Is there a document in place that allows easy reading of communication and planning involved in maternal or neonatal transport?
- Are there ongoing, continuing education programs for nurses and physicians in problem areas such as interpretation of fetal monitoring strips?
- Is there a documented chain of command in place that sets forth the appropriate personnel to notify in the event of problem situations on the unit?

Policies and Procedures

- Do obstetrical policies and procedures conform to the standard of care set forth in ACOG, Nurses Association of the American College of Obstetricians (NAACOG) and Gynecologists and Joint Commission on Accreditation of Hospitals Standards? Are those policies and procedures actually followed?
- Is there a policy that states that, in situations where there has been a serious birth trauma, the placenta is routinely examined? (A genetic and chromosomal analysis of the placenta may indicate a congenital defect and therefore the absence of malpractice.)[13]
- Is there a policy that defines high-risk mothers? Is there a procedure that defines how to respond to the various high-risk situations?
- Is there a policy regarding maternal transfer?
- Is there a policy regarding Pitocin administration? Does the policy require the presence of the obstetrician?
- Is there a policy for requesting a pediatrician or neonatologist at delivery?

- Have policies been developed regarding the management of emergency cesarean sections?

Emergency Department The emergency department is one of the most common locations in the hospital for injuries that lead to claims to occur. In addition, the types of occurrences that take place in the emergency department are often quite serious, resulting in either serious bodily injury or death. Cases involving failure to diagnose are the most common, particularly with regard to fractures, myocardial infarction, meningitis, and appendicitis. Failure to treat, delay in treatment, and failure to remove a foreign body are also common allegations.[14]

Although these allegations indicate physician negligence, actual liability often belongs to, or is shared by, the hospital. Emergency department physicians are frequently full-time hospital employees rather than independent contractors, and the hospital is therefore liable under the doctrine of *respondeat superior.* During the past several years, some hospitals have contracted with physician groups to run their emergency departments, and although this technically creates an independent contractor relationship, some courts have nevertheless found the hospital liable for the emergency physician's negligence under the theory of ostensible agency; that is, since the plaintiff perceived the emergency physician to be a hospital employee, and therefore, an agent of the hospital, then for all intents and purposes the physician is a hospital employee.[15]

The extent of the services that an emergency department offers also determines its malpractice risk. Departments with more comprehensive facilities (e.g., at least one full-time physician, with 24-hour laboratory, x-ray, and pharmacy available) are likely to treat more cases overall and more serious cases, and therefore are at greater risk for malpractice lawsuits. Hospitals with less extensive facilities are at less risk.

The nature of emergency department work also contributes to its lawsuit-prone environment. The work is an unpredictable mixture of lulls and frenzied periods, of providing care in true emergencies and in nonemergencies. A significant percentage of the population uses emergency departments as clinics for basic, nonemergency medical care. The burden of deciding whether or not something is an emergency rests with a single person: the one doing triage. His or her mistake could mean the difference between life and death. Furthermore, there is no prior (or future) physician-patient relationship, and patients and families, already tense, have no personal context in which to place the emergency department physician. Thus, the impression the staff gives as to whether they are caring and efficient can make a difference as to whether a patient sues.

Patient Care Issues

- Have audits been conducted for claims or occurrences involving failure to diagnose or misdiagnoses of myocaroial infarction, meningitis, fractures, and appendicitis?

- Have audits been conducted for serious delays in treatment, failure to treat, or failure to remove a foreign body?
- Who is responsible for triage? Is this person (or persons) adequately trained?
- What is the procedure for the patient who leaves against medical advice?
- What are the protocols for managing the disruptive or intoxicated patient?
- Are sufficient instructions provided to all patients? Are these instructions documented in the medical record?
- Does the staff have sufficient linguistic capabilities to meet the needs of a multilingual patient population?

Equipment and Safety

- Are defibrillators, oxygen flowmeters, sphygmomanometers, and other instruments calibrated and periodically checked? Are checking and maintenance documented?
- Is the appropriate equipment, including pediatric equipment, on the crash cart at all times?
- Are drugs stored in a secure location to avoid easy theft?
- What types of restraints are used on disruptive patients? Are staff trained in the proper use of restraints?
- Are security personnel sufficiently skilled? Are enough security personnel present, especially at night and on weekends?

Staffing

- Do the physicians in the emergency department have sufficient credentials to practice medicine? (It is preferable to use board-certified emergency physicians, but since this is a new specialty it is not always possible to do so. Avoid "moonlighters.")
- If audits and other evidence reveal that a physician is practicing below the standard of care, are his or her privileges restricted?
- Are on-call physicians responding promptly when summoned?

Documentation

Because documentation in emergency department records is often more sparse than in other departments, documentation is a key risk management strategy. Are the following items always documented?[16]

- Name, addresses, age of patient
- Next of kin
- Allergies and tetanus status

- Vital status (documented frequently if the patient is unstable)
- Chief complaints
- History and physical examination
- Test results and medication responses
- Patient discharge instructions
- Formal discharge summary, including diagnosis.

Administrative Responsibilities

- Is a procedure in place and followed for x-ray or abnormal test result call-backs?
- How are lost belongings handled?
- Are Joint Commission on Accreditation of Hospitals (JCAH) standards being met? Did the report from the JCAH on-site visit include any comments about the emergency department?

Policies and Procedures

Are policies and procedures written and followed for

- Triage
- Patients leaving against medical advice
- Managing the intoxicated patient
- Equipment status and maintenance
- Treatment of minors and substitute consent
- Patients dead on arrival
- Patients injured while driving while intoxicated.

Radiology The most frequent allegations in claims against radiologists are failure to diagnose and delay in diagnosis.[17] Other frequent allegations include misdiagnosis, injuries resulting from invasive procedures (e.g., mild to severe reactions to contrast media, extravasation of contrast media, perforations), injury on the x-ray table, and radiation injuries.[18] For a variety of reasons, occurrences relating to these allegations are more difficult for the hospital to avert than occurrences in other high-risk areas. First, the responsibility for diagnosis is solely the physician's, not that of hospital employees such as nurses or technicians (unless, of course, the radiologist is an employee of the hospital). In fact, when a radiologist is named in a suit, he or she is most frequently named along with the attending or emergency physician and any other physician consultants, all of whom shared in the alleged negligence. Thus, the degree of risk of liability is largely contingent on the skill level of medical staff members.

Second, there appears to be a high risk of error inherent in interpreting radiographs.[19] At least one commentator has observed that the fact that a reasonable radiologist could misread a particular radiograph has not served to make negligence more difficult to prove; instead it appears that missed diagnoses or misdiagnoses are being treated as prima facie malpractice.[20] Third, as a result of new technologies, the practice of radiology is rapidly branching into subspecialties such as neuroradiology, angiography, interventional radiology, ultrasonography, and computed tomography. Consequently, the present profile of allegations in radiology claims cannot be used as a sufficient indicator of the types of claims that will arise in the future, nor, as a corollary, of the types of risk prevention activities that ought to be taking place now to avert those future claims.

All of these factors underscore the importance of appointing only qualified radiologists to the medical staff and reappointing current staff members only after their performance has been assessed. Also, because suits involving radiologists usually involve other physicians, a concerted effort must be made to improve communications between radiology and other departments.

Last, there is an ongoing controversy as to what should be told the patient regarding the 1-in-40,000 risk of death associated with the use of contrast media for such procedures as intravenous pyelography, computed tomography, and intravenous angiography.[21] Some physicians have argued that the anxiety produced by knowing that the procedure carries with it a risk, however slight, of death may in fact trigger the reaction.[22] These physicians maintain that they are entitled to claim the therapeutic privilege exception to informed consent. The issue is further clouded by whether the radiologist is in a jurisdiction where the informed consent standard is based on what a reasonable person would want to know or on what reasonable physicians would inform their patients in similar circumstances. In any case, the hospital should address the issue of informed consent forthrightly, rather than wait for a crisis, by developing with the assistance of legal counsel the necessary informed consent procedures and ensuring that they are followed.

Patient Care Issues

- Have audits been conducted for reaction to extravasation of contrast media, injury during patient transport, wrong test/wrong patient, cardiac or respiratory arrest, missed diagnosis, differences in interpretation between the emergency department physician and the radiologist, injury or repair of organ or structure as a result of radiologic procedure, and other problems?

- Is every female of childbearing age asked if she is pregnant prior to radiographic exposure?

- Are patients transported from radiology by trained personnel? Is the patient properly identified? If the patient is left unattended in radiology, are safety precautions taken? Is there a protocol for patient transport?

Equipment and Safety

- Is radiologic equipment checked for leakage and correct placing of secondary radiation filters? Is equipment calibrated regularly?
- Are patient and visitor areas clearly marked to minimize radiation exposure?
- Is the protocol for use, handling, and disposal of radioisotopes enforced?
- Are radiation areas properly marked?
- Is there a radiation accident procedure?

Staffing

- Is the skill level of initial applicants for radiology privileges assessed prior to appointment?[23]
- Is the skill level of staff radiologists assessed prior to reappointment?[24]
- Is the skill level of x-ray technicians assessed prior to hiring, and is it evaluated periodically?
- Are radiologists sufficiently available during off-hours to meet the hospital's inpatient and emergency department needs?
- Do the emergency physicians have sufficient skills in interpreting x-rays?
- Are there periodic conferences with radiology and emergency room physicians to review discrepancies in interpreting films?
- Are continuing education programs attended regularly by staff?

Documentation

- Does the record include an x-ray requisition and a brief but thorough clinical history?
- Are the time the patient is sent to radiology, the time of return, the wet reading, and the name of person who performed the wet reading recorded?
- Is the film read within a reasonable amount of time after the x-ray was taken? Is the radiologist's report typed and in the record within 24 hours?

Administrative Responsibilities/Policies and Procedures

- Is there a special consent form for invasive procedures? Who explains the procedure to the patient?
- Is there good communication between radiology and the emergency department?
- Are there policies and procedures for release of x-ray films? Are copies rather than originals released? Are films stored in a secure and fireproof place?
- Are JCAH standards followed?

Surgery and Anesthesia The severity of injuries that can occur in the operating room and the recovery room makes both surgery and anesthesia high-risk areas. The types of surgical claims seen include surgery on the wrong body part, retained instrument or sponge, failure to follow preoperative protocol, postoperative wound infection, iatrogenic injury during surgery, and negligent performance of surgery. Anesthesia claims include wrong agent administered, reaction to anesthetic agent, incorrect drug dose, transfusion error, equipment failure, obstructed tracheal tube resulting in tachycardia, trauma to patients' eyes or teeth, and severe central nervous system injury resulting in failure to regain consciousness, blindness, or paralysis.[25]

Using the survey form for the previously described initial assessments in obstetrics, the emergency department, and radiology, similar surveys should be developed for both surgery and anesthesia. Articles that would be helpful in developing surveys in these two areas are listed at the end of this chapter.

Defining and Identifying Other Risks

In addition to the typical high-risk areas, numerous other risks in hospitals and health facilities merit the risk manager's attention. If the time were available, every department (e.g., infection control, pharmacy) could benefit from a risk assessment survey. In lieu of the survey (or in addition to it), the risk management database (which should include claims history, incident reports and other occurrence reports, and quality assurance information) will identify the significant risks. For example, the data may show that the hospital has had a series of medication errors that resulted from the nurses' repeated confusion of two medications with similar-sounding names.

Although a database is clearly useful in identifying risks, the risk manager should not overlook information that is anecdotal and cannot be quantified. Some issues arise spontaneously and must be addressed immediately. For example, in 1983 several children were fatally injured as a result of getting caught in the raising-and-lowering mechanism of pediatric beds manufactured by a certain company. The situation received nationwide attention. A good risk manager would have seriously investigated the use of those beds in his or her hospital without waiting for an injury to occur. Another dramatic example is the current AIDS crisis in which the legal rights and obligations of the hospital, the providers, and patients are just beginning to be formulated.[26] A good risk manager knows that policies and procedures should be developed in this area as quickly as possible.

The Importance of Credentialing

As a result of the *Darling* case[27] and the subsequent development of the doctrine of corporate liability, hospitals can be found liable for the negligent appointment and retention of unqualified physicians to the medical staff. It is therefore important that every hospital implement a comprehensive procedure for the initial appointment, granting of clinical privileges, and reappointment and reappraisal of its physicians. A thorough credentialing mechanism is one of the most effective risk prevention techniques available to hospitals in that it helps minimize the risk of patient injury by allowing only competent physicians to practice, and it prevents potential hospital liability under the doctrine of corporate negligence. (See the next section for a brief discussion of developing a credentialing system, and Chapter 5 on the law of corporate negligence).

Addressing Institutional Priorities

Interdepartmental Functions in Risk Prevention

For a risk prevention program to function effectively, it must be hospital-wide and must include the participation of numerous hospital staff and personnel, in addition to the risk manager. The cooperation and participation of the medical staff, nursing, quality assurance, and medical records are essential. The roles of the medical staff, nursing, and quality assurance are discussed below. The role of the medical record department is discussed in Chapter 9.

The Medical Staff Since the actions of the medical and nursing staff are the major source of potential liability in the hospital, it logically follows that they are the major source of liability prevention. It is particularly difficult to enlist the effort of physicians in a risk prevention program, especially if they are independent contractors who are not insured under the hospital policy and therefore see their legal interest as distinct from, and potentially adverse to, the hospital's legal interests. In addition, many physicians are used to practicing in a highly independent fashion without anyone evaluating, much less questioning, their medical judgment.

The risk manager must therefore make staff physicians realize that risk prevention activities are in their own best interest as well as the hospital's. This can be accomplished in a variety of ways. First and foremost, risk management should encourage physicians to sit on the risk management committee and on other committees involved in risk management issues. Second, the risk management department should have a philosophy of ongoing physician outreach by being an informal source of medicolegal information. Establishing a risk management lending library, and a risk management newsletter, circulating articles and court decisions of interest to the medical staff, conducting in-service programs and inviting physicians to attend outside risk management seminars are all ways of encouraging physician response to and involvement in risk prevention.

Nursing Since nurses are in constant contact with patients, they are the risk manager's major source of formal incident reports. If the risk manager has a good relationship with nursing, he or she can also utilize the nurses' knowledge of what is happening on the floor as a way of "taking the pulse" of a particular unit, or in other words, identifying potential problems before they become incident reports. Nurses also play an important role in patient relations.

Developing a good relationship with nursing is not usually as complicated as with physicians, since nurses are employees of the hospital and are covered under the hospital's insurance policy. As with the physicians, offering regular in-service programs and providing an information clearinghouse are good ways to encourage nursing involvement in risk prevention.

Quality Assurance As the center of hospital data collection activities, the quality assurance department is a vital resource for identifying risks in the hospital. The data that the quality assurance department routinely gathers in its review commit-tees and through generic screenings can be invaluable in detecting patterns of injury, which should be investigated to determine whether there have been re-peated breaches in the standard of care. In addition, quality assurance data are useful in indicating whether a particular medical staff member is providing subop-timal care. Special risk management studies and audits are often best accomplished through the quality assurance department, since their data collection mechanisms are already established throughout the hospital.

Given the role that quality assurance plays in risk identification, it is imperative that good communication take place between risk management and quality assur-ance, particularly in institutions where the quality assurance coordinator does not report to the director of risk management. It is advisable to establish a formal structure that includes periodic meetings and/or the exchange of monthly reports so that each department is regularly apprised of the activities of interest in the other department.

Patient Relations The patient's perception of his or her care often determines whether or not the patient files a lawsuit. Many hospitals have a patient relations department and patient representatives whose role is to address patient problems. Patient representatives can serve as major participants in risk prevention because individual patient complaints are initially addressed to them.

Whether or not the hospital has a separate department of patient relations and designated patient representatives, all medical and nursing staff and allied health professionals have a role to play in patient relations. When the hospital staff are consistently attentive and caring, the likelihood of patient claims being filed is greatly reduced. Communicating well with patients and responding to their physi-cal and emotional needs throughout their hospital stay is an important part of risk prevention. A patient who is kept abreast of the specifics of his or her treatment plan is in a better position to notice and object to any improper deviations from that plan.

Continuing Education

Continuing education is a key component of risk prevention. Continuing education programs in risk prevention generally fall into three areas:

1. Basic introduction to risk management for the new employee
2. Preventive legal strategies
3. Instruction in clinical areas

A basic introduction to risk management should be presented to all new employees as part of the hospital's regular orientation program. The risk manager should give a brief talk explaining what risk management is and how to complete an incident report. The obvious advantage of speaking to all employees, not just nurses and physicians, is that the potential sources of information will be much more extensive. By speaking to new employees at orientation, the groundwork is being set at the earliest possible moment for hospital-wide risk prevention.

Continuing education in the area of preventive legal strategies takes the form of in-service programs or seminars for target audiences, usually physicians and nurses. Depending on the particular risk management problems in the hospital and the level of medicolegal knowledge of the audience, topics could include:

- Fundamentals of liability law (negligence, respondeat superior, doctrine of corporate liability, ostensible agencies)
- Fundamentals of documentation in the medical record
- Patients' rights, informed consent, and informed refusal
- The nurse's role in patient relations
- Nursing chain of command
- Improving the physician-patient relationship, improving physicians' communication skills
- Scope of nursing practice
- Conforming to policies and procedures
- Confidentiality of patient records
- Discoverability of hospital records
- Civil procedure, mock depositions, mock trials
- Professional liability insurance mechanisms
- Antitrust law.

All of these topics can be tailored to issues in a given department.

Clinical instruction should take place as a result of claims history and/or audits that have identified the clinical area or areas in which staff skills are weak. For example, the hospital's claims history may indicate that physicians and nurses have difficulty interpreting fetal monitoring strips. An in-service program could be organized in which hands-on instruction is provided to obstetrical staff on fetal monitor strip interpretation.

Since the purpose of clinical instruction is to build the skill level of the student, it is important that every clinical instruction program have as part of its structure a mechanism that evaluates whether each student has in fact learned from the instruction. If the student has not attained the appropriate skill level, he or she should take the instruction again. If most students do not attain the skill level, the course should be examined and revised to make sure the information is being communicated in the most effective way possible.

Depending upon the importance of the skill being learned, risk management may want to consider periodic reassessment of the information or skill learned. If the newly acquired skill is not frequently being used in practice, periodic reassessment and/or offering a refresher course may be appropriate.

In addition to the three categories of continuing education, the risk management department also has an educational role in the provision of risk management information. As mentioned above, developing a risk management lending library is one of the most effective ways to accomplish this. At the end of this chapter is a partial list of newsletters, journals, and books of particular interest.

Developing a Credentialing System

Although the responsibility of developing a credentialing procedure and screening physicians belongs to the medical staff and the hospital's governing board,[28] risk management should make sure that the procedure is designed to elicit a complete and accurate picture of the applicant's competence. Important risk prevention elements of the credentialing procedure include:

- Verification from sources other than the applicant of all information that the applicant submits. (This can be done by directly contacting the medical school, specialty board, or state licensure department, or through the American Medical Association). Any unexplained time gaps should be further investigated.

- Reference letters and/or telephone references that elicit specific information about clinical competence (clinical skills and judgment, outcomes, use of consultants, ethics).

- Notarization of all documents submitted. Any documents in foreign languages should be translated into English. Those who review the application should be alert to any unusual markings or color or type variations on presumably official documents.

- Inquiry as to whether and under what circumstances the applicant has had medical staff membership terminated or privileges terminated or reduced at other institutions or a state license suspended or revoked.

- Inquiry as to whether the applicant has had any settled or pending malpractice lawsuits against him or her.

- Submission of proof of liability coverage including an amount of coverage adequate for the applicant's specialty.

Once the physician has received an appointment to the medical staff, and clinical privileges have been applied for, they should be granted provisionally until the new member has been proctored (formally observed and assessed) and his or her clinical competence assured.

JCAH standards mandate that physicians be reappointed and their skills reappraised every 2 years. Although most hospitals approach this phase of credentialing in a proforma fashion, it is the hospital's opportunity to determine whether the physician up for review is posing a new risk to the hospital (e.g., through lack of skill in a particular procedure, impairment due to age or substance abuse, or a series of related malpractice suits). Quality assurance data should be used to profile the physician's track record to see whether he or she merits reappointment.

Consultants and External Programs

As a cost-containment measure, many hospitals are hiring outside consultants to handle their risk prevention and claims administration activities or are having their insurers provide these services as part of the insurance package. In either situation, substantial risk management activities take place outside the hospital and therefore may severely limit the amount of risk prevention activity that takes place.

If the hospital decides that it is necessary to utilize an external program in lieu of an in-house risk manager, the hospital must be sure that the consultant makes frequent on-site visits and clearly understands the scope of his or her responsibilities. The hospital should closely monitor the performance of the consultant to make sure that he or she is fulfilling the contract and that the contract continues to meet the hospital's needs. Any risk management program, whether in-house or through consultants, should also include an evaluation mechanism. Although it is impossible to assess the number of maloccurrences or lawsuits that have been avoided as a result of implementing a risk management program, the effectiveness of the incident reporting system, and the skill level of staff are among the things that can and should be measured.

At present, a listing of hospital risk management consultants is not available. Sources for finding consultants include insurance brokers, hospital associations, physician-owned professional liability companies, multihospital self-insurance organizations, and the American Society for Hospital Risk Management and its state and local chapters. Contributors to this text also engage in risk management consulting services.

A Selection of Literature on Risk Management, Law, and Quality Assurance

The following newsletters, journals, and books cover a broad range of topics related to risk management, health care law, and quality assurance. They are recommended reading for all personnel involved in these activities and are worthwhile additions to any risk management lending library. Titles followed by an asterisk are of primary interest to those individuals responsible for the day-to-day functioning of the hospital's risk management program.

Newsletters

Forum (bimonthly)
Risk Management Foundation of the Harvard Medical Institutions, Inc.
Cambridge, Massachusetts

Occurrence (quarterly)
Chicago Hospital Risk Pooling Program
Chicago, Illinois

Health Law Digest (monthly)
National Health Lawyers Association
Washington, DC

Hospital Risk Management (monthly)*
American Health Consultants, Inc.
Atlanta, Georgia

Medical Liability Advisory Service (monthly)
Capitol Publications
Arlington, Virginia

Malpractice Digest (quarterly)
St. Paul Fire and Marine Insurance Co.
St. Paul, Minnesota

Legal Aspects of Medical Practice (an official publication of the American College of Legal Medicine; monthly)
Pharmaceutical Communications
Long Island City, New York

Malpractice Reporter (monthly)
Leader Publications
New York, New York

Action Kit for Hospital Law (monthly)
Pittsburgh, Pennsylvania

Regen Reports (on hospital, medical, and nursing law; monthly)*
Medica Press
Providence, Rhode Island

Hospital Law Newsletter (monthly)
Aspen Publications
Rockville, Maryland

*QRC Advisor/Managing Hospital Quality, Risk and Cost**
Aspen Systems Corporation
Rockville, Maryland

Malpractice Lifeline (monthly)
Malpractice Lifeline, Inc.
Chicago, Illinois

Journals and Other Periodicals

Law, Medicine and Health Care (monthly)
American Society of Law and Medicine
Boston, Massachusetts

Journal of Law and Medicine (quarterly)
American Society of Law and Medicine
Boston, Massachusetts

Journal of Legal Medicine (an official publication of the American College of
Legal Medicine; quarterly)
Long Island City, New York

Books

Medical Risk Management: Preventive Legal Strategies for Health Care Providers
Edward Richards, III, and Katherine C. Rathbun
Aspen Systems Corporation
Rockville, Maryland

*Risk Management: A Guide for Health Care Professionals**
John F. Monagle
Aspen Systems Corporation
Rockville, Maryland

Risk Management HPL (Hospital Professional Liability Primer)*
Ronald D. Wade
Ohio Hospital Insurance Co.
Columbus, Ohio

The Rights of Doctors, Nurses and Allied Health Professionals
George J. Annas, Leonard H. Glantz, and Barbara F. Katz
American Civil Liberties Union (an ACLU handbook)
New York, New York

The Rights of the Critically Ill
John A. Robertson
American Civil Liberties Union (an ACLU handbook)
New York, New York

Problems in Hospital Law, 4th Edition
Robert D. Miller
Aspen Systems Corporation
Rockville, Maryland

Risk Management for Hospitals: A Practical Approach
Bernard L. Brown, Jr.
Aspen Systems Corporation
Rockville, Maryland

*Health Law Manual** (multivolume looseleaf service)
Health Law Center
Aspen Systems Corporation
Rockville, Maryland

*Medical Management Analysis, A Systematic Approach to Quality Assurance
and Risk Management, Vols. 1 and 2** (deals with generic screening criteria)
Joyce W. Craddick, M.D.
Auburn, California

*ECRI Risk Control** (multivolume looseleaf service with hotline to consultants)
Plymouth Meeting, Pennsylvania

Handbook of Health Care Risk Management
Glen T. Troyer and Steven L. Salman
Aspen Systems Corporation
Rockville, Maryland

Summary

Risk prevention activities fall within two major categories, patient care related and those that are not directly related to patient care. Patient care activities are those with direct impact on the person receiving health services and include many tasks, including physician credentialing. An activity not directly related to patient care would typically include physical plant safety.

All health care facilities have areas that by their very nature can be classified as high risk. These are traditional service areas such as obstetrics, where there is a high probability of both sustaining a claim or suit and the incurrence of high damages associated with the event. The common high risk areas of an acute care general hospital are obstetrics, emergency department, radiology, surgery, and anesthesia. Many policies, procedures, standards, and other criteria are offered for risk managers to use in assessing the degree of exposure for each high-risk area. The concept of occurrence screening is the technique of applying known criteria to an exposure area to help identify potential sources of misadventures and the claims or lawsuits that can result.

A successful risk prevention program for a health care facility will require the close monitoring and coordination of risk prevention activities of many departments. It will also require a professional risk management staff with access to literature and the experiences of others available through communications in professional societies. The organization's risk manager should be active in both a local and national association of hospital risk managers to keep abreast of changes in the environment.

Chapter Exercise

You are the administrative officer of a health care facility. You are concerned that the risk prevention program at your facility is spread out among many units and that therefore a lack of coordination exists. You desire to streamline the function and have been thinking of some way of improving risk prevention linkage between departments.

1. Discuss and, if necessary, draw a diagram of a hypothetical system that will fulfill your plans.

2. Discuss each unit in the new system and what its role will be in the new program.

3. Decide which department will serve as the focal point of the system.

4. List some steps that can be used to verify the credentials of applicants to the medical staff, and any additional steps that can be taken with graduates of foreign medical schools and hospitals.

References

1. Press, Irwin. "The Predisposition to File Claims: The Patient's Perspective." *Law, Medicine and Health Care* 12 (April 1984): 53-62.

2. Sowka, M. Patricia, Editor, *NAIC Malpractice Claims: Medical Malpractice Claims 1975-1978*. Kansas City, MO: National Association of Insurance Commissioners Vol. II, No. 2 (September 1980).

3. Localio, A. Russel. "Variations on $962,258: The Misuse of Data on Medical Malpractice." *Law, Medicine and Health Care* 13 (June 1985): 126-127.

4. *Injury Valuation Reports No. 253*. Solon, Ohio: Jury Verdict Research, Inc., 1982

5. "Malpractice Suits Affect OB/Gyn Fees and Practices." *Medical Liability Advisory Service*. 8 (September 1983): 1.

6. *Interim Report of the PIAA Committee to Study Claims Involving Infants With Neurologic Deficit*. Lawrenceville, NJ: Physicians Insurers Association of America, 1984; Barry S. Schifrin et al., "Electronic Fetal Monitoring and Obstetrical Malpractice." Law, Medicine and Health Care (13) (June 1985): 100.

7. Schifrin, et al., pp. 100-105.

8. *PIAA Interim Report*, p. 2.

9. *Guidelines for Perinatal Care*. American Academy of Pediatrics Washington, DC: American College of Obstetricians and Gynecologists, 1983; Standards for Obstetric-Gynecologic Services. 6th ed. American College of Obstetricians and Gynecologists, 1985.

10. "Summary of ASHRM Annual Conference: Brain-Damaged Infant Claims The Plaintiff's Perspective." Occurrence 6 (September-October 1985): 3; "Experts Reveal Sources of Perinatal Liability, Solutions." *Hospital Risk Management* 7 (9 September 1985): 109-119.

11. *Guidelines for Perinatal Care*. (ref. 9)

12. "Risk Management in Perinatal Services: Documentation Criteria," *Help News* (June 1985).

13. "Placenta/Cord Pathology Can Aid Malpractice Defense", *Malpractice Digest* (June 1985):1-2; Adam P. Wilczek, and Karl T. Franzoni. Umbilical Artery Blood Gas Studies: A Tool for Defending the 'Defensible' Brain Damage Case?" *Specialty Reporter for Obstetrics,* 3 (July 1985): 1-2; Marvin Cornblath and Russell L. Clark. "Neonatal 'Brain Damage'—An Analysis of 250 Claims." *Western Journal of Medicine,* 140 (February 1984): 302.

14. Rogers, John T. *Risk Management in Emergency Medicine*. Dallas, Texas: American College of Emergency Physicians, 1985, p. 4; "Risk Management—Emergency Department." *Help News* (August 1984): 1; Joseph J. Trautlein et al. "Malpractice in the Emergency Department—Review of 200 Cases." *Annals of Emergency Medicine* 13 (September 1984): 103-105.

15. *Badeaux v. East Jefferson Hospital*. 364 So 2d 1348 (La. App. 1978); Theodore D. Sawyer and Mary Sawyer Pickers. "The Emergency Room—Unique Legal Problems." *For the Defense* 23 (1981): 32.

16. "Documentation on the Emergency Department Record." *Help News* (August 1984).

17. "Radiology Claims Experience." *Norcal Claims Rx* (April 1985); "High Radiology Losses Related to Invasive Procedures," *Forum* 6 (July-August 1985): 2.

18. Ibid.

19. "Is a Radiologic 'Miss' Malpractice? An Ominous Example." *AJR* Vol. 140 (May 1983): 1031.

20. Ibid.

21. Reuter, Stewart R. "Legal Aspects of Angiography and Interventive Radiology." *Legal Aspects of Medical Practice* 13 (January 1985): 2.

22. Rosoff, Arnold J. *Informed Consent: A Guide for Health Care Providers*. Rockville, MD: Aspen Systems Corp., 1981, pp. 305-306.

23. Baltaxe, Harold A., and Robert C. Stadalnik. "A New Look at Hospital Clinical Privileges As They Apply to Radiology," *JAMA* 249 (June 3, 1983): 2907-2908.

24. Ibid.

25. Risk Management in Anesthesia, *Help News*, 5 (September 1982).

26. Tarr, Amy. "AIDS: The Legal Issues Widen." *The National Law Journal* 8 (November 25, 1985): 1, 28-29.

27. *Darling v. Charleston Community Memorial Hospital*, 33 Ill. 2d 326, 211 N.E. 2d 253 (1965).

28. *Accreditation Manual for Hospitals AMH-83*. Chicago: Joint Commission on Accreditation of Hospitals, 1983, p. 106.

CHAPTER NINE

THE MEDICAL RECORD AND RISK MANAGEMENT

Joan T. Rines

The importance of the medical record and the reliance of a health facility's risk management program on it cannot be overstated. This chapter will provide some insight as to why the medical record is so critical to a successful risk management program. How the risk manager and other members of the risk management team use the record will also be explained, as well as the role of the medical record department and practitioners. Last, suggestions for improving medical record maintenance will be offered.

The Importance of the Medical Record

A full, complete, and accurate medical record is the physician's best defense against a malpractice claim.[1] Completeness, objectivity, consistency, and accuracy are four components of a good medical record. If a physician has kept poor medical records, a plaintiff's attorney will pursue a malpractice claim even if it appears defensible.[2] In 1980, Jorgenson wrote that, " . . . Something as complex as a medical malpractice action can be avoided by something as simple as the maintenance of medical records in a proper, accurate, and systematic manner." Lanham and Orlikoff agreed and suggested that poor medical records and depersonalization of medical care are equally important reasons for malpractice suits.[3]

Documentation problems exist in all types of health care facilities. "Bad records make good care look bad, bad care look worse, and can make a case indefensible."[4] In his article describing psychiatric record liability, Joseph contended that documentation continues to be the most important risk management problem that mental health facilities have. He cited two instances of astronomical settlements that could have been avoided with proper documentation. In the first case, a hospital paid $3.6 million for tampering with a record after the patient suffered an adverse outcome. Another facility settled for $3.3 million after a mental patient died in a secluded room. The staff members had failed to document the regular monitoring of the patient. After the patient's death, the staff tried to provide evidence of regular monitoring, but since timely documentation did not exist, their defense was unsuccessful.

The law is stern. If the records do not contain information on a particular point, and if the physician does not have a sound recollection of that needed information, then the patient's version of the happening is credible. Many actions are not filed until years after the incident; thus medical records must be completed quickly, must be timely, and must be as close to the events as is reasonably possible.[5]

The Purpose of the Medical Record

The medical record is the property of the hospital and is the basic document for all quality assurance and risk management activities. The medical record department and its personnel occupy an important position in ensuring that hospital staff members who have the right either to document in the record or review its content do so in accordance with applicable laws, regulations, and accreditation standards.[6]

In 1984 the Joint Commission on Accreditation of Hospitals (JCAH) enumerated the following purposes of the medical record:[7]

1. The medical record serves as the basis for planning patient care and for continuity in the evaluation of the patient's condition and treatment. It is a record of ongoing care on which medical treatment decisions are based and justified. Consequently, its purpose is consistent with the hospital's quality assurance responsibility to audit and evaluate the care rendered a patient.

2. The medical record furnishes documentary evidence of the course of the patient's medical evaluation, treatment, and change in condition during the hospital stay, during an ambulatory care or emergency visit to the hospital, or while being followed in a hospital-administered home health care program. This is important from a risk management standpoint because in the event a patient makes a claim against the hospital, the record documentation serves to demonstrate that care was rendered in accordance with appropriate standards. For instance, the JCAH and various state hospital licensing laws require that a written record be maintained on each patient seen in the emergency room regardless of whether or not he or she is admitted to the hospital. Such written records provide proof in court that standards of emergency care have been followed.[8]

3. The medical record documents communication between the treating physician and any other health care practitioner involved in the treatment plan. Different sections of the record do not exist in isolation, and it is a legitimate quality assurance/risk management function to see that there are no discrepancies and inconsistencies in the information flow.

The JCAH listed two additional purposes of the medical record that are related to quality assurance and risk management activities, namely, to protect the legal interests of the patient, hospital, and the responsible practitioners; and to provide data for continuing education and research activities.

Failure to Comply with Minimum Requirements for Medical Record Keeping

A definite correlation exists between liability and medical record keeping. The possibility is remote that hospitals may lose licensure or accreditation because of failure to meet the minimum standards of record keeping. However, if that failure were coupled with other substandard conduct, there could be grounds for such loss.[9]

Mishandling of or failure to read records correctly could result in negligence liability. The medical record documents what happens to the patient, and an expert witness testifying to standards met uses the documentation to prove whether the standards were or were not met. For instance, improper writing of the physician's order such as occurred in *Norton v. Argonaut Insurance Co.*,[10] lack of use of the medical record for reading the patient's history as alleged in *Favalora v. Aetna Casualty and Surety Company*,[11] and the failure of the nurse to observe and record eclampsia symptoms in the *Hansch v. Hackett*,[12] case are all illustrations of how crucial proper medical record documentation is to liability and risk prevention.

It is an almost unanimous opinion that in almost every case the medical record is both a decision-making aid and a deterrent to decisions to determine the hospital's legal liability for injuries sustained by patients. In a jury trial, the medical record determines whether or not standard care has been given. The medical record can answer questions about the probability of medical risk. For example, did the doctor order an IV? Is there evidence that he or she checked to ensure that the patient benefited from that IV? Jury surveys have shown year after year that many cases were decided on the basis of the quality of the medical records introduced as evidence in trials.[13] In the absence of a clear and accurate medical record, the decision as to who is telling the truth in a malpractice case is decided by the jury, judge, or arbitrator. Even though it is the plaintiff who must prove that negligence occurred, the medical record's accuracy, or lack of it, becomes an ally of whomever it favors.

The medical record is primarily a tool for continuity of care, but its role as a legal document is increasing.[14] It provides the simplest and most economical defense against medical malpractice claims.[15] As long as reasonable medical care has been delivered, a medical record serves as an impenetrable barrier between the physician and the dissatisfied patient. Errors or sloppily kept records signal dollar signs to attorneys. Also, poor documentation can prevent the risk manager from developing a true profile of the institution's exposure to liability.[16]

Rules of Medical Record Keeping

Before discussing further the relationship of the medical record, the medical record department, and the medical record professional to risk management, proper medical record documentation rules must be enumerated. The following list of documentation do's and don'ts is quoted directly from Ronald G. Wade's book, *Risk Management HPL: Hospital Professional Liability Primer.*[17] According to Wade these documentation rules are probably more important to claims settlements than the actual rendering of professional services.

1. Medical records are permanent documents, and as such, all entries should be typewritten or by ball-point pen. No soft felt pens or lead pencils should be used as recording instruments.

2. Each entry should be placed in the appropriate column, beginning without any indentation at the immediate left of the column.

3. For space remaining at either the left or right side of the entry, a straight, unbroken line should be extended to each margin, the purpose of which is to prevent entries at a later date.

4. Each entry should be documented by date and time and each medical record page identified by patient name and the date. (Usually, an imprint of the patient's identification card appears in the upper right hand corner of each page.)

5. All entries should be in chronological order and entered on consecutive lines.

6. A new entry should be recorded for each new time and a new time for each topic.

7. Each entry should be signed by the individual making the entry. The signature should include the first name initial, complete surname, and status (e.g., R. Brown, R.N.). The signature should follow the completion of the entry.

Care should be taken with medical chart checklists such as doctors' orders, medication record sheets, fluid intake/output, and lists of provisional diagnoses and treatment plans. Nurses should check and initial each order and avoid using blanket initialing meant to cover a series of orders, according to Karp.[18]

8. No one should ever chart or sign the medical record for another individual.

9. Individuals should never countersign an entry without having first read and checked the entry for accuracy. The countersignature attests to the authenticity of what was recorded and shares equal responsibility with the signature being countersigned.

Attorneys can use the Medical Staff's Bylaws on countersigning to prosecute physicians. When a physician countersigns in the medical record, he or she is attesting to the chart's historical accuracy. If questioned on the witness stand, the physician must testify that he or she knows and understands this bylaw provision or he or she will be accused of being in violation of the hospital's protocol on countersigning. Countersigning "is no mere act of cosmetics," Shrager wrote.[19]

10. No entry should ever be made in advance of the procedure performed.

There should be no precharting of medications and completion of proposed treatment. Events may intervene before the precharted time, and uncharting looks suspicious.

11. Documentation to the chart does not have to be a long narrative, but it should be complete and record precisely what was seen, heard, felt, smelled, or otherwise observed through the senses and also what professional services were rendered to the patient.

The less precise and the more subjective and incomplete the documentation is, the more successful an attorney will be in convincing a jury that his or her client was harmed, Karp wrote. Completeness and accuracy are two of the four components that according to Karp comprise a good medical record.[20]

12. The first word of every statement should be capitalized. Periods should be used at the completion of each thought. Though complete sentences are not necessary, correct grammar and spelling are mandatory. There are several drugs with almost identical spelling but with very different characteristics and applications.

13. Medical records must be legible. Printing is preferred with letters of uniform size and words evenly spaced. If an entry cannot be read, it can be argued that that which was being documented did not occur.

This item has been emphasized by other authors, as well.[21-23] Karp added that illegible entries may be overlooked or misinterpreted. A misplaced decimal point can be critical. According to Jorgenson, legibility is the most abused premise to preparing a good medical record. A record that cannot be read is meaningless. The failure to insist upon legibility defeats the whole purpose of maintaining a medical record. Illegibility may force the physician to rely on his or her recall, which may be far removed from the incident, thus detracting from the credibility of the defense. Legibility also relates to the proper, timely recording of observations of patients' conditions and/or the administration of medications. Many times the exact timing of these details is crucial to the case's defense. Notes that fail to record exact times may misrepresent the patient's treatment course. It may appear that the patient did not receive the proper treatment, when in fact proper treatment was administered, but was improperly recorded, with the result that there is no concrete evidence that it happened. Even if both the hospital and the physician are eventually absolved of any negligence, nevertheless, if a suit was filed, the legal work has been done, and costs were incurred on what may have been an otherwise unmeritorious claim. It does not take very many of these instances to raise insurance premium costs.

14. All entries should be consistent and noncontradictory. Some duplicity [duplication] in medical record documentation cannot be avoided. Therefore, the information recorded in one section of the record must be the same as that in other record locations. Once a pattern has been established in documentation, the pattern should not be changed. Variance in spacing between entries or before the signature hints that the record might have been altered. (Consistency is a third component of a good medical record, according to Karp.[25])

15. Only hospital-approved and authorized abbreviations should be used in medical records documentation. Abbreviations should not be used in recording diagnoses, surgical procedures, and medications administered to patients. Abbreviations with duplicate meanings should be avoided.

16. Charting must be accurate. Any inaccuracy intentional or unintentional, will be discovered by the claimant/plaintiff attorney who will use the error to discredit the reliability of the record and the one who made the error.

It is highly likely that at some point the court will order that the patient's attorney be given at least a copy of his or her record. For that reason alone, documentation should be accurate and timely, according to Glass.[26]

17. The medical records should be documented where they are located and under no circumstances removed from the area.

18. When it becomes necessary to copy a page of the medical record, a diagonal line should be drawn across the page to be recopied and the word "original" written at the top of the page. The word "copy" should be written on the new page. Both sheets then should be maintained and kept in the records. NEVER SHOULD THE ORIGINAL PAGE BE DISCARDED OR THROWN AWAY.

19. Entry corrections. Corrections to a medical record should be few in number and done so carefully and correctly in order that the correction cannot be used by the claimant/plaintiff to cast doubt or suspicion on the reliability and credibility of the record and the one doing the charting. Entries should be corrected only when the entry information is inaccurate. Correction procedures should be as follows:
    a. A single, thin line should be drawn through each word or line which is

inaccurate, but ensuring the incorrect material is still legible.

b. The correction should be dated and initialed.

c. A note should be placed in the margin stating why the previous entry had to be corrected.

d. The correcting entry should be entered on the chart in chronological order and the charter should assure it is clear which entry is being corrected.

e. In questionable situations, the corrected entry should be witnessed by a colleague.

Grayson[27] wrote that because a plaintiff's attorney may subpoena a record before a case is filed, it behooves the physician, who may want to reexamine the record in order to jot down whatever else he or she can remember about that case after being named a defendant, to write and attach a separate addendum to the record and send it to his or her attorney. Such actions may prevent the plaintiff and his or her attorney from suspecting chart tampering. However, Jorgenson[28] said that amended original entries indicate that treatment was omitted or was not rendered properly in the first place. If proper time and careful thought are employed when documenting in the record, addendums can be avoided. A record that appears altered will be suspect even if the alteration was the innocent correction of a spelling error, and a prior entry should never be obliterated, according to Glass[29].

20. All atypical treatments should be recorded with explanation as to why the treatments were rendered to patients.

21. All unusual occurrences/incidences such as falls, medication incidents, equipment malfunctions, and emergency situations should be documented to the record.

22. All patient injuries must be charted. If a patient injury is not recorded, the claimant/plaintiff attorney has a free rein to allege "coverup." In all incidents, the recorder should objectively document just what was actually seen, heard, or witnessed through the senses. Conclusions should not be drawn as to what happened, just what was actually witnessed. Patient comments should be recorded and clearly indicated as patient quotes. Subsequent to a patient injury situation, the record must reflect the record of the patient's vital signs, physical condition, noting abrasions, swelling, hematomas, etc., the patient's mental condition and subjective complaints, time physicians were notified, and time of physician arrival, and the details of treatments rendered or ordered.

The medical record could be a definite obstacle to a risk management program if incident reports are a part of the record. Incident reports have been described as an administrative record, which should be kept separately from the clinical record.[30] Some risk managers discourage completing these documents and insist that, especially in patient injury cases, these incidences or occurrences be reported directly and orally to the risk manager. As long ago as 1978, Grayson warned that, regardless of the severity or type of incident reported, confidentiality is a mainstay of incident reporting.[31] The fact that a report has been filed should never be noted in either the medical section or the nurse's notes section of the medical record. Section 24.2 of the California Hospital Association *Consent Manual*,[32] for instance, states that the incident report itself should not be a part of the record because it contains information not applicable to patient treatment. However, mention of the incident and how the patient was affected should be documented in the patient's record to facilitate treatment by the health care team. In 1982, Dwyer wrote that keeping the incident report separate from the medical record was one of three ways hospitals could minimize the likelihood of discovery of the incident report.[33] Although keeping the report separate does not preclude discovery, it does provide the hospital with an arguable position of privilege and/or work done by the hospital attorney in anticipation of litigation.

Groah and Reed wrote that incident reports are designed to communicate patient care information either within a department or to other areas of the hospital, and nurses should distinguish them from documented medical records.[34] However, these authors are a bit vague in their directions to nurses on how to document incidents. They prescribe documenting the incident in the record and recording what steps were taken to correct or report the situation. A documented incident is better than a gap in the record, which is likely to cause legal difficulties. A report, they continued, is written briefly, concisely, and factually, and is separate from the record. They do not, however, give examples of proper documentation in either the record or the separate report, which leaves the reader confused. They do instruct nurses that the patient's chart should contain baseline patient data, patient problems, patient goals, evaluative criteria for assessing goal achievement, nursing interventions, actual patient outcomes, information about postoperative care, and the nurse's signature. Note that reports of incidents are not mentioned in this list of basic documentation elements.

As mentioned earlier, one of the record's purposes is to portray ongoing patient care and evidence of treatment furnished. It is the information that is not needed for patient care (i.e., that part that is of interest to the administration) that is intended to be preserved separately under the attorney-client privilege, and since a patient's medical record can be subpoenaed, it is paramount that this report not be filed with the record.

23. Informed consent for surgery and special procedures must be included in the records.

In general, there are two types of consent, a general consent to admission and nursing care and a surgical consent.

Detailed information is a key to obtaining an informed consent that will stand up in court.[35] In addition, careful documentation should reflect the risks of the procedure that were explained to the patient and when these were explained. Alternative procedures that may be performed should be mentioned and it is imperative that the consequences of failure to perform the procedure be made clear to the patient. Only the physician should communicate these informed consent elements to the patient, and he or she should document having done so. It is dangerous practice for a nurse or any other health care professional to discuss these elements in lieu of the physician. Many lawsuits are brought because the physician-patient relationship breaks down, and much of this relationship is based on communication and subsequent trust.

Karp urged that when forms are to be completed, each nonapplicable blank should be marked either "nonapplicable" or a single line should be drawn through the area.[37] Joseph wrote that medical record forms should be designed to encourage thorough documentation,[36] but often the opposite is true, and poor documentation is often the result of a poor forms design. In some malpractice claims alleging lack of consent for a specific procedure, the plaintiff has attempted to claim that although he or she signed a consent form, some blanks were filled in after surgery, which amounted to an unauthorized consent.

In 1983, Noreen M. Clark at the University of Michigan's School of Public Health reported her study of consent forms in seven Michigan hospitals.[38] Consent forms serve two purposes: 1) legal, to make sure that the patient is aware of and agrees to the treatment decisions; and 2) educational, to inform that patient so that he or she can make an informed decision about his or her own mode of treatment. In Clark's study, all seven hospitals' consent forms complied with the legal purpose of the form, but only one served the educational purpose. She wrote that it is reasonable to assume that hospitals want to protect themselves and their patients legally. However, studies show that where there is more patient involvement, the patient tends to be more satisfied with his or her treatment. Although this patient satisfaction benefits the physicians and the hospitals, there is no proof that better informed patients are less likely to sue when they experience an adverse outcome. Nevertheless, when hospitals ask patients to sign a difficult-to-read consent form, they place themselves in legal jeopardy, Clark wrote.[39] If the names of the procedures and the language used to explain those procedures are not written in lay terms, the courts may say that the patient had little chance to make an informed decision.

Ethicists argue that the lack of an informed consent violates the principle of autonomy: the right of a patient to choose what shall be done to his or her own body. However, because a consent form, signed by both the patient and the physician, is present in the record it does not mean that the patient truly understands and has made an informed decision. The form merely represents evidence that the physician discussed the procedures with his patient, nothing more.

24. Nurses should record death-bed statements.

25. The medical records should document accountability for patients' personal effects and valuables.

26. Physician, specialist, consultant visits to the patient and the professional services rendered should be charted.

27. Insertion and removal of drains and radium should be documented.

28. Patients' personal and medical responses to professional services rendered to include patients being uncooperative and/or not following instructions. [This is especially important when a patient insists upon leaving the hospital before being officially discharged by the physician. The documentation should read that "patient left against medical advice."]

29. Medications, treatments, vital signs, specimens obtained and where sent must be noted in the record.

30. Assessments of patients' mobility, appetite, orientation, mental attitude, and degree in independence should be documented.

31. Documentation of the times and sites of intramuscular, subcutaneous, intradermal, and intravenous injections, sites of infusions and appearances, type and amount of fluids, medications added, rate administered, IV sites, and number of drops per minute by shift should be documented.

32. Specifically, in regards to the documentation of times, the medical records should be documented to reflect the exact time all professional care and treatments are rendered to patients and the exact times physicians are contacted by nurses, supervisors are contacted, consent forms/releases obtained, and doctors' orders validated.

33. A patient's condition should be documented to the chart upon initial admission to the floor, prior to and upon return from the operating room or other special treatment areas, and at discharge. Joseph wrote that this is especially applicable to psychiatric patients' charts.

34. Nurses should chart their observations of patients' conditions prior to their leaving the floor for any extended period of time such as for breaks, etc.

35. Patients' histories and physicals should be documented to charts within 24 hours of the date of their admissions.

According to Jorgenson, the patient's history is a major area of the medical record in which preventive steps can be taken to avoid liability exposure and subsequent litigation.25 Circumstances leading to treatment must be obtained and recorded accurately. That a patient "complained of chest pains" upon entering a facility is insufficient documentation. Such items as time of onset, nature, and location of the pains should be included also. Accuracy and substance should not be sacrificed for the sake of expediency. In addition, histories must be consistent. Many times patients are asked to repeat their history to various medical personnel when they enter the hospital. These histories should not reflect contradictions or conflicting statements.

36. Surgical notes by surgeons should be entered to charts immediately after the completion of surgery. The formal Operative Report should be dictated and entered to the charts no later than 24 hours of the surgeries performed.

37. Operating room records should include:

   a. Patient identification, level of consciousness and understanding of procedures to be performed.

   b. Consent forms.

   c. Authorized observers in the operating room.

   d. Pre-operative checklists.

   e. Verification of allergies, NPO status, and any physical limitation.

   f. Skin condition and skin preparation.

   g. Patient support mechanism and position.

   h. Identification of prosthetic implants, medical devices, wound drains, catheters, packing, medical equipment and location.

   i. Sponge, needle and [instrument] count verification.

   j. Specimen disposition.

   k. Patient monitoring device identification and location.

   l. Condition of patient and time of patient arrival in the recovery room.

   m. Anesthesiologist's record.

   n. Surgeon's operative note.

38. Telephone and verbal orders of physicians to nurses should be countersigned by the ordering physician within 24 hours of the order. The nurse who takes a telephone order from a physician should first write down the order on a scratch pad and then re-read the order back to the physician. The order should then be recorded in the chart to include the name of the physician, the time and manner the order was received, and details of the order.

39. Discharge orders. It is extremely important that the medical records are

carefully and diligently documented as to the discharge instructions and instructional material given to a patient and/or patient family at discharge time. The documentation should include the instructions given pertaining to diet, patient activity and exercise, medications (what the medication is for, when and how it is to be taken and side effects to look for), applicable skin care and hygiene, specific treatments the patient will have to do such as wound dressing, injection and injection site care, Foley catheter care and usage, colostomy care, etc., patient follow-up appointments, and applicable agency referrals. The documentation should record the indication of patient and family's understanding of the discharge instructions received, patient's demonstrated ability to perform what was taught, and the names of all instructional booklets, pamphlets, etc. given to the patient. The chart should also contain all signed transfer forms should the patient be transferred to an extended care facility.

Joseph wrote that this element is particularly important in psychiatric record documentation.[41] Failure to state the patient's ability to be discharged has been the basis for legal action against mental health facilities.

40. Charting must be objective and void of conclusions. The choice of the patient is very important. Words should be carefully chosen so that there isn't any room for conjecture, doubt, or misunderstanding of what is being recorded. Claimant/plaintiff[s'] attorneys will look for all such verbiage and use them to discredit or cast doubt on what was observed or professionally done for the patient, all of which just adds an additional burden for the defense. Words such as unintentionally, inadvertently, somehow, unexplainably, [and] unfortunately are not good choices because they reflect a judgment of something that took place and can call for additional explanation. Words such as appeared, seems to be, [and] apparently, are not definitive and can be used by the claimant/plaintiff['s] attorney to cast doubt as to what was actually observed.

Many words can have different meanings to any number of different people. The charter who writes that the patient "feels better" or "appears confused" is open to criticism and questioning, for different interpretations can be applied to both phrases. The charting has to be specific. If these phrases are used, they should be accompanied by a description of the observed specific behavior of the patient which led to the assessments.

Words should be chosen carefully. There is a big difference between "Patient slipped on wet floor, fell, and broke hip" and "Patient incontinent of urine on way to BR, slipped and broke right hip at 10:30 a.m. Dr. B was notified." Entries of findings should contain enough information to identify the treatment as it evolves, according to Jorgenson.[42] Words such as *negative* or *positive* should not be used.

Instead, supplementary data should accompany these statements to determine the steps taken to reach these conclusions. All steps taken to rule out all provisional diagnoses should be documented. This thorough documentation supports the physician's and the hospital's attempt to treat the patient properly prior to his or her discharge from the hospital.

41. Patient transfers to another facility should be documented by:

    a. Date and time of transfer.

    b. Conveyance and name of transporting organization.

    c. Name of the facility to which the patient is being transferred.

    d. Name of the person talked to at the receiving facility, time and means of contact.

    e. Information afforded the person at the receiving facility.

    f. Services requested.

    g. Time the patient can be expected.

42. The medical record should be documented of all nursing and physician contacts, both in person and telephone conversations. The documentation should include:

    a. The complete names and titles of nurses and physicians involved.

    b. Means of communication.

    c. Time of the contact and who initiated.

    d. Details of the discussion.

    e. Response of each to the discussion.

The substance of all notes in the record between the physician and hospital personnel should be documented in clear language.[43] Entries such as "Dr. B. called" do not indicate whether the nurse initially contacted the physician or whether or not the physician called the hospital to inquire about the patient's progress.

43. Documentation should never mention that an Incident Report was completed. [See the previous discussion on reporting incidents].

44. Personal positions or points of view should never be argued or complaints about working conditions entered into the medical records. Such documentation activity can be construed as unprofessionalism and that less than full attention was given to patients' conditions and needs.

45. The medical record should never be the forum for belittling, criticizing, placing blame, or casting doubt on the professionalism of another member

of the health care team. Professional in-fighting documented to a medical record guarantees litigation and escalates settlement/jury verdict values. This type of documentation provides the plaintiff a built-in expert.

Self-serving statements inconsistent with the end result only serve to encourage the initiation of malpractice claims. Concise, professional, objective language should be used at all times. Subjective, derogatory, or sarcastic wording should be avoided at all times. Too often in instances where criticisms have been made, there has not been a thorough review of prior records or discussions with prior treating physicians. Any criticism that a patient makes must be referenced to that patient to avoid such confusion, Karp wrote.[44]

46. Frivolous, extraneous, or humorous remarks which have nothing to do with patient care should never be charted. They infer inattention to duty and bespeak of unprofessionalism.

47. Biased or personal feelings about a patient being cared for should never be entered to the chart. Even should those feelings be true, the claimant/ plaintiff attorney can use those remarks to give an unfavorable opinion of the charter and to infer the patient possibly did not receive the best of care from the involved individual.

Joseph warned against the use of such extraneous remarks as "bonkers" in psychiatric records.[45] It is best to quote the patients directly rather than paraphrase their remarks, he wrote.

48. Time gaps in a medical record are very difficult to explain and justify. The claimant/plaintiff attorney can raise significant questions as to what was or was not professionally observed during the unrecorded period of time or what was or was not done of a professional nature to the patient. The best possible way to avoid medical record time gaps is for charting to be performed timely and without delay, preferably as soon as possible subsequent to patient observation and/or care and treatment rendered to patients.

Examples of problems in time gaps and delays are failure to respond in a timely manner to emergencies and code blue orders. Wade is very critical of nurses who wait until the end of their shifts to document the records. Their rationale is that the ratio of nurses to patients is such that there is insufficient time to document more frequently. However, Wade believes it is physically impossible for nurses to recall totally and accurately their observations and acts of professional care and treatment rendered over an 8-hour period. Lapsed time between observation and treatment promotes errors, omissions, and gaps, which would be detrimental to any defense.

49. Late entries to the chart should be identified as such, reflecting the date

and time of the actual entry and then in the body of the late entry, state the date and time the entry should have been recorded. Guidelines for late entries should be available in the medical record department.

50. Omissions are to be avoided at all cost. Omissions can be a deadly tool in the hands of an adroit attorney. Even if adequate professional services were rendered to a patient, if for some reason the chart does not provide a record of those services, the attorney can allege they were not performed. In almost every instance when a jury has to decide who to believe, the witness or the chart, it will go with the chart.

   Although omissions are sometimes done at the patient's request, it could affect the method of treatment chosen. When such information is omitted and a patient is injured, the person responsible for the omission may be held liable. Sensitive information should be objectively recorded and identified as history from the patient or as a medical diagnosis.

51. Obliterating an entry or portions thereof can serve the claimant/plaintiff attorney in the same way as omissions. Medical record entries should never be made non-legible by pencil, pen, typewriting markings, or by "white out" or any other way.

Wade wrote that these criteria are not all-inclusive, but merely represent sources of problems for those who have represented the interests of both the hospital and those responsible for record documentation in malpractice claims and suits.

In mental health facilities, the families' and patients' expectations of outcome of care should be documented, according to Joseph.[46] Care should be used in the treatment plan area of the record to make sure that the documentation shows that a treatment plan was derived following the needs assessment identified earlier. The patient's contribution to the plan should be documented also. Goals should be defined and a statement should be made as to how they are to be met. Periodic review and update of the goals should be documented also. The patient's record should be used to show that the hospital has placed the patient in the least restrictive environment possible and incorporated the use of precautions, restrictions, or other behavior controls with documentation of the justification for their use. The patient's readiness to be moved to a less restrictive environment or to be discharged should also be evidenced in the record. Contradictions and inconsistencies in this documentation can arouse suspicion, for example, when the physician writes a discharge-to-home order but the therapist documents that the patient is still mentioning suicide.

Risk Management Uses of the Medical Record

The following are just a few of the activities that rely on the medical record as a source document.

Generic Screening

Although generic screening is usually described in the quality assurance literature, the mere fact that it is a quality assurance activity makes it also a risk management function. The California Medical Insurance Feasibility Study identified 20 criteria that can be used by medical record practitioners to screen records for potential compensable events (PCEs). Hospitals use either this same list or a modified, more hospital-specific version.[48]

Kennedy described the use of record screening for PCEs. Records in her setting were screened using a set of generic outcome-screening criteria adapted to the hospital's abstracting system. She wrote that the medical record professional is the most qualified to perform this quality assurance activity for several reasons: 1) the medical record is the only source document that details the treatment program of the patient; 2) the medical record is a document that applies equally to all patients regardless of the sources of or persons responsible for care; and 3) if the screening method is applied equally to all patients, more time becomes necessary to do a complete, accurate job. Physicians and other direct patient care personnel do not have this time. Therefore, since medical record professionals perform final chart analyses and assembly, logically they are the ones who should use the generic screening process. Reports are generated according to criterion numbers, which identify trends, as well as specific departments and personnel. Screening becomes both a quality assurance and a risk management tool. Kennedy emphasized that generic screening performed by medical record professionals is an identification process only, and the judgments of responsibility for these potential problems are left to be made via the peer review process.[49]

Lanham and Orlikoff[50] wrote that conflicting or missing documentation in the medical record can be used as a generic screening criterion to detect professional negligence. The criterion is intended to identify problems in documentation recorded by different health care professionals that may affect the patient's care or the record's status as a legal document . These authors found most documentation discrepancies to be the result of a professional's failure to document accurately, a patient's failure to reveal consistently the same information to all providers, or problems in the data management systems. The results of the screening should be compared with incident reports to ensure that all adverse outcomes have been reported. Gaps in the incident reports then can be reported to the risk manager for follow-up.

White added that generic screening has eliminated the need for periodic audits, death reviews, and utilization review and tissue review committees in one of Arizona's hospitals.[51] In addition to the generic screening advantages that Kennedy mentioned, White listed some criticisms of the process. Some argue that the criteria are too broad. Others say that it is easy to see where things could or should have been done differently when one knows the outcome. One critic said that, in day-to-day patient care, decision making is not that simple, and often decisions that went awry can be justified. At the hospital described by White, all agreed that this quality assurance activity had helped control malpractice risks. White added, however, that skepticism still exists as to whether occurrence screening helps reduce physician liability.

Generic screening is used in all areas and is the basis for many peer review activities (P. L. Spath, personal communication, October 15, 1985). Policy and procedure manuals should be used as criteria when screening records for risk exposure (J. Fainter, personal communication, October 15, 1985). One should make sure that any procedure documented in the record is also a part of that department's rules and regulations. Regardless of the source or effectiveness of the criteria used, medical record professionals use them for either concurrent or retrospective, upon-discharge record analyses. Screening the record helps close the information gap and helps the risk manager investigate the event while the facts are still fresh in the minds of those involved.

Infection Control

Salman and Click[52] believe that risk managers should interact with infection con-trol experts because of increasing patient awareness of the rights of health care consumers and the knowledge of the potential for acquiring infections resulting from their hospital stay. These authors described how the infection control practi-tioner and the risk manager can work together to reduce liability risks resulting from infections. The infection control expert reviews all records, and all records revealing such infections are kept in a permanent file. As soon as a patient complaint is received, and there is no record of that patient having an infection, the patient's medical record is pulled to confirm whether or not the patient acquired a nosocomial infection. After all data have been reviewed, the risk manager and/or the medical incident review committee decide whether or not this infection could have been prevented, and if so, what type of compensation or bill adjustment should be offered the patient. Perhaps a more efficient way of handling this procedure would be through the screening done by medical record professionals as they routinely analyze charts. Why wait to pull records to confirm a patient's complaint? The medical record professional could alert both infection control and the risk manager as soon as the patient record is screened. Of course, if the infection is not documented, it is as if it did not happen, and no amount of chart searching is going to defend the hospital.

Professional Credentialing

Credentialing committees can use information abstracted from the medical record to make sure that all physicians are properly credentialed, licensed, and have privileges for conducting the procedures documented. For instance, when a physician performs a procedure, the record can be checked to see if he or she has been granted privileges to perform such operations. Credentialing committees should carefully research applicants' records to make sure that they have received sufficient training to qualify them for those privileges. If this had been done in *Darling v. Charleston Community Memorial Hospital*,[53] the physician would not have been allowed to perform surgery on Darling (D. H. Mills, personal communication, October 15, 1985).

Billing

The medical record can be used to identify problems arising from the patient's bill. In this era of cost containment, authors and lecturers constantly illustrate ways to cut costs. In a recent lecture, a scheme for charge coding was described that can cross-reference with the medical record and identify possible risks in drug usage, for example. It works in this fashion: Using the uniform billing abstracting device, the medical record practitioner can capture data that will compare procedures and treatments with the patient's bill. If, for instance, one expects certain drugs to be administered for certain problems, the bill can be checked to confirm that these drugs were used. If patterns begin to show that perhaps improper drugs or untested drugs are being used, risks are identified, and the pattern can be broken. This scheme does several things: 1) it produces a more detailed bill, which identifies not only what drug was used, but also through what route it was administered, if this was a routine treatment or a special case, and so on; 2) it is a useful technique to identify excessive costs; and 3) it becomes a quality assurance/risk management tool (S. Mendenhall, personal communication, October 15, 1985).

Many other uses of the medical record could be identified, but these examples simply serve to confirm that most risk management activities depend on this source document.

The Medical Record and Confidentiality of Patient Information

The medical record and the medical record practitioner are involved directly with policies and procedures involving the confidential nature of patient information. Requests for records or copies of records are handled by the medical record department, and there are usually rather elaborate ways of determining a legitimate request. If the medical record practitioner suspects that the request is more than just a routine patient request, he or she alerts the risk manager, and the original record is sequestered in a separate place, usually in the medical record department.

Physicians should not release the patient's medical record without the patient's specific consent unless the information is required by a specific statute, as in cases that fall under the purview of reportability statutes.[54] If written consent for release cannot be obtained, then an oral authorization will suffice, provided it is appropriately and carefully documented in the record. Extreme care should be used when accepting an oral consent for release, however. Records should be available in answer to legitimate requests, because a lost record impedes the physician's ability to defend himself or herself.

The confidentiality and release of psychiatric records constitute a special situation. In general, the regulations set out in Part 2 of Title 42 CFR, and which apply to drug and alcohol abuse programs assisted by the federal government, do not allow release of patient information without authorized patient consent even in cases where a subpoena or court order has been issued; they merely permit the release of ordered information.[55] The regulations apply to the entire record even though the drug or alcohol treatment is secondary or incidental to the primary diagnosis. However, these regulations are presently under review, because for all practical purposes they are impossible to comply with literally. Generally, states have confidentiality statutes that allow for release only upon the patient's written consent except in cases where court orders or subpoenas are issued. Cases in which a claim is made on behalf of a patient to facilitate his or her transfer to another institution or for continued treatment do not require patient authorization for release. Some states have statutes granting patients the right to access their records, but in the absence of such statutes a patient has no such right. The rationale for denial is that a patient can hire an attorney to secure a release of the record. Often mental health records are excluded under these right-to-access statutes because their release could be detrimental to the patient, according to Root.[56]

Most states have reporting regulations for child abuse and infectious disease cases. The information reported is kept to just that amount of information that is absolutely necessary to fulfill reporting requirements. A medical record practitioner must have a keen sense of applicable state regulations, because there is some disagreement as to whether child abuse should be reported if doing so violates the confidentiality of federal drug and alcohol abuse cases.

Communications between patients and physicians or therapists in psychiatric or drug and alcohol abuse cases, are considered confidential and therefore as privileged information not to be disclosed. However, there are always exceptions, and the following apply in these cases:

1. Consent given by patient or his or her personal representative (e.g., guardian.)

2. Court orders and subpoenas requesting information about a lawsuit in which the patient has put his or her physical condition at issue.

3. Requests from other health care providers for information necessary for continued patient care.

Since the medical record communicates information to members of a treating team, the above exceptions apply to the entire record. Unless there is a state law to the contrary, no records may be released to police officers, school representatives, employers, probation officers, or social workers who do not have the right to consent to the patient's medical treatment, or to clinical staff members not involved with the patient's treatment. It must be remembered that if the facility is not a party involved in the action, the record belongs to the hospital and is not the property of the patient or the requesting parties. The hospital does not produce the record unless it receives proper authorization for its release.

Most states have separate mental health statutory schemes that generally prohibit revelations of any medical information concerning any type of patient with a mental disorder. Again, exceptions always exist, and the medical record practitioner as well as the risk manager must keep abreast of applicable legislation and regulations.

Root advised that to avoid risk when served with a subpoena *duces tecum* there are definite steps to be followed by a medical record practitioner to ensure compliance with regulations and state statutes governing release.[57] Each consent for release form should contain the information required in the federal regulations on drug and alcohol abuse: the name of the patient, the name of the party to whom the information is to be released, the reason for the release, what specific information is to be released, and the consent's termination date. All of this information should be documented in the patient's medical record. Even in cases where a consent to release is not required, consents should be obtained, except, of course, in child abuse cases or in cases where the patient has indicated his or her intent to do bodily harm to another.

Often state statutes provide that when a medical record practitioner is served with a subpoena *duces tecum,* a declaration can be signed stating that he or she is the custodian of the record and that the record is the one sought by the subpoena. If compliance with the subpoena becomes a problem, the facility must contact the requesting party and give reasons for the noncompliance. Then the institution can offer an alternative procedure with which it will comply (i.e., obtain a court order or secure the proper patient authorization). According to Root, the following constants apply to official requests for records:

1. The records belong to the hospital;

2. The requesting party must show justification for its request, and

3. The requesting party must be kept informed of what the facility is or is not doing to comply with that request.[58]

What a medical record practitioner or the facility should avoid, says Root, is appearing in court every time a subpoena *duces tecum* is served, and subsequently being held in contempt of court for failure to comply or to state reasons for noncompliance before the required date of compliance. It is also recommended that envelopes containing the released information indicate clearly to whom the information is being sent, to prevent the information from passing into the wrong person's hands and issues from arising as to which party violated the confidentiality rules.

The key element underlying confidentiality rules is the patient's interest, according to Root.[59] As a communication device, the medical record is for those parties who contribute to the patient's treatment. It is not prepared for litigation, claims adjustment, or as a keepsake for the patient. The question to be answered when release of information is requested is how it will help the patient or, in some cases, the public.

The American Medical Record Association has set out specific guidelines for confidentiality in its position statement, last revised in 1981, and encourages each of its members to work diligently to implement the letter and spirit of the position statement not only for themselves but also for all health care providers.[60] Using these guidelines, medical record practitioners should conduct staff in-house training sessions, especially with new employees, on the importance of maintaining confidential information. Only by explaining the consequences of violation of confidentiality rules will there be better compliance with the law and patient rights. At the conclusion of this orientation, an employee often signs an oath to maintain records confidential, but Root warns that unless state laws make the employee's signature a condition of employment, this procedure is often difficult to enforce.[61] Nevertheless, such an act at least arouses the employees' awareness of the seriousness of the issue.

In the Ohio case of *Pacheco v. Ortiz*,[62] the judge ruled that a hospital did not need to release records in cases where a patient had not waived his or her privilege either expressly or implicitly. The judge attached to his opinion a letter from the hospital attorney in which the attorney cited specific federal and state statutes and case law as the basis for the hospital's noncompliance with the subpoena *duces tecum* and, in addition, for why the hospital should not be held in contempt of court. Hersey said that in effect this is a memorandum of law that is relevant to hospital records access and also serves as a model for hospitals to use when responding to a subpoena *duces tecum*.[63] As a practical matter it shifts the burden to the requesting party to show a legal basis for obtaining a patient record. A hospital need not release patient records, absent a court order, unless it has received a waiver of privileges from the patient, or has reason to believe, through its attorney, that there has been an implied waiver of privileges by the patient, Hersey wrote. This letter points out that certain privileges regarding confidentiality ordinarily asserted by the patient may be asserted by the medical record practitioner in certain circumstances. However, in the absence of a specific authorization for release of this information, the hospital and the medical record practitioner could be held liable for improper release. The mere filing of a personal injury suit constitutes neither an authorized release of information nor a waiver of the patient's right.

Rita Finnegan[64] wrote that confidentiality of patient information needs to be watched carefully because more and more people are studying medical records. Third-party payors now demand documentation that it was medically necessary that the care be given in the hospital and could not more appropriately have been administered in an alternative setting. Employers are demanding that their employees receive care at the appropriate level (utilization management). Within the hospital, physicians, nurses, unit clerks, data processors, medical record personnel, quality assurance personnel, therapists, pathologists, radiologists, and those personnel who review records for administrative purposes all have access to the record. Finnegan highly recommends a written policy stating who has record access. Each employee should sign a statement indicating that he or she agrees to hold the information confidential and that breach of this policy shall result in some type of punitive action.

Now that the government through the system of professional review organizations (PROs) is reviewing records and requesting that the records be reviewed on the premises (many are also mailed to reviewers), the patient has very little privacy. Finnegan recommends restricting what the PRO reviewer sees. One should give the reviewer a list of all Medicare patients' names and request that he or she ask for the chart by name, and only the hospital employee should fill that request. This procedure would prevent reviewers from seeing non-Medicare patient charts, Finnegan believes.[65] She also suggests that the hospital should develop a Memorandum of Understanding with its PRO whereby the hospital maintains control as tightly as possible and, in turn, the PRO agrees to hold the record in a confidential and secure manner. Each medical record practitioner should meet with the PRO to determine how and where records will be reviewed and what procedures will be implemented to maintain confidentiality.

The Medical Record Department's Role in Risk Management

From this discussion of the purposes and roles of the medical record, it follows logically that the following functions should constitute the medical record department's and the medical record practitioner's roles in hospital risk management activities:[66]

1. Supervision of data gathering, with documentation of the data produced at all levels.

2. Training of clerical personnel engaged in locating the most useful sources of required information.

3. Determination of the incidence of relevant data requested for the use of committees and individuals.

4. Screening of medical records for compliance with established clinical criteria and designated exceptions or equivalents as established by the medical staff.

5. Participation in the selection and design of forms used in the medical record, and in the determination of the sequence and format of the contents of the medical record.

6. Suggesting to the professional staffs methods of improving the primary source data that will facilitate their retrieval, analysis, tabulation, and display.

7. Performing ongoing informational surveillance of practice indicators or monitors for medical staff review.

8. Ensuring the provision of a mechanism to protect the privacy of patients and practitioners whose records are involved in quality assessment activities.

9. Reviewing all requests for access to or copies of medical records by patients and third parties to determine their validity under applicable state law.

10. Reviewing all medical records for which requests for access to or copies of medical records have been received from, in particular, patients, attorneys, and court orders or subpoenas, to determine whether it is apparent from the medical record that the hospital has potential exposure to liability.

Durkin and Korsak[67] earlier elaborated on these same functions.

Inservice Education

The medical record practitioner has the major responsibility for educating hospital staff in the correct methods for correcting errors and recording procedures; appropriate entries and signatures of health care providers, especially physicians; proper means of documentation (handwritten or typewritten); recording pre- and post anesthesia visits and orders; and documentation of evidence of informed consent.

Data Collection and Dissemination

The medical record department sits on a wealth of data, which must be disseminated to those in the hospital to whom the data are relevant. Disease indices and operative and physician indices are maintained, the records are coded and abstracted, and the data are stored in the medical record department.

Information Searches

Medical record personnel often take the initiative and search for needed information even when they have not been requested to do so.

Quality Assurance

The medical record department may or may not be responsible for quality assurance. Utilization management, quality assessment, and risk management are interconnected, and reviewers are often on the floors screening medical records to discern patterns emerging from documentation often before the risk manager does. Focused review can be performed on areas proven by the traditional utilization review activities to be sources of potential institutional problems and risks. This focused review can be substituted for the traditional utilization management activities, which study any problem the hospital chooses to review. The results of these activities are valuable information sources for the risk manager.

Sources of potential liability within the medical record department center around confidentiality. Outside transcription, paper destruction, microfilming, and off-site storage services should have written contracts for confidentiality, with an agreed-upon liability for breach of that contract. Students who do clinical affiliations in medical record departments may also create liability. Institutions and schools should have written contracts that assign responsibility for confidentiality as well as for student illness or injury.

Diener[68] wrote that routine examination of attorneys' requests for medical record information is one way in which medical record departments contribute greatly to liability control in the area of claims prevention. She suggested that these departments redesign their correspondence logs to capture events that may have initiated the patient's request for an attorney. In this manner, incidents not reported by hospital staff can be identified.

Discharge analyses performed by the medical record department are excellent ways of providing information for both quality assurance and risk management. However, Diener felt that these functions would be more timely and useful if they were performed on the floor and incorporated into the ongoing concurrent review process. Today, concurrent monitoring is used more and more to identify problems such as failure to verify verbal orders or failure to include in the chart a proper history and physical examination before surgery. In addition, the discharge diagnosis can be obtained from the physician to determine the accuracy of the information recorded in the chart before the record is sent to the medical record department for final analysis, coding, and filing.

In general, the medical record department's actual role in risk management most likely depends on what the facility decides to include in the risk management program. Data collection, record documentation, in-service education, and legal correspondence are the main areas in which medical record departments contribute to the risk management function.

The Role of Medical Record Practitioners in Risk Management

Essentially, the prevention of injury and/or liability, whether related to physician behavior or other causes, depends on adequate, reliable data.[69] It is in this area that the role of the medical record professional is extremely important. He or she is the keeper of the hospital records. Individually, these records reflect the care of the patient during the course of his or her hospital stay. Collectively, these records reflect the hospital's business and reason for existence.

Medical record professionals know the strengths and weaknesses of the hospital as portrayed by the record documentation, and often they know them more accurately and in more detail that any other member of the health care team. Medical record professionals also know the quality and quantity of information needed in the record. Because the information systems designed to collect and analyze data pertaining to patient injury prevention are record intensive, the medical record practitioner becomes an essential component of the risk management program.

To educate the medical staff about documentation is no small task, and because of the medical record practitioner's relationship with the medical staff he or she becomes vital to the risk management program. Medical record professionals participate in many medical staff committee activities, mostly by collecting and displaying data needed for committee functions. This relationship places the medical record professional in a strategic position to effect change in and to influence the content and outcome of those committee activities. It is logical that by this same process medical record professionals can foster more effective risk management activities. For example, if standard medical practice dictates that certain procedures necessitate a particular activity, these activities should be documented in the record to prove that standard care was given. The medical record professional can detect, through either concurrent or retrospective chart analyses, whether or not such activities have been charted. If the documentation is absent, and it is known that absence of such activity entails a definite risk of loss, the medical record professional can and should bring this to the attention of the medical record committee and exert a considerable influence on the committee members to change documentation practices. Sometimes medical record practitioners work with the individual physician. However, effecting change between the medical record professional and the physician personally is not always successful. Willetts wrote that when the chairman of the medical staff committee questions whether an issue is something with which they must be concerned, the medical record professional must be ready to respond appropriately. At this point, the institution can be a leader rather than a follower in risk management activities. It is imperative that timely, accurate data be available to prevent a crisis before it happens rather than waiting until a crisis occurs to realize that these data were needed to ensure appropriate, effective hospital decision making.[70]

Medical record professionals know the content and mechanics of medical data systems, which can produce appropriate data to aid risk management activities, and therefore the medical record professional is able to lead the hospital into a position from which it can deal with problems revealed by any effective data analysis. The medical record practitioner understands the importance of data systems to risk management activities and can effect the use of these systems to perform these activities. Thus, the medical record practitioner is an invaluable benefit to the institution in general and the risk manager in particular.

Actually, medical record practitioners have been involved in risk management activities for years. One review of the chart can accomplish quality, utilization, and risk management activities simultaneously according to Crane and Reckard,[72] Huffman,[73] and Rodger.[74] Legal correspondence, incomplete records, missing records, illegible handwriting, complications of medical procedures, record inconsistencies, and inappropriate documentation are areas in which the medical record practitioner contributes to risk management activities. Specific risk management activities are included in the Professional Practice Standards for quality assurance, highlighted in Chapter 2. The medical record practitioner notifies the risk manager, or whomever is responsible for risk prevention, of potential problems and provides access to the record for review purposes. Risk management is notified when subpoenas are received and when attorneys and/or patients request information from the record. Release of information policies and procedures are carefully maintained to avoid hospital liability. Often the medical record department is the coordinating unit for release of all patient information, including admissions, discharges, x-rays, social service information, and ambulatory care records.

Finally, the medical record professional contributes to risk prevention activities through in-service education delivered to all hospital department staffs. Record policies and procedures, documentation requirements, and confidentiality comprise the outline for such education sessions.

Changing societal values of life and health care constantly demand new patient record documentation policies, for example with respect to the decision to withhold or withdraw life-sustaining treatment from the terminally ill patient and living wills.[75] Therefore, medical record practitioners must remain abreast of current literature and legislation describing up-to-date methods of record keeping.

Because of its emphasis on quality data, the prospective payment system has propelled the medical record professional to the forefront in health care delivery environments. It follows, then, that by providing these quality data, these professionals are more likely to advance their careers in risk management. These are just a few of the examples brought out in the literature that demonstrate the medical record practitioner's role in risk management and prevention.

In the recent survey of selected medical record practitioners previously mentioned in the quality assurance section of Chapter 2, practitioners were asked to answer the same set of questions pertaining to their roles in the risk management programs in their facilities. Of those respondents whose facility had a risk management program, 58 percent felt that their risk management expertise was underutilized. Suggestions for their increased participation clustered into three distinct areas: 1) the need for increased department staff; 2) better use of the medical record practitioner's documentation knowledge and expertise in the planning stages of the risk management programs; and 3) increased respect and support from administration and the risk manager for the practitioner's role in the quality assurance/risk management plan. A few respondents felt that their expertise was adequately utilized. Some wanted no further responsibility. Others felt that the hospital staff, including the risk manager, needs more educational programs on documentation and confidentiality and that medical record practitioners are the best qualified personnel to educate these professionals. Even though over half of the respondents felt they were underutilized in risk management functions, only one respondent actually believed that the medical record department could assume more specific risk management responsibility, and only two respondents felt that there were poor communication lines between the two departments.

Evaluation of these results needs to be treated with caution, however, because it must be realized that in the current health care environment medical record practitioners simultaneously have had to learn and implement procedures to capture reimbursement information and have had to cope with other implications of the prospective payment system. This has all transpired in a relatively short period of time. At the same time, medical record practitioners have experienced the same reductions in staff as other areas of the hospital. Naturally, these practitioners tend to want to master this new role before accepting additional responsibilities. The majority of these respondents seemingly do not realize the medical record practitioner's potential role in the risk management function, or maybe it is that at this point they do not want to realize this potential. Also, it may be that administration needs to recognize the medical record department's and practitioner's contributions to risk management.

The medical record department has begun to climb out of its basement location, and maybe the department should climb even higher in the organization. Some medical record departments report to directors of fiscal services. The medical record practitioner can be an assistant administrator of health information services and be in the same position horizontally as fiscal services, nursing, and administrative services. Or the medical record department's relationship to risk management could be line or staff with quality assurance, utilization management, and other related areas. However, according to these respondents, added responsibilities could be assumed only with ample staff and perhaps some additional educational preparation.

Suggestions for Improved Medical Record Maintenance

Several authors have described ways to improve quality patient record keeping. Nathanson and Bazzoli[76] described a pilot project carried out in two southeast Michigan hospitals. Bedside terminal systems connected to seven minicomputers have been installed. Part of the available software programs used are for medical record documentation, still another stab at the paperless record. Physicians, nurses, and other health care professionals enter the patient's room, insert their card into the terminal, and then enter their identification number. Next, the terminal displays what treatment the patient needs. The user enters the tasks that were performed on the patient and, when finished, removes his or her card. This method eliminates the nurses' end-of-the-day charting, and because the computer recognizes the physicians' codes, all orders are signed simultaneously through the terminal. Supposedly, the system will enhance quality of care, freeing the nurses so that they can spend more time with patients.

Storing sensitive medical records in the risk manager's office can create rather than solve legal problems.[77] Ideally, records should be placed in a designated area in the medical record department.[78] Part of the medical record practitioner's Code of Ethics dictates that he or she will maintain confidentiality of patient information. Logically, the medical record department is the place in which to store these files. The record's copy should be placed in the open file. This procedure serves two purposes: 1) the record is available should the patient be readmitted, and 2) the copy will show that the original is sequestered, which will prevent tampering. Another way to discourage tampering is to number each page and every test result. Also, when anyone asks to review the chart—physician, nurse, or whoever—a medical record professional should be present while the chart is reviewed, especially when charts are being reviewed for physician credentialing and quality of care delivery. Many people review a host of records during an audit procedure, and any tampering of any record can falsify the audit, allowing the physician to remain on staff regardless of the study's revelations.

Following approximately the same format as the clinical pathological conferences, which meet to discuss patient mortalities, Goodman[79] proposed that a clinical legal pathological conference be implemented to review each lost malpractice case. Review of the case would concentrate on administrative and procedural failures rather than medical faults. For instance, the case would be reviewed for physician documentation failure (uses of prejudicial language in the physician's favor, inadequate progress notes, improper corrections, etc.). Goodman, a physician, suggested that the legal pathologist be an attorney, preferably a defense attorney, who carefully reviews the record and then discusses his or her findings with the attending physicians. It seems appropriate, although Goodman does not mention it, to include a medical record professional in this open meeting to represent documentation expertise. These conferences, if properly conducted, would educate and benefit all physicians without recriminations. Proper documentation does not compromise the quality of care rendered, and guidance from medical record documentation experts as members of this conference enhances risk prevention.

Finally, the use of patient-written progress notes is a recent concept described in the literature. It has been suggested that patients participate in documenting their record, thereby contributing to the ongoing quality care assessment. Patients could be trained to self-assess their treatments and record their findings similar to the way in which physicians and nurses document these findings. The added touch would be the patient's own subjective feelings about his or her hospital stay. These notes could be filed either with the record or separately, depending on facility policy. Institutions with active risk management programs might find these patient-written progress notes a valuable and perhaps a truer tool for concurrent patient complaint identification.[80]

Summary

The roles of the medical record, the medical record department, and the medical record professional in quality assurance and risk management have been described. It is hard to differentiate quality assurance roles from those of risk management. Is a medical record practitioner who screens the record for inconsistencies and PCEs assessing quality or contributing to liability reduction? Obviously, the answer is both. A properly kept medical record assesses quality of care and reduces the risk of loss to the hospital. This dual role further supports the concept of overlapping responsibilities of the quality assurance and risk management functions. Accurate maintenance of the medical record prevents the attorney from having to rely on the client's subjective comments. The record should provide the objective evidence necessary to determine the standard of care. It should not create further questions regarding that standard.

Medical record professionals as custodians of the record play key roles in quality assurance/risk management programs. Their expertise should be recognized and utilized so that quality records make quality care unsurpassable and hold risks to a minimum.

Chapter Exercises

1. As a hospital risk manager, you receive notice from the medical records admin-

istrator that a certain attorney in your city has sent a letter requesting the medical record of a former patient, who is engaged in a workers' compensation claim against an employer in town whom he represents. There is no evidence of authorization for the record. Outline in letter form your response to the attorney's request.

2. What are the primary purposes of the medical record?

3. What programs can the risk manager use the medical record for?

4. Outline a risk prevention function that the risk manager could delegate to the medical records administrator.

5. Make one argument why a medical record should not be computerized.

References

1. Grayson, M. A. "Risk Management: New Focus for Traditional Functions". *Hospital Medical Staff* 7 (May, 1978): 12-17.

2. Karp, D. "Medical Records and Malpractice Claims." *Medical Malpractice Cost Containment* 1 (January 1980): 303-313.

3. Lanham, G. B., and J. E. Orlikoff. "Full Coverage of Issues Reflects Importance of Risk Management." *Hospitals* 55 (April 1, 1981): 165-168.

4. Joseph, E. "Improved Psychiatric Records Cut Liability." *Hospital Risk Management* 5 (April 1983): 41-45.

5. Glass, L. S. "The Medical Record: Shield or Sword of Damocles?" *Alaska Medicine* 26 (April 1984): 48-49.

6. Roach, W. H., S. N. Chernoff, and C. L. Esley. *Medical Records and the Law.* Rockville, Md.: Aspen Systems Corporation, 1985.

7. Joint Commission on Accreditation of Hospitals. *Accreditation Manual for Hospitals/AMH 84.* Chicago, Ill.: JCAH, 1984.

8. Southwick, A. F. *The Law of Hospital and Health Care Administration.* Ann Arbor, Mich.: Health Administration Press, 1978.

9. Huffman, E. *Medical Record Management.* Berwyn, Ill.: Physicians' Record Company, 1981.

10. *Norton v. Argonaut Insurance Co.*, 144 So.2d 249, (La. App. 1962).

11. *Favalora v. Aetna Casualty and Surety Company,* 144 So.2d 544 (La. App. 1962).

12. *Hansch v. Hackett,* 66 P.2d 1129 (Wash. 1937).

13. Karp, p. 304.

14. Durkin, E., and A. Korsak. "A Risk Management Primer for Medical Record Practitioners." *Medical Record News* 51 (June, 1980): 37-41.

15. Glass, p. 48a.

16. Joseph, p. 43.

17. Wade, R. D. *Risk Management HPL.* Columbus, Ohio: Ohio Hospital Insurance Company, 1983.

18. Karp, p. 310.

19. Shrager. D. S. "Using Hospital Records to Prove Liability." *Hospital Risk Management* 5 (July 1983): 85-86.

20. Karp, p. 308.

21. Jorgensen, T. "Reducing Malpractice Claims Through Proper Maintenance of Medical Records." *Medical Malpractice Cost Containment* 1 (January 1980): 303-313.

22. Joseph, p. 42.

23. Karp, p. 312.

24. Jorgenson, p. 85.

25. Karp, p. 308.

26. Glass, p. 48a.

27. Grayson, p. 16-17.

28. Jorgensen, p. 300.

29. Glass, p. 48a.

30. Dwyer, J. "Hospital Incident Reports: Protected From Discovery?" *Hospital Progress* 63 (October 1982): 38-39.

31. Grayson, p. 14.

32. California Hospital Association *Consent Manual* Section 24.2. Sacramento, Calif.: California Hospital Association, 1981, p. 452.

33. Dwyer, p. 39.

34. Groah, L., and E. A. Reed. "Your Responsibility in Documenting Care." *Association of Operating Room Nurses* 37 (May 1983): 1174-1188.

35. Grayson, p. 16.

36. Joseph, p. 43.

37. Karp, p. 306.

38. Clark, Noreen M. " Consent Forms, As Written Confuse Patients, Study Says." *Hospital Risk Management* 5 (August 1983): 109-111.

39. Clark, p. 110.

40. Jorgenson, p. 297.

41. Joseph, p. 43.

42. Jorgensen, p. 298.

43. Karp, p. 313.

44. Ibid., p. 312.

45. Joseph, p. 42.

46. Ibid.

47. California Medical Association/California Hospital Association. *A Report on the Medical Feasibility Study.* San Francisco: Sutter Publications, 1977.

48. Kessler, P. K., and E. D. Joseph. *The Risk Management Primer.* Chicago: Care Communications, Inc., 1979.

49. Kennedy, B. G. "Use of Generic Outcome Screening Criteria for Problem Identification." *Topics In Health Record Management* 1 (December 1980): 53-62.

50. Lanham and Orlikoff, p. 166.

51. White, J. S. "Is This the Ultimate Step in Quality Control?" *Medical Economics* 60 (February 1983): 204, 206, 210, 212, 214-215.

52. Salman, S., and N. Click. "Risk Manager Must Interact with Infection Control Expert." *Hospitals* 54 (March 16, 1980): 52-54.

53. *Darling v. Charleston Community Memorial Hospital* 211 N.E.2d 253 (1965).

54. Glass, p. 48-49.

55. Root, G. L. Psychiatric Health Record Practitioners: The Enforcers." *Topics in Health Record Management* 5 (June 1985): 1-8.

56. Ibid., p. 2.

57. Ibid., p. 6.

58. Ibid., p. 7.

59. Ibid., p. 8.

60. *Confidentiality of Patient Health Information: A Position Statement.* Chicago: American Medical Record Association, 1981.

61. Root, p. 5.

62. *Pacheco v. Ortiz,* 463 N.E.2d 670 (Ohio Ct. C.P. 1983).

63. "An Effective Response to a Request for Hospital Records." N. Hersey, editor, *Hospital Law Newsletter,* 2 (August 1985): 1.

64. Finnegan, R. "DRGs Pose Problems on Keeping Medical Records Confidential." *Prospective Payment Survival* (March 1984): 31-32.

65. Finnegan, p. 32.

66. Roach, et al., p. 187.

67. Durkin and Korsak, p. 40-41.

68. Diener, J. "Data Collection—New Tools for Quality Assurance." *Topics in Health Record Management* 1 (1980): 63-68.

69. Willetts, J. W. "Risk Management and the Medical Record Professional." *Journal of the American Medical Record Association* 53 (October 1982): 68-70.

70. Ibid., p. 70.

71. Ibid.

72. Crane, E. J. and J. M. Reckard. "Hospital Liability, Risk Management, and the Medical Record." *Topics in Health Record Management* 2 (September 1981): 49-59.

73. Huffman, p. 533-534.

74. Rodger, C. Z. "Medical Records' Role in Risk Management." *Michigan Hospitals* 20 (November 1984): 36-37.

75. Miller, R. D. "The Decision to Withhold or Withdraw Life-Sustaining Treatment from Terminally Ill Patients." *Hospital Law Newsletter* 2 (November 1984): 1-8.

76. Nathanson, M., and F. Bazzoli. "Bedside Terminals Will Save Work, Cut Staff." *Modern Healthcare* 15 (April 26, 1985): 44-48.

77. Heydman, F. " Tighten Medical Records' Security to Reduce Incidence of Tampering." *Hospital Risk Management* 5 (January 1983): 8-9.

78. Crane and Reckard, p. 55.

79. Goodman, R. S. "The Clinical-Legal-Pathological Conference." *Legal Aspects of Medical Practice* 13 (September 1985): 1-2, 8.

80. "Patient Progress Notes: A Measure of Patient Satisfaction." *QA Section Connection* 3 (October 1985): 3.

CHAPTER TEN

RISK MANAGEMENT IN THE FUTURE

In Chapter 1 we learned that risk management was adopted by health providers out of necessity caused by external circumstances, primarily the increase of financial losses attributed to malpractice, workers' compensation, and other forms of tort liability. Once again, changes in external circumstances will require risk managers to adopt new methods in order to better protect their organizations in various exposure areas.

In this chapter we will review the current liability crisis, particularly as it pertains to professional malpractice, so that the reader can better understand its causes and effects. By understanding the source of a phenomenon, managers can better predict the future and perhaps make administrative changes in the organization so that the negative impact is prevented or reduced.

This chapter will also review recent reforms made in tort law and some changes suggested by legislators and others. Last, a hypothetical model for an internal dispute resolution program for a health care facility is included as an alternative to traditional claims administration processes.

The Liability and Malpractice Crisis

The decade of the 1980s may prove to be of particular significance in the history of professional liability. During this period, the second malpractice crisis accelerated, reached its peak, and now appears to be waning. Some may take issue with the prediction that the crisis may have reached its high point; however, the passage of tort reform legislation in California, Illinois, and other states, plus pending bills in 18 other states[1] and the Congress, are strong indicators that the end may be in sight. When statistics for the last years of this decade are published, they may show record losses; thereafter, however, changes in the law should begin to take effect.

Risk managers are obviously interested in the effects of the liability crisis because it has a direct impact on their positions. In fact, many would have no job if the crisis environment had not existed. It is very important for those making risk management decisions to understand the source of the current problem and its effects so that they can better predict the future and adjust their administrative strategy accordingly. Also, it is important for a professional to possess this knowledge for its own sake.

If one solicits the opinions of the primary actors in the malpractice scenario, one finds each placing the blame on the others, until an endless circle results. Health care providers blame the lawyers; the lawyers blame the providers and insurance companies;[2] the insurers blame the market, juries, and patients; and the patients blame the provider and so forth and so on.

Placing blame on any one class of individuals is too simplistic for a phenomenon as complex as the current malpractice crisis. The fact is that there is a crisis in all areas of liability, not just in health care. Health providers have simply felt the impact sooner and longer. The problem spills over to many markets. Because of large losses and the number of actions, Directors' and Officers' insurance is either un-affordable or unavailable.[3] Accounting firms and accountants have seen large increase in insurance premiums because of class action suits brought by investors in troubled companies whose business reports are alleged to have been negligently compiled. Tavern owners have seen their liability insurance increase by 200 and 300 percent in a year because of suits by victims of drunk drivers who seek to redress their grievance against the party who sold the inebriate driver liquor. Manufacturers of all sorts of goods are seeing their product liability insurance increase to the point that tort reform addressing the problem has been introduced in the Congress.[4] The problem is so pervasive that all who purchase liability insurance are feeling the impact, including attorneys. Recently, the San Francisco law firm of Melvin Belli, the so-called "king of torts," had a $5.8 million judgment rendered against it in a case of legal malpractice.[5] With a crisis this pervasive, one must probe deeply to find the source of the problem; once found, the real challenge will be how to solve it without eroding the public's right to justice.

There would be no malpractice crisis if people did not sue over misadventures they sustained; therefore, one must first look to the reason why some people sue and some do not. Below are some reasons why people file lawsuits:

1. The increasing mobility of society. Many people feel no sense of community and do not establish roots in new communities.

2. The increased specialization of medicine. Patients do not become acquainted with their doctors. Each medical specialist concentrates on a single organ system, without looking after the whole person. This is a problem especially in teaching hospitals.

3. Overexpectation of the capabilities of medical science. In a phenomenon sometimes called the "Marcus Welby syndrome," years of watching heroic doctors portrayed on television have led people to believe that once they place their bodies in the hands of a doctor or a hospital, a successful outcome is guaranteed. Anything less is malpractice.

4. The "lottery syndrome." The quest for easy money attracts large segments of society, who see others become rich with the luck of the draw. A medical misadventure is looked upon as a financial opportunity.

5. A better educated public. A medical complication is no longer accepted as bad luck, but as having been caused by doctors, nurses, or other providers.

To explore these causes in depth would be beyond the scope of this text. For more information see the article on this subject by Press.[6]

The legal profession is very much involved in the crisis. The abundance of attorneys in this country no doubt contributes to the problem, since the competition for cases probably results in suits that are frivolous or marginal at best. Also, abuses of the law of damages, evidence (expert witnesses), and rules of civil procedure contribute to the problem (see next section). The judiciary must also accept a share of the blame. Many of the horror stories related to outrageous verdicts occur because many judges will not judge.

Insurance companies have precipitated the crisis, since it was their sudden, large, and dramatic increases in premiums that have raised the greatest outcry by providers. Also, the retreat from many liability markets, such as the secondary market in malpractice insurance, has intensified the problem. Why insurance companies have behaved as they have is subject to speculation, but the following reasons have been suggested:[7]

- The expected cost of the exposure insured. This means that the insurance company did not accurately value the potential damages sustained and claimed against the insured party or organization

- The length of the claim reporting tort. This means that plaintiffs have a long time to bring an action, particularly with regard to children. Therefore, the effect of time and resulting effects of inflation and higher health care costs, as well as changing jury attitudes cause an increase in the value of an injury. The insurance company, however, may have sold the policy too inexpensively in relation to the risk or exposure covered.

- The underwriting cash flows (premium, expense, and loss payments)

- The rates of return and reinvestment risks associated with the underwriting cash flow

- The necessary margins for profit relative to the risk assumed.

Last, health care providers must take a certain amount of responsibility for the crisis. The quest for profit on the part of some has led many patients to believe that they as persons are of secondary importance. Until recently, the medical profession has had a poor record of policing itself. The result is that a small number of incompetents mar the image of doctors in the eyes of the public. State licensing boards have not shown interest in quality-of-care issues but concentrate on such acts as abuse of drugs and other nonprofessional overt behavior as the focal point of their activities. With diagnosis related groups (DRGs) and prospective payment being emphasized by government and third-party payors, there is a greater danger that hospitals will place more pressure on doctors to reduce the number of tests and other diagnostic procedures as well as shorten stays in order to improve profitability. The chances of error in such an atmosphere are predictable.

Considering the nature of the liability crisis and the fact that it is being felt in all areas, it appears that the cause does not rest with any one class of individuals or groups but with all of society. The crisis in health care malpractice is symptomatic of the attitude of society, with some professionals exploiting it to the detriment of others. Ultimately, the consumer suffers the impact in the form of higher costs as well as mistrust and an erosion of confidence in health care providers.

The health care provider is the most obvious target and to an extent the victim of the crisis. Physicians and other providers of care are being sued in record numbers and with increasingly higher losses. The figures that follow provide insight into the degree of the problem as it pertains to physicians. In one state, California, the data are of interest because they may indicate a partial effect of tort reforms. According to data provided by the Insurance Information Institute, Pacific Coast Region (Table 10-1), the number of malpractice cases in California was lower, but the average reward substantially higher in 1983 than in 1976. One can speculate that the reforms help screen out frivolous or borderline claims, but those that make it through the system result in greater losses.

Data from the American Medical Association's Social Economic Monitoring System tend to support the position of physicians that they are being sued in record numbers (Table 10-2).[9]

Information provided by Best's Insurance Management Report shows that the insurance industry sustained record losses during the period 1977 to 1983. Their data indicate that although premiums increased by 30.8 percent during the period, losses increased by 144.8 percent. These figures translate to an increase in premiums from $1.20 billion in 1979 to $1.57 billion in 1983, while losses soared from $817 million in 1979 to $2 billion in 1983.[10]

Data from Jury Verdict Research, Inc., indicate that the median and mean malpractice settlements rose from $75,000 and $192,344 in 1976 to $200,000 and $962,258 in 1982, respectively.[12] The number of verdicts over $1 million rose from 4 in 1976 to 45 in 1982 (Table 10-3).[11]

Although the accuracy of these data is subject to debate[12], there is little doubt that a crisis does exist. We have seen that besides the effects of higher insurance rates, higher health care costs to consumers, and an erosion of confidence in providers, some specialists such as obstetricians are leaving the profession, thus leaving the consumer to be cared for by the less trained. Another effect of the problem may be that the aberration will become institutionalized, and a service

Table 10-1 California Superior Court Verdicts in Medical Malpractice Cases, 1973–1983

Year	Total No. of Verdicts	Defendant Verdicts*	Plaintiff Verdicts*	Total Amount Awarded	Average Plaintiff Award
1972	137	82 (60)	55 (40)	$11,016,305	$200,296
1973	165	115 (70)	50 (30)	10,642,391	212,848
1974	215	142 (66)	73 (34)	9,768,628	133,817
1975	215	156 (73)	59 (27)	9,025,248	152,970
1976	226	168 (74)	58 (26)	9,661,795	166,582
1977	205	146 (71)	59 (29)	16,066,354	272,311
1978	204	147 (72)	57 (28)	11,456,873	200,998
1979	204	133 (65)	71 (35)	24,961,427	351,569
1980	180	110 (61)	70 (39)	21,607,739	308,682
1981	146	94 (64)	52 (36)	20,548,490	395,163
1982	163	103 (63)	60 (37)	15,433,327	257,222
1983	152	103 (68)	49 (32)	31,811,292	649,210

*Numbers in parentheses represent percentage of all verdicts for that year.
Source: American Medical Association Special Task Force on Professional Liability and Insurance.

Table 10-2   Average Liability Claims Per 100 Physicians

Practice Area	1978–1983	1978 and before
Surgery	11.8	4.8
Medical	4.5	2.3
General and family practice	8.2	3.8
All physicians	8.0	3.3

Source: American Medical Association Special Task Force on Professional Liability and Insurance.

Table 10-3   Median and Mean Malpractice Settlements and Settlements Over $1 Million, 1976–1982

Year	Median	Mean	No. of Settlements Over $1 Million
1976	$ 75,000	$192,344	4
1977	150,000	364,396	19
1978	105,000	419,372	16
1979	165,000	367,319	14
1980	200,000	404,726	20
1981	300,000	850,396	50
1982	200,000	962,258	45

Source: Jury Verdict Research, Inc.

industry may grow to such a size that, because of political pressure, changes will never be forthcoming. These issues will be discussed in the next section.

Legislative Reforms and Curative Measures

Physicists teach that for every cause there is an effect and for every effect a cause. To a certain degree this rule also applies to the social sciences and is often seen in human behavior. We have learned that higher costs of patient care are the practical result of the malpractice crisis, because of increased insurance rates charged providers. Actually, the impact on rates is more of a domino effect, since increased health care costs are partially the result of providers passing their costs on to the patient. The risk management profession has grown and expanded in importance as a result of the crisis, and although it would not be accurate to say that the legal profession sustained the same degree of growth, those attorneys who specialize in liability, either through prosecution or defense, have certainly felt the impact.

Besides the impact on the primary professions, another important aspect of the liability crisis is the development of collateral service organizations that rely on it as a source of business. Specifically, persons or organizations who furnish such support services as expert witnesses, structured settlements and other financial services, actuarial and statistical data, and consulting services have grown and thrived as a result of the size and intensity of the problem. One has only to look in any legal journal to find numerous advertisements for the services of witnesses and other specialists. Some advertisements raise ethical questions, particularly those that boast of cases that resulted in settlements over a million dollars.[13] One must question the objectivity of an expert from an organization that suggests that its fees will be contingent on the outcome.[14] Considering the number and intensity of advertisements for experts and other services, it appears that a lucrative and competitive support industry has developed.

The danger of having a support industry that thrives on what many see as an anomaly is that those in the industry will resist reforms necessary for the good of all. The current debate over tobacco advertising is an example. The outcry in favor of continued cigarette advertising is not coming from the manufacturers alone, but from magazine publishers and ad agencies who see a lucrative source of revenue threatened.

It is predictable that those who feel victimized by a problem will attempt to do something about it. Their action usually takes the form of pressure on professional associations to request changes by the legislatures of the states and the Congress. Almost half the states as well as the Congress have had bills introduced designed either to reform the tort system or to offer some curative measure.[15] Although each bill is different, most include common elements. The proposed legislation can be classified into two major categories, tort law reform and no-fault liability.

Tort Reforms

Tort reforms are designed to correct perceived abuses in the current system without radical changes in the advocacy court system. The most common suggested reforms found in many bills are the following:

1. Restructuring state health professional licensing boards so that they incorporate a quality assurance role. Reform laws usually require hospitals and insurance companies to notify licensing boards of claims, lawsuits filed against physicians, or denial or diminishing of staff privileges due to issues of competency.

2. Limiting noneconomic losses. The proposed statutes generally set a dollar limit that is recoverable for such noneconomic damages as pain and suffering or loss of consortium. In California the figure is $250,000.

3. Setting an absolute cap on awards. Some bills set a maximum amount allowable regardless of the damages sustained. This is probably unconstitutional and certainly unfair unless all future expenses and costs can be frozen.

4. Forbidding punitive damages in medical malpractice absent the showing of willful, wanton or outrageous conduct.

5. Eliminating the collateral source rule. Bills introduced to address this issue prohibit a plaintiff from claiming as damages medical expenses paid by third parties such as Blue Cross and Blue Shield or other insurance companies.

6. Use of structured settlements for payments of a judgment over certain limits. Some bills require reversionary clauses in these agreements whereby damage payments not used by the victim because of death are returned to the defendant, rather than providing a windfall to next of kin.

7. Apportionment of fault. This reform requires juries to determine how much fault each party to the suit contributed, including that of the plaintiff. Damages paid by a defendant cannot exceed his or her degree of fault.

8. Repealing joint and several liability. This reform is an attempt to correct a situation in which one defendant can be made to pay the damages of another defendant if the latter has no insurance or other attachable assets. Those in the hospital industry are especially interested in this reform because they feel that uninsured doctors cause hospitals to be named as joint defendants because of their "deep pockets."

9. Limiting attorneys' fees.[16] Many providers feel that attorneys' shares of settlements and judgments are too large in proportion to the work performed. Also, they feel that, with no cap on fees, lawyers ask for damages that are unreasonable, hoping for a windfall.

10. Reducing the statutes of limitation to reasonable periods, which will allow insurance companies to better estimate their tail and establish rates accordingly.

11. Establishing fair and appropriate standards for expert witnesses. The abuse of the expert witness is serious and does not reflect the reality of the industry. In essence, anyone with a medical education can claim to be an expert even if he or she does not practice the same specialty as the defendant or has never performed the procedure at issue.

12. Establishing screening panels to certify claims with merit and discourage those deemed frivolous. These panels are usually made up of an attorney, a physician or other provider(s), and community members. The defendants in cases deemed to have merit are strongly encouraged to settle rather than litigate. The panel's findings can be used as evidence.[17]

13. Requiring plaintiffs to file affidavits by an expert that the case has merit within a short time of filing a suit. This reform, recently introduced in

Missouri, is designed to discourage frivolous claims because plaintiffs must spend money to obtain the expert's opinion that the case has merit before they can go forward with the lawsuit.[18]

14. Protecting peer review and other provider information from discovery. This provision is designed to strengthen the confidentiality of quality assurance programs.

15. Mandating risk management programs in health facilities (currently the law in Florida).[19]

Few if any legislation contains all of the above reforms once it has passed through the political process. Nevertheless, the incorporation of only a few of the suggested changes in a state's statutes should have a positive impact on the problem.

No Fault Liability

In the spring of 1984, Representatives Richard A. Gephardt of Missouri and W. Henson Moore of Louisiana introduced into Congress H.R. 5400, known as the Alternative Medical Liability Act. The bill's basic provision creates incentives for providers of health care to avoid litigation and concomitantly high verdicts by offering to compensate injured patients for all economic losses.[20] The proposed legislation, which failed to pass in 1984, was a substantial change in the traditional litigation system. It would have worked as a modified no-fault program because there is no requirement of claimants to show negligence. The bill would have required the states to adopt the proposed federal statute by January 1987 or establish a more stringent law that covers all third-party payors. In those states not passing reform legislation H.R. 5400 would become the law. This would affect such federal programs as Medicare, Medicaid, the Veterans Administration, and others.

Some of the other provisions of H.R. 5400 are as follows:

1. A provider's offer of compensation would foreclose the individual from filing a lawsuit.

2. Other providers jointly responsible can be joined by the provider making the offer.

3. Damages are limited to economic losses only, including offset from collateral sources.

4. Patients who make bad-faith claims could be made to pay defendants' expenses.

5. Provider must make tender within 180 days.

6. Benefits must be paid within 30 days of the time proof of losses is submitted.

7. Patients lose their right to compensation benefits after 5 years if no claim is made.

8. Compensation benefits are free from demand from creditors of the claimant.

9. Both sides have certain discovery rights for proving losses and injuries.

10. Disputes between provider and patient are referred to a court but only for issues of damages.

11. Settlements over a certain size ($5,000) must be approved by a court and may be required to be paid by installments.

12. Structured settlements can be modified if grounds are shown for doing so.

13. Patients are assured payments.

Although H.R. 5400 did not pass, a new bill, H.R. 3084, called the Medical Offer and Recovery Act of 1985, was introduced by the same congressmen. The new bill contains several changes from the original, but the basic provisions remain.[21]

The basic premise of the new bill is that patients can request and receive binding arbitration to cover net economic losses. For states that enact tort reform legislation, a more expansive waiver provision is provided. Individuals are also encouraged to report incompetent or impaired physicians, and providers must carry sufficient insurance or post bonds in order to participate.

Critics of the no-fault approach fear that the system would be overwhelmed as every person who sustained a bad outcome would come forward to collect an award. The focal point of criticism is thus the potential volume of claims. The California Medical Insurance Feasibility Study showed that nearly 5 percent of hospitalized patients suffered an adverse outcome, and 17 percent of the 5 percent would have prevailed in court had they sued. However, only ten percent of the 17 percent ever file a suit.[22] Under the proposed system, if the other 90 percent filed claims, it could overburden the program and actually result in greater losses to providers and their insurers.[23] Critics also feel that an emphasis on risk prevention should be incorporated in the bill.[24] Hospital-based programs to control and manage the risk of malpractice are suggested as a solution to a crisis that is rapidly becoming insupportable.[25]

One may assume that the federal government will eventually pass some sort of no-fault malpractice law, which would cause hospitals and other health providers concern, and perhaps substantial losses, if they have not conceptualized a total claims administration system that will easily interface with the law. In the following section we will explore a model for an internal program for early dispute resolution that could serve as the focal point for handling claims under any new law.

Early Dispute Resolution: Model for an Internal Program

Alternative dispute resolution (ADR) appears to be the popular buzz word for the second half of the 1980s. Attorneys are hearing more about it in professional journals,[26] and it is being touted in seminars and becoming a part of some law school curricula. It would appear that many in the legal profession are becoming disenchanted with the traditional court system with its delays and perceived injustices. They are also being advised of the opportunities offered by ADR for employing their legal and negotiating skills.[27]

ADR is not new but has been part of the way this nation resolves its differences for decades. It is simply enjoying a resurgence for reasons discussed elsewhere in this text. Essentially, the explosion in litigation is overwhelming our traditional court system to the point that leaders both in and out of government are suggesting alternatives.[28] Despite the fact that some forms of ADR adapt well to particular industries or business environments, such as arbitration to contract disputes or mediation to labor relations, none seems to be a panacea for all situations. It is highly doubtful whether any form of ADR could fit all situations, and one can argue that this may be one reason why our traditional form of adjudication is under siege. Our society is too pluralistic and integrated with other nations to expect that all forms of human behavior and business endeavors can be effectively served by only one form of dispute resolution process. It appears reasonable, therefore, that the health care industry should consider a system that has been designed to fit its particular needs and experiences, while still serving the interest of justice.

Common Forms of Alternative Dispute Resolution

Minitrial In a minitrial the parties themselves create a tribunal, with lawyers presenting their cases to a panel of top executives from each organization, and a neutral party serving as mediator.[29]

Private Tribunals In a private tribunal, parties voluntarily submit their case to an individual (usually a retired judge) hired to serve on the tribunal. This system can eliminate delays, and the proceeding can be somewhat customized.[30]

Arbitration Arbitration is a form of ADR that is used extensively in contract disputes. The American Arbitration Association (AAA) publishes rules for arbitration and will serve as the third-party organizer. From a list furnished by the AAA, each side agrees on an individual who will serve as the arbitrator. Each party or its advocate presents its case, and the arbitrator decides the issue.

Mediation Mediation has various forms but essentially uses a neutral party to mediate a dispute. Each side presents its arguments or position to the mediator, who attempts to effect a compromise. The mediator is simply a facilitator and has no authority to make a decision. This approach is sometimes called conciliation.[31]

Mediation-Arbitration This process starts as mediation, but if no solution is reached and accepted by both parties to the dispute, it then proceeds to arbitration, with the mediator or sometimes a new individual making the decision.[32]

Ombudsman An ombudsman is an individual employed by an organization, often a hospital or other health facility, who listens impartially to a complaint of a patient or customer, investigates it, and offers a solution.

Malpractice Screening Panels Parties, through their attorneys, present their case before a panel made up of a lawyer, a health provider, and perhaps a judge or a community representative. Decisions are made about the merits of a case, and the plaintiff, if he or she loses, is encouraged to drop the matter. If the plaintiff wins, he or she can proceed to court, unless the defendant accepts the decision and settles the case.[33]

Although each of the above methods of ADR works in certain environments, a weakness in all of them, including adjudication of disputes as it applies to a perceived no-fault format, is that they stand alone. For a no-fault plan to work it has to be part of a totally integrated system. The hypothetical early dispute resolution system, as it is conceived, requires that it be integrated within the health care organization environment. A precedent condition, required to make the process work, is that it must be sanctioned by the law, with the authority to resolve the dispute, not simply to screen for merit or recommend a solution for others to implement.

Another precedent condition is that the system be known and accepted. If a no-fault law is passed, then this requirement will be taken care of by the media and common knowledge; however, if the system were voluntarily incorporated into some type of health care delivery system such as a health maintenance organization (HMO), then the membership must be advised of the plan in advance and accept it through contract provisions. It may also be advisable that the provider tout the program through internal and external media.

Model for Early Dispute Resolution Program

The contending parties find themselves more effectively ruined by the delay than they could have been by the injustice of any decision. (Edmund Burke, 1759)[34]

Timeliness is a critical element of the dispute resolution process (see diagram of

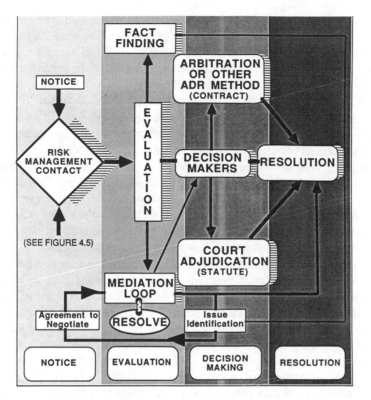

Figure 10-1 A model for early dispute resolution.

a model system for early dispute resolution in Figure 10-1). To avoid the delay Burke complained of in 1759, which still plagues the adjudication process today, the system must go into action immediately after the occurrence of the misadventure. This does not mean the total process will be completed by the time the patient leaves the health facility, although this could happen with minor cases that are undisputed. In most situations, the process should begin while the patient is still in-house or, in ambulatory care cases, soon after treatment. The purpose is to begin the process of mitigation in order to head off those claims that can be resolved by simple apologies, by explanations from doctors and other providers, or by correcting perceived failures or shortcomings in patient care.

Therefore, a model must contain the element of early notification of adverse occurrences. One could simply incorporate into the model system the risk management early-notice process, if it exists, which has been discussed in Chapter 4 and elsewhere in this text. The first major element of an early dispute resolution system is therefore "early notice." The notification point can be the office of the risk manager, the patient relations representative, the ombudsman, or another person designated by the administration as the contact person and known by all staff, employees, or others. It is entirely possible, and recommended in certain environments such as government facilities and not-for-profit organizations, that the person to be notified, although employed by the organization, be clearly designated as neutral. This aspect of the plan is essential to maintain fairness.

Once the institution has been placed on notice of the existence of an iatrogenic misadventure by news of the event being communicated to the designated contact person, the second phase of the model, called case evaluation, is implemented. The evaluation process contains two major parts: fact finding and mediation. Fact finding incorporates the aspects of investigation discussed in Chapter 6. The degree to which each case is investigated of course depends on the severity of the event. Some will be simple and require very little fact finding; others that are more serious can require extensive investigation, including having various elements evaluated by specialists with expertise in a particular area at issue.

There is an unknown element that must be taken into consideration when designing an early dispute resolution program: that of establishing fault or causation. This point will depend on the legal requirement, or lack of one, in the enabling statute. If a law is passed that is a total no-fault statute, then it will not matter if the misadventure was caused by the negligence of the provider, or was simply an accepted risk of the procedure with just a bad outcome, or was partially caused by the patient. In such a situation, the fact-finding process would not have to dwell on cause, but would concentrate on the degree of damages sustained. If, of course, the early dispute resolution program is not mandated by some new law and has been implemented by a health provider voluntarily under contract law provision, then the causation and negligence issue would certainly need to be thoroughly investigated, since a program to compensate all bad outcomes could be financially impractical. Considering the criticism directed at the Alternative Liability Act,[35] it is highly unlikely that any statute would be passed that is purely no-fault; it is more likely to be designed according to a modified no-fault provision. Consequently, hospital misadventures would be covered so long as they were not caused by the patient. In such a case, fact finding will therefore have to be extensive enough to address this issue.

The second and perhaps more important part of the evaluation phase is mediation. The two parts should occur concurrently, with emphasis given to early intervention in hopes of mediating a dispute and perhaps heading off a claim by providing the patient or family with a forum to address issues of concern. As stated above, early intervention with negotiation and perhaps apologies and explanations might be all that is needed to dispose of the matter.

The mediation process may contain a closed loop or may have to be referred to others for decisions. It is hoped that the mediation will dispose of most small cases, with only the major problems being referred to a decision-making body. If the quality of the care is such that the policy and procedures do not require input from the decision group, as shown in Figure 10-1, then by completing those stages outlined in the mediation closed loop the case should be resolved.

Within the closed loop the three stages of 1) identifying and agreeing on what is the central issue of the dispute, 2) reaching an agreement to resolve the dispute, and 3) concluding an agreement are necessary for final resolution. During the mediation aspects of the program, the fact-finding process plays a critical role in providing the necessary information for identifying the central issue and providing data about damages in order to assist in reaching an agreement. If the dispute can be disposed of within the closed loop of the mediation process, the resolution of the conflict has been achieved directly (see direct line to resolution in Figure 10-1). In more serious matters, when substantial funds may change hands or other serious issues cannot be disposed of in the mediation process, they will be referred to the decision body as indicated in the figure. The mediation and fact-finding processes would most likely be carried out by the health facility risk manager, patient relations representative, ombudsman, attorney, or perhaps by more than one party.

The decision body should be a blue-ribbon group made up of members of the facility administration, the medical staff, and the board of directors. In governmental, not-for-profit, and other public organizations, members of the public should also be considered. There is no reason why community representatives could not be included in all types of organization, both public and proprietary. The primary role of the decision body is exactly what the title implies, and it should serve as a tribunal for final resolution of the case. The risk management committee discussed in Chapter 2 could fulfill this role, if properly authorized.

Two additional unknowns that appear in Figure 10-1 are labeled *arbitration* and *adjudication*. Which, if any, of these is implemented in the system will once again depend on the specifics of the enabling statute or contract provision that serves to establish and enforce the program. If, for example, the system were established according to a law such as the Alternative Medical Liability Act, then only issues of damages could be adjudicated, and therefore, if the matter could not be resolved in either the mediation process or by the decision body, it would then be sent to court. From the court, the case would flow toward resolution as seen in Figure 10-1. On the other hand, if the system is not supported by statutes but by a contract provision in a HMO or other provider agreement, then a requirement for impasses to be arbitrated could be included, and therefore the dispute would flow toward arbitration as shown in Figure 10-1. Thereafter, the case would flow from the arbitration toward final resolution. Arbitration can be replaced with other established forms of ADR such as a private tribunal, a screening panel with decision-making power, or even a minitrial. It is possible and perhaps wise for all options to be made available to the parties in order to enforce the element of justice. The options available might depend on the seriousness of the case or the amount of money at issue.

In conclusion, the strength of the model for early dispute resolution is that it is totally contained within the confines of the health care organization, with the exception of the few cases that may have to be adjudicated, such as disagreements over damages as required by statute. The arbitration process could, however, be contained within the organization since the contract agreement would spell out the specifics of this process.

Summary

A crisis exists in all liability exposure areas, not just in medical malpractice. The problem is most vocal among the medical community because of increased numbers of lawsuits and the size of awards. The evidence seems to support doctors' claims that their premiums have been raised to a point where many no longer can afford insurance. In some parts of the nation excess insurance is not available. The crisis was caused by a combination of factors and developed over a long period of time.

Reforms have been passed in some states and have been introduced in several others including the U. S. Congress. Curative legislation usually takes the form of either no-fault liability or reform in tort laws.

There are several methods of alternative dispute resolution that are used in different environments. These include arbitration, mediation, or private tribunals. It is suggested that the health industry establish a tailor-made system that would incorporate the aspects of early notification and evaluation previously discussed in this text. Regardless of the form taken, the program must contain early notice, investigation, decision making, and resolution phases.

Chapter Exercises

1. Discuss the basic factors that create a predisposition to file a lawsuit on the part of a patient.

2. What factors, if controlled, could possibly cause stabilization in liability rates?

3. Discuss which reforms would be most desirable to a) health providers, b) insurers, c) providers' attorneys, d) plaintiffs' attorneys.

4. In a no-fault liability reform statute, what danger could result if the law were not thoughtfully designed?

5. Name the four major phases of an alternative dispute resolution program for the internal use by a health care facility.

References

1. "Professional Liability Legislation: Looking to 86." *Medical Staff* 14 (October 1985): 2.

2. Perlman, Peter. "President's Page." *Trial* 21 (December 1985): 5.

3. Cooper, Randall. "Directors and Officers Liability, the War." *Emphasis* (July 1985): 1.

4. Moody, Michael J. "Tort Reform for Products Liability." *Emphasis* (November 1985): 4.

5. "Look Who's Getting Sued Now," *Newsweek* 106 (August 26, 1985): 58.

6. Press, Irwin. "The Predisposition to File Claims: The Patient's Perspective." *Law, Medicine and Health Care* 12 (April 1984): 53.

7. Krause, Gustone A. "Long Tail Casualty Lines: After the War." *Emphasis* (November 1985): 8.

8. American Medical Association Special Task Force on Professional Liability and Insurance. "Professional Liability in the 80's." Chicago: AMA: October 1984, p. 21 (quoting the Insurance Information Institute, Pacific Coast Regional Office, San Francisco, 1983, p. 21).

9. Ibid., p. 15.

10. Ibid., p. 9 (quoting *Best's Insurance Management Reports,* January 1984).

11. "Claims, Premiums on the Way Up." *Modern Healthcare* (April 1984): 70 (quoting Jury Verdict Research, Inc.).

12. Localio, A. Russel. "Variation on $962,258: The Misuse of Data on Medical Malpractice." *Law, Medicine and Health Care* 13 (June 1985): 126.

13. Advertisement in *Trial* 21 (November 1985): 112.

14. Advertisement in *ABA Journal* (December 1985): 96.

15. "Professional Liability Legislation" (ref. 1).

16. Griffith, James. "What It Will Take To Solve the Malpractice Crisis?" *Medical Economics for Surgeons* (October 1982): 122.

17. "New York Okays Use of Medical Malpractice Panels." *ABA Journal* 71 (December 1985): 101 (commenting on *Treyball v. Clark,* Sept. 1985, No. 516, New York Appeals Court, Albany, N.Y.).

18. The Missouri Bar, letter to members (December 5, 1985). Chapter 383.110, Section 1-5. RSMo. 1978.

19. Section 768.41 Fla. St. 1976, Supp.

20. H.R. 5400, The Alternative Medical Liability Act. U.S. Cong. 1984.

21. "Tort Reform Bill Introduced in Congress." *Occurrence* 5 (September—October 1984): 1.

22. Ibid.

23. Testimony by Patricia M. Danzon, Ph.D., before the Committee on Labor and Human Resources, U.S. Senate, July 10, 1984.

24. "Tort Reform Bill Introduced in Congress" (ref. 21).

25. Ibid.

26. Coulson, Robert. "Alternative Dispute Resolution, Threat or Invitation?" Trial 21 (October 1985): 21.

27. Ibid.

28. Burger, Warren E. "The State of the Judiciary Address, February 17, 1985." *ABA Journal* (April 1985): 88.

29. Coulson, p. 21.

30. Riskin, Leonard and James Westbrook. *Materials on Alternative Dispute Processing and Lawyers.* University of Missouri-Columbia, School of Law, 1985, pp. 1-3. Typescript.

31. Ibid, pp. 1-4.

32. Ibid, pp. 1-5.

33. Holder, A. *Medical Malpractice Law* 408-13 (2d. 1977).

34. Quoted in Falsgraf, William W. "President's Page: Toward Swifter Justice." *ABA Journal* (November 1985): 8.

35. "Tort Reform Bill Introduced in Congress" (ref. 21).

GLOSSARY OF LEGAL AND INSURANCE TERMS

Abate To put a stop to a nuisance; to reduce or cancel a legacy because the estate of the testator is insufficient to make payment in full.

Absolute Liability Liability for an act that causes harm even though the actor was not at fault.

Absolute Privilege Protection from liability for slander or libel, given under certain circumstances to statements regardless of the fact that they are false or maliciously made.

Acceptance Unqualified assent to the act or proposal of another, such as the acceptance of a draft (bill of exchange), of an offer to make a contract, of goods delivered by the seller, or of a gift or a deed.

Accessory after the Fact One who after the commission of a felony knowingly assists the felon.

Accessory before the Fact One who is absent at the commission of a crime but who aided and abetted its commission.

Accident An event that occurs even though a reasonable person would not have foreseen its occurrence, because of which the law holds no one legally responsible for the harm caused.

Accident Insurance Insurance that indemnifies the policyholder for loss due to some accidental personal injury he or she has suffered.

Acknowledgment An admission or confirmation, generally of an instrument and usually made before a person authorized to administer oaths, such as a notary public, the purpose being to declare that the instrument was executed by the person making the instrument, or that it was his or her free act, or that he or she desires that it be recorded.

---

*Insurance terms by permission of Gwathmey Tyler of Reagan and Harris, Louisville, Kentucky, published in *Risk Management and Insurance, a Handbook of Fundamentals,* by Claudina Modsen and John H. Walker, 1983, Washington, DC: National Association of College and University.

Action A proceeding brought to enforce any right.

Action in Rem An action brought to declare the status of a thing, such as an action to declare the title to property to be forfeited because of its illegal use.

Action of Mandamus A common-law action brought to compel the performance of a ministerial or clerical act by an officer.

Action of Quo Warranto A common-law action brought to challenge the authority of an officer to act or to hold office.

Action of Replevin A common-law action brought to recover the possession of personal property.

Action of Trespass A common-law action brought to recover damages for a tort.

Act of Bankruptcy Any of the acts specified by the national bankruptcy law which, when committed by the debtor within the 4 months preceding the filing of the petition in bankruptcy, is proper ground for declaring the debtor a bankrupt.

Act of God Something beyond human control that happens to property. Lightning, for example, would be such, and damage done by it would not be the responsibility of a bailee, although he or she might be responsible for many other calamities. Acts of God are excluded by the usual bill of lading and, to the extent not specifically assumed, by insurance policies.

Actual Cash Value The replacement cost of property less an allowance for depreciation. Usually the measure of indemnity in an insurance contract.

Administrative Agency A governmental commission or board given authority to regulate particular matters.

Administrator (Administratrix) The man (woman) appointed to wind up and settle the estate of a person who has died without a will.

Admission A concession as to the truth or falsity of a particular proposition, or the existence or nonexistence of a particular fact or set of facts.

Admitted Company An insurance company that has been licensed by the insurance department of the state in question.

Advertisers' Liability Insurance Insurance that covers an insured party against claims for libel, slander, defamation, infringement of copyright, invasion of privacy, etc., arising out of its advertising program. Also available for radio and television stations and advertising agencies.

Advisory Opinion An opinion that may be rendered in a few states when there is no actual controversy before the court. The matter is submitted by private persons, or in some instances by the governor of the state, to obtain the court's opinion.

Affidavit A statement of facts set forth in written form and supported by the oath or affirmation of the person making the statement, setting forth that such facts are true to his or her knowledge or to his or her information and belief. The affidavit is executed before a notary public or other person authorized to administer oaths.

Affirmative Defense A matter that, if proved, means that the plaintiff cannot recover in his or her suit. The term applies to matters unrelated to the primary claim that offer independent reasons why the plaintiff may not recover.

Agency The relationship that exists between a person identified as a principal and another, called the agent, by virtue of which the latter may make contracts with third persons on behalf of the principal.

Agent One who is authorized by a principal or by operation of law to make contracts with third persons on behalf of the principal.

Agreed Amount Clause A provision in a policy whereby the policyholder agrees to carry a specified amount of insurance under penalty of being a coinsurer for the deficit. Used in lieu of coinsurance in certain policies.

All Risk Policy A policy of insurance against damage to property may be written to insure against "named perils," i.e., the various hazards against which the policy insures are listed. However, policies may be issued in certain cases to insure against "all risks of loss or damage" and are then termed "all risk" policies. The term is not strictly correct, because all policies exclude insurance against certain hazards.

Alteration Any material change of the terms of a writing fraudulently made by a party thereto.

Ambulatory Not effective and therefore able to be changed, as in the case of a will that is not final until the testator has died.

Amicable Action An action that all parties agree should be brought and which is begun by the filing of such an agreement, rather than by serving the adverse parties with process. Although the parties agree to litigate, the dispute is real, and the decision is not an advisory opinion.

Amicus Curiae Literally, a friend of the court; one who is appointed by the court to take part in litigation and to assist the court by furnishing his or her opinion in the matter.

Amount of Insurance The limit of payment a company can be liable for under a policy. A house, for example, may be "insured for $10,000." The $10,000 is the greatest amount the company will have to pay.

Annuity A contract by which the insured party pays a lump sum to the insurer and later receives fixed annual payments.

Antitrust Acts Statutes prohibiting combinations and contracts in restraint of trade, notably the Federal Sherman Antitrust Act of 1890, now generally inapplicable to labor union activity.

Appeal To take a case to a reviewing court to determine whether the judgment of the lower court or administrative agency was correct. (Parties: appellant, appellee.)

Appellate Jurisdiction The power of a court to hear and decide a given class of cases on appeal from another court or administrative agency.

Arbitration The settlement of disputed questions, whether of law or fact, by one or more arbitrators by whose decision the parties agree to be bound. Increasingly used as a procedure for labor dispute settlement.

Arbitration Clause A clause in an insurance policy that provides that in the event the company and the policyholder are unable to agree on the amount due after a loss, the matter shall be submitted to disinterested parties for solution. One is appointed by the insured party, one by the insurance company, and these two together pick a third, or "umpire."

Assignment Transfer of a right. Generally used in connection with personal property rights, such as rights under a contract, commercial Paper, an insurance policy, a mortgage, or a lease. (Parties: assignor, assignee.)

Assumption of Risk The common-law rule that an employee cannot sue an employer for injuries caused by the ordinary risks of employment on the theory that he or she had assumed such risks by undertaking the work. The rule has been abolished in those areas governed by workmen's compensation laws and most employers' liability statutes.

Assured The party who has purchased a policy of insurance and is protected by it (same as "insured" or "policyholder").

Attachment The seizure of property of, or of a debt owed to, the debtor by the service of process upon a third person who is in possession of the property or who owes a debt to the debtor.

Attractive Nuisance Doctrine A rule imposing liability on a landowner for injuries sustained by small children playing on his or her land when the landowner permits a condition to exist or maintains equipment that he or she should realize would attract small children who could not realize the danger. The rule does not apply if an unreasonable burden would be imposed on the landowner in taking steps to protect the children.

Automatic Sprinkler A device to protect property from damage by fire in which water is piped to devices called sprinkler heads, which melt with heat and release water to extinguish the fire. Extensively used to protect valuable properties, and property so protected normally is charged a much lower fire insurance rate than property not so protected.

Automobile Insurance Plan Many states either 1) require that an automobile owner carry liability insurance or 2) have "unsatisfied judgment" or "financial responsibility laws" that make the purchase of insurance mandatory. Some motorists cannot buy insurance for some reason. To make it possible for them to be insured, there are "automobile insurance plans," in which such risks are insured. These risks are rotated among the subscribing companies in proportion to the amount of automobile liability insurance each writes in the state. All companies writing this class of insurance are required to participate in this activity. Long identified as "assigned risk plan."

Automobile Liability Insurance A form of liability insurance (see definition) specifically designed to indemnify for loss incurred through legal liability for bodily injury and damage to the property of others caused by accident arising out of ownership or operation of an automobile.

Automobile Physical Damage Insurance Insurance covering loss or damage to the policyholder's automobile. Also called "material damage insurance."

Bail Variously used in connection with the release of a person or property from the custody of the law, referring a) to the act of releasing or bailing, b) to the persons who assume liability in the event that the released person does not appear or it is held that the property should not be released, and c) to the bond or sum of money that such persons furnish the court or other official as indemnity for nonperformance of the obligation.

Bailee One who has custody of the property of another. Bailees "for hire" have certain responsibilities to care for the property of others in their custody.

Bailees' Customers' Insurance Insurance arranged by a bailee for the account of his or her bailors or customers. An example is the insurance of furs for those who store furs in a storage warehouse arranged by the storer for the benefit of the owners of the furs. Laundry bundle insurance is similar.

Bankruptcy A procedure by which someone unable to pay his or her debts may be declared a bankrupt, after which all assets in excess of his or her exemption claim are surrendered to the court for administration and distribution to his or her creditors, and the debtor is given a discharge that releases him or her from the unpaid balance due on most debts.

Beneficiary The person to whom the proceeds of a life insurance policy are payable, a person for whose benefit property is held in trust, or a person given property by a will.

Binder A memorandum of an agreement to insure issued to record the transaction pending the writing of a policy. A policy to "close out" is issued to replace it shortly thereafter.

Blanket Crime Policy A blanket policy insuring against employee dishonesty, losses inside and outside the premises, money orders and counterfeit currency, and depositor's forgery. The policy covers money, securities, and other property with a single limit of insurance applying to all coverages, none of which may be eliminated. Similar to the 3D policy wherein the same coverages are afforded but on an optional basis.

Blanket Insurance A single amount of insurance that covers several items. For example, one may write one amount of insurance to cover two buildings, or one building and its contents. Such policies usually require the fulfillment of certain restrictions, which may not be required in "specific" or "itemized" policies, such as the use of a 100 percent coinsurance clause. "Blanket rates" are rates that apply to blanket policies.

Blanket Position Bond A bond that insures an employer against loss from dishonest acts by his or her employees. As the name implies, this is a blanket coverage for all employees in the regular service of the employer during the term of the bond. The bond is issued for a fixed sum, and each employee is covered up to the full amount of the bond. The maximum amount payable for any one embezzlement involving more than one employee would thus be the amount of the bond multiplied by the number of employees involved. See "Commercial Blanket Bond."

Blanket Rate Fire insurance rates normally apply to one particular building or its contents. These are "specific" rates. When a rate is made to apply to more than one building, or a building and its contents, or, in general, more than one subject of insurance, it is a blanket rate. It normally requires the use of a higher percentage of coinsurance than a specific rate.

Blue-Sky Laws State statutes designed to protect the public from the sale of worthless stocks and bonds.

Boardinghouse Keeper One regularly engaged in the business of offering living accommodations to permanent lodgers or boarders.

Bodily Injury Injury to a human being, as opposed to injury to property.

Boiler and Machinery Insurance Insurance against loss arising from the operation of boilers and machinery. It may cover loss suffered by the boilers and machinery itself, or include damage done to other property and business interruption losses. Also called "machinery breakdown insurance."

Bona Fide In good faith; without any fraud or deceit.

Bond An obligation or promise made in writing and sealed, generally of corporations, personal representatives, trustees; fidelity bonds.

Boycott A combination of two or more persons to cause harm to another by refraining from patronizing or dealing with the other person in any way or inducing others to so refrain; commonly an incident in labor disputes.

Broker-Agent Large and successful insurance agents at times operate both as brokers representing the policyholder and as agents representing the company. Or they may have an office in one city, which operates strictly on a brokerage basis, and one in another city, in which they are agents.

Builders' Risk The risk exposure associated with building or a ship in the course of construction.

Building Rate A fire insurance rate made separately for the insurance of the building itself as opposed to its contents.

Burden of Proof The obligation of a party to produce evidence establishing his or her contention. The term is used in several senses, the primary ones being the burden to produce a preponderance of the evidence in civil cases, or the burden to offer evidence countering evidence offered by the opponent.

Business Interruption Insurance When a business owner experiences a calamity of some kind that prevents the normal carrying on of business, he or she loses profits and has certain continuing expenses that may not be avoided. The insurance of this loss against any hazard is called "business interruption insurance," or often "use and occupancy insurance."

Camera Floater An inland marine form designed to insure cameras and related equipment.

Cancellation A crossing out of a part of an instrument or a destruction of all legal effect of the instrument, whether by act of one party upon breach by the other party, or pursuant to agreement or decree of court.

Capacity The measure of an insurer's ability to issue contracts of insurance, determined usually by the largest amount it will accept for a given risk or, in certain other situations, by the maximum volume of business that the company is prepared to accept.

Capital The net assets of a corporation.

Capital Stock The declared money value of the outstanding stock of a corporation.

Cause of Action The right to damages or other judicial relief when a legally protected right of the plaintiff is violated by an unlawful act of the defendant.

Caveat Emptor "Let the buyer beware." This maxim has been restricted by warranty and strict tort liability concepts.

Cede When one company reinsures its liability with another, it "cedes" business.

Certificate of Insurance A certificate of insurance is in the usual sense of the word a copy of a policy. When a policy is issued covering a piece of property that is mortgaged with a "mortgagee clause" attached, as is often the case with properties such as houses, the mortgagee usually insists that he or she be given the original policy. In such cases a certificate is issued by the agent or the company and is given to the owner for his or her records. Also the document that gives the specific details of property insured by "master" or "open" policies. Ocean marine cargo insurance is usually handled by the use of certificates referring to an open master policy.

Certiorari A procedural device to obtain review when normal channels are not available.

Charter The grant of authority from a government to exist as a corporation. Generally replaced today by a certificate of incorporation approving the articles of incorporation.

Chartered Property and Casualty Underwriter (CPCU) The degree conferred by the American Institute for Property and Liability Underwriters. A parallel term, "chartered life underwriter" (CLU), is found in life insurance practice.

Chattels Personal Tangible personal property.

Chattels Real Leases of land and buildings.

Circumstantial Evidence Evidence relating to circumstances surrounding the facts in dispute from which the trier of fact may deduce what happened.

Civil Action In many states, a simplified form of action combining all or many of the former common-law actions.

Civil Court A court with jurisdiction to hear and determine controversies relating to private rights and duties.

Claim The amount that a policyholder believes he or she is due from an insurance company as the result of some happening that is insured against. After its amount has been determined, it becomes a "loss." In practice, the terms "claim" and "loss" are synonymous.

Codicil An additional writing by someone who has made a will, which is executed with all the formality of a will and is treated as an addition or modification to the will.

Coinsurance Clause A clause contained in some fire and burglary policies, requiring the insured to carry insurance equal to a stated percentage of the value of the insured property if he or she is to collect his or her partial losses in full up to the limits of the policy.

Collision The striking of a vehicle or a ship against another object or another vehicle or ship. Collision insurance insures against loss so caused.

Collusion An agreement between two or more persons to defraud the government or the courts, as by obtaining a divorce by collusion when no grounds for a divorce exist, or to defraud third persons of their rights.

Commercial Blanket Bond A bond to insure an employer against loss through dishonest acts committed by his or her employees, covering all employees in the regular service of the employer during the term of the bond. A commercial blanket bond is issued for a fixed amount, which is the maximum sum payable for any one embezzlement, whether one or more employees are involved. See "Blanket Position Bond."

Commission The share of an insurance premium allowed to the producer for having produced the business.

Commissioner of Insurance The official of a state charged with the duty of enforcing the insurance laws. Also sometimes called the "insurance superintendent" or "director of insurance."

Common Carrier One who offers to transport merchandise for hire and must accept shipments from anyone who wishes to use his or her services. Different laws and rules govern common carriers than private or contract carriers who only transport the goods of those with whom they have made agreements.

Common Law The body of unwritten principles originally based on the usages and customs of the community, which were recognized and enforced by the courts.

Common Stock Stock that has no right or priority over any other stock of the corporation as to dividends or distribution of assets upon dissolution.

Community Property The cotenancy held by husband and wife in property acquired during their marriage under the law of some of the states, principally in the southwestern United States.

Complaint The initial pleading filed by the plaintiff in many actions, which in many states may be served as original process to acquire jurisdiction over the defendant.

Completed Operations The liability a contractor might incur from improperly performed work after he or she has completed a job. At one time regarded as a part of product liability, but now more properly regarded as a separate coverage.

Comprehensive Automobile Coverage An item of coverage in an automobile physical damage policy insuring against loss or damage resulting from numerous miscellaneous causes such as fire, theft, windstorm, flood, vandalism, etc., but normally not including loss by collision or upset.

Comprehensive General Liability Policy A policy particularly suited to a manufacturer, contractor, or large wholesaler or retailer providing broad coverage for claims made against him or her for bodily injury or damage to property of others for which he or she may become liable and which arise out of the entire business operation. Automobile liability coverages may be included in this policy.

Comprehensive Personal Liability A form of liability insurance that reimburses the policyholder in the event he or she has become liable to pay money for damage or injury he or she has caused to others. This form does not include automobile liability, but does include almost every activity of the policyholder except such as arise from the operations of his or her business; hence "personal" liability.

Concealment In insurance, failure to disclose a material fact. Concealment may void an insurance policy. In law, failure to volunteer information not specifically requested.

Confession An admission of guilt, usually used in a formal sense.

Confidential Relationship A relationship in which, because of the legal status of the parties or their respective physical or mental conditions or knowledge, one party places full confidence and trust in the other and relies upon him or her entirely for guidance.

Conflict of Laws The body of law that determines the law of which state is to apply when two or more states are involved in the facts of a given case.

Consanguinity Relationship by blood.

Consideration The promise or performance by the other party that the promisor demands as the price of his or her promise.

Contents Rate The insurance rate on the contents of a building as distinguished from the rate for insurance of the building itself.

Contingent Business Interruption Insurance Insurance against loss due to interruption of business by fire or other insured catastrophe occurring at another's premises, such as those of a supplier or a large customer. Sometimes called "contingent use and occupancy insurance."

Contingent Liability A liability that may be incurred by an insured party as a result of negligence on the part of independent persons engaged by him or her to perform work. The most common example is the contingent liability of a principal contractor, that may result from construction operations undertaken by subcontractors. In property damage insurance, the possibility of financial loss to a policyholder resulting from damage or loss to the property of another, e.g., a supplier or a customer.

Contract A binding agreement based upon the genuine assent of the parties, made for a lawful object, between competent parties, in the form required by law, and generally supported by consideration.

Contractor's Equipment Floater An inland marine form to insure the equipment, tools, and materials of a contractor.

Contractual Liability Liability as set forth by agreements between people as distinguished from liability imposed by law (legal liability).

Contribution The right of a co-obligor who has paid more than his or her proportionate share to demand that the other obligor pay him or her the amount of the excess payment.

Contributory Negligence Negligence of the plaintiff that contributes to his or her injury and at common law bars the plaintiff from recovery, even though the defendant may have been more negligent than the plaintiff.

Conveyance A transfer of an interest in land, ordinarily by the execution and delivery of a deed.

Corporation An artificial legal person or being created by government grant, which for many purposes is treated as a natural person.

Costs The expenses of suing or being sued, recoverable in some actions by the successful party, and in others subject to allocation by the court. Ordinarily they do not include attorney's fees or compensation for loss of time.

Counterclaim A claim that the defendant in an action may take against the plaintiff.

Crime A violation of the law that is punished as an offense against the state or government.

Cross-Complaint A claim that a defendant may take against a plaintiff.

Cross-Examination The oral examination of a witness during a trial by the attorney for the adverse party.

Culpable Responsible for; liable for.

Damages A sum of money recovered to redress or make amends for the legal wrong or injury done.

Declaratory Judgment A procedure for obtaining the decision of a court on a question before any action has been taken or loss sustained. It differs from an advisory opinion in that there must be an actual, imminent controversy.

Decree A judgment of a court, in written form, specifying what the parties to a lawsuit must do or not do.

Deductible Some insurance policies are written to pay only after the policyholder has suffered an agreed amount of loss. This amount is "deducted" from the total of the damage to determine the amount the company must pay and thus becomes the "deductible."

Deed An instrument by which a grantor (owner of land) conveys or transfers the title to a grantee.

De Facto Existing in fact as distinguished from as of right, as in the case of an officer or a corporation purporting to act as such without being elected to the office or having been properly incorporated.

Defendant A party who is accused of a crime by the state, or against whom suit is brought by a private litigation, in which complaint is made that the party violated his or her duty or is responsible for a breach of duty or for negligence.

Demonstrative Evidence Evidence that consists of visible, physical objects.

Demurrer A pleading that may be filed to attack the sufficiency of the adverse party's pleading as not stating a cause of action or a defense.

Deposition A proceeding whereby questions are asked of a person, relating to the subject matter of a lawsuit, and in advance of trial, the questions and answers being recorded in written form.

Depositors' Forgery Bond A bond whereby a person or corporation can insure against losses by reason of forgery or alteration of any check, draft, etc.

Depreciation The difference between the value of an item of property when new and its reduced value at any subsequent time.

Devise A gift of real estate made by will.

Differences in Conditions Insurance A policy insuring against losses not usually covered by fire and business interruption policies, such as those caused by flood, earthquake, landslide, and other unusual, accidental occurrences. Applicable mostly to large commercial and industrial organizations and performing much the same function in property insurance that the umbrella liability policy (see definition) does for liability coverage.

Directed Verdict A direction by the trial judge to the jury to return a verdict in favor of a specified party to the action.

Directors The persons vested with control of a corporation, subject to the elective power of the shareholders.

Directors' and Officers' Liability Insurance Insurance that protects officers and directors of a corporation against damages from claims resulting from negligent or wrongful acts in the course of their duties. Also covers the corporation for expenses incurred in defending lawsuits arising from alleged wrongful acts of officers or directors. These policies always require the insured party to retain part of the risk uninsured.

Discharge in Bankruptcy An order of a bankruptcy court discharging the bankrupt debtor from the unpaid balance of most of the claims against him or her.

Discharge of Contract Termination of a contract by performance, agreement, impossibility, acceptance of breach, or operation of law.

Discovery Proceedings The full procedures of asking oral and written questions, and providing oral and written answers, as well as giving another party access to relevant documents and things, all undertaken prior to a trial.

Dismiss To terminate an action on the ground that the plaintiff has not pleaded a cause of action entitling him or her to relief.

Domestic Corporation A corporation that has been incorporated by the state in question rather than by another state.

Domicile The home of a person or the state of incorporation of a corporation, to be distinguished from a place where a person lives but that the person does not regard as his or her home, or a state in which a corporation does business but in which it is not incorporated.

Double Jeopardy The principle that a person who has once been placed in jeopardy by being brought to trial at which the proceedings progressed at least as far as having the jury sworn cannot thereafter be tried a second time for the same offense.

Drive-Other-Cars Clause A provision in an automobile policy to protect the policyholder when driving cars other than the one described in the policy.

Due Care The degree of care that a reasonable person would exercise to prevent the realization of all harm that under the circumstances would be reasonably foreseeable in the event that such care were not taken.

Due Process of Law The guarantee by the Fifth and Fourteenth Amendments to the U.S. Constitution and by many state constitutions that no person shall be deprived of life, liberty, or property without due process of law. As presently interpreted, this prohibits any law, either state or federal, that sets up an unfair procedure or a procedure the substance of which is arbitrary or capricious.

Duress Conduct that deprives the victim of his or her own free will, which generally gives the victim the right to set aside any transaction entered into under such circumstances.

Earned Premium When a premium is paid in advance for a certain time, the company is said to "earn" the premium as time advances. For example, a policy written for 3 years and paid for in advance would be one-third "earned" at the end of the first year of its life.

Eleemosynary Corporation A corporation organized for a charitable or benevolent purpose.

Embezzlement A statutory offense consisting of the unlawful conversion of property entrusted to the wrongdoer with respect to which he or she owes the owner a fiduciary duty.

Employers' Liability Legal liability imposed on an employer making him or her responsible to pay damages to an employee injured by the employer's negligence. Generally replaced by worker's compensation, which pays the employee whether the employer has been negligent or not.

Endorsement After a policy has been written, it often is necessary to modify it. Such modification, called an "endorsement," is written, typed, or printed on the policy or on a small piece of paper and attached to the policy.

Equity The body of principles that originally developed because of the inadequacy of the rules then applied by the common-law courts of England.

Errors and Omissions Insurance A type of insurance that steps in to take the place of insurance that has not been effected due to a mistake or forgetfulness. Issued to concerns such as mortgage concerns or others engaged in the routine insurance of many properties.

Estate The extent and nature of one's interest in land; the assets constituting a decedent's property at the time of his or her death, or the assets of a bankrupt.

Estoppel The principle by which a person is barred from pursuing a certain course of action or of disputing the truth of certain matters when his or her conduct has been such that it would be unjust to permit the person to do so.

Evidence That which is presented to the trier of fact of a case as the basis on which the trier is to determine what happened.

Exception An objection, such as an exception to the admission of evidence on the ground that it is hearsay; a clause excluding certain property from the operation of a deed.

Excess Insurance Insurance that does not pay until the loss exceeds an agreed amount, which may or may not be insured elsewhere. Excess policies are not subject to the basic principle of contribution with nonexcess policies, although they may contribute or share the loss with other excess policies.

Exclusion Something not covered and so set forth in the wording of a policy.

Ex Contractu A claim or matter that is founded upon or arises out of a contract.

Ex Delicto A claim or matter that is founded upon or arises out of a tort.

Execution The carrying out of a judgment of a court, generally directing that property owned by the defendant be sold and the proceeds first used to pay the execution or judgment creditor.

Exemplary Damages Damages in excess of the amount needed to compensate for the plaintiff's injury, which are awarded in order to punish the defendant for his or her malicious or wanton conduct so as to make an example of the defendant; also called "punitive damages."

Exoneration An agreement or provision in an agreement that one party shall not be held liable for loss; the right of the surety to demand that those primarily liable pay the claim for which the surety is secondarily liable.

Expense Constant A flat premium loading, mostly used in worker's compensation insurance, based on the fact that, for smaller policies, the expense factor in the basic premium is inadequate to cover the cost of issuing and handling the policy.

Experience Rating The establishing of rates based on what the past history of the insured risk has been.

Expert Witness One who has acquired special knowledge in a particular field through practical experience, or study, or both, which gives him or her a superior knowledge so that his or her opinion is admissible as an aid to the trier of fact.

Expiration The date on which the time for which a policy was written runs out.

Ex Post Facto Law A law making criminal an act that was lawful when the act was done or that increases the penalty for an act that was subject to a lesser penalty when done. Such laws are generally prohibited by constitutional provisions.

Exposure The danger of loss (particularly by fire) arising from what happens to another risk close by. Also the sum total of values, which if damaged or destroyed would cause loss under a policy, i.e., the value of everything a policy insures. Also used as a measure of the rating units or premium basis of a risk, e.g., payroll exposure or an exposure of a number of automobiles.

Extra Expense Insurance Insurance purchased to reimburse the policyholder for the additional money beyond the loss, which he or she may be forced to spend because of a fire or other inaured calamity. It is written either as a separate policy or as an addition to an ordinary policy.

Fair Plan A program recommended by the President's Advisory Panel on Insurance in Riot-Affected Areas to provide fair access to insurance for property owners who experience difficulty in buying insurance on property located in blighted or deteriorating urban areas. Basically the plan assures a property owner of a physical inspection of his or her property and a promise to provide fire and allied lines insurance if the property insurable have been made. Many of these plans have been extended to statewide coverage.

Family Automobile Policy An automobile policy insuring against liability, medical expense, physical damage, and uninsured motorists, available only for individually owned private passenger cars and some small trucks. It is somewhat similar to the combination automobile policy, but provides broader coverage.

Family Protection Coverage (Automobile) If a person has a bodily injury claim against a motorist who has no automobile liability insurance and is also financially irresponsible, the injured person could not collect damages. Family protection coverage protects the policyholder and his or her spouse and family by paying the amount that should have been collected from the uninsured motorist up to the bodily injury limits fixed by the financial responsibility laws of the state in which the policy was issued. This coverage also protects the insured party in case of injuries caused by a hit-and-run driver. Determination of who was responsible for the accident and how much the injuries are worth is a matter for agreement between insured and insurer, with any disputes settled by arbitration. This coverage originated as the "uninsured motorist endorsement."

Fellow-Servant Rule A common-law defense of an employer that bars an employee from suing the employer for injuries caused by a fellow employee.

Felony A criminal offense that is punishable by confinement in prison for a substantial term or by death, or that is expressly stated by statute to be a felony.

Fidelity Bond A bond that makes good if an employee steals or embezzles or otherwise robs his or her employer.

Fiduciary A person or a corporation that has an obligation to act for another, produced by a trust. For example, the executor of an estate is a fiduciary.

Financial Responsibility Laws Laws enacted by most states to keep reckless and financially irresponsible drivers off the highways. These acts vary from state to state, but generally speaking they suspend the driving license of any person a) who cannot pay a judgment arising out of an automobile accident, or b) who has been involved in any automobile accident causing bodily injury or property damage, or c) who has been convicted of a serious traffic violation. In cases b) and c), the operator recovers his or her license upon filing proof of his or her ability to pay claims up to certain fixed amounts for injury he or she may subsequently do to others, but under a) in many states the person cannot drive again until he or she has paid the outstanding judgment and filed proof of financial responsibility for future accidents. The required proof is usually supplied by a certificate filed by an insurance company or sometimes by a bond or deposit of cash or securities. Sometimes referred to as "safety responsibility" laws.

Fine Arts Insurance Insurance covering works of art. Usually written by inland marine underwriters on an "all risks" and a "valued" basis.

Fire While a fire is a fire in ordinary language, by the insurance definition there must be accompanying flame to make it so qualify. For example, a fire policy is not liable for losses caused by scorches by cigarettes, unless a flame is actually produced at the same time.

Fire Insurance Insurance that covers losses from fire and lightning and also the resultant damage caused by smoke and water. Usually supplemented by extended coverage.

Fire-Resistive Refers to the construction of a building built of steel and concrete or other noncombustible materials. The proper term for "fireproof."

Floater A policy that covers property at any location; i.e., the protection "floats around" with the value.

Flood Overflow of water from its natural boundaries. More specifically defined by the National Flood Insurance Act of 1968 as "a general and temporary condition of partial or complete inundation of normally dry land areas from 1) the overflow of inland or tidal waters or 2) the unusual and rapid accumulation or runoff of surface waters from any source."

Food, Drug, and Cosmetic Act A federal statute prohibiting the interstate shipment of misbranded or adulterated food, drugs, cosmetics, and therapeutic devices.

Foreign Corporation A corporation incorporated under the laws of another state.

Forgery The fraudulent making or altering of an instrument that apparently creates or alters a legal liability of another.

Fraud The making of a false statement of a past or existing fact with knowledge of its falsity or with reckless indifference as to its truth with the intent to cause another to rely thereon, and the other person does rely thereon to his or her injury.

Free On Board (F.O.B.) When goods are shipped F.O.B. the place of origin, the shipper is responsible only until the goods have been placed on board the vessel, freight car, truck, or other means of transport; after that, the risk belongs to the consignee. When they are shipped F.O.B. destination, the risk belongs to the shipper.

Furniture and Fixtures In insurance language, the contents of a building excepting merchandise for sale or in the course of manufacture (stock) and excepting machinery. Fixtures are the pieces that are "fixed," that is, attached to the building.

Garagekeepers' Legal Liability The liability that the operator of a garage has to preserve the cars that are stored there. There is a special form issued by automobile insurers covering this risk.

General Damages Damages that in the ordinary course of events follow naturally and probably from the injury caused by the defendant.

General Partnership A partnership in which the partners conduct as co-owners a business for profit, and each partner has a right to take part in the management of the business and has unlimited liability.

Gift Causa Mortis A gift made by the donor because the donor believed he or she faced immediate and impending death, which gift is revoked or is revocable under certain circumstances.

Glass Insurance Insurance against the breakage of glass.

Grand Jury A jury not exceeding 23 in number that considers evidence of the commission of crime and prepares indictments to bring offenders to trial before a petty jury.

Grievance Settlement The adjustment of disputes relating to the administration of existing labor contracts as compared with disputes over new terms of employment.

Guaranty An undertaking to pay the debt of another if the creditor first sues the debtor or principal and is unable to recover the debt. In some instances the liability is primary, in which case it is the same as suretyship.

Guest Laws In some states, legislation provides that the right of action of an injured guest passenger against the driver of an automobile is subject to proof that the driver was guilty of and "willful and wanton" negligence. Apart from such laws, known as "guest laws," the guest passenger would have the same rights as any other member of the public and only be required to prove "ordinary" negligence.

Habeas Corpus Frequently called the "great writ," it means "you have the body." The writ of habeas corpus has a varied use in criminal and civil contexts and is basically a procedure for obtaining a judicial determination of the legality of an individual's custody.

Hearsay Evidence Statements made out of court that are offered in court as proof of the information contained in the statements; subject to many exceptions, hearsay evidence is not admissible as evidence in court.

Heirs Those persons specified by statute to receive the estate of a decedent not disposed of by will.

Hold-Harmless Agreement A company may wish to pay a loss but is not entirely sure that it may not be called upon to pay a second time to some other party. The payee may be asked to execute an agreement whereby the company will be reimbursed or held harmless by the payee if such should happen. The principal in a large construction project will frequently demand hold-harmless agreements from all subcontractors in respect to claims made against him or her arising out of the subcontractors' negligence. The principal often stipulates the purchase of a liability policy by the subcontractor to support the hold-harmless agreement.

Holographic Will A will written by the testator in his or her own hand.

Homicide The killing of a human being.

Hotelkeeper One regularly engaged in the business of offering living accommodations to all transient persons.

Hung Jury A petty jury that has been unable to agree upon a verdict.

Ignorantia Legis Non Excusat Ignorance of the law is not an excuse.

Impeachment Demonstration that testimony or statements made are false or substantially inaccurate.

Implied Contract A contract expressed by conduct or implied or deduced from the facts. Also used to refer to a quasi-contract.

Implied Warranty A warranty is a representation by the policyholder that certain conditions exist or will be met. Even without having this warranty in writing, it may exist as an "implied" warranty, e.g., that a building is not on fire when insured, or that a vessel is seaworthy.

Imputed Vicariously attributed to or charged to another; for example, the knowledge of an agent obtained while acting in the scope of his authority is imputed to his principal.

Incest Sexual intercourse or cohabitation among family members.

Incidental Authority The authority of an agent that is reasonably necessary to execute his or her express authority.

Incurred Losses Losses are "incurred" when they happen. The total of all such losses (whether paid or not) makes up this figure as it appears in operating statements. Since this figure is one used frequently for various periods as well as in the annual statement, and it would take much work to keep track of the losses by both date of occurrence and payment, the figure is arrived at by subtracting from the period's paid losses those that were on the books unpaid at the beginning of the period and adding those that are on the books unpaid at the end of the current period.

In Custodia Legis In the custody of the law.

Indemnity The right of a person secondarily liable to require that a person primarily liable pay him or her for a loss when the secondary party discharges the obligation that the primary party should have discharged; the right of an agent to be paid the amount of any loss or damage sustained by him or her without his or her fault because of the agent's obedience to the principal's instructions; an undertaking by one person for a consideration to pay another person a sum of money to indemnify that person when he or she incurs a specified loss.

Independent Contractor A contractor who undertakes to perform a specified task according to the terms of a contract but over whom the other contracting party has no control except as provided for by the contract.

Indictment A formal accusation of crime made by a grand jury, which accusation is then tried by a petty or trial jury.

Inheritance The interest that passes from a decedent to his or her heirs.

Injunction An order of a court of equity to refrain from doing (negative injunction) or to do (affirmative or mandatory injunction) a specified act. Its use in labor disputes has been greatly restricted by statute.

Inland Marine Insurance The insurance of a property that is in the course of transportation or is of such a nature that it may easily be transported. There is a long list of such coverages.

Innkeepers' Legal Liability Hotel and motel operators are legally liable for the safekeeping of guests' property. The extent of the liability is established by various state laws. Innkeepers' legal liability policies insure against this liability, usually with a limit of $1,000 for any one guest, and with an appropriate aggregate limit.

In Pari Delicto Equally guilty; used in reference to a transaction as to which relief will not be granted to either party because both are equally guilty of wrong-doing.

Insolvency An excess of debts and liabilities over assets.

Installation Risk Certain inland marine policies are issued to protect the manufacturers or sellers of machinery while they are installing it on the premises of the purchaser.

Insurable Interest No policy should be issued to insure anyone who will not actually be out of pocket if the calamity that is insured against should happen. The policyholder must have an interest in the subject. He or she must own it or lose if it be damaged or lost by the insured peril; i.e., he or she must have an "insurable interest."

Insurance The making of a legal and enforceable contract between one party (called the insurer or underwriter) and another (called the insured) whereby in consideration of a sum of money (called the premium) the insurer agrees to pay an agreed amount of money to the insured if and when the latter may suffer some loss or be injured by some event, the happening of which is described in the contract of insurance (which is usually a "policy"). Also, the contract may be one that indemnifies the insured for claims made against him or her by third parties. (See "Liability Insurance.")

Insurance Rating Board (IRB) An association of insurance companies writing automobile, general liability, theft, and glass insurance. Organized in January 1968 to make rules; to develop policy forms, rates, and rating plans; and to handle all other related matters for these classes of business. Formed as a merger of the National Bureau of Casualty Underwriters and the National Automobile Underwriters Association. Headquarters in New York. Now part of the Insurance Services Office (see definition).

Insurance Services Office (ISO) A voluntary nonprofit association of property and casualty insurance companies providing a great variety of services on a national basis. Among its operations are rating, statistical, actuarial, and policy form services for all classes of property and casualty business. The association also functions, as provided by law, as an insurance rating organization. In addition, where applicable, ISO acts as an advisory organization or as a statistical agent. Established in 1971 by the consolidation of numerous associations and bureaus performing these services for separate classes of business and in various parts of the country. Headquarters in New York.

Insured The person who has purchased a policy of insurance and is protected by it. Same as "assured."

Interlocutory An intermediate step or proceeding that does not make a final disposition of the action and from which ordinarily no appeal may be taken.

Interpleader A form of action or proceeding by which a person against whom conflicting claims are made may bring the claimants into court to litigate their claims between themselves, as in the case of a bailor when two persons each claim to be the owner of the bailed property, or an insurer when two persons each claim to be the beneficiary of the insurance policy.

Inter Se Among or between themselves, as the rights of partners inter se or as between themselves.

Inter Vivos Any transaction that takes place between living persons and creates rights prior to the death of any of them.
Intestate The condition of dying without a will as to any property.
Intestate Succession The distribution made as directed by statute of property owned by the decedent of which he or she did not effectively dispose by will.

Ipso Facto By the very act or fact in itself without any further action by anyone.

Irrebuttable Presumption A presumption that cannot be rebutted by proving that the facts are to the contrary; not a true presumption but merely a rule of law described in terms of a presumption.

Joint and Several Contract A contract in which two or more persons are jointly and severally obligated or are jointly and severally entitled to recover.

Joint Contract A contract in which two or, more persons are jointly liable or jointly entitled to performance under the contract.

Joint Venture A relationship in which two or more persons combine their labor or property for a single undertaking and share profits and losses equally unless otherwise agreed.

Judgment The final sentence, order, or decision entered into at the conclusion of the action.

Judgment Nonobstante Veredicto (N.O.V.) A judgment that may be entered after verdict upon the motion of the losing party on the ground that the verdict is so wrong that a judgment should be entered the opposite of the verdict, or "nonobstante veredicto" (notwithstanding the verdict).

Judgment on the Pleadings A judgment that may be entered after all the pleadings are filed when it is clear from the pleadings that a particular party is entitled to win the action without proceeding any further.

Judicial Sale A sale made under order of court by an officer appointed to make the sale or by an officer having such authority as incident to his or her office. The sale may have the effect of divesting liens on the property.

Jurisdiction The power of a court to hear and determine a given class of cases; the power to act over a particular defendant.

Jurisdictional Dispute A dispute between rival labor unions, which may take the form of each claiming that particular work should be assigned to it.

Laches The rule that the enforcement of equitable rights will be denied when the party has delayed so long that rights of third persons have intervened or the death or disappearance of witnesses would prejudice any party through the loss of evidence.

Land Earth, including all things imbedded in or attached thereto, whether naturally or by act of man.

Landlord's Protective Liability If an owner of a property leases the entire premises to others who assume full control, his or her chance of being held liable for accidents occurring on the premises is diminished. The owner can insure this liability as "landlord's protective liability" at rates less than for the normal owners', landlords', and tenants' form of policy.

Last Clear Chance The rule that if the defendant had the last clear chance to have avoided injuring the plaintiff, he or she is liable even though the plaintiff was also contributorily negligent. In some states also called the humanitarian doctrine.

Law of the Case Matters decided in the course of litigation that are binding on the parties in the subsequent phases of the litigation.

Lease An oral or written contract whereby a person having a legal estate in real property or personal property grants its use or interest to another for consideration.

Leasehold Insurance The right to occupy a building set forth in a lease may be valuable and may be subject to loss if certain contingencies arise (such as severe fire). The insurance against the loss of such value is "leasehold" insurance against whatever peril it may be written.

Legal Remedy A means provided by law for the redress of a wrong committed; generally implies a court proceeding.

Lessee A tenant who has signed a lease.

Lessor A person who owns property and rents it to another under the terms of a contract called the "lease."

Letters of Administration The written authorization given to an administrator as evidence of his or her appointment and authority.

Letters Testamentary The written authorization given to an executor as evidence of his or her appointment and authority.

Levy A seizure of property by an officer of the court in execution of a judgment of the court; in many states it is sufficient if the officer is physically in the presence of the property and announces the fact that he or she is "seizing" it, although the officer then allows the property to remain where he or she found it.

Liabilities Money owed; the two columns in an insurance company financial statement are 1) its "assets" (the things it owns) and 2) its "liabilities" (the amount it owes or expects to owe) and capital.

Liability Insurance A form of insurance that protects the insured party from liability imposed by law for bodily or other personal injury or damage to property; legal liability normally results from negligent acts or omissions.

Libel The publishing of defamatory statements about another person. The general distinction between libel and slander is that the former must be in writing or similar permanent form, whereas the latter is oral. The distinction at law is not as simple. In maritime law, also a legal action directed against a ship.

License A personal privilege to do some act or series of acts upon the land of another, as the placing of a sign thereon, not amounting to an easement or a right of possession.

Lien A claim or right against property existing by virtue of the entry of a judgment against its owner or by the entry of a judgment and a levy thereunder on the property, or because of the relationship of the claimant to the owner of the property, such as an unpaid seller.

Limited Liability Loss of contributed capital or investment as maximum liability.

Limited Partnership A partnership in which at least one partner's liability is limited to the loss of the capital contribution that he or she has made to the partnership, and such a partner neither takes part in the management of the partnership nor appears to the public to be a partner.

Lineal Consanguinity The relationship that exists when one person is a direct descendant of the other.

Liquidated Damages A provision stipulating the amount of damages to be paid in the event of default or breach of contract.

Litigant A party to a lawsuit.

Lloyds A group of individuals who, each on his or her own, agree to share in making contracts of insurance. The best known is "Lloyds of London," although there are others.

Lloyds Syndicate A group of underwriters at Lloyds London who have entrusted their business to the handling by one underwriter on behalf of all in the group.

Loss In insurance, the amount the insurer is required to pay because of a happening against which it has insured. A happening that causes the company to pay. Also, the overall financial result of some operation, as opposed to "profit."

Loss Payable Clause A condition in a policy whereby the company is directed by the policyholder to pay any loss that may be due to some other person designated in the policy. Usually the payment is made by check or draft payable to the insured and the designated payee both.

Loss Ratio The fraction arrived at by dividing the amount of losses by the amount of premiums. Expressed as a percentage of the premiums. There are various ways of figuring, e.g., "earned premium loss ratio," "written premium loss ratio," etc.

Loss Reserve An estimate of the amount an insurer expects to pay for any reported loss or claim. The total of these estimates constitutes the loss reserves of an insurance company.

Lost Policy Release The normal way of canceling a policy is by returning it to the company, where it is marked "canceled" and placed on file. A policyholder who has lost his or her policy may still cancel it by executing a "lost policy release," which is a document designed to accomplish this purpose.

Majority Of age, as contrasted with being a major; more than half of any group, as a majority of stockholders.

Malice in Fact An intention to injure or cause harm.

Malice in Law A presumed intention to injure or cause harm when there is no privilege or right to do the act in question, which presumption cannot be contradicted or rebutted.

Maliciously Inducing Breach of Contract The wrong of inducing an employee to break his or her contract with the employer or inducing the breach of any other kind of contract with knowledge of its existence and without justification.

Malpractice Improper professional actions or failure to exercise proper professional skills by a person practicing a profession, such as a physician or dentist.

Malum In Se An offense that is criminal because it is contrary to the fundamental sense of a civilized community, such as murder.

Malum Prohibitum An offense that is criminal not because it is inherently wrong but is prohibited for the convenience of society, such as overtime parking.

Manslaughter The intentional taking of a human life without malice or premeditation.

Manufacturers' and Contractors' Liability Insurance (M&C) Insurance of liability arising from business operations including ownership and maintenance of premises. Applicable mainly to persons or corporations engaged in manufacturing, construction, and installation work. Such policies always exclude automobile liability.

Marine Insurance One of the major divisions of insurance (life, fire, casualty, marine, fidelity and surety). Has to do primarily with property in transit. If by sea, called "ocean" marine. If otherwise, "inland" marine.

Market Value Clause A clause whereby the company agrees that the amount it will pay in the event of loss shall be the value of the destroyed merchandise "on the market," i.e., what can be realized by selling it. Obviously, this thereby includes the seller's profit. Therefore, the clause is used with caution to avoid the creation of a moral hazard.

Medical Payments Insurance An agreement to pay the cost of medical care to an injured party irrespective of whether or not the policyholder is liable to do so. Written in conjunction with general liability policies. A similar coverage, automobile medical payments, is available in automobile liability policies.

Mens Rea The mental state that must accompany an act to make the act a crime. Sometimes described as the "guilty mind," although appreciation of guilt is not required.

Misdemeanor A criminal offense that is neither treason nor a felony.

Misrepresentation A false statement of fact made innocently without any intent to deceive.

Moratorium A temporary suspension by statute of the enforcement of debts or the foreclosure of mortgages.

Mortgage An interest in land given by the owner to a creditor as security for the payment to the creditor of a debt, the nature of the interest depending upon the law of the state where the land is located. (Parties: mortgagor, mortgagee.)

Mortgagee Clause A mortgagee lends money on the security of the value of the property mortgaged. If the property burns, the mortgagee could find himself or herself without collateral. The mortgagee therefore insists on a clause in the policy that makes any loss incurred payable to him or her and safeguards his or her rights in other ways. Such a clause is a "mortgagee clause."

Mutual Atomic Energy Reinsurance Pool A pool formed by mutual casualty and fire companies to provide bodily injury and property damage liability and physical damage insurance for private nuclear reactor installations. The Nuclear Energy Liability and Nuclear Energy Property Associations are similar to stock companies.

Mysterious Disappearance Disappearance of insured property in an unexplained manner. Mysterious disappearance is now an insured peril under broad-form personal theft policy. Previously there were disputes under theft policies as to whether property mysteriously lost had or had not been stolen. To avoid contention, insurers stated in such policies that mysterious disappearance was presumed to be due to theft. Mere disappearance of property such as an article dropped from a boat is not covered since the disappearance is not mysterious.

Named Insured The person designated in the policy as the insured, as opposed to someone who may have an interest in a policy but is not named.

National Flood Insurance Act of 1968 An act establishing a basis for flood insurance as a joint venture between the private insurance industry and the federal government. See "National Flood Insurers Association."

National Flood Insurers Association A voluntary pool of property insurers formed to provide flood insurance for dwellings in specified areas in collaboration with the U.S. Department of Housing and Urban Development (HUD). This joint venture produces a market for flood coverage hitherto almost nonexistent. The association was formed in 1968 with headquarters in New York.

Natural and Probable Consequences Those ordinary consequences of an act that a reasonable person would foresee.

Negative Covenant An undertaking in a deed to refrain from doing an act.

Negligence The failure to exercise due care under the circumstances in consequence of which harm is proximately caused to one to whom the defendant owed a duty to exercise due care.

Negligence Per Se An action that is regarded as so improper that it is declared by law to be negligent in itself without regard to whether due care was otherwise exercised.

No-Fault Automobile Insurance "No-fault" is a term coined to describe a system for improving the compensatory process for automobile accident victims by eliminating costly and lengthy litigation. The concept was developed by lawyers Keeton and O'Connell, but a variety of so-called "no-fault" plans substantially retaining lawsuits and introduced into state legislatures have rendered the term almost meaningless.

Nominal Damages A nominal sum awarded the plaintiff to establish that his or her legal rights have been violated although the plaintiff has not sustained any actual loss or damages.

Nonownership Automobile Liability Insurance against the liability incurred while driving an automobile not owned or hired by the policyholder.

Nonsuit A dismissal of an action without determination of the merits.

Noon Clause Some fire policies start and end at noon on a given day, and so state. A noon clause may be used to make clear what kind of time is meant, i.e., standard time at place of risk, or Eastern Standard Time, or some such provision.

Nuclear Energy Liability Insurance Association (NELIA) A syndicate of stock casualty writing companies formed to underwrite nuclear energy liability hazards on industry-operated nuclear reactors and related operations. Liability covers "third party" bodily injury and property damage. Headquarters in New York.

Nuisance Any conduct that harms or prejudices another in the use of his or her land or that harms or prejudices the public.

Nuisance Per Se An activity that is in itself a nuisance regardless of the time and place involved.

Obligee The person or persons protected by a bond.

Occurrence A happening or event. A basis for coverage in liability policies much broader than the accident basis, which requires the injury or damage to be due to a specific accident.

Operation of Law The attaching of certain consequences to certain facts because of legal principles that operate automatically, as contrasted with consequences that arise because of the voluntary action of a party designed to create those consequences.

Opinion Evidence Evidence not of what the witness himself or herself observed but the conclusion that the witness draws from what he or she observed, or in the case of an expert witness, also from what he or she is asked or has heard at the trial.

Owners' and Contractors' Protective Liability Insurance Insures the legal liability of contractors and other persons against the negligent acts of independent contractors engaged by them and also, in some cases, for their own negligent supervision of the work performed.

Owners', Landlords', and Tenants' Liability (0 L & T) Liability that arises from the ownership, operation, or maintenance of premises.

Package Policy A package policy is a combination of the coverages of two or more separate policies in one contract with one premium. A move toward economy and efficiency by giving the policyholder one document instead of several.

Parole Evidence Rule The rule that prohibits the introduction in evidence of oral or written statements made prior to or contemporaneously with the execution of a complete written contract, deed, or instrument, in the absence of clear proof of fraud, accident, or mistake causing the omission of the statement in question.

Partial Loss Loss involving less than all of the values insured or calling on the policy to pay less than its maximum amounts.

Payroll Audit Some insurance, notably workers' compensation, charges its premium on the basis of the policyholder's payroll. The company sends out "payroll auditors" to determine the accuracy of the policyholder's figures.

Penal System The system of prisons, probation departments, and other formal state organizations designed to implement the imposition of sanctions in the criminal law.

Per Curiam Opinion An opinion written "by the court" rather than by a named judge when all the judges of the court are so agreed on the matter that it is not deemed to merit any discussion and may be simply disposed of.

Per Se In, through, or by itself.

Person A term that includes both natural persons, or living people, and artificial persons, such as corporations which are created by act of government.

Personal Injury Liability Sometimes synonymous with bodily injury liability. An additional coverage in a liability policy relating to other than bodily injury to the person, including such actionable wrongs as false arrest or imprisonment, malicious prosecution, libel, slander, and invasion of privacy.

Personal Property Property other than "real" property, which consists of buildings and land. Also called "chattels."

Personal Property Floater (PPF) A broad form of inland marine policy issued to the owners of furniture and other household effects, which protects against "all risks" with certain exclusions. Covers the insured property wherever it may be. With the advent of homeowner's insurance, separate PPFs are seldom written, since the coverage is included in homeowner's policies.

Petty Jury A 12-member trial jury. Also called "petit jury."

Plaintiff One who initiates a lawsuit and claims that he or she has a right to recover from the defendant.

Pleadings The papers filed by the parties in an action in order to set forth the facts and frame the issues to be tried, although under some systems the pleadings merely give notice or a general indication of the nature of the issues.

Policy Power The power to govern; the power to adopt laws for the protection of the public health, welfare, safety, and morals.

Polling the Jury The process of inquiring of each juror individually in open court as to whether the verdict announced by the foreman of the jury was agreed to by them.

Preferred Risk A risk of a class considered to be particularly desirable.

Premium The amount of money an insurance company charges to provide the coverage that the policy describes.

Preponderance of Evidence The degree or quantum of evidence in favor of the existence of a certain fact when from a review of all the evidence it appears more probable that the fact exists than that it does not. The actual number of witnesses involved is not material, nor is the fact that the margin of probability is very slight.

Pressure Vessel Something designed to contain gas or vapor (such as steam) under pressure. A steam boiler is an excellent example.

Presumption A rule of proof that permits the existence of a fact to be assumed from the proof that another fact exists when there is a logical relationship between the two or when the means of disproving the assumed fact are more readily within the control or knowledge of the adverse party against whom the presumption operates.

Presumption of Death The rebuttable presumption that a person has died when he or she has been continuously absent and unheard of for a period of 7 years.

Presumption of Innocence The presumption of fact that a person accused of crime is innocent until it is shown that he or she in fact is guilty of the offense charged.

Pretrial Conference A conference held prior to the trial at which the court and the attorneys seek to simplify the issues in controversy and eliminate matters not in dispute.

Prima Facie Evidence Such evidence as by itself would establish the claim or defense of the party if the evidence were believed.

Primary Liability The liability of a person whose act or omission gave rise to the cause of action and who in all fairness should therefore be the one to compensate the victim for his or her wrong, even though others may also be liable for his or her misconduct.

Principal One who employs an agent to act on his or her behalf; the person who as between himself or herself and the surety is primarily liable to the third person or creditor.

Private Passenger Car An automobile primarily operated by the owner for his or her personal use, as distinguished from commercial use such as would be the case with a truck or taxicab.

Privileged Communication Information that the witness may legitimately refuse to testify to because of the relationship with the person furnishing the information, such as husband-wife, attorney-client.

Privilege from Arrest The immunity from arrest of parties, witnesses, and attorneys while present within a jurisdiction for the purpose of taking part in other litigation.

Privity A succession or chain of relationship to the same thing or right, such as a privity of contract, privity of estate, or privity of possession.

Probate The procedure for formally establishing or proving that a given writing is the last will and testament of the person purported to have signed it.

Product Liability Liability imposed upon the manufacturer or seller of goods for harm caused by a defect in the goods, embracing liability for 1) negligence, 2) fraud, 3) breach of warranty, and 4) strict tort.

Promoters The persons who plan the formation of a corporation and sell or promote the idea to others.

Proof The probative effect of the evidence; the conclusion drawn from the evidence as to the existence of particular facts.

Property The rights and interests one has in anything subject to ownership.

Property and Casualty Insurance There is a broad insurance distinction between companies writing life and health insurance and those writing the "nonlife" classes such as fire, casualty, surety, inland marine, etc. Numerous and varied descriptive titles have been employed to describe this "nonlife" area of operation, and although no one definition has yet been firmly established, the tendency is to adopt the generic title "property and casualty insurance." In 1965, the Commission on Insurance Terminology recommended the term "property and liability," a*ed in some quarters there is a feeling that the word "liability" is too restrictive to properly represent classes of casualty business such as burglary, glass, physical damage, boiler and machinery, etc.

Property Damage Liability Insurance Insurance that covers the insured party's legal liability for negligent damage to the property of others. A form of third-party insurance.

Property Insurance The insurance of real and personal property against physical loss or damage. A form of indemnity insurance not to be confused with property damage liability insurance (see definition).

Pro Rata Proportionately, or divided according to a rate or standard.

Proximate Cause The act that is the natural and reasonably foreseeable cause of the harm or event that occurs and injures the plaintiff.

Proximate Damages Damages that in the ordinary course of events are the natural and reasonably foreseeable result of the defendant's violation of the plaintiff's rights.

Proxy A written authorization by a shareholder to another person to vote the stock owned by the shareholder; the person who is the holder of such a written authorization.

Public Charge A person who because of a personal disability or lack of means of support is dependent upon public charity or relief for sustenance.

Public Policy Certain objectives relating to health, morals, and integrity of government that the law seeks to advance by declaring invalid any contract that conflicts with those objectives even though there is no statute expressly declaring such contract illegal.

Punitive Damages Damages in excess of those required to compensate the plaintiff for the wrong done, which are imposed in order to punish the defendant because of the particularly wanton or willful character of his or her wrongdoing. Also called "exemplary damages."

Quorum The minimum number of persons, shares represented, or directors who must be present at a meeting in order that business may be lawfully transacted.

Railway Subrogation Waiver If a railroad installs a siding on property belonging to another, it will demand an agreement that no claims for damages will be made against the railroad for damages because of the siding's existence. The waiver of the right of subrogation would void a fire policy unless the policy gave such permission by attaching the railway subrogation waiver. (See "Sidetrack Agreement.")

Rate The price of $100 of insurance, usually for 1 year. Expressed in dollars and cents or in percent.

Real Evidence Tangible objects that are presented in the courtroom for the observation of the trier of fact as proof of the facts in dispute or in support of the theory of a party.

Real Property Land and all rights in land, including buildings.

Reasonable Care The degree of care that a reasonable person would take under all the circumstances then known.

Rebuttable Presumption A presumption that may be overcome or rebutted by proof that the actual facts were different than those presumed.

Receiver An impartial person appointed by a court to take possession of and manage property for the protection of all concerned.

Reinstatement Some policies provide that the payment of a loss reduces the amount of insurance by the amount paid. When the amount of insurance is restored by endorsement or other agreement, the policy is said to have been reinstated. Most fire policies contain an automatic reinstatement clause.

Reinsurance The process whereby a company may share its risk with another, paying to such sharing company a portion of the premium it receives. This is done in many ways. Reinsurance contracts pay only the company that reinsures, not the policyholder.

Reinsurance Treaty An agreement between companies whereby reinsurance is shared on terms set forth therein.

Release The granting or giving of a right, claim, or privilege by the person in which it exists or accrues to another individual against whom it could be demanded or enforced by law.

Remand An order given by an appellate court sending a case back to the trial court for further action.

Remedy The action or procedure that is followed in order to enforce a right or to obtain damages for injury to a right.

Renewal Certificate It is the practice in many cases to issue a short form certificate instead of writing a whole new policy to replace an expiring one. This form is a "renewal certificate" and contains merely references to the original policy rather than its complete terms.

Rental Value Insurance Insurance that reimburses the owner of a building who occupies it for the cost of renting some other place if his or her own building should be rendered unusable by some peril insured against.

Rent Insurance If a person owns a building and rents it to another, a fire or other insured happening may make it impossible to collect rent from the tenant until the building has been replaced or repaired. Insurance against such loss is "rent insurance" and is one of the "time element" coverages.

Replacement Most policies of insurance of property give the company the right to substitute other property of like kind and quality for insured property that has been damaged or destroyed. This is called making a "replacement."

Replacement Insurance Insurance that pays the sound value of damaged or destroyed property without deduction for depreciation.

Representations Statements, whether oral or written, made to give the insurer the information it needs in writing the insurance, and which if false and relating to a material fact will entitle the insurer to void the contract.

Representative Capacity Action taken by a person not on his or her own behalf but on behalf of another, as an executor acting on behalf of the decedent's estate, or action taken both on one's behalf and on behalf of others, such as a stockholder bringing a representative action.

Reserve A sum set aside to meet some future obligation. (See "Loss Reserve.")

Res Ipsa Loquitur "The thing speaks for itself." The permissible inference that the defendant was negligent when the circumstances are such that ordinarily the plaintiff could not have been injured had the defendant not been at fault.

Res Judicata The principle that once a final judgment is entered in an action between the parties, it is binding upon them and the matters cannot be litigated again by bringing a second action.

Respondeat Superior The doctrine that a principal or employer is vicariously liable for the unauthorized torts committed by his or her agent or employee while acting with the scope of his or her agency or the course of his or her employment, respectively.

Reversible Error An error or defect in court proceedings of so serious a nature that on appeal the appellate court will set aside the proceedings of the lower court.

Risk The chance of loss. Specifically, the possible loss or destruction of property or the possible incurring of a liability. Sometimes refers to the subject of an insurance contract when talking of a "good risk" or a "poor risk."

Sacrifice In marine insurance, certain things may be done for the welfare of all interests such as the throwing overboard (jettisoning) of part of a cargo to keep the ship from sinking. This is a "sacrifice."

Sanction A penalty or punishment established by the state imposed upon a person after the commission of a crime.

Scheduled Property Floater An inland marine form designed to insure various specific items with a specific amount of insurance on each. Any articles of unusual value may normally be written on such a form provided they are movable (so they may qualify as inland marine). Such forms usually insure against many hazards or often are written against "all risks."

Scienter Knowledge, referring to those wrongs or crimes that require a knowledge of wrong in order to constitute the offense.

Scope of Employment The area within which an employee is authorized to act, with the consequence that a tort committed while so acting imposes liability upon the employer.

Seal At common law an impression on wax or other tenacious material attached to an instrument. Under modern law, any mark not ordinarily part of the signature is a seal when so intended, including the letters "L.S." and the word "seal," or a pictorial representation of a seal, without regard to whether they had been printed or typed on the instrument before its signing.

Sealed Verdict A verdict that is rendered when the jury returns to the courtroom during an adjournment of the court, the verdict then being written down and sealed and later affirmed before the court when the court is in session.

Self-Insurance The assumption of one's own risk through internal financing mechanisms rather than by purchase insurance.

Selling Price Clause A provision in a policy whereby it will pay the price for which the owner expected to sell his or her merchandise instead of what it would cost the owner to replace. Includes the merchant's profit.

Short Rate Cancellation When a policy is canceled by the policyholder before it reaches its natural expiration, the company pays a return premium less than the proportionate or pro rata part, that is still unearned. The policy is canceled "short rate," not "pro rata."

Sidetrack Agreement When a railroad builds a track or spur on private property to facilitate the shipping of goods, the business involved is normally required to hold the railroad harmless for personal injuries and property damage due to the use or existence of the siding. In such event, any applicable fire policy should carry the "railway subrogation waiver clause," recording the insurer's consent to such waiver of rights, and the user can also purchase sidetrack liability insurance to cover the third-party liability assumed under the sidetrack agreement.

Silverware Floater An inland marine form designed to insure valuable silverware against practically all risks wherever it may be.

Sine Qua Non Literally, "without which not." An absolutely necessary prerequisite to the occurrence of an event.

Slander Per Se Certain words deemed slanderous without requiring proof of damages to the victim, such as words charging a crime involving moral turpitude and an infamous punishment, a disease that would exclude from society, or words that tend to injure the victim in his or her business, profession, or occupation.

Social Security Acts Statutes providing for assistance for the aged, blind, unemployed, and similar classes of persons in need.

Special Damages Damages that do not necessarily result from the injury to the plaintiff but at the same time are not so remote that the defendant should not be held liable therefor, provided that the claim for special damages is properly made in the action.

Specific Insurance Insurance that describes what is insured more definitely than "blanket" insurance; e.g., a policy covering building and contents would be blanket, whereas one covering a certain amount on the building and another amount on the contents would be specific.

Specific Performance An action brought to compel an adverse party to perform his or her contract on the theory that merely suing for damages for its breach will not be an adequate remedy.

Sprinkler Leakage Insurance Insurance against the damage done by water leaking from automatic sprinklers and similar fire prevention devices.

Stare Decisis The principle that the decision of a court should serve as a guide or precedent and control the decision of similar cases in the future.

Statement of Values When a risk is rated with a blanket rate, that is, when a single rate is to cover more than one item or building, the rating bureau requires that the policyholder give the amount of value in each separate risk and usually in the contents of each so that a correct average may be arrived at. The information required is a "statement of values."

Status Quo The requirement that before a contract may be rescinded, the status quo must be restored; that is, the parties must be placed in their original positions prior to the making of the contract.

Statute An act of a legislature set forth in writing that declares, requires, or prohibits certain conduct.

Statute of Limitations A statute that restricts the period of time within which an action may be brought.

Stock Merchandise for sale or in the process of manufacture, as distinguished from furniture, fixtures, or machinery.

Stop Loss Reinsurance A company wishing to protect itself in the event its net loss ratio for a given year rises above a certain percentage may buy reinsurance which pays in excess of that figure up to a higher agreed percentage beyond which the company is once more liable. In short, a plan that ameliorates an above-average net loss ratio.

Strict Tort Liability A product liability theory that imposes liability on the manufacturer, seller, or distributor of goods for harm caused by goods that are dangerously defective.

Subpoena A court order directing a person to appear as a witness. In some states it is also the original process that is to be served on the defendant in order to give the court jurisdiction over his or her person.

Subrogation The right of a party secondarily liable to stand in the place of the creditor after having made payment to the creditor and to enforce the creditor's right against the party primarily liable in order to obtain indemnity from him or her. Insurance companies have a right of subrogation after paying an insured.

Subsidence Damage due to the movement of the land on which property is situated. A house built on the side of a hill may slide down the hill as a result of heavy rain or some similar cause. Earthquake damage is not considered subsidence damage.

Substantive Law That portion of the law which deals with matters of substance rather than matters of procedure; substantive law deals with the definition and regulation of rights and duties. Its opposite is "adjective law," which deals with the legal remedies and modes of procedure for obtaining redress for the violation of rights or the breaches of duties.

Summary Judgment A judgment entered by a court when no substantial dispute of fact is present, the court acting on the basis of affidavits or depositions which show that the claim or defense of a party is a sham.

Summons A writ by which an action is commenced under the common law.

Surety The underwriter who guarantees something under a bond.

Surplus Line Originally a risk or part thereof where the interested broker or agent had no available market. In recent years, the definition has broadened to describe any business normally subject to state regulations as to rate and form written by a nonadmitted insurer in accordance with the surplus line laws of the relevant state.

Testamentary Designed to take effect at death, as by disposing of property or appointing an executor.

Testate The condition of leaving a will upon death.

Testate Succession The distribution of an estate in accordance with the will of the decedent.

Testimony An oral statement made under oath at a trial.

Theft The wrongful taking of the property of another.

Time Element A phrase used to describe a kind of insurance that reimburses the policyholder for the loss of use of property. The amount of loss depends on the length of time it will require to rebuild or repair or recover.

Toll the Statute To stop the running of the period of the statute of limitations by the performance of some act by the debtor.

Tort A private injury or wrong arising from a breach of a duty created by law.

Tort-Feasor One who commits a tort.

Total Loss Loss of all the insured property. Also, a loss involving the maximum amount for which a policy is liable.

Transcript of Proceeding A written record that records verbatim testimony and statements made in a proceeding.

Trier of Fact In most cases a jury, although it may be the judge alone in certain classes of cases, as in equity, or in any case when jury trial is waived, or an administrative agency or commission.

Ultra Vires An act or contract that a corporation does not have authority to do or make.

Undue Influence The influence that is asserted upon another person by one who dominates that person.

Vacation of Judgment The setting aside of a judgment.

Valid Legal.

Verdict The decision of a trial or petty jury.

Void Of no legal effect and not binding on anyone.

Voidable A transaction that may be set aside by one party thereto because of fraud or similar reason but that is binding on the other party until the injured party elects to void the contract.

Voir Dire Examination The preliminary examination of a juror or a witness to ascertain that he or she is qualified to act as such.

Volenti Non Fit Injuria The maxim that the defendant's act cannot constitute a tort if the plaintiff had consented thereto.

Voluntary Nonsuit A means of the plaintiff's stopping a trial at any time by moving for a voluntary nonsuit.

Waiver "The intentional relinquishment of a known right" is the definition adopted by some important courts. To illustrate, an insurance policy may set forth certain conditions with which a policyholder must comply under penalty of voiding his or her insurance; e.g., the policyholder may have accepted a policy in which it is stated that he or she must maintain a watchman on the premises or keep a sprinkler system in working condition. The company may forego its right to avoidance of the policy arising from the insured's failure to comply. Such a waiver may be conveyed by implication as well as by direct statement.

Wanton Conduct Conduct undertaken in reckless disregard of the consequences.

Warranty A statement by an insured party on the literal truth of which the validity of the insurance contract depends. Warranties may relate to matters existing at or before the issuance of the policy (affirmative warranties) or may be undertakings by the insured that something will be done or omitted after the policy takes effect and during its continuance (promissory warranties). Many states have restricted by statute the common-law rule that "any breach of warranty avoids an insurance policy"; e.g., under New York law (150), a breach of warranty to avoid the policy must have "materially increased the risk of loss, damage, or injury within the coverage of the contract."

Water Damage Insurance Insurance against loss due to the accidental presence of water in places where it is not supposed to be. It is one of the coverages of the additional extended cover endorsement, and also is written on special water damage policies by both fire and casualty companies.

Willful Intentional as distinguished from accidental or involuntary. In penal statutes, with evil intent or legal malice, or without reasonable ground for believing one's act to be lawful.

Windstorm Insurance Insurance against damage done to property by unusually high winds or by cyclones, hurricanes, or tornadoes. Today most such liability is assumed by the "extended coverage" endorsement.

Witness A person who has observed the facts to which he or she testifies, or an expert who may testify on the basis of observation, the testimony presented in the court, or hypothetical questions put to him or her by the attorneys in the case.

Workers' Compensation A system providing for payments to workers who have been injured from a risk arising out of the course of their employment while they were employed or have contracted an occupational disease in that manner, payment being made without consideration of the negligence of any party. Workers' compensation insurance is a common method of protecting an employer for losses arising out of a workplace injury.

Writ of Mandamus A procedural device for obtaining review of a lower court's decision when ordinary channels of review are not available or are too slow.

Year and a Day The common-law requirement that death result within a year and a day in order to impose criminal liability for homicide.

INDEX

Italicized numbers indicate figures, exhibits, or tables.

Italicized numbers indicate figures, exhibits, or tables.

Italicized numbers indicate figures, exhibits, or tables.

Italicized numbers indicate figures, exhibits, or tables.

Italicized numbers indicate figures, exhibits, or tables.

Italicized numbers indicate figures, exhibits, or tables.

Italicized numbers indicate figures, exhibits, or tables.

Italicized numbers indicate figures, exhibits, or tables.